Philosophy Born of Struggle

Anthology of Afro-American Philosophy from 1917

Edited with an Introduction and Select Bibliography of Afro-American Works in Philosophy by

Leonard Harris

KENDALL/HUNT PUBLISHING COMPANY
2460 Kerper Boulevard   P.O. Box 539   Dubuque, Iowa 52004-0539

Acknowledgments

Robert C. Williams. "W. E. B. DuBois: Afro-American Philosopher of Social Reality." *Bicentennial Symposium on Philosophy*, New York: City University of New York Graduate Center, 1976, pp. 99–107. Reprinted by permission of the author.

Alain L. Locke. "Values and Imperatives." *American Philosophy Today and Tomorrow*. Edited by Horace M. Kallen and Sidney Hook. New York: Lee Furman, 1935.

William T. Fontaine. " 'Social Determination' in the Writings of Negro Scholars." *American Journal of Sociology* 49 (January 1944), pp. 302–315. University of Chicago Press, Chicago, Illinois. Reprinted by permission of the University of Chicago Press, Chicago, Illinois.

Cornelius L. Golightly. "Ethics and Moral Activism." *The Monist* 56 (October 1972), pp. 576–86. Reprinted by permission of Hegeler Institute, La Salle, Illinois.

Bernard R. Boxill. "Self-Respect and Protest." *Philosophy & Public Affairs* 6 (Fall 1976), pp. 58–69. Reprinted by permission of Princeton University Press, Princeton, New Jersey.

Alain L. Locke. "The New Negro." *The New Negro*. Edited by Alain L. Locke. New York: Atheneum, 1969, pp. 3–16. (Original 1925)

Houston A. Baker. "On the Criticism of Black American Literature: One View of the Black Aesthetic." *Reading Black: Essays in the Criticism of African, Caribbean, and Black American Literature*. Edited by Houston A. Baker. Monograph Series No. 4, University of Pennsylvania, Afro-American Studies Program and Cornell University, Africana Studies and Research Center, 1976, pp. 47–58. Reprinted by permission of the University of Pennsylvania, Afro-American Studies Program and Cornell University, Africana Studies and Research Center.

Thomas F. Slaughter. "Epidermalizing the World: A Basic Mode of Being Black." *Man & World* 10 (1977), pp. 303–308. Reprinted by permission of the author.

Figure Design

Figure designed for this anthology by Edward L. Pryce, Tuskegee Institute, Alabama. According to the artist, "The central figure is the spirit of man with his roots in various cultures over time and struggling to understanding and joy."

Photographs

Frederick Douglass, courtesy of the Moorland-Spingarn Research Center, Howard University.

William Edward Burghardt DuBois, © 1920, Brown Brothers, private collection.

Alain LeRoy Locke, © 1938, Philadelphia Society for Negro Records and Research, courtesy of Moorland-Spingarn Research Center, Howard University.

Eugene Clay Holmes, © 1942, courtesy of the Moorland-Spingarn Research Center, Howard University.

William Thomas Fontaine, © 1962, courtesy of the University of Pennsylvania Archives.

Cornelius Lacy Golightly, © 1972, private collection.

The research opportunities provided to me as a Fellow of the Robert R. Moton Center for Independent Studies, 1976–77, and my receipt of the Portia Washington Pittman Fellowship, Tuskegee Institute, 1980–81, made this anthology possible. I am indebted to these agencies and their representatives who so graciously withstood my idiosyncracies and unfailingly encouraged my research.

To my extended family, AESOP Inc., and the Association for Caribbean Transformation, I remain as one with our multiphasial efforts, of which this anthology is but one contribution to our collective movement.

For Agnes Chappell Harris who spoke to me with her eyes. When all is written, it will fall short of the messages I received.

Having believed I over-slept an exam, I sat outside a door at Cornell University, ashamed that I failed Eugene Harris Sr. who arose at 5 A.M. six days a week to feed five of us.

For my partner in life, Sherron Jones-Harris, and the future, Leonard Nawatu, Jarrard Lemir, and Jamila Rehema—A Luta Continua

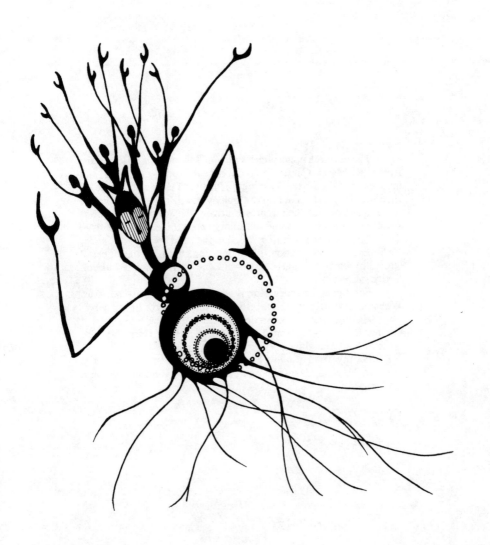

Let me give you a word of the philosophy of reform. The whole history of the progress of human liberty shows that all concessions yet made to her august claims, have been born of earnest struggle.

This struggle may be a moral one, or it may be a physical one, and it may be both moral and physical, but it must be a struggle. Power concedes nothing without demand. It never did and it never will.

Frederick Douglass, 1857

Contents

III
Experience Interpreted

Introduction

Philosophic texts, if products of social groups doggedly fighting to survive, are texts born of struggle. They must cut through the jungle of oppressive deeds to the accompanying labyrinth of words masking the nature of the deeds. Fraught with controversial intuitions that reflect the coming accepted beliefs of the new world, such texts challenge prevailing ways of viewing the world.

Independent of a particular Afro-American's philosophy, the preconditions for admission to American institutions of higher education as students or teachers were battles for opportunity fought by militants of various persuasions. Whether it was W. E. B. DuBois, who rejected the speculative character of William James' pragmatism as unfit to guide a real program of social change for Afro-Americans, and thereafter pursued the study of sociology and history; Broadus N. Butler who applied for a teaching position at a predominately white university after completing requirements for a doctorate degree in 1952 at the University of Michigan, learned that his advisers accompanying letter of reference stated ". . . a good philosopher, but of course, a Negro", and the one-line response, "Why don't you go where you will be among your own kind"; or Angela Y. Davis, who, although recommended by the Department of Philosophy, University of California, Los Angeles, for a renewed teaching contract was denied it by the regents of the university, and after their decision was overturned by the federal courts, the university simply declined to renew her contract; the same results were sustained—Afro-Americans steered and pushed away from one of America's spheres of culture-interpreting, image-making, and conception-shaping activities. If the content of American philosophy has not been sufficiently repugnant, the instructors and institutions have. The profession of philosophy, however, has hardly been the sole source of philosophic texts. Nor has the rising tide of Afro-American philosophers been long stayed by tinsel-town theories and tin soldiers, well-meaning or not.

That tide has been perennially confronted by a world that refuses to see Afro-Americans as humans and as peers. It is a world unduly reluctant to embrace, and unwilling to avow, messages of truth, insight, sound arguments, or cogent methods because of their source. Yet that world fraudulently prides itself on color-blindness and universality. The works of Afro-Americans are trapped, as it were, in a labyrinth where even the walls are white. Nonetheless, philosophic texts by Afro-Americans, taken as a group, attest to participation in America's philosophic panorama; to a world of intellectual activity separate from the barren bastions of the profession; and to ways of explaining and interpreting the way the world is despite a hostile environment of veiled contempt.

Races, countries, and cultures are not homogeneous, static, or *sui generis*. Any particular Afro-American need not be associated with the Afro-American social experience as a general phenomenon. Nor is social philosophy always done by Afro-Americans with a sense of responsibility for looking at issues through the prism of, or with examples drawn from, Afro-American culture. The common language of Afro-Americans, as with all common customs, changes over time. And the truth of a proposition is not necessarily a function of some historical or cultural circumstance, nor are universally true propositions (if there are any) true because they are unassociated with some context.

Contexts convey meaning, and only sometimes are meanings in the form of propositions. Propositions are most naturally expressed in the flow of a text. Arguments designed to be therapeutic, reasoning methods for arriving at warrantedly assertable claims, or methods of analysis purporting to correspond to the movement of things in the world, are also expressed in the flow of a text. That flow is the cultural medium of some particularity. It orders the kinds of questions considered important. It structures what is taken as more or less intuitively sound. It delivers unspoken needs that help make an argument therapeutic or convincing. It tells us what kinds of connecting premises, carrying what sort of information, count as rational. What is commensurable between mediums, and what is unique about a medium, are both taken into account when looking at the meaning of a text. Just as there is more than one meaningful way of interpreting a text, and more than one way of interpreting a culture, there is more than one use of a medium. A text has only so many pages, and a culture its parameter. Doing philosophy from the foundations of Afro-American culture is thus doing philosophy through a medium; a medium from which examples are taken, a medium considered valuable, a medium itself under scrutiny, a medium through which the way the world is can be understood. This anthology brings the mediums and messages central to the modern history of philosophy done in the context of Afro-American culture together as a family of texts.

These texts have lived on the edge of a less-than-cogent conception about philosophy and culture: that there is an inherent conflict between doing philosophy and doing philosophy from the foundations of a particular culture. If races, countries, and cultures were not distinguished and did not perform various roles in the world, then the doing of philosophy from the foundations of such particularities would be at least suspect. But that is not the way of the world. What counts as universal, whether it is a proposition, appealing argument, meaningful distinction, a valuable method, or material interest is said to be universal through some medium. Mediums are languages, sets of examples, and bevies of concerns. An argument concerned with what is commensurable between languages, theories, questions, and argument techniques is an argument occurring through some medium we can all theoretically understand. Assuming, however, that there is an Archemedian point, Afro-American culture can be its medium. What we all have in common may be well explicated through the conceptual contours that form Afro-American culture. This anthology is predicated on the belief that it would be a good thing if we all took into account Afro-American cultural mediums and the philosophies germane to them.

Precursors to this anthology are Carter G. Woodson's *Negro Orators and Their Orations* (1925) and Alain L. Locke's *The New Negro* (1925).

Negro Orators and Their Orations consists of speeches, lectures, and proclamations originally delivered orally. They capture much of the Afro-American oral tradition as a dialogical art form. Those forms were, among other things, argument methodologies only partially conveyed in writing. The word, as power, as force, as intonation and nuance, carried justificatory modalities and constituted an arguing tradition rarely engrained by contemporary secular philosophers. The theologians' pulpit, the politicians' soap box, the actors' stage, and the civil rights leaders' platform continue as rostrums for the oral traditions' argument form. This anthology heralds the emergence of the word in another form, alien to its roots here, an intentional extension of its roots there, foreign to the soil that nurtured its founding here, and a praise of that soil there. As with all successful births, traumatic or gentle, there comes new life alike and different from its source. This anthology captures the tenor of a growing body of written texts.

The first anthology published by an Afro-American professional philosopher, *The New Negro* epitomized an intellectual movement. That movement, the Harlem Renaissance, as seen through Locke's eyes was grounded on value pluralism characterized by a pronounced rejection of value absolutism. According to Locke, absolutism condones, if not directly at least tacitly, racist judgments of black culture and the denegration of positive forms of race consciousness. Value pluralism, however, held an ontology that accepted diversity without hierarchial judgments of human worth according to racial and cultural characteristics. Both color blindness and ethnocentrism were eschewed by Locke in favor of a DuBoisian conception of self-respect and a communicative theory of race relations explicated in DuBois' "Conservation of Races" (1897). This anthology does not tender the 'Negro mind', the 'Negro spirit', or the 'Negro mood'. It tenders different, and sometimes conflicting, interpretations, explanations, and judgments of the world by Afro-Americans using or seeing through mediums germane to Afro-American culture. It heralds not one movement, but several.

Philosophies are products endemically associated with some time, place, and social group. A given text may nonetheless effect more than one time period, place, social group, or cadre of intellectuals. Relationships between texts can be conceived consequently in more than one meaningful way. Philosophic texts by Afro-Americans are both relevant to Afro-American culture, taken separately and apart, and to American culture in general. As such, *Afro-American philosophic texts form a unidimensional text of divergent components*. The doing of professional philosophy, and thereby the direct partaking in and creating of works through the cultural peculiarities associated with the field, had its genesis in 1917.

The year 1917, as with most dates used to mark a trend, is suggestive. Thomas N. Baker (1860–1940), for example, received his doctorate in philosophy in 1903 from Yale with a dissertation on the mind-body problem. Baker, as with most students of philosophy during the period, pursued a career in the ministry.

Rufus L. M. Perry (1833–1895), was awarded an honorary Doctor of Philosophy degree in 1887 from the State University of Kentucky, Louisville. He authored a standard introduction to classical authors in 1889, *Sketch of Philosophical Systems*. Perry's 'Sketch' was followed by *The Cushite or the Descendants of Ham* (1893), a history of blacks as a race. 'Race' as Perry conceived it in his history was not a social creation, but providentially ordained. Race pride held ontological status. Black, yellow, and white races were separate and equal types for Perry, and each type a constitutive component of being. African culture, and by implication Afro-American cultural carryovers, represented civilization equivalent to any other.

Jerome R. Riley, a New York lawyer, authored *Philosophy and Negro Suffrage* (1895), and later, *Evolution . . . or . . . Racial Development,* 1901. Riley championed a popular defense of black equality, e.g., that the low social status of blacks was not evidence of innate inferiority or inalterable consequences of natural selection, and that the black educated elite was evidence of the race's adaptability and potential. The power of rational persuasion carried for Riley "all the material forces" needed to change racist beliefs and practices. As a moral suasionist, Riley believed that character improvement would be convincing. Riley argued against black suffrage on grounds of meritocracy and political efficiency. Attainment of civilized character on a broad basis, for Riley, warranted full suffrage.

Given this background of diverse perspectives, scholarly associations, and philosophic interests predating 1917, it may seem a bit truncated to concentrate an anthology primarily on the works of professional philosophers over the last sixty-five years. As late as 1962, however, E. Franklin Frazier critically appraised Afro-American philosophers: "We have no philosophers or thinkers who command the respect of the intellectual community at large. I am not talking about the few teachers of philosophy who have read Hegel or Kant or James and memorized their thoughts. I am talking about men who have reflected upon the fundamental problems which have always concerned philosophers such as the nature of human knowledge and the meaning or lack of meaning of human existence." The "intellectual community at large" for Frazier meant the Euro-American community.

A survey I conducted between 1976 and 1977 suggests that such critics are less knowledgeable of the history of Afro-American philosophers than lay intellectuals, librarians, theologians, social activists, and older university administrators. Respondents not employed by predominantly white educational institutions were subject to greater influence by Afro-American philosophers during the historical period Frazier considered. Moreover, the character of activity by Afro-American philosophers at historically black institutions reflects a different matrix of issues and spheres of influences than those Frazier considered relevant.

Analysis of American professional philosophy normally marks its beginnings with the rise of institutionalized teaching and the promulgation of theories not directly reliant upon European authors and traditions. The profession was barely marketable at white universities in the late 1900s. Philosophy courses, when taught, were taught most often under the auspices of religion or psychology departments. Blacks were rarely admitted to white colleges. Philosophy, considered an intellectual field for the better minds, was not one blacks were considered either capable of mastering or one that would make them useful employees. As a specialized discipline, philosophy was not endemic to African traditions. Historically black colleges offered philosophy and theology courses but few offered majors in the field. Introduction to philosophy, logic, and classical readings were the main fare. On more than one occasion the few blacks with degrees in philosophy were drafted into administration. The institutionalization of philosophy at historically black colleges, and the rising number of Afro-American certified philosophy teachers at those colleges, had its moorings at Howard University. Alain L. Locke (1886–1954), Eugene C. Holmes (1905–1980), William T. Fontaine (1909–1968), Carlton L. Lee (1913–1972), Cornelius L. Golightly (1917–1976), Winston K. McAllister (1920–1976), Forest O. Wiggins, and Broadus N. Butler, to name a few, were teaching doctors of philosophy prior to 1962 at most often different historically black colleges. None of these could be properly described as simply Hegelian, rationalist, or pragmatist. But the story is only half told.

Alain L. Locke, the most noted Afro-American philosopher to date, spent three years at Oxford University as a Rhodes Scholar, 1907–1910, and one year at the University of Berlin, 1910–1911, prior to joining Howard University in 1912 as Assistant Professor of the Teaching of English and Instructor in Philosophy and Education. Locke was appointed Professor of Philosophy and head of the department in 1917, and a year later received his doctorate from Harvard. Although Locke is the most noted Afro-American philosopher, he was predated at Howard by Lewis B. Moore. Moore, Professor of Philosophy and Education and Dean of the Teachers College, was the principle teacher and architect of the philosophy program at Howard from 1898 until his departure in 1917. Howard University under Locke's guidance would become the principle base for Afro-American social philosophers with an active interest in social problems facing the black community from the early 1900s until the early 1970s. Several authors in this anthology were his students, colleagues, or associates. A modest increase in Afro-American students of philosophy throughout the country brought a concern for doing social philosophy with interest in understanding the Afro-American experience in a variety of arenas. This development was concretized, not through the aegis of one department, but through conferences. Black philosophy conferences were held at the University of Illinois, Chicago Circle (1971); Tuskegee Institute, Alabama (1973/76), Wingspread Conference Center, Racine, Michigan (1976), Morgan State University, Maryland (1979), the University of the District of Columbia, Washington D.C. (1980), and Haverford College, Pennsylvania (1982). The Robert R. Moton Center for Independent Study Postdoctoral Fellowships, Virginia, and the Department of Philosophy, Tuskegee Institute's DuBois Fellows and Portia Washington Pittman Fellowship, have provided more research opportunities for Afro-American philosophers than any other sources. The Committee on Blacks in Philosophy, American Philosophical Association, holds yearly sessions on various topics under the rubric of black philosophy and the New York Society for Black Philosophy holds several discussions sessions yearly. The Afro-American Studies Department at the University of Illinois, Urbana, supports research in the history of Afro-American philosophers. These various conferences, institutions, and associations are the current sources of support and centers of scholarly activity concerned with the Afro-American heritage in philosophy.

American philosophers, with Afro-American cultural roots, have been particularly associated with African and Caribbean independence movements, social revolutions, state formations, and constitution designs. Alain L. Locke, for example, was influential in the formation of the Negritude movement and *The New Negro* was in concert with Jean Price-Mars' Haitianism. In 1943 Locke was an Inter-American Exchange Professor to Haiti and is memorialized on Senegalese stamps among other recognitions. It is well known that W. E. B. DuBois was a close associate of Kwame Nkrumah, but it is not well known that Nkrumah was a philosophy major and student of William T. Fontaine at the University of Pennsylvania; that as a member of the American Society of African Culture, Fontaine attended the 1956 Paris Negro Artists and Writers Conference, the follow-up 1959 Rome conference, and a 1962 African Socialism conference convened by President Leopold S. Senghor in Senegal. The Pan-African connection continues, for example, with Broadus N. Butler's Directorship of the NAACP's International Affairs Committee and consultancy to the Federal Republic of Nigeria's constitution deliberations; Lucius T. Outlaw's Africana Philosophy-International Philosophy Conference, Haverford, 1982; and Angela Y. Davis' international lecture tours. This tradition has roots running as deep as Frederick Douglass' use of Toussaint L'Ouverture's overthrow of the French to argue for an end to slavery; Alexander Crummel teaching moral philosophy in Liberia from 1853–1873 after sojourning there to aid in the building of a homeland for the security of African people; Paul Cuffee's repatriation of Afro-Americans to avoid the hellish influences of American slavery; and Anton Wilhelm Amos, first African educated in philosophy after the advent of chattle slavery, returning to the Gold Coast in 1747. Frazier focused on the wrong intellectual community.

The most active and influential Afro-American thrust has been Pan-Africanist. The classical Anglo-American social philosophers such as C. S. Pierce (1839–1914), William James (1842–1910), John Dewey (1859–1952),

Josiah Royce (1855–1916), C. I. Lewis (1883–1964), and George H. Mead (1863–1931), were influenced by the German traditions of Hegel and Kant, but, like James, moved in theoretical directions uniquely their own and in important ways severed from the European heritage. Making the African connection, rejoining roots, and building common bonds have carried far more weight among Afro-American scholars than severing roots or decrying heritage influence. The cultural roots more likely disdained are those festered by the corrupting and deprivational circumstances of slavery and racism. Identities are most likely not based on the pioneer image of rugged pragmatic individualism, but on images associated with protest and management of hardship.

The distinction between Afro and Anglo-American traditions is not hard and fast. Afro-Americans have studied widely in Europe and not a few hold theoretical positions associated with European and Anglo-American authors. The same might be said of not a few European and Anglo-American authors in relation to African peoples. Moreover, the source of a claim or process of thinking is neither true nor valuable simply by virtue of its origin. The point is that there are at least two cultural foundations of American philosophy. Each has a different association with its heritage and each has concretized its views on an international level in different arenas. The principle, though not exclusive, thrust of Afro-American theories involve confrontation with unfulfilled democracy, human ravages of capitalism, colonial domination, and ontological designation by race. Liberation from such social consequences and critiques by theories tending to legitimize reprehensible conditions are the distinguishing marks of the Afro-American heritage. That heritage is reflected in this anthology.

Black philosophy conferences, representing the professional side of the Afro-American philosophic heritage, had as their overriding concerns what is, or should be, the character of philosophy and the social role of Afro-American philosophers. Philosophy—understood as what professionals do, as what conceptions guide men of letters, and as what (or whether) the fundamental concepts held by society at large count as a form of black philosophy—framed considerations. The first section, **Philosophy Experienced,** offers articles that tender perspectives on what is, or should be, the nature of American philosophy; that explore the life and works of particular thinkers; and that argue for a given approach to the doing of philosophy.

Broadus N. Butler's "Frederick Douglass: A Commentary on the Black Philosopher in the United States," argues that the role of the black philosopher has been both "formidable and paradoxical;" formidable because it has always been taken into account and paradoxical because once taken into account, denied full status. The core thrust of black philosophic works according to Butler, argue for human equality. The resistance to a general acceptance of this stance has been unyielding. Whether Thomas Jefferson or more contemporary liberal American philosophers immersed in the dominant culture and its European moorings, the mind-set associated with this reluctance has been all too common. Indominatable figures such as Frederick Douglass have consistently offered ways of viewing the world founded in a basic presupposition of human equality. The African grounding of this Afro-American thrust, Butler suggests, is not to be taken lightly.

The works of W. E. B. DuBois are occasionally divided between an early NAACP period and a later, socialist-communist period. Robert C. Williams, in "W. E. B. DuBois: Afro-American Philosopher of Social Reality," explicates the consistent themes and principles that DuBois constructed to guide his works. The nature of human society, in Williams' interpretation of DuBois, is an order of mutual interdependency. It is also the notion of mutual interdependency that undergirds DuBois' view of identity. DuBois criticized, used, or developed theories in accordance with their utility for understanding social change as a dynamic process of interdependent agents and the racism that separates the human community.

According to Alain L. Locke's "Values and Imperatives" (1935), "All philosophies are in ultimate derivation philosophies of life and not abstract, disembodied 'objective' reality. . . ." Locke constructs a value theory based on a notion of 'feeling modes' that avoids the ill consequences of all absolutisms, explicit or implicit, as a guide for the resolution of conflicts. This theory, functional relativism, argues for mutual respect between cultural sentiments and tolerance as a *modus vivendi* for human progress and peace.

"Eugene C. Holmes: A Commentary on a Black Marxist Philosopher," by John H. McClendon, reviews Holmes' sojourn through the study of pragmatism, naturalism, and evolutionary theories of society to Marxism and Holmes' role as an activist black philosopher. Holmes chaired the Department of Philosophy at Howard after Locke for eighteen years, retiring in 1970. Holmes withstood the McCarthy era, wrote numerous articles on Locke and DuBois as social philosophers from a materialist perspective, which appreciated their positive activism, and addressed the problem of space and time from a materialist perspective (the first extensive work published by an Afro-American philosopher on the subject). McClendon takes issue with Holmes' materialist explication of space and time. McClendon covers Holmes' contribution to the continuing black Marxist tradition of historical materialism. He considers Holmes as a "philosopher who gained his intellectual insights from the persistent and militant struggle of Black people."

Cornell West, in "Philosophy, Politics and Power: An Afro-American Perspective," queries what the calls for the end of philosophy represent and what the significance of the calls mean in relation to Afro-Americans in general and particularly those engaged in the enterprise of philosophy. West considers the western philosophic panorama as a reflection of a cultural crisis, a crisis appropriately characterized as a repetition of Hegel's historicizing efforts but with an emphasis on language and impotence. West argues for a revolution of philosophy, not its end, in terms of a genealogy of "moral and political technologies, a genealogy that lays bare the workings of structures of domination and mechanisms of control," and a vocation of service for the construction of a revolutionary future.

"Philosophy, Hermeneutics, Social-Political Theory: Critical Thought in the Interest of African-Americans", by Lucius T. Outlaw, places the relation of universal interest and African-American interest in the context of a dynamic and dialectical relationship. The doing of philosophy, in universal and African-American interest for Outlaw requires a global theory "within which the particularity of African-Americans is properly situated." That interest is situated in the context of critical social theory. The theory is guided by a value commitment to serve emancipatory praxis, conditioned by a hermeneutical interpretation of culture as text, a proper appreciation of nationalist concerns, and a critical theoretic explanation of events.

Experience Explained, Explanatory Theory, explores viable ways of elucidating the social and intellectual character of Afro-American situations and forms of legitimation associated with theories of oppression and liberation. Explanatory theories tend to weigh descriptions and causal explanations for the purpose of both judging and understanding human experience. Just as there is more than one facet of the doing of philosophy, there is more than one side of the Afro-American experience to be explained, and more than one mode of so doing. The nature of an explanation that accounts for both racism and class conflict, and the appropriate intellectual and practical stance that should be adopted, are the concerns of articles in this section.

William T. Fontaine's " 'Social Determination' in the Writings of Negro Scholars" (1944), holds that social theories are themselves the consequence of human interactions with their environment. Grounded on the sociology of knowledge, Fontaine queries whether, and in what way, dominant theories of Afro-Americans are determined, and what approach, unconditioned by a defense psychology or white American ideology, could form the basis of rational theory construction.

Bernard R. Boxill, in "The Race-Class Questions," takes to task classical Marxian ways of explaining racism, particularly the use of historical materialism as an explanadum. Distinguishing what is not at issue, in terms of whether racial designations or class designations are ever significant influences, Boxill queries whether it is necessarily "the case that persons always acquire ideas that tend to secure and justify their *true* interests"? Doubts are raised concerning the supposition that persons are or will be disposed to act in their true interests. Given that the white workers of advanced capitalist countries, for example, are embourgeoisified relative to blacks and the Third World, Boxill argues that they are not likely to perceive their true interest nor hold the same sentiments of justice as others. Attaching criteria of rationality to how things work in the world is implicitly taken into account by Boxill.

Lucius T. Outlaw, in "Race and Class in the Theory and Practice of Emancipatory Social Transformation," addresses the historically inadequate way theorists have handled race-class questions. Outlaw describes Marx's philosophic anthropology, e.g., the production and reproduction of the means of existence, which are the principle historical determining characteristics of human existence. Outlaw argues that Marx's philosophic anthropology held as a general outlook is partial and thereby misleading if it does not "appreciate the (always historically conditioned) absolute and relative autonomy of the racial/ethnic national character of humans in their particularity." Outlaw eschews reductionism and paternalism. He notes the strengths and weaknesses of James Q. Wilson's analysis of the significance of class positions over race as a determining factor and suggests criteria for an adequate approach that incorporates the nationalist movement and a viable class analysis.

Angela Y. Davis' "Unfinished Lecture on Liberation—II" is the second installment in an ongoing analysis; the first "Unfinished Lecture on Liberation" was presented as a lecture in her first course, "Reoccurring Philosophical Themes in Black Literature." In this new version, Davis focuses on "the nature of freedom, its extents and limits" particularly through the literature and struggles of Frederick Douglass. Bourgeois ideology traditionally emphasizes freedom and equality although refusing to acknowledge its perpetuation of servitude and inequality. Black literature reveals the progressive "transformation of the principle of freedom into a dynamic, active struggle for liberation." Religion, for example, is the opium of the masses as Marx explicates; it also happens, as Davis explicates, that religion as "wish dreams of the oppressed" can revert to their original bases, e.g., placed in the framework of the real world, directed toward real needs, and thereby performing potentially revolutionary roles. The experience of slavery and class oppression, understood in this context for Davis, reflect the transformation of the ideal of freedom, through real struggles, into an active movement as exemplified by Frederick Douglass.

Experience Explained, Ideal Theory, consists of articles that principally, but not exclusively, judge and understand through clarification and analysis of concepts. In this sense, ideas are weighed. The problems of central focus are thereby different. The same problems can be addressed by an explanatory or ideal tendency, since these are heuristic distinctions, but this section concentrates on problems not always the same as those under explanatory theory. The intent is to provide a fair spread of issues and approaches concerned with the general problem of explaining the Afro-American experience.

"Ethics and Moral Activism" (1974), by Cornelius L. Golightly argues for a "descriptive, normative, analytical ethics in a single conceptual system" that would afford substantive direction for scholars, as citizens, to be activists. Golightly suggests that rather than examples using disagreements between individuals, we construct examples of disagreements between cultures to explore ethical principles. In this fashion, theories would be more amenable to appreciation and testing in the laboratory of life.

Alain L. Locke's voluminous literary analyses and criticisms can be interpreted through his philosophy of value relativism and cultural pluralism. Locke's original contributions to value theory are explored and challenged in

Johnny Washington's "Alain L. Locke's 'Values and Imperatives'." Locke rejected prevailing theories of pragmatism, relativism, and pluralism that, by themselves, did not provide substantive direction for the resolution of conflicts and the avoidance of absolutism. 'Feeling modes' on Locke's account infused all theories that tendered different ways the world is; that is, the world is in no small measure the different ways our feeling modes suggest. But the subordination of absolutism, which threatens all ways of viewing for Locke, requires an active effort to interject mutual respect and tolerance. Washington argues that Locke's view of tolerance is an insufficient base for the resolution of real conflicts.

Essie A. Eddins and Berkeley B. Eddins, in "Liberalism and Liberation," examine liberalism's implications for liberation and defend a classical form of liberalism not akin to contemporary distortions of liberal theory. The Eddins' hold "that the individual is of worth, intrinsically, apart from any contractual relationship into which he might enter." The Eddins' take a different tack than interest-group liberals or revisionist democrats. A classical form of liberalism that appreciates recent critical standpoints and practical difficulties is tendered.

"Self-Respect: Theory and Practice", by Laurence Thomas, holds that an individual has self-respect "if and only if he has the conviction that he is deserving of full moral status, and so the basic rights of that status, simply in virtue of the fact that he is a person." This article centers our attention on self-concepts of individuals. Self-esteem, for Thomas, is a function of our successes in relation to our aspirations. Thomas believes that his view of self-respect can be seen as the social analogue, for adults, to parental love and that this analogue provides us with additional insight. Thomas uses Rosa Parks' resistence to segregation to demonstrate good and bad reasons for submitting to unfair treatment and argues for the significance of self-respect as distinct from self-esteem.

Booker T. Washington and W. E. B. DuBois held conflicting views over "whether protesting injustice, when one could do nothing to right it oneself, was self-respecting." Bernard R. Boxill, in "Self-Respect and Protest," argues, in concert with W. E. B. Du Bois, that protesting wrongs in hard straits is a vital condition for having self-respect and being respected—and this not strictly as a function of assured success.

"Racial Integration and Racial Separatism: Conceptual Clarifications," by Howard McGary, Jr., reviews major propositions associated with racial integrationist and separatist movements as a means of focusing on their arguably strong and weak features and the sorts of considerations public policy makers should be cognizant of. McGary focuses our attention on programmatic concerns and holds that the separatists' emphasis on "controlling one's resources and the need to avoid being deprived of one's culture" are substantive considerations. Moreover, McGary notes that whether individual welfare is a function of group self-determination requires careful consideration in decision making.

One of the founding assumptions in Maulana Karenga's "Society, Culture and the Problem of Self-Consciousness" is that "the human being is essentially a cultural being." Karenga argues for the resolution of the problem of self-consciousness, i.e., the lack of general self-consciousness, through an appreciation of the context within which it arises and through, in part, the development of an ethos, and a self-realization that involves both knowing and producing one's self. Karenga argues on behalf of not a general theory first and foremost, but an Afro-centric theory as handmaiden in the struggle.

William R. Jones considers the preconditions for change through human activism, particularly Martin L. King's theories and strategies of change in light of black theology developments in "Liberation Strategies in Black Theology: Mao, Martin or Malcolm?" The efficacy of King's nonviolent civil disobedience direct action philosophy, to be practical on Jones' account, requires the oppressor's acceptance of "my co-humanity" because this undergirds what could be the oppressor's eventual repulsion with his own inhumanity. But in a racist society, the presupposition of co-humanity is absent and the effect of self-sacrificing love, on Jones' account, is mute. Consequently, "where racism is present the belief that black suffering is undeserved is absent." This both explains and clarifies what Jones tenders as an appropriate strategy and its association to Mao and Malcolm.

Experience Interpreted consists of articles that look at a body of texts and cultural patterns and tell us what they mean and how they should be understood. These articles engage in the act of interpreting as well as saying what approach we should use to interpret. Insofar as the act of interpreting 'what does it say, how does it say it, and what does it mean' is an act of explaining how and why the saying, among other things, came about, interpreting is explaining. Conversely, our understanding of how and why a given 'what' came about contributes to a conveyance of what the 'what' means. It is not a matter of which comes first, but of both adding to our comprehension of the Afro-American experience.

"The New Negro", originally Alain L. Locke's introduction to the book by that name, is an early application of Locke's functional relativism and cultural pluralism views. Locke notes that the 'old Negro' was more stereotypical images than reality. The use and promotion of idioms Locke associated with Afro-American folkways and the emergence of a race consciousness are presented by Locke as positive developments.

The article "On the Criticism of Black American Literature: One View of the Black Aesthetic," by Houston A. Baker, considers the notion of black aesthetics, its limitations, and positive aspects. Baker, in the process, "stresses the primacy of being/language/meaning" and a "concern for the historical aspects of the critical process". Baker explores the wider meaning of the black aesthetic as a movement beyond the narrow ideational forms characteristic of American literature.

Among the least regarded features of the African heritage has been magic. Albert G. Mosley, in "Negritude, Magic, and the Arts: A Pragmatic Perspective," explores magic's offerings to our conception of rationality. Mosley considers the association of magic with aesthetic and linguistic forms and tenders a view of magic as alternative communication.

Using a phenomenological approach focused on language and self-consciousness, Thomas F. Slaughter Jr. in "Epidermalizing the World: A Basic Mode of Being-Black" moves inside of what the experience of being black in a racist world is. For Slaughter, "The world is never merely given. It is given always already as a racist world." This conditions, for Slaughter, a given mode of being that is quintessentially a black mode.

The areas covered by this anthology represent a limited range of general problems—the nature of philosophy, explanation, interpretation—and do not include all works or fields of interest to Afro-American authors. As a family of texts, with various perspectives offered, this anthology is intended as a guide to the ideas of modern Afro-American philosophers, while serving as a historical resource directory for their works.

I

Frederick Douglass
1817–1895
c. 1880

I

Philosophy Experienced

Frederick Douglass: The Black Philosopher in the United States: A Commentary

Broadus N. Butler

The role of the Black philosopher in the United States has been both formidable and paradoxical. It has been formidable, because it always has had to be taken into account. It has been paradoxical, because once taken into account it generally has been either co-opted or denied full status and recognition. The preponderance of Black American philosophical inquiry, analysis, and philosophically oriented oral, literary, and political work has been directed primarily toward change in the human condition and toward social and legal change in pursuit of a clarification and perfection of the democratic ideal of justice. That pursuit always has combined ontological analysis with moral prescription—the analysis of what is with the analysis of what ought to be. Black American thinkers, with few exceptions, have not indulged themselves in the luxury either of pure speculative pursuit or of phenomenological analysis that disclaims consequences of analysis. This has been a matter of their historical attitude toward the relationship between knowledge and social responsibility.

Their methodology and their goals of inquiry have been different from and often disquieting to those who are accustomed to the accepted academic pursuit of philosophy. The most profound and penetrating philosophical contributions by Black Americans have emerged in the context of social analysis, social decision and/or social action in pursuit of national social change. That role for philosophy generally has been either shunned or unheralded in the academic annals of the profession in America. It may be for the reason that time has not diminished the immediacy of its impact, and it cannot yet be looked upon from the distant neutrality of historical retrospect.

1

In the main, Black American thinkers have contributed profound insights into what America ought to be and, by extension, what the universal condition and quality of existence of humankind ought to be. Their concentration has been upon American ontological conditions rather than only phenomenological possibilities—upon the achievement of an appropriate humane and democratic quality of life based in the proper universalization of the norms of equality, fraternity, and justice both in law and in the reality of the social contract. They have sought simultaneously a universal normative basis for unity, belonging, and governmental humaneness in the mediate realm and a similar basis for global cultural respect and just peace among the nations and institutions of humankind. This is in contrast to theories and postulations that have as their ultimate effect the support of systems of acquisitiveness, power, and dominance. Those insights, in the main, have met resistance among professional philosophers.

The professional resistance within the field has generally taken the form of ignoring or excluding from anthologies and other compilations of philosophical, literary, and poetic works the work of Black Americans. In other cases, there have been attempts to deny their theoretical uniqueness and purpose as ideas and contributions to the advancement of knowledge. In the more extreme cases, such as article I, sections 2 and 9, and article IV, section 2, of the original American Constitution, there was denial of the status of Black Americans as full-statured human beings within the legal and political premises of the American Constitution.

Yet, in spite of the alienations and denials, it has been recognized that no critical decision regarding the national existence and continued unity, security, governance, or quality of life throughout the history of this nation has ever been made without facing both the existence and the importance of Black Americans and Black American thought. At every major juncture in that history, Black Americans have been at the crucial decision point about both the existence of the nation and the quality of American life.

The first draft of the American Declaration of Independence recognized the contradiction between the existence of the institution of slavery and the quest by the colonists for independence in the name of liberty. The elimination of that passage from the final draft displayed such a contradiction even of theory that British and American commentators addressed the matter as an absurdity, and the British used that fact to belittle the whole effort of the colonists to be free. Although the paragraph that would have been the vehicle for the elimination of slavery was itself eliminated from the Declaration, the meaning of it and the significance of the institution to the history of thought in the nation has not diminished. Had that paragraph been retained, the drafting of the Constitution may have taken a different course. As it was, the 1787 Constitution provided for the perpetuation of the slave trade for twenty years; the classification of slaves as taxable property or chattel; the denial of citizenship to free and slave Blacks, and hence their exclusion from the intended meaning of "We the people of the United States." It also provided for the mandatory return of fugitive slaves by any state upon claim by a slaveholding state.

By contrast, and in the same year 1787, another document created as the Northwest Territorial Ordinance was drafted and adopted by the Confederation Congress. It was promulgated to govern the first territory, to provide the conditions for the establishment of new states and territories, to establish a commitment to education, and to provide that neither slavery nor involuntary servitude would prevail in that first territory or in any subsequent state or territory. There was no intention actually to carry out that mandate, even in the Northwest Territory. But the ordinance rather than the Constitution did become the pivotal document for addressing the question of the unity or dissolution of the nation itself seventy-five years later when President Abraham Lincoln finally put the issue squarely:

> My interest is in uniting the nation. If I can do that by freeing no
> slaves, I will do that. If to do that I must free some and leave others, I
> will do that. If to do that I must free all slaves, I will do that. But my
> interest is in uniting the nation.

Had the provisions of the Northwest Ordinance been made articles of the original Constitution, American history would have seen a different role for the nation and the Black philosopher.

The basic contradiction inherent in the circumstance of the formulation and promulgation of the original Constitution and in the attitude of the American nation toward the institution of slavery and involuntary servitude has dominated the textual framework and the contextual role of Black American philosophers. Thus, as philosophers, for all of the eloquence of their speech or writing and the profundity and universality of their thoughts; they have not enjoyed detachment from concerns about the American and world human condition in their engagement in philosophical speculation and analysis. Even as Black scholars organized their first national scholarly organization in 1897, the American Negro Academy, its preamble addressed its purpose to advance knowledge and culture, but also ". . . to protect ourselves from vicious assault." Those scholars subsequently used the route of learning and scholarship to enter the arena of constitutional challenge as the Niagara Movement, which itself subsequently became the National Association for the Advancement of Colored People. The second article of the charter of the Niagara Movement read:

> To organize thoroughly the intelligent and honest Negroes throughout
> the United States for the purpose of insisting on *manhood rights,*
> *industrial opportunity, and spiritual freedom.*

Those concerns have been most pervasive and deeply consuming, and they are based in a profound understanding of the very nature of our nation.

The Dred Scott decision of the United States Supreme Court in 1857 had demonstrated conclusively how fundamental was the distinction between the Euro-American minds and the Afro-American minds as they conceptualized reality and as each perceived the meaning of America. It also demonstrated that Euro-Americans perceive institutions, social systems, the Constitution, the Declaration, legal systems, and even moral and ethical propositions as relating to conceptual systems and to systems-determined phenomenology in complete abstraction from the realities that are or should be norms of human existence. Hence, flat human contradictions, for example as between freedom and slavery, can completely escape their recognition in philosophical analysis. That case further demonstrated that in spite of the eloquence of the Declaration of Independence and the specificity of the Northwest Ordinance, the Constitution itself did not contemplate the peer status of Black Americans or of women or of native Americans within the purview of the polity addressed as "We the people of the United States. . . ."

The tragedy, as witnessed just a few years later as a Civil War, is that the interpretation of the Constitution and the law of the land (except the Northwest Ordinance) at that time by that court was valid. Moreover, history bears out that it also was a true reflection of the intent of the framers of the Constitution even as expressed by Thomas Jefferson, the principle drafter of both the Declaration of Independence and the Northwest Ordinance.

That interpretation of the Constitution is still the dominant philosophical and psychological orientation of the Euro-American scholars, as there still is pervasive, though a bit more subtle, denial of peer status not only to Afro-Americans, but also to women, to native Americans, and to most classes of immigrants who are not northern or western Europeans—including Orientals.

When one looks at this basic systemic and constitutional paradox within which the American Black cultural, intellectual, political, social, and ontological status is conceptualized in both the foundational thought and the intellectual traditions of this nation, there should be no wonder that the Black American philosophical orientation to America and hence to the universe would differ from the prevailing norms. Typical of that difference is the particularity that Frederick Douglass gives to America in expressing his world view in the following passage:

> To build up a nation here, sacred in freedom as an example to the
> world, every man equal in the law and equally exercising all rights,
> political and civil . . . is the surest way to civilize humanity.

The philosophical context from which the metaphysical and social world outlook of a Frederick Douglass emerged in the nineteenth century United States is very different from that of Thomas Jefferson even when interpreting the same words of the same fundamental documents and ideas. Yet each purported to define the deepest meaning of America. The difference is the same as between Virgil and Cicero, between St. Paul and St. Augustine, between

4

Spinoza and Descartes, between Frederick Douglass and Lloyd Garrison, or even between W. E. B. Du Bois and John Dewey. In essence, there is a difference (not to be overgeneralized) of both epistemological and psychological context between philosophers who think within the dominant position and those who think as aliens within. Whether victim of a slave system, a member of an underclass or an outcast, or even a peer who empathises with the outcast; he or she conceptualizes from a consciousness of his or her own exemplification of the paradoxes and the contradictions that define the real charter of the larger society.

The difference was captured again by Douglass when he related the role-function of the Afro-American to the existence of the nation itself in the following way:

> . . . for the Negro and the nation are to rise and fall be killed or cured together. Save the Negro and you save the nation, destroy the Negro and you destroy the nation, and to save both you must have but one great law of Liberty, Equality and Fraternity for all Americans without respect of color.
>
> I base no man's right upon his color and plead no man's right because of his color. My interest in any man is objectively in his manhood and subjectively in my manhood.

Those constructions were not part of the mind set of the Jeffersons or even of the more recent liberals among traditional American philosophers. Frederick Douglass as distinguished from Thomas Jefferson in the realm of political thought or William James, John Dewey, Alfred North Whitehead, George Mead, or George Santayana in the philosophical arena addressed conceptual and analytical questions from a humanicentric perspective. That is, a perspective that presupposes that all human beings are equal qua humans and does not base human equality upon political and economic premises. The others, by contrast, address such matters from a systems-centric and an institutional analysis based upon European political, philosophical, and economic theories and systems rather than the broader human universalities. James Madison, among the Founding Fathers, like Douglass, saw mankind as peers, not property. He provided the closest linkage between the conceptual content of the Declaration and the Constitution and promulgated the first ten amendments, which are now enshrined as the Bill of Rights.

Jefferson could espouse eloquently the Declaration's commitment to creator-endowed equality of man while eschewing peership and advocating the return of Afro-Americans to Africa. President Abraham Lincoln could separate out his purposes in writing the Emancipation Proclamation by clearly and explicitly relating the document to the system of slavery, not to slaves, and to the effect of rebellion upon the nation, not upon the maintenance of slaves.

In an earlier address and in direct reference to the question of peership, Mr. Lincoln had made a carefully prepared speech that was the antithesis of his immortal Gettysburg Address. This was in Peoria, Illinois, in 1854:

What next? Free them and make them politically and socially our equal? My own feelings will not admit of this, and if mine would, we will know that those of the great mass of whites would not. Whether this feeling accords with justice and sound judgment is not the sole question, if indeed it is any part of it. A universal feeling whether well or ill founded, cannot be safely disregarded. We cannot then make them equal.

Exactly the same attitude was expressed even by the fiery abolitionist William Lloyd Garrison who stated that his opposition was to the existence of the institution of slavery, not in behalf of the peership of Negroes. Douglass, by contrast, was known to oppose all of those views and to view mankind as one and indivisible except by institutions and conditions that affect them. Thus, his address to the slavery institution took the following form:

My sympathies are not limited by my relation to any race. I can take no part in oppressing and persecuting any variety of the human family. Whether in Russia, Germany or California, my sympathy is with the oppressed, be he Chinaman or Hebrew.

Thus, whether consciously engaged in formal philosophy or making philosophical expression through poetry, speech, or literature, Black American cosmological, metaphysical, epistemological, ethical conceptions, and modalities tend in the final analysis to be humanicentric as distinguished from system-centric thought. Theirs is a metalogical more than a propositional function. Thus no matter what logical system is used, he characteristically infuses into the context a transcendent requirement that is not easily reducible to a common logical syntax. That is, that the logic gives as much attention to the value and consequence of the truth or falsity of premises as to the validity of conclusions drawn from the premises.

One may speculate with some substantial justification that this difference of orientation is itself a carryover from indigenous African philosophy and such family and political philosophies as ubuntuism of Zimbabwe or the fundamental concept of "belonging," which prevades the ancient traditions of African thought and still constitutes a dominant element of Black American thought and literature. A very recent documentary exhibition of the distinction is found in the October 1979 Nigerian Constitution, which was conceived in the framework of the American document but which made elaborate and carefully structured improvements over the American Constitution by the avoidance of the inherent contradictions between the systems address and the human address of the American Constitution.

To illustrate, the preamble to the 1787 Constitution of the United States was recast in the 1979 Constitution of Nigeria with the following fundamental difference of orientation.

American:

We, the people of the United States in order to form a more perfect union, establish justice, insure domestic tranquality, provide for common defense, promote general welfare . . . do ordain and establish . . .

Nigerian:

We the people of the Federal Republic of Nigeria firmly resolve: TO LIVE in harmony as one individual and indissoluble Sovereign Nation under God dedicated to the promotion of inter-African solidarity, world peace, international cooperation and understanding:

AND TO PROVIDE for a constitution for the purpose of promoting the good government and welfare of all persons in our country on the principles of Freedom, Equality and Justice and for the purpose of consolidating the unity of our people:

DO HEREBY make, enact and give to ourselves the following constitution.

The constitution itself is replete with propositions such as:

The State shall foster a feeling of belonging and involvement among the various peoples of the Federation to the end that loyalty to the nation shall override sectional loyalties.

Every citizen shall have equality of rights, obligations and opportunities before the law:

The sanction of the human person shall be recognized and human dignity shall be maintained and enhanced.

Government actions shall be humane:

It is a legitimate philosophical question to ask whether this or the original American Constitution is more commensurate to what the American nation is or ought to be, was or ought to have been. It is clear that this is what some perceive America all the time should have been and, as is their wish, in the future will be. Paradoxically, America framed the philosophical model that Nigeria adopted, but psychologically America still leans toward the Platonic *Republic* model that its own document rejected.

The Nigerian model and Zimbabwean humanism, based in the ordering of the concept of belonging and the extension of the family symbol into political organization, translate American documents into nationhood rather than statism. This, from the standpoint of the Black American philosophic tradition, represents the larger meaning of its conflict with the mainstream of American academic philosophy. That also is one of the larger meanings of the profound conflict generally suggested by the phrase "Black experience."

7

However, in spite of the Black philosophers' dilemma in America and in the stream of European thought, and even in spite of their struggle against perpetual alienation and intellectual assault, their posture in behalf of what America ought to be and may yet become is neither cynical nor tragic in projection of outcome. It vests a profound faith in the belief that if the highest moral and political objectives as they perceive them were pursued in America, then the totality of humankind would be the beneficiary and even more largely the emulator.

Black American philosophy and activism has as its final goal the fulfillment of the hope that is inherent in true democracy—not a dispair for the consequences of the contradictions and absurdities that yet must be fully overcome. They say that mankind faces a clear choice at this juncture; the choice is between elevation of humankind and the destruction of human existence. For the first time in human history, humankind has both the technology for utter and complete destruction of all of life on the planet and the human and natural resources to enhance the totality of humankind to the highest quality of existence that has ever been experienced on this planet. In the Black tradition, the choice is clear; and it has been consistent over time. Humankind must be elevated in equality or humanity will be destroyed. Others must be persuaded to this wisdom.

Note on the Author

Broadus N. Butler is a highly regarded educator and scholar. He is the former President of Dillard University and Robert R. Moton Memorial Institute, which sponsored post-doctoral research for many Afro-American philosophers under the auspices of the Moton Center for Independent Studies. His philosophical focus is value theory, but his mode is more the educator, practioner, historian, and civil rights advocate, than the ivory tower academecian. Dr. Butler was Board member and Director for International Affairs, National Association for the Advancement of Colored People, and Board Member, National Institute of Public Management. He is presently Vice President for Academic Affairs of the University of the District of Columbia.

II

William Edward Burghardt Dubois
1868–1963
c. 1920

W. E. B. DuBois: Afro-American Philosopher of Social Reality

Robert C. Williams

During the tenth decade of his unusually eventful and scholarly life, the Afro-American thinker William Edward Burghardt DuBois (1868–1963) uttered insightful and prophetic words which summarized his view of American social reality:

> Government is for the people's progress and not for the comfort of an aristocracy. The object of industry is the welfare of the workers and not the wealth of the owners. The object of civilization is the cultural progress of the mass of workers and not merely of the intellectual elite.
>
> (from a speech to the world over
> delivered in Peking, China, on his
> ninety-first birthday, 1959)
>
> No universal selfishness can bring social good to all . . . [or] restore democracy in [the USA] . . . [the path of social progress in America] will call for:
>
> 1. Public ownership of natural resources and of all capital.
> 2. Public control of transportation and communications.
> 3. Abolition of poverty and limitation of personal income.
> 4. No exploitation of labor.
> 5. Social medicine, with hospitalization and care of the old.
> 6. Free education for all.
> 7. Training for jobs and jobs for all.
> 8. Discipline for growth and reform.
> 9. Freedom under law.
> 10. No dogmatic religion.
>
> (from letter of application for membership in
> the Communist Party of the USA, 1961)

In this all too brief essay I will not attempt to challenge the above assertions since I regard them as well-founded. Instead, I will argue that the writings of DuBois support the above observations as characteristic of his evolving social philosophy. His views, as expressed above, are substantiated in at least two ways. First, they relate to the realities of politics and social change/stratification which he repeatedly experienced in twentieth century America. Second, they convey his sense—expressed in numerous ways throughout his writings—that some form of democratic or radical socialism will constitute the basis of political thought and the organization of national life in America's future. These two ways of assessing DuBois' philosophical analysis of social reality relate to present-day endeavors to articulate the necessity, legitimacy and content of social philosophy in the Afro-American context. In fact, mutual interdependence—forged upon the anvil of human

11

equality, economic opportunity and liberty for all—was regarded by DuBois as the basis of real democratic or social life. This concept (i.e., mutual interdependence) is the central theme in DuBois' social philosophy.

Thus in discussing his philosophical vision of the social dimension of the American experience, I will limit my comments to three things:

1. his encounter with American philosophical ideals and liberalism;
2. his view of social reality; and 3. the relation of his ideas to the emerging black perspective in philosophy.

DuBois and American Philosophical Ideals

Much of the philosophical interpretation of the American experience has been unduly formalistic and, from the perspective of ethnic and class minorities, antiquarian. In the process of interpreting the American reality vis-a-vis letters, few major questions regarding the prevasive ethnic/pluralistic character of the national spirit have been raised. Within the American philosophical establishment, for example, there is a paucity of comment—with Josiah Royce being perhaps the most classic exception[1]—concerning the diversity of ethnic and racial interests axiomatic to the New World venture in republicanism, industrialism, and democracy.

By 1910 DuBois (a product of Fisk, Harvard, and Berlin Universities) was the most articulate Afro-American voice in the area of philosophy and the social sciences. Early in his career, DuBois espoused, in the Enlightenment tradition of moral suasion, a social philosophy of freedom, creative protest, and manhood rights for Africans and their descendents in the New World. His social philosophy, paradoxically, is as much a critical comment on the collective aspects of the American experience as it is a straightforward description/analysis of the dehumanizing predicament of black people in America and the world. In his role as Afro-American philosopher of social reality, DuBois was both an incisive thinker and a "lyric historian." Yet, he was more history-maker than an historian or social scientist.[2] He was, to summarize his life activities in brief compass, an activist/advocate as well as a creative and productive thinker. In fact, DuBois emerges at the end of the second century (1976) of the evolving American mind, in its philosophical and aesthetic dimensions, as one of the most insightful and gifted men of letters to come from the American soil.[3] Whereas he ardently believed that human beings function, via their social roles, in direct relation to historical-social circumstances, he was also convinced that human beings created and influenced social circumstances. His faith in human progress, by means of the American cultural reality, enabled him to spawn a social philosophy based upon egalitarianism, hope for progressive change, self-development on the part of disadvantaged groups, and the universal rights of all peoples.

Heir to philosophies of the Enlightenment, the American experiment in egalitarian democracy and *laissez faire* economics was initially intended to answer the pressing needs of various classes and races. By the middle of the nineteenth century both the Jeffersonian and Jacksonian versions of American political aspirations had lost the spirit of the Enlightenment, had bartered with strange bedfellows in order to pursue the economic/philosophical interests of certain dominant political groups, and had thereby become functionally (though perhaps not ideologically) disengaged from all significant humanitarian concerns.[4]

But the latter part of the nineteenth century saw the rise of a critical-realistic perspective in the assessment and espousal of the political and social dimensions of American life. This perspective enabled observers, dreamers, and critics of the nation to view the processes of industrialism and the concomitant spread of the workings of scientific thought as the basis for forging a more adequate view of the complex evolving American cultural fabric. Economics, psychology and history were three of the major forces operating in the dominant thought at this time (1890–1910).[5]

It is noteworthy that the Afro-American thinker W. E. B. DuBois came upon the American intellectual scene during this very creative and troublesome era. He pioneered in and championed the new empirical emphasis in social science and history. He achieved this distinction by stressing class and social environment as major causal agents in personality formation and the sociological understanding of reality.[6] His emergence as a social theoretician and critic/activist came about as he was in the process of ferreting out his philosophical views on the nature of community and social change.

When DuBois completed his graduate work in 1896 he was totally immersed in the rigors of scientific research and had made a personal commitment (contrary to his earlier wish to do philosophy[7]) to undertake a career as a writer and teacher in the social sciences. *The Philadelphia Negro* (1899) was his great work in the social sciences, being an impressive monograph that deals with social stratification as an index into understanding the plight and social condition of the Negro population. In this seminal sociological study, DuBois observed that

> Notwithstanding the large influence of the physical environment of
> home and ward, nevertheless there is a far mightier influence to mold
> and make the citizen, and that is the social atmosphere which surrounds
> him: first his daily companionship, the thoughts and whims of his class;
> then his recreations and amusements; finally, the surrounding world of
> American civilization.[8]

The "surrounding world of American civilization" in 1900 was an existential reality that the thinker DuBois could not cavalierly dismiss or arrogantly wish away. DuBois could not turn his back upon this facet of the American reality because the problem it posed was his problem (the problem of being back in a world dominated by whites).

> My life had its significance and its only deep significance because it was
> part of a problem; but that problem was, as I continue to think, the
> central problem of the greatest of the world's democracies and so the
> problem of the future world.

13

> The problem of the twentieth century is the problem of the colorline,—
> the relation of the darker to lighter races of men in Asia and Africa, in
> America and the islands of the sea.[9]

This world of color-paradox; wherein the apotheosis of evil made havoc of the democratic aspirations of the post-Civil War era, was the world from which black folks, newly emergent from slavery, were drawing their self-consciousness, self-realization, and self-respect. This was the world of the sombre forests of American's enduring internal contradiction: oppression and freedom, liberty and bondage—a situational vortex that constituted the American reality of two world-races: the darker, oppressed race and the lighter, oppressor race.[10] The darker Negro-African race tended to perceive itself through the eyes of others, via a bipolar identity and/or a "double-consciousness,"[11] though the realization that as the darker of the American races it is both African and American in its essential character.

This divided "world of American civilization" impacted upon DuBois' sensibility via its contradictions in custom, temper, and thought—revealing itself as "a terribly complex moral condition" (with its characteristic bursts of work, longings for progress, cries of revolution and exploitation of the black masses). This peculiar cultural syndrome, inspired by greed and ethnocentrism, generated in the young DuBois, as in many of his contemporaries, its own social contagion of optimism, individualism, roughness, and distrust.[12] It is therefore no mere wonder that the diffident philosopher Santayana confessed to a non-American audience that "To be American is of itself almost a moral condition . . ."[13] a juxtaposing of materialism and idealism in day-to-day life (the striving for a kind of moral idealism realized by means of an ideational conjoining of nature and spirit). Like Santayana, DuBois clearly saw that moral freedom as manifested in the social realm "is not an artificial condition"[14] sustained merely by the life of the mind. But unlike Santayana who eschewed American philosophical ideals (as these were embodied in the actualities of American culture and especially in the reflections of James and Royce), DuBois remained in America and resigned himself to work toward disclosing the essence of its postenlightenment moral bankruptcy and the double standard it espoused for citizenship, justice, and community. The American ideal of national unity by means of community—an ideal never applied to the condition and social development of black folks—caused DuBois to sense that the price of liberty was less than the price of bondage: for "oppression costs the oppressor too much if the oppressed stand up and protest."[15]

DuBois' disappointment with the American practice of racial discrimination and his refusal to dogmatically embrace established liberalism supplied the animus for his creation of a social philosophy of interdependence (anticipating in some respects Charles Hartshornes's *Reality As Social Process*). Thus, the concept of mutual interdependence became the basis of his critique of the American liberal and intellectual establishment: i.e., no form of universal selfishness can generate social stability or economic/racial justice.

Social Philosophy

Rights and duties are inextricably interwoven into the cultural fabric of American democracy. DuBois' philosophical perspective on the social life of Afro-Americans was a reflection upon the chief problematic of the American identity both in actuality and in terms of its ideal creed: the reality of the American people in community and national vocation. And this crisis of identity in community and collective purpose is, as DuBois sensed all too clearly, was inadequately treated in the philosophical probings of American intellectuals. This is what made DuBois' encounter with American philosophy so dissatisfying.

It was both Royce and DuBois who emerged in the American intellectual tradition as articulate voices treating the problematic of the American identity (vis-a-vis rights and duties) in its collective and social dimensions. Royce's philosophical studies treated the motif of community-in-loyalty as the creative perspective by means of which the American experiment is to be understood; and DuBois' massive historical study of the attempt to democratize the American nation through the actualities of the Reconstruction era looms as a classic example of probing that period in the American experience in all of the departments of its social-political-economic life. Those who read DuBois' *Black Reconstruction* and Royce's *The Hope of the Great Community* back-to-back are in for a real intellectual challenge. And yet Santayana's comment that Royce "seemed to view everything in relation to something else that remained untold"[16] is not an apt delineation of DuBois' evolving view of things social, for DuBois' view entailed his sensing that detached inquiry was not enough and that the truth alone did not encourage or enhance social reform.[17] Royce the philosopher was a blend of the necessarily moral and the detached observer ("Moralism and an apology for evil could thus be reconciled and merged in the praises of tragic experience").[18] But DuBois the scholar was in actuality really only a graft on DuBois the Negro, thus prohibiting him from being merely a cool, calm, and detached scientist ("My life had its significance . . . because it was part of a problem . . . the problem of the colorline.")[19] Royce's idea of community was couched in optimistic terms (i.e., that the diversity of ideas and the pervasiveness of human error could only be handled by means of the coexistence of all types of human beings who exist via a principle of loyalty).[20] This view of community was, in the final analysis, too sentimental and tame to guide the searchings and social analysis developed by DuBois. For DuBois, the problematic of the Black American identity through time was not infused with a calculated and measured idealism. His analysis was more radical—based as it was upon the reality and ambiguity of black existence in pursuit of justice, of a loyalty and mutual interdependence that demanded the American people grant real equity, liberty, and opportunity to every citizen.

What DuBois espoused in his personal philosophy he firmly believed to be incumbent upon the American people: "I am by birth and law a free black American citizen. As such I have both rights and duties. If I neglect my duties my rights are always in danger. If I do not maintain my rights I cannot perform my duties."[21] This dialectic of rights and duty formed the basis of DuBois' analysis/criticism of America's moral-philosophical ideas and its strange sense of social justice.

As early as 1907, DuBois published his first sentiments on socialism, and, though at that time he did not claim to be a disciple of socialism, it was his belief that socialism was one reliable path leading to the ideal of human brotherhood, equality of opportunity, and self-respect.[22] But later in his life DuBois felt strongly that American black folk should come to understand the nature of Marx's panacea for the plight of the working class—in England, France, and Germany—if they really intended to plan effectively for the future.[23] In this and other sympathetic articles on the relevance of the Marxian analysis to the class struggle DuBois saw its potential relation to the problem of discrimination against Negroes (even given the fact that there was rampant racism within the ranks of the white working class).[24] In DuBois' view of American society the class struggle of exploiter and exploited was indeed grounded in reality, but a different reality for whites and blacks respectively.

Even though his thought underwent considerable change, DuBois consistently believed in democracy and equity for all citizens. His embrace of radical socialism during his last decade is the most telling fact that the concept of mutual interdependence formed the crux of his social philosophy as well as his assessment of the American experiment in liberty and citizenship.[25]

DuBois and Black Philosophy

DuBois' early encounter with the Harvard philosophers James, Royce, and Santayana made a significant and lasting impression upon him. In fact he had wanted to be a philosopher, but, as he reports, "it was James with his pragmatism and Albert Bushnell Hart with his research method, that turned me back from the lovely but sterile hand of philosophic speculation, to the social sciences as the field for gathering and interpreting that body of fact which would apply to my program for the Negro."[26] There was manifest upheaval in DuBois' thinking during his days at Harvard, Berlin, and Pennsylvania Universities.

> To understand this revolution in DuBois' thinking one must understand
> what happened to the hopes of the American Negro. The Emancipation
> and the period of the Reconstruction following the Civil War—the
> period of DuBois' childhood—had brought dreams of equality and for a
> time, some actual power to the Negro. But then the reaction had set in,
> and by the turn of the century the dreams had been shattered, and
> what DuBois saw around him was the steady—and apparently
> accelerating—deterioration of the position of the Negro in American
> life.[27]

With his characteristic knack for analysis, DuBois argued early in this century that blackness and black consciousness were significant components of black reality—were of the essence and ambiguity of being black in America. He cited a double-consciousness as descriptive of black people and stipulated that this myopia of a dual or bipolar consciousness/identity produced a fundamental alienation in black folks: caused them to view themselves both through their own eyes and "through the eyes of others."[28] This self-consciousness in alienation is problematic because it embodies both the seeds of self-disregard and self-liberation (it is, as DuBois clearly recognized, the self in realization of itself—the self in search of its own identity and fulfillment through the presence of the other. More often than not, this 'other' was the pervasive hand of white oppression). Hence a pervasive contradiction and/or ambiguity is the factor upon which the dual consciousness of the Negro is structured—a phenomenon related to the yes and no of black life as it encounters in reciprocity white life ("Self-consciousness attains its satisfaction only in another self-consciousness"—Hegel, *Phenomenology of Spirit*). This insight is indispensable for articulating the totality of the American—and the black—experience in the New World. Such a view is relevant and necessary to any viable program in American philosophy. For an analysis of consciousness—of an epoch, a nation, or a people—is one reliable means of carrying out the task of philosophy. An analysis of American consciousness that excludes black consciousness is flawed.

And a black philosophy would assume the fundamental value of an ethnic perspective and/or identity. Even assuming that philosophy is an undertaking committed to a search for the general and regulative principles of human existence, then a black and/or Afro-American philosophy would enhance such an endeavor by elucidating the ambiguities and particularities of black life. Accordingly, the social dimension of the black experience would be a very important factor in such a task. To the degree that it succeeds in shattering the illusion of a possible freedom in racial bondage and individual self-determination, and to the degree that it provides a corrective to those philosophies that support ethnic oppression and the cultural/cognitive invisibility of black people, black philosophy will enhance the task of philosophy in general and will also stand in the sociological/philosophical tradition of DuBois. That is, that no form of universal or individual selfishness will yield a social good and that the basis of social solidarity is mutual interdependence. If it follows the polemical and searching tradition of the Afro-American thinker DuBois, a black and/or Afro-American social philosophy would be the means of correcting all attempts at linguistic sovereignty, conceptual imperialism, and the espousal of the view that philosophizing is alien to the black imagination/sensibility. This is simply a way of saying—and DuBois said it in many different ways—that black existence and black reflection merit status, authority, and consideration in the philosophical arena: that the existence of black Americans is a legitimate and necessary means of pursuing philosophy through the idiom of American social reality.

The immediate challenge facing a black philosophy—an outlook on human existence that accents what it means to be black, that discloses all attempts to subordinate black existence and that lays bare the rights and obligations of Americans—is for it to serve as a means of liberation and enlightenment to the economically dispossessed, politically exploited, and racially oppressed peoples of the world. Such a view, in the final analysis, is neither racist nor parochial, for in DuBois' terms, it will serve as an appropriate means of elucidating the "surrounding world of American civilization."[29] And it may be the case that a black social philosophy, spawned in the American intellectual milieu, will stress mutual interdependence and individual collective unselfishness as the basis of a workable social contract.[30]

Notes

1. Josiah Royce, *Race Questions, Provincialism, and Other American Problems* (New York: The Macmillan Company, 1911); *The Hope of the Great Community* (New York: The Macmillan Company, 1916); and *The Letters of Josiah Royce* (ed. by John Chendenning, Chicago: The University of Chicago Press, 1970).
2. Herbert Aptheker, unpublished lecture titled "DuBois' Philosophy of History," delivered at Vanderbilt University, April 12, 1976.
3. DuBois was the author of nineteen books, editor of eighteen books, founder of four leading magazines, contributor of weekly columns to newspapers, and producer of hundreds of articles in scholarly journals and publications throughout the world. See the *Annotated Bibliography of the Published Writings of W. E. B. DuBois* by Herbert Aptheker (Millwood, New York: Araus-Thomson Organization Limited, 1973), which cites approximately 1,975 items. For examples of his philosophical/historical writing, compare his *Souls of Black Folk* with Santayana's *Reason in Society* or his *Black Reconstruction* with Royce's *The Hope of the Great Community*. He wrote five novels and many poems of the social protest genre.
4. Vernon L. Parrington, *Main Currents in American Thought*, volume 3 (New York: Harcourt, Brace and World, Inc., 1958), pp. 189–203.
5. Ibid., p. XXVIII. At this time a decay of the older theological forces, which dominated political minds, was evident, making way for the emergence of an urban mind that would, in many instances, begin to champion proletarian hopes.
6. DuBois, *The Philadelphia Negro* (1899). See his famous "Atlanta Studies" (1897–1910) published in sixteen monographs, and especially his *Black Reconstruction* (1935).
7. DuBois "My Evolving Program for Negro Freedom" in Rayford W. Logan, ed., *What the Negro Wants*, p. 42.
8. DuBois, *The Philadelphia Negro*, p. 309.
9. DuBois *Dusk of Dawn*, 1940, p. vii, and *Souls of Black Folk*, 1903, p. 23.
10. *Souls of Black Folk*, p. 20.
11. Ibid., pp. 16 and 17.
12. George Santayana, *Character and Opinion in the United States* (New York: Doubleday, 1920), p. 105.
13. Ibid., p. 104.
14. Ibid., p. 118.
15. DuBois, *John Brown*, 1909, p. 395.
16. Santayana, *op.cit.*, p. 60.
17. DuBois, *Souls of Black Folk*, Introduction by S. Redding, Fawcett Publications, Inc., 1961, p. viii.

18. Santayana, *op.cit.*, pp. 80–81 and 76.
19. See note 9 above. Also, *Souls of Black Folk.*
20. Royce, *The Hope of the Great Community*, pp. 49, 52.
21. DuBois, "A Philosophy for 1913", published in *The Crisis*, January, 1913.
22. *The Horizon* (Vol. I, No. 2, February, 1907), p. 7 and 8.
23. *The Crisis* (Vol. XI, No. 3, March 1933), p. 56.
24. Blacks, he once argued, "Theoretically . . . are part of the world proletariat in the sense that (they) . . . are mainly an exploited class of cheap laborers; but practically (they) . . . are not a part of the white proletariat and are not recognized by that proletariat to any great extent." (*The Crisis*, August, 1921, pp. 151–152).
25. Herbert Aptheker (ed.), *The Correspondence of W. E. B. Du Bois* (University of Massachusetts Press, 1976), vol. II, pp. 92 and 76–103.
26. Logan, *op.cit.*, p. 42—see note 7 above.
27. S. Redding, *op.cit.*, p. ix—see note 17 above; also, Robert C. Williams "Moral Suasion and Militant Aggression in the Theological Perspectives of Black Religion", *The Journal of Religious Thought*, Vol. XXX, No. 2, Fall-Winter, 1973–74, pp. 32–34.
28. *Souls of Black Folk*, chapter I.
29. See note 8 above.
30. These two concepts could be enlarged upon by contrasting them with the notion of distributive justice (John Rawls, *A Theory of Justice*) and the theory of entitlement (Robert Nozick, *Anarchy, State, and Utopia*).

Note on the Author

Robert C. Williams is Associate Professor of Philosophy, Vanderbilt University. He teaches in the area of the philosophy of religion and American and African philosophy. He is a former chairman of the Committee on Blacks in Philosophy, American Philosophical Association. His works have been published in theological and philosophical journals.

III

Alain LeRoy Locke
1886–1954
c. 1938

Values and Imperatives
[1935]

Alain L. Locke

All philosophies, it seems to me, are in ultimate derivation philosophies of life and not of abstract, disembodied "objective" reality; products of time, place and situation, and thus systems of timed history rather than timeless eternity. They need not even be so universal as to become the epitomized *rationale* of an age, but may merely be the lineaments of a personality, its temperament and dispositional attitudes projected into their systematic rationalizations. But no conception of philosophy, however relativistic, however opposed to absolutism, can afford to ignore the question of ultimates or abandon what has been so aptly though skeptically termed "the quest for certainty". To do that is not merely to abdicate traditional metaphysics with its rationalistic justification of absolutes but also to stifle embryonic axiology with its promising analysis of norms. Several sections of American thought, however, have been so anxious to repudiate intellectualism and escape the autocracy of categoricals and universals that they have been ready to risk this. Though they have at times discussed the problems of value, they have usually avoided their normative aspects, which has led them into a bloodless behaviorism as arid as the intellectualism they have abandoned or else resulted in a completely individualistic and anarchic relativism which has rightly been characterized recently as "philosophic Nihilism". In dethroning our absolutes, we must take care not to exile our imperatives, for after all, we live by them. We must realize more fully that values create these imperatives as well as the more formally super-imposed absolutes, and that norms control our behavior as well as guide our reasoning. Further, as I shall later point out, we must realize that not in every instance is this normative control effected indirectly through judgmental or evaluational processes, but often through primary mechanisms of feeling modes and dispositional attitudes. Be that as it may, it seems that we are at last coming to the realization that without some account of normative principles, some fundamental consideration of value norms and "ultimates" (using the term in a non-committal sense), no philosophical system can hope to differentiate itself from descriptive science or present a functional, interpretive version of human experience.

Man does not, cannot, live in a valueless world. Pluralism has merely given temporary surcease from what was the central problem of monism,— the analysis and justification of these "ultimates", and pragmatism has only transposed the question from the traditional one of what ends should govern life to the more provocative one of how and why activity creates them. No philosophy, short of the sheerest nominalism or the most colorlessly objective

21

behaviorism, is so neutral that it has not some axiological implications. Positivism least of all; for in opposing the traditional values, positivism has set up countervalues bidding us find meaning in the act rather than project meaning from the plane of reason and the subjective approach; and further, as pragmatism and instrumentalism, has set up at the center of its philosophy a doctrine of truth as itself a functional value. So, by waiving the question of the validity of value ultimates as "absolutes", we do not escape the problem of their functional categorical character as imperatives of action and as norms of preference and choice.

Though this characteristically American repudiation of "ultimates" was originally made in the name of the "philosophy of common sense", common sense and the practical life confronts us with the problem all the more forcefully by displaying a chronic and almost universal fundamentalism of values in action. Of this, we must at least take stock, even if we cannot eventually justify it or approve of it. The common man, in both his individual and group behavior, perpetuates the problem in a very practical way. He sets up personal and private and group norms as standards and principles, and rightly or wrongly hypostasizes them as universals for all conditions, all times and all men. Whether then on the plane of reason or that of action, whether "above the battle" in the conflict of "isms" and the "bloodless ballet of ideas" or in the battle of partisans with their conflicting and irreconcilable ways of life, the same essential strife goes on, and goes on in the name of eternal ends and deified ultimates. Our quest for certainty, motivated from the same urge, leads to similar dilemmas. The blind practicality of the common man and the disinterested impracticality of the philosopher yield similar results and rationalizations. Moreover, such transvaluations of value as from time to time we have, lead neither to a truce of values nor to an effective devaluation; they merely resolve one dilemma and set up another. And so, the conflict of irreconcilables goes on as the devisive and competitive forces of our practical imperatives parallel the incompatibilities of our formal absolutes.

We cannot declare for value-anarchism as a wishful way out, or find a solution in that other alternative blind alley of a mere descriptive analysis of interests. That but postpones the vital problems of ends till the logically later consideration of evaluation and post-valuational rationalizations. To my thinking, the gravest problem of contemporary philosophy is how to ground some normative principle or criterion of objective validity for values without resort to dogmatism and absolutism on the intellectual plane, and without falling into their corollaries, on[1] the plane of social behavior and action, of intolerance and mass coercion. This calls for a functional analysis of value norms and a search for normative principles in the immediate context of valuation. It raises the question whether the fundamental value modes have a way of setting up automatically or dispositionally their end-values prior to evaluative judgment. Should this be the case, there would be available a more direct approach to the problem of value ultimates, and we might discover their primary normative character to reside in their functional rôle as stereotypes of feeling-attitudes and dispositional imperatives of action-choices, with this character reenforced only secondarily by reason and judgment about them as "absolutes". We should then be nearer a practical understanding of the operative mechanisms of valuation and of the grounds for our agreements and conflicts over values.

Normally, one would expect a philosophical tradition dominated, as contemporary American thought has been, by an activist theory of knowledge, to have made a problem like this central. We might very profitably pause for a moment to take stock of the reasons why this has not been so. In the first place, in the reaction away from academic metaphysics, there has been a flight to description and analysis too analagous to science and too committed to scientific objectivism. It is impossible to reach such problems as we have before us effectively in terms of pure positivism, of the prevalent objectivism, or of the typical view that until quite recently has dominated American value theory,—the view namely that end-values exist only in so far as values are rationalized and mediated by processes of evaluation and formal value judgments. Added to this, is our characteristic preoccupation with theories of meaning limited practically to the field of truth and knowledge. Because of this logico-experimental slant, we again have made common cause with the current scientific attitude; making truth too exclusively a matter of the correct anticipation of experience, of the confirmation of fact.[2] Yet truth may also sometimes be the sustaining of an attitude, the satisfaction of a way of feeling, the corroboration of a value. To the poet, beauty is truth; to the religious devotee, God is truth; so the enthused moralist, what ought-to-be overtops factual reality. It is perhaps to be expected that the typical American philosophies should concentrate almost exclusively on thought-action as the sole criterion of experience, and should find analysis of the emotional aspects of human behavior uncongenial. This in itself, incidentally is a confirming example of an influential value-set, amounting in this instance to a grave cultural bias. When we add to this our American tradition of individualism, reflecting itself characteristically in the value-anarchism and *laissez faire* of which we have already spoken, it is easy to explain why American thought has moved tangent to the whole central issue of the normative aspects and problems of value.

In saying this, do we say anything more than that values are important and that American philosophy should pay more attention to axiology? Most assuredly;—we are saying that but for a certain blindness, value-theory might easily have been an American forte, and may still become so if our predominantly functionalist doctrines ever shed their arbitrary objectivism and extend themselves beyond their present concentration on theories of truth and knowledge into a balanced analysis of values generally. Ironically enough, the very type of philosophy which has insisted on truth as a value has, by rigid insistence on the objective criterion and the experimental-instrumental aspects of thought, disabled itself for pursuing a similarly functional interpretation of the other value modes and their normative principles.

Human behavior, it is true, is experimental, but it is also selectively preferential, and not always in terms of outer adjustments and concrete results. Value reactions guided by emotional preferences and affinities are as potent in the determination of attitudes as pragmatic consequences are in the determination of actions. In the generic and best sense of the term 'pragmatic', it is as important to take stock of the one as the other.

Fortunately, within the last few years a decided trend toward axiology and the neglected problems of value has developed, properly enough under the aegis of the *International Journal of Ethics*, promising to offset this present one-sidedness of American philosophical interests. Once contemporary American thought does turn systematically to the analysis of values, its empirical and functionalist approach will be considerably in its favor. Such a philosophic tradition and technique ought to come near to realizing the aim of Brentano, father of modern value-theory, to derive a functional theory of value from a descriptive and empirical psychology of valuation and to discover in value-experience itself the source of those normative and categorical elements construed for centuries so arbitrarily and so artificially in the realm of rational absolutes.

There is little or no hope that this can be obtained *via* a theory of value which bids us seek whatever objectivity and universality values may have outside the primary processes of valuation, whether in the confirmations of experience or the affirmations of evaluative judgments. For these positions lead only, as far as the direct apprehension of value goes, to Protagorean relativism,—each man the measure and each situation the gauge of value, and then an abysmal jump to the objective criterion of the truths of science, valid for all situations, all men and all times.

What seems most needed is some middle ground between these extremes of subjectivism and objectivism. The natural distinctions of values and their functional criteria surely lie somewhere in between the atomistic relativism of a pleasure-pain scale and the colorless, uniformitarian criterion of logic,— the latter more of a straight-jacket for value qualities than the old intellectualist trinity of Beauty, Truth and Good. Flesh and blood values may not be as universal or objective as logical truths and schematized judgments, but they are not thereby deprived of some relative objectivity and universality of their own. The basic qualities of values should never have been sought in logical classes, for they pertain to psychological categories. They are not grounded in types of realms of value, but are rooted in modes or kinds of *valuing*.

In fact, the value-mode establishes for itself, directly through feeling, a qualitative category which, as discriminated by its appropriate feeling-quality, constitutes an emotionally mediated form of experience. If this be so, the primary judgments of value are emotional judgments—(if the inveterate Austrian term *"feeling-judgments"* is not allowable philosophical English), and the initial reference for value predication is based on a form-quality revealed in feeling and efficacious in valuation through feeling. Though finally validated in different ways and by different criteria, beauty, goodness, truth (as approval or acceptance), righteousness are known in immediate recognitions of qualitative apprehension. The generic types of value are basic and fundamental feeling-modes, each with its own characteristic form criterion in value perception. For the fundamental kinds, we can refer to inveterate common-sense, which discriminates them with approximate accuracy—the moral and ethical, the aesthetic, the logical and the religious categories with their roughly descriptive predicates. For an empirical psychology of values, however, they need to be approached directly from the side of feeling and value-attitudes, and re-descriminated not in terms of formal definition but in terms of technical description of their affective-volitional dimensions and factors.

Normally a value-mode is conveyed while the value is being apprehended. Otherwise the quality of the value would be indeterminate, and this is usually contrary to fact. Though we may still be in doubt regarding its validation, its quantity, place in the value series and other specific issues of the value situation, we are usually certain of the value-mode. This is why we should think of a value-quality primarily in terms of feeling or attitude and not of predicates of judgment; why we should speak of a value-reference rather than a value claim. And if the value type is given in the immediate apprehension of the particular value, some qualitative universal is given. It supplies the clue to the functional value norm,—being felt as good, beautiful, etc.—and we have this event in mind when we say that in the feeling-reference to some value-mode, some value ultimate becomes the birthmark of the value. If values are thus normatively stamped by form-qualities of feeling in the original value experience, then the evaluative judgment merely renders explicit what was implicit in the original value sensing, at least as far as the modal quality of the value is concerned. This could only be true on one of two assumptions, *viz.*, that some abstract feeling-character functioned dispositionally as a substitute for formal judgment, or that the feeling-attitude itself moulded the value-mode and reflected sympathetically its own pattern. If the latter be the case, a value-type or category is a feeling-mode carved out dispositionally by a fundamental attitude.

Of course, this notion of a feeling-reference or form-quality constituting the essential identity and unity of a value-mode is not easily demonstrable; it may be just a hypothetical anticipation of what an experimental analysis of valuation might later establish and prove. However, the main objection to such a conception of a value form-character has been undermined, if not overthrown, by the Gestalt psychology, which has demonstrated the factual reality of a total configuration functioning in perceptual recognition, comparison and choice. There is therefore nothing scientifically impossible or bizarre in assuming a form-quality felt along with the specific value context and constituting its modal value-quality and reference. In the absence of direct evidence of this configurational element in valuation, the most corroborative circumstantial evidence is to be found in the interchangeability or rather the convertibility of the various kinds of value. The further we investigate, the more we discover that there is no fixity of content to values, and the more we are bound, then, to infer that their identity as groups must rest on other elements. We know that a *value-genre* often evades its definition and breaks through its logical barriers to include content not usually associated with it. The awe-inspiring scene becomes *"holy,"* the logical proof, *"beautiful,"* creative expression, a "duty," and in every case the appropriate new predicates follow the attitude and the attitude cancels out the traditionally appropriate predicates. For every value coupled by judgmental predication, thousands are linked by identities of feeling-mode; for every value transformed by change of logical pre-suppositions, scores are switched by a radical transformation of the feeling-attitude. We are forced to conclude that the feeling-quality, irrespective of content, makes a value of a given kind, and that a transformation of the attitude effects a change of type in the value situation.

In this connection, a competent analyst concludes[3]: "We are compelled to recognize that in the aesthetic value situation anything animate or inanimate, natural or artificial, deed or doer, may be the object. This consideration alone makes it clear that beauty and goodness cannot always, if ever, be the same." Yet with all this qualitative distinctness, the artist may feel duty toward his calling, obligation toward his unrealized idea, because when he feels conflict and tension in that context, he occupies an entirely different attitude toward his aesthetic material. Instead of the repose or ecstasy of contemplation or the exuberant flow of creative expression, he feels the tension and pull of an unrealized situation, and feeling obligation and conflict, senses along with that a moral quality. The changed feeling-attitude creates a new value; and the type-form of the attitude brings with it its appropriate value category. These modes co-assert their own relevant norms; each sets up a categorical imperative of its own, not of the Kantian sort with rationalized universality and objectivity, but instead the psychological urgency (shall we say, necessity?) to construe the situation as of a particular qualitative form-character. It is this that we term a functional categorical factor, since it operates in and through feeling, although it is later made explicit, analyzed and validated by evaluative processes of judgment and experiential test.

The traditional way of accounting for the various kinds of value, on the other hand, starting out as it does from the side of evaluation, leans too heavily upon logical definition. It substitutes the terminology of predicates for the real functional *differential*. A comparison, even in incomplete, suggestive outline, between a logical and a psychological classification of values will show how much more neatly a schematization of values in terms of the mechanics of value-feelings fits the facts than the rough approximations of the traditional logical classification. More than this, such a classification not only states the basis on which the primary value groups generically rest, but reveals the process out of which they genetically arise.

Taking feeling-modes as the basic factor of differentiation, the religious and ethical, moral, logical and aesthetic types of value differentiate very neatly on the basis of four fundamental feeling-modes of exaltation, tension, acceptance, and repose of equilibrium. There are sub-divisions for each value-mode determined by the usual polarity of positive and negative values, and also for each mode a less recognized but most important sub-division related to the directional drive of the value-feeling. This latter discriminates for each type of value an 'introverted' and an 'extroverted' variety of the value, according as the feeling-reference refers the value inward toward an individualized value of the self or projects it outward toward value-sharing and the socialized plane of action. We may illustrate first in terms of the moral values. Every definition of the moral or ethical situation recognizes the characteristic element of conflict between alternatives and the correlated sense of tension. The classification we are discussing would transpose a typical pragmatic definition such as "the conflict of mentally incompatible goods defines a moral situation" into a psychological category of value grounded in the form-feeling of tension, inducing the moral attitude toward the situation irrespective of content. Where the value reference is introverted or directed inwardly toward the self, this tension expresses itself as a compulsion of inner restraint or as "conscience": where an extroverted reference directs the tension toward a compulsion outward to action, the tension becomes sensed as "duty" or obligation. Or, to illustrate again, in the mode of the religious values, we have the mechanisms of introverted exaltation determining positively the ecstasy and sense of union of the religious mystic and negatively his sense of sin and separation, with the outward or extroverted form of the religious value expressing itself in the convictions of "conversion" and salvation (active union with God) and the salvationist crusade against evil (the fear and hate of Satan).

This view, if correct, leads to the conclusion that there is a form-feeling or form-quality characteristic of each fundamental value-type, and that values are discriminated in terms of such feeling factors in the primary processes of valuation. The view further regards these modalities of feeling as constituting the basic kinds of value through the creation of stereotyped and dispositional attitudes which sustain them. The substantial agreement of such a table with the traditional classification of values merely indicates that the established scheme of value judgments has traced the basic value modes with fair correctness. However, there are differences more significant than the similarities. These differences not only make possible a more accurate classification of the types of value, but make evident a genetic pattern of values by which we may trace more accurately their interrelations, both of correlation and of opposition.

Tabular illustration follows:

Modal Quality Form-Quality and Feeling-Reference	Value Type or Field	Value Predicates	Value Polarity	
			Positive	*Negative*

Exaltation: (Awe-Worship)
a. Introverted: (Individualized):
    Inner Ecstasy
b. Extroverted: (Socialized):
    Religious Zeal
	Religious	Holy—Unholy
		
		Good—Evil
			Holiness
			
			Salvation
				Sin
				
				Damnation

Tension: (Conflict-Choice) a. Inner Tension of "Conscience" b. Extrovert: Outer Tension of "Duty"	*Ethical* *Moral*	Good—Bad Right—Wrong	Conscience Right	Temptation Crime
Acceptance or **Agreement:** (Curiosity—Intellectual Satisfaction) a. Inner Agreement in Thought b. Outer Agreement in Experience	*Logical Truth* *Scientific Truth*	True (Correct) and Incorrect True—False	Consistency Certainty	Contradiction Error
Repose or **Equilibrium** a. Consummation in Contemplation b. Consummation in Creative Activity	*Aesthetic* *Artistic*	Beautiful—Ugly Fine— Unsatisfactory	Satisfaction Joy	Disgust Distress

a: Value: introverted type.
b: Value: extroverted type.

Over and above greater descriptive accuracy in value analysis, then, this view may be expected to vindicate itself most effectively in the field of the genetics and the dynamics of values. Here it is able to account for value conversions and value opposition in terms of the same factors, and thus apply a common principle of explanation to value mergings, transfers and conflicts. It is with this range of phenomena that the logical theories of value experience their greatest difficulties. We are aware of instances, for example, where a sequence of logical reasoning will take on an aesthetic character as a "beautiful proof" or a "pretty demonstration", or where a moral quality or disposition is appraised not as "good" but as "noble", or again, where a religious ritual is a mystical "reality" to the convinced believer but is only an aesthetic, symbolic show to the non-credal spectator. The logical way of explaining such instances assumes a change of the judgmental presuppositions mediating the values, or in other cases, puts forward the still weaker explanation of the transfer of value predicates through metaphor and analogy. But by the theory that values are constituted by the primary modal quality of the actual feeling, one does not have to go beyond that to explain the accurate appropriateness of the unusual predicates or the actuality of the attitude in the valuation. They are in direct functional relation and agreement. As a *quod erat demonstrandum*, the proof or demonstration is an enjoyed consummation of a process, and is by that very fact aesthetic in quality. Likewise, the contemplation of an ethical deed, when the tension of the act is not shared, becomes a detached appreciation, though it needs only the sharing of the tension to revert to the moral type of valuation. In fact, moral behavior, when it becomes dispositional, with the smooth feeling-curve of habit and inner equilibrium, normally takes on a quasi-aesthetic quality, as reflected in the criterion of taste and *noblesse oblige* rather than the sterner criterion of "must" and of "duty". And of course, to the disinterested spectator, the religious ritual is just like any other work of art,—an object of reposeful, equilibrated projection. Once a different form-feeling is evoked, the situation and the value type are, *ipso facto*, changed. Change the attitude, and, irrespective of content, you change the value-type; the appropriate new predicates automatically follow.

The same principles hold, moreover, in explaining the conflicts and incompatibilities of values as value-groups. Of course, there are other types of value conflicts, means-ends and value-series problems, but what concerns us at this point are those graver antinomies of values out of which our most fundamental value problems arise. One needs only to recall the endless debate over the *summum bonum* or the perennial quarrel over the respective merits of the value Trinity. How, even after lip service to the parity of Beauty, Truth and Good, we conspire for the priority of one pet favorite, which usually reflects merely our dominant value interest and our own temperamental value bias. The growth of modern relativism has at least cooled these erstwhile burning issues and tempered the traditional debate. Indeed from our point of view, we see these grand ultimates, for all their assertion of fraternal harmony, as doomed to perpetual logical opposition because their basic value attitudes are psychologically incompatible. Repose and action, integration and conflict, acceptance and projection, as attitudes, create natural antinomies, irresolvable orders of value; and the only peace a scientific view of value can sanction between them is one based not upon priority and precedence but upon parity and reciprocity.

As we dispose of this traditional value feud, we become aware of the internal value conflicts within the several value fields, those schisms within common value loyalties which are becoming all the more serious as the traditional value quarrel subsides. There is the feud between the mystic and the reformer in religion, between the speculative logician and the inductive experimentalist in the pursuit of truth, yes,—even the one, less sharp and obvious, between the aesthete and the artist. An affective theory of valuation throws these internal dilemmas into an interesting and illuminating perspective. In each of these cases, the modal value-feeling is, of course, held in common and the same ideological loyalties shared, but these sub-groups are still divided by the basic difference in their orientation toward their common values. Here we see the functional importance of that distinction in feeling-reference or feeling-direction which so closely parallels the Jungian polarity of introversion and extroversion that these terms have been adopted to describe it. These directional drives, determined emotionally in the majority of cases, deciding whether the value is focussed inwardly or outwardly, individuated or socialized, are of the utmost practical importance. For they are the root of those civil feuds within the several value provinces between the saint and the prophet, the mystic and the reformer, the speculative theorist and the practical experimentalist in the search for truth, the aesthete and dilettante versus the creative and professional artist, and finally between the self-righteous moral zealot and the moral reformer. And as each of these attitude-sets becomes dispositional and rationalized, we have the scientific clue to that pattern of value loyalties which divides humanity into psychological sub-species, each laying down rationalizations of ways of life that, empirically traced, are merely the projections of their predominant value tendencies and attitudes.

Thus our varied absolutes are revealed as largely the rationalization of our preferred values and their imperatives. Their tap-root, it seems, stems more from the will to power than from the will to know. Little can be done, it would appear, either toward their explanation or their reconciliation on the rational plane. Perhaps this is the truth that Brentano came near laying hands on when he suggested a love-hate dimensionality as fundamental to all valuation. Certainly the fundamental opposition of value-modes and the attitudes based upon them has been one of the deepest sources of human division and conflict. The rôle of feeling can never be understood nor controlled through minimizing it; to admit it is the beginning of practical wisdom in such matters. As Hartmann[4] has well observed,—"Every value, when once it has gained power over a person, has a tendency to set itself up as a sole tyrant of the whole human *ethos*, and indeed at the expense of other values, even of such as are not inherently opposed to it." We must acknowledge this, though not to despair over it, but by understanding how and why, to find principles of control from the mechanisms of valuation themselves. Without doubt many value attitudes as separate experiences are incompatible and antithetic, but all of us, as individuals, reconcile these incompatibilities in our own experience when we shift, for variety as often as for necessity, from one mode of value to the other. The effective antidote to value absolutism lies in a systematic and realistic demonstration that values are rooted in attitudes, not in reality and pertain to ourselves, not to the world. Consistent value pluralism might eventually make possible a value loyalty not necessarily founded on value bigotry, and impose a truce of imperatives, not by denying the categorical factors in valuation, which, as we have seen, are functional, but by insisting upon the reciprocity of these norms. There is not necessarily irresolvable conflict between these separate value modes if, without discounting their emotional and functional incommensurability, we realize their complementary character in human experience.

At the same time that it takes sides against the old absolutism and invalidates the *summum bonum* principle, this type of value pluralism does not invite the chaos of value-anarchy or the complete *laissez faire* of extreme value individualism. It rejects equally trying to reduce value distinctions to the flat continuum of a pleasure-pain economy or to a pragmatic instrumentalism of ends-means relations. Of course, we need the colorless, common-denominator order of factual reality and objectivity (although that itself serves a primary value as a mechanism of the coordination of experience), but values simply do not reduce to it. To set values over against facts does not effectively neutralize values. Since we cannot banish our imperatives, we must find some principle of keeping them within bounds. It should be possible to maintain some norms as functional and native to the process of experience, without justifying arbitrary absolutes, and to uphold some categoricals without calling down fire from heaven. Norms of this status would be functional constants and practical sustaining imperatives of their correlated modes of experience; nothing more, but also nothing less.

Such "ends" totalize merely an aspect of human experience and stand only for a subsistent order of reality. They should not confuse themselves with that objective reality nor attempt to deny or disparage its other value aspects and the subsistent orders they reflect. This totalizing character is purely functional in valuation, and it is a mockery of fact either to raise it to the level of transcendental worship or to endow it with objective universality. This conceded, there is little sense and less need to set facts and values over against

31

each other as antagonistic orders; rather should we think of reality as a central fact and a white light broken up by the prism of human nature into a spectrum of values. By proposing these basic value-modes as coordinate and complementary, value pluralism of this type proposes its two most important corallaries,—the principles of reciprocity and tolerance. As derivative aspects of the same basic reality, value orders cannot reasonably become competitive and rival realities. As creatures of a mode of experience, they should not construe themselves in any concrete embodiment so as to contradict or stultify the mode of which they are a particularized expression.

Should such a view become established,—and I take that to be one of the real possibilities of an empirical theory of value, we shall then have warrant for taking as the proper center of value loyalty neither the worship of definitions or formulae nor the competitive monopolizing of value claims, but the goal of maximizing the value-mode itself as an attitude and activity. The attitude will itself be construed as the value essence,—which it really is, and not as now the intellectualized *why* or the traditional and institutionalized *how* associated with the value category. In such a frame of reference, for example, romanticism and classicism could not reasonably think of themselves as monopolizing the field of art, nor Protestantism, Catholicism or even Christianity conceive themselves the only way to salvation. In such a perspective, Nordicism and other rampant racialisms might achieve historical sanity or at least prudential common-sense to halt at the natural frontiers of genuinely shared loyalties and not sow their own eventual downfall through forced loyalties and the counter-reactions which they inevitably breed. Social reciprocity for value loyalties is but a new name for the old virtue of tolerance, yet it does bring the question of tolerance down from the lofty thin air of idealism and chivalry to the plane of enlightened self-interest and the practical possibilities of effective value-sharing. As a working principle, it divorces proper value loyalty from unjustifiable value bigotry, releases a cult from blind identification with creed and dogma, and invests no value interest with monopoly or permanent priority.

However, no one can sensibly expect a sudden or complete change in our value behavior from any transformation, however radical, in our value theory. Relativism will have to slowly tame the wild force of our imperatives. There will be no sudden recanting of chronic, traditional absolutisms, no complete undermining of orthodoxies, no huge, overwhelming accessions of tolerance. But absolutism is doomed in the increasing variety of human experience. What over a century ago was only an inspired metaphorical flash in the solitary universal mind of a Goethe,—that phrase about civilization's being a fugue in which, voice by voice, the several nations and peoples took up and carried the interwoven theme, could in our day become a systematic philosophy of history like Pareto's. His historical and functional relativism of cultural values, with

32

persistent normative constants ("residues") and variable and contingent specific embodiments ("derivatives"), is but an indication of the possibilities of relativism extended to historical and social thought. Cultural relativism, to my mind, is the culminating phase of relativistic philosophy, and it is bound to have a greater influence than any other phase of relativism upon our conception and practise of values.

Our present way of socializing values on the basis of credal agreement, dogmatic orthodoxies, and institutionally vested interests is fundamentally unsound and self-contradictory. As a practise, it restricts more than it protects the values that have called institutions into being. Organized for value-sharing and value promotion, they often contradict their own primary purposes. One way of reform undoubtedly is to combat the monopolistic tradition of most of our institutions. This sounds Marxian, and is to an extent. But the curtailing of the struggle over the means and instrumentalities of values will not eliminate our quarrels and conflicts about ends, and long after the possible elimination of the profit motive, our varied imperatives will still persist. Economic classes may be absorbed, but our psychological tribes will not thereby be dissolved. So, since there may be monopolistic attitudes and policies with respect to ends and ideals just as well as monopolies of the instrumentalities of human values—(and of this fact the ideological dogmatism of contemporary communism is itself a sad example), it may be more effective to invoke a non-Marxian principle of maximizing values.

Contrary to Marxian logic, this principle is non-uniformitarian. It is the Roycean principle of "loyalty to loyalty", which though idealistic in origin and defense, was a radical break with the tradition of absolutism. It called for a revolution in the practise of partisanship in the very interests of the values professed. In its larger outlines and implications it proclaimed a relativism of values and a principle of reciprocity. Loyalty to loyalty transposed to all the fundamental value orders would then have meant, reverence for reverence, tolerance between moral systems, reciprocity in art, and had so good a metaphysician been able to conceive it, relativism in philosophy.

But if reciprocity and tolerance on the large scale are to await the incorporation of the greater community, the day of our truce of values is far off. Before any such integrations can take place, the narrowness of our provincialisms must be broken down and our sectarian fanaticisms lose some of their force and glamor. A philosophy aiding this is an ally of the larger integration of life. Of this we may be sure, such reconstruction will never bring us to a basis of complete cultural uniformity or common-mindedness about values. Whatever integrations occur, therefore, whether of thought or social system,—and undoubtedly some will and must occur,—cultural and value pluralism of some sort will still prevail. Indeed in the atmosphere induced by relativism and tolerance, such differentiation is likely to increase rather than just continue. Only it is to be hoped that it will be less arbitrary, less provincial and less divisive.

One thing is certain,—whatever change may have occurred in our thinking on the subject, we are still monists and absolutists mainly in our practise of value, individual as well as social. But a theoretical break has come, and seems to have set in simultaneously from several quarters. Panoramically viewed, the convergence of these trends indicates a new center for the thought and insight of our present generation, and that would seem to be a philosophy and a psychology, and perhaps too, a sociology, pivoted around functionalistic relativism.

Notes

1. Compare Professor Frank H. Knight's comment on Charner Perry's,—*The Arbitrary as Basis for Rational Morality*—Inter. Journal of Ethics, Vol. 53—No. 2—Jan., 1933—p. 148:—"In the present situation of the western mind, the crying need is to substantiate for social phenomena a middle ground between scientific objectivity and complete skepticism. On the one hand, as Scylla, is the absurdity of Behaviorism. . . . On the other side is the Charybdis of Nihilism, perhaps momentarily the nearer and more threatening of the two reefs. Of course, the two are related; nihilism is a natural correlate of "scientificism." . . . In any case, there is no more vital problem (pragmatically) than that of distinguishing between utterance that is true or sound and that which is effective in influencing behavior."
2. Compare Dewey—*The Quest for Certainty*,—p. 21:—Are the objects of desire, effort, choice, that is to say, everything to which we attach value, real? Yes,—if they can be warranted by knowledge; if we can know objects having their value properties we are justified in thinking them real. But as objects of desire and purpose they have no sure place in Being until they are approached and validated through knowledge."
3. "Beauty and Goodness"—Herbert E. Cory—*International Journal of Ethics*, July, 1926.
4. Hartmann, *Ethics*, Vol. II, p. 423.

Note on the Author

(This note is Locke's own self-description that accompanied "Values and Imperatives", 1935)

Curriculum vitae: Born 1886, Philadelphia—Harvard A.B., 1907; graduate student Oxford 1907–10—Rhodes scholar from Pennsylvania—University of Berlin, 1910–11; Assistant Professor English and Philosophy, Howard University, 1912–16; Harvard Graduate School 1916–17—Ph.D. Harvard, 1918; Professor of Philosophy (Howard) 1918 to date. Author:—Race Contacts and Inter-racial Relations (1916); The Problem of Classification in Theory of Value (1918); The New Negro (1925); The Negro in America (1933); Frederick Douglass; a Biography of Anti-Slavery (1935).

I should like to claim as life-motto the good Greek principle,—"*Nothing in excess*," but I have probably worn instead as the badge of circumstance,— "*All things with a reservation.*" Philadelphia, with her birthright of provincialism flavored by urbanity and her petty bourgeois psyche with the Tory slant, at the start set the key of paradox; circumstance compounded it by decreeing me as a Negro a dubious and doubting sort of American and by reason of the racial inheritance making me more of a pagan than a Puritan, more of a humanist than a pragmatist.

Verily paradox has followed me the rest of my days: at Harvard, clinging to the genteel tradition of Palmer, Royce and Munsterberg, yet attracted by the disillusion of Santayana and the radical protest of James: again in 1916 I returned to work under Royce but was destined to take my doctorate in Value Theory under Perry. At Oxford, once more intrigued by the twilight of aestheticism but dimly aware of the new realism of the Austrian philosophy of value; socially Anglophile, but because of race loyalty, strenuously anti-imperialist; universalist in religion, internationalist and pacifist in world-view, but forced by a sense of simple justice to approve of the militant counter-nationalisms of Zionism, Young Turkey, Young Egypt, Young India, and with reservations even Garveyism and current-day "Nippon over Asia." Finally a cultural cosmopolitan, but perforce an advocate of cultural racialism as a defensive counter-move for the American Negro, and accordingly more of a philosophical mid-wife to a generation of younger Negro poets, writers, artists than a professional philosopher.

Small wonder, then, with this psychograph, that I project my personal history into its inevitable rationalization as cultural pluralism and value relativism, with a not too orthodox reaction to the American way of life.

IV

Eugene Clay Holmes
1905–1980
c. 1942

Eugene C. Holmes: A Commentary on a Black Marxist Philosopher

John H. McClendon

Eugene C. Holmes was a central, though relatively unknown, figure as a philosopher in Black intellectual history. Born in Patterson, New Jersey, on October 12, 1905, he died of cancer in 1980.[1]

This essay will briefly outline Holmes' philosophical outlook and his contribution to Black intellectual history and the Afro-American liberation struggle. I will discuss Dr. Holmes' philosophical work in the following areas:

1. Holmes' dissertation on American intellectual history;
2. his philosophical work in Black art and aesthetics;
3. his contribution to Black intellectual history; and
4. his materialist approach to physical science and the question of the philosophical implication of space and time.

Holmes' undergraduate study was undertaken at New York University. There he began to explore the field of literary criticism. During this time he published his first article in the August 1932 issue of *Opportunity,* "Jean Toomer: Apostle of Beauty".[2] After he had completed his work at New York University, he simultaneously pursued graduate work in philosophy at Columbia University (1932) and was an instructor of philosophy at Howard University. He was attracted to Howard's philosophy department because Alain L. Locke, chairperson of the department, was the leading critic of Black literary expression of the time,[3] and there were few other places a professional academic philosopher could work and teach.

The Great Depression (1929–1939) provided the social grounds for increased radical political and intellectual fermentation. The economic crisis of the world capitalist system in general, and U.S. capitalism in particular, had a profound impact on intellectual, theoretical, and ideological formulations.

Holmes was in a unique position. As he began the formal process of training to becoming a professional philosopher, he came under the influence of John Dewey and pragmatism at Columbia University. On the other hand, at Howard University, and primarily through the Division of Social Science, he established a relationship with a number of Black intellectuals increasingly influenced by Marxism. William Alpheus Hunton, Doxey Wilkerson, Abram

This paper is an expansion of an article appearing in the 1982 spring issue of *Freedomways.* A special thanks goes to the staff of the Afro-American Studies and Research Program, University of Illinois-Urbana, its Director, Gerald A. McWorter, for the technical and intellectual assistance received in the preparation of this article.

Harris, and Ralph Bunche were involved in a left critique of capitalism, racism, and bourgeois scholarship. Thus, from 1932 to 1942 (1942 was the year he completed his doctoral dissertation) the philosophical outlook of Eugene C. Holmes was forged in the context of the struggle between dialectical materialism and pragmatism, the latter being the leading expression of bourgeois philosophy in America.[4]

It is important to note that pragmatism as a philosophical school of thought had decidedly attached itself to the populist, and later the progressive, movements, which gave it the appearance of being in democratic opposition to monopoly capitalism. In the period of the Depression, pragmatism was to lean even more leftward, with philosophers such as Sidney Hook, a student of Dewey, trying to merge pragmatism with Marxism. But despite this left form, its content remained bourgeois through and through.[5]

The New Deal of Roosevelt, with its subsequent compromises to the working class upsurge via the Welfare State, found in pragmatism the philosophical tool for reformist measures. Pragmatism's methodology of trial and error and a piecemeal approach to particular problems was a theoretical underpinning of New Deal legislation. The greater emphasis of New Deal reformism was on resolving particular and individual problems of capitalist crisis rather than the resolution of the general crisis. This was philosophically compatible with the pragmatic denial of the need for a generalized conception of reality. New Deal thought sought not an explanation of capital crisis in general and its logical consequence—i.e., revolutionary change—but ways to insure the survival of capitalism with reforms.[6]

Holmes was critical of pragmatism, and he rendered a critique of its emergence in his doctoral dissertation. This dissertation, privately printed in 1942, and entitled, "Social Philosophy and Social Mind: A Study of the Genetic Methods of J. M. Baldwin, G. H. Mead and J. E. Bodin," was a short, but comprehensive tract detailing how ruling philosophies of the late nineteenth century had been transformed into a new type of liberalism, which espoused a naturalist, evolutionary theory of a society. The amalgamation of Darwinism and pragmatism as a "scientific" social philosophy, according to Holmes, led to the demise of both theological/Hegelian idealism and Spencerian speculative philosophy. Pragmatism pointed the way for the emergence of a social reformism that rested on the findings of psychology in the last decade of the nineteenth century. The "genetic" method of these pragmatists upheld evolution but viewed the dialectic between "organism" and "environment" from the viewpoint that both were fundamentally social entities. The political implication was philosophical apology of bourgeois democracy. Holmes in his critique of this philosophical trend states:

> During the period before the World War, the leaders who made
> democracy synonymous with a republican form of government did not
> realize that it was not in reality the democracy it professed to be.
> Philosophers had adequately explored the philosophies of democracy,
> but they were not critical of these philosophies.[7]

Eugene Holmes was not the typical "ivory tower" philosopher. He was an activist/scholar whose chief aim was to unite the scientific world outlook of dialectical materialism to the practical struggle for Black liberation and socialism.

Holmes' entire academic career was at Howard University, where he taught for thirty-eight years in the Department of Philosophy. He followed his mentor and colleague Alain Locke as chairperson of philosophy and held that position for eighteen years, retiring with emeritus status in 1970.[8] The radical posture of Howard University scholars led to a reluctance (especially during the 1930s and 1950s) by large foundations to give grants for social science research, and there were governmental attempts to attack Howard University for alleged communist influences. Yet, the Division of Social Science, in spite of McCarthyist hysteria, sponsored a conference in 1953 on "Academic Freedom in the United States" and a lecture by W. E. B. DuBois in 1958. The DuBois lecture characteristically upheld peace and socialism and condemned the execution of the Rosenbergs. This lecture was the subject of government pressure for almost four years prior to its presentation. Eugene Holmes, as a member of the Division of Social Science (the Philosophy Department was included in this division), played no small part in these efforts. He was indeed a contributor to and an editor of the proceedings of the division's conference of 1955 on "The New Negro Thirty Years Afterwards," a tribute to Alain Locke.[9] The influence of Locke on Holmes after many years of collaboration as colleagues explains why he wrote several articles and gave many public lectures on Alain Locke's philosophy. He had even written a manuscript on Locke, "Alain LeRoy Locke—Life and Times," which Holmes had hoped would be published by Howard University Press. However, it is the understanding of this author that the manuscript today remains unpublished.[10]

Holmes published in a wide range of scholarly journals. It is instructive to note that along with writing in "traditional" scholarly journals such as *Journal of Philosophy, Philosophy and Phenomenological Research,* and *Journal of Physics,* he also sought to reach a more politically oriented audience by publishing works in Marxist journals such as *Science and Society* and *New Masses.* But because Holmes had an abiding interest in the application of dialectical materialism to the Black experience, his most frequent contributions appeared in the pages of *Freedomways.* His first essay in *Freedomways,* "The Legacy of Alain Locke", appeared in the summer of 1963. In this article, Holmes displayed his keen awareness of the dynamics and nuances of Black intellectual history.

He combined a historical approach to the role that Locke had played in the Harlem Renaissance with a literary criticism of the Renaissance writers, giving special attention to the social-historical basis of the poetry and novels

39

of this period. Although Holmes extolled the positive role of the "Renaissance", his materialist perspective made it possible to be critical of its socio-economic basis. He stated:

> The post-war decade which ushered in the Harlem Renaissance was the age of the triumph for big business and the consolidation of industry and monopoly capitalism on a world scale. This was conducted by white capital with Negro and immigrant labor, a mass of cheap and potentially efficient labor, unlimited natural power and a use of unequaled technique, reaching all of the markets of the world and leading to the emergence of America as a force in twentieth century world imperialism.[11]

Holmes was equally critical of the class character of the Renaissance movement and its incipient bourgeois nationalism. Holmes contends that:

> . . . there was being cultivated a middle-class nationalism within the protective folds of the capitalist ethos. The majority did not rebel, but rather hearkened to the voice of bourgeois authority. American capitalism had prospered in the revision of the profits and spoils of war. In too many instances, the "New Negro" has served in too large measure as a means of amusement, to be frowned upon and idolized. Many of the New Negroes were unwilling victims of an inverted racialistic nationalism, looking upon themselves as having arrived, and priding themselves that they could sing, paint and write as well as their white-skinned patrons.[12]

Holmes' next article for *Freedomways* was in the special issue devoted to the dean of Black scholarship, W. E. B. DuBois. Holmes focused on "W. E. B. DuBois—Philosopher" by initially giving a biographical account of DuBois' early development as a student and scholar. Declaring that "literally and historically, there had not been any philosophies of freedom until DuBois." Holmes recaptured Du Bois' analysis of the Black liberation struggle from slavery to reconstruction, emphasizing DuBois' class approach.[13]

Holmes accentuated the point that, philosophically, DuBois was a materialist and a scientific historian and sociologist. He argued that the political upshot of this led DuBois to struggle for equality, democracy, peace, and the destruction of imperialism. He cited the fact that DuBois was among the first American scholars to teach a course on Marxism at an American university and showed how DuBois' scholarship and life work pointed to the necessity for socialism.[14] Since Holmes was himself a dialectical materialist philosopher he could fully appreciate the importance of DuBois' stance and how dialectical materialism was a scientific world outlook guiding revolutionary practice.

A later contribution to *Freedomways,* in the spring 1968 issue, was on "Langston Hughes—Philosopher-Poet." Following the format of his two previous essays, he began with a biographical description and historical account of Hughes' life and work. Holmes highlighted the fact that Hughes' art grew directly from the masses. Holmes described Hughes as a "social poet." Holmes argued that this led Hughes "to eschew all of the old formalism of traditional poetry. He was disposed always to link this profession with his people and to use his poetry as a weapon in his activist alliance with the oppressed."[15] For Holmes, Hughes had successfully understood the dialectic of aesthetic theory of Black masses as subject material and uncovering its universal content. Although Hughes was not expressly concerned with the elaboration of this theory (Holmes thought this was more a concern of Locke and DuBois), he was nevertheless, a crucial person in inspiring the outgrowth of the Black art movement during the 1960s.[16]

Another philosophical domain that Holmes explored was the philosophy of science. An able philosopher of science, his work on the highly complex topic of space/time displayed his mastery of higher mathematics, physics, and the history of philosophy. Holmes' production on the topic of space and time numbered three articles. They were "The Main Philosophical Considerations of Space and Time", which appeared in the *American Journal of Physics* (December 1950); "The Kantian Views of Space and Time Reevaluated" in *Philosophy and Phenomenological Research* (September-June 1955–1956), and "Philosophical Problems of Space and Time," which appeared in *Science and Society* (Summer 1960). The objective of each of these articles was to confirm materialism's opposition to various idealist philosophical formulations relating to the conceptualization of space and time. My main focus here will be on Holmes' "The Main Philosophical Considerations of Space and Time." It should be noted that the subject matter, space and time, significantly alters Holmes' method of exposition and abstraction.

Holmes begins this essay by stating it was very recent when "space and time or space/time were not thought of as having real existence."[17] The exceptions were certain materialists, such as Galilei, Gassendi, and Descartes among others. However, in the materialism of Bacon, Hobbs, and Priestly, "space and time were taken for granted." It was the agnostic Kant who sought to scrutinize the philosophical significance of space and time, only to render it to a subjective epistemology. Neo-Kantianists have not moved beyond the muddle of Kant's agnosticism and idealism. Mach, Avenarius, Cohen, Natorp, Pearson, and Poincare ultimately became positivists of some sort. Holmes adds that their contemporary counterparts are Schlick, Neuman, Carnap, and Russell.[18]

It is noteworthy that Holmes recognized the philosophical continuity of this reactionary trend. On the one hand, it explicitly anchors his own work in the tradition of Lenin. For Lenin had subjected the former group to a scathing critique in his *Materialism and Empirio-Criticism.* On the other hand, Holmes had anticipated the need for a Marxist-Leninist analysis of the latter group, a task that was also undertaken by Maurice Cornforth in *Science versus Idealism,* which was published in 1955, five years after Holmes wrote his essay.[19]

Geometry's emergency in Africa (Egypt) was used as an example by Holmes for historical evidence to support his argument. He states, "No consciously theoretical notions about space were supported until men learned that

41

such theories had practical purposes." Geometry, in turn, developed in Egypt in response to the objective problems of agricultural production and the flooding of the Nile River. Yet, the general level of science and the limits of scientific work were a reflection of the specific development of the productive forces (Bronze Age) and production relations (class/caste structure) of Egypt. The aim of science narrowly became control and prediction. However, the mixture of theology with science was the product of the relations between clerk and priest.[20]

The Ionian philosophers (the first materialists in the Western World) were not circumscribed by production to the degree of the Egyptian forerunners. The Ionians advanced to a more abstract conception of space. In part, Holmes reveals that this advancement was due to the progressive evolution of the productive forces from bronze to iron instruments. The Marxist philosopher, Theodore Oizerman, I might add, points out that the division of labor resulting in the separation of mental and manual labor, gave a relative independence to theory in Ionia. Relative independence from production meant a great possibility for abstract, theoretical thought.[21]

Theories developed by Ionian philosophers were a substantial aid toward a materialist cognition of reality. Democritus' atomistic materialism, for example, was naive and speculative, yet it gave us a notion of matter—the atom—and of space-the void. Holmes indicates that Democritus saw time as objectively real but viewed it separate from matter. Time, for Democritus, was absolute and metaphysical.[22] In Holmes' view, some materialists of the seventeenth century, like Gassendi, not only were influenced by Democritus but merely parrotted the pioneering materialist. Gassendi was a materialist for whose philosophy the ideas of Democritus, Lucretius, and Epicurus were central. Gassendi's notion of the relationship of space to time was initially the same as his materialist progenitors, i.e., a conception of space and time as disunited.

Holmes believed Descartes was more important to the progress of a clear idea of space and time than Gassendi. For Holmes, the importance of Descartes' mechanical materialism lies in his notion of space as "the property of material bodies in extension."[23] According to Holmes, Descartes had not seen, however, the unity of space and matter, i.e., space as the mode of matter's existence, but identified matter with space.

Holmes, by giving greater weight to the philosophy of Descartes over Gassendi, I contend, had failed to see that the contribution to materialism made by Gassendi was the very basis of Gassendi's criticism of Descartes. Although Holmes did recognize the dualism of Descartes' philosophy, viz. that it was idealist in its epistemology but materialist in regard to physics, he did not go far enough to recognize that Descartes' metaphysics was precisely what Gassendi attacked.

The founders of dialectical materialism, Karl Marx and Frederick Engels, in their work, *The Holy Family,* remarked,

"the metaphysics of the seventeenth century represented in France by Descartes, had materialism as its antagonist from its birth. The latter's opposition to Descartes was personified by Gassendi, the restorer of Epicurean materialism. French and English materialism closely related to Democritus and Epicurus. Cartesian metaphysics had another opponent in Hobbes. Gassendi and Hobbes triumphed over their opponents long after their death. . . ."[24]

Holmes' summation of Newton's mechanistic materialism is instructive because Holmes brings into focus how mechanistic materialism can collapse into idealism. On an epistemological plane, Newton (along with Galileo and Locke) held to agnosticism. He separated qualities available to perception from properties of matter, which Newton thought could not be known. (Of course, this agnosticism would find full measure in Kant's "thing-in-itself.") Newton's mechanical materalism had deprived matter of intrinsic motion; thus, matter remained inert. Additionally, Newton separated matter from space and time. Thus, the catalyst for mechanical motion became the "prime mover"— God. Also, space was seen by Newton as the "senorium of God."

The mechanical physics of Newton was raised to the level of a world outlook, i.e., mechanistic materialism. However, to the degree that Newton had advanced materialism, we must distinguish his physics from his metaphysics, as was necessary with Descartes earlier. Holmes did not grasp this fact and consequently missed the import of Newton's role in the history of materialism.

Because Kant's conception of space and time was consciously developed from Newtonian physics (and Euclidean geometry as well), Holmes' treatment of Kant is extremely important. Holmes argues, "Kant raised the philosophical problems of space and time to their highest metaphysical-idealist expression." Kant, in countering Hume's skepticism of the empirical source of knowledge, grounds his epistemology in subjectivity. Space and time were conceived by Kant as intuitive constructs, as subjective forms of sensibility that were a priori, i.e., logically prior to and a condition of experience (perception).

For Kant, says Holmes, the infinity of space and time was not a reflection of the unity of material reality but something imposed on experience intuitively. Holmes goes on to say, Neo-Kantian philosophers "were just as concerned as Kant with the problems generated by regarding space and time as modes of thought or as reflections of objective reality.[25]

But then Holmes (incorrectly) identifies Mach and Avenarius (two leading Neo-Kantians) as "materialist" philosophers that "disguise" their materialism under the cover of "empirio-criticism." Yet, Holmes contradicts himself, for he states that, "Mach regarded consciousness and sensation as the ultimate elements of the world . . . he regarded space and time as subjective consciousness, conditioned by sensation. Holmes further states that this was "an idealist operation performed by mechanical materialism upon physics by destroying any vestige of an independent reality which had been preserved by Kant's noumena."[26]

The central confusion in Holmes' argument, namely, that Mach was a mechanical materialist, lies precisely in his attributing to Mach, Kant's dualism. Kant, by arguing for the existence of "noumena," i.e., the "thing-in-itself", was pointing to materialism. Yet, by denying the knowability of "noumena" and making time and space subjective categories, Kant was decidedly an idealist. Kant's critical philosophy was an effort to merge two irreconcilable opposites, materialism and idealism. Mach and Avenarius, by rejecting Kant's thing-in-itself, were in fact negating the materialist side of Kant's ontology. They were upholding Kant's idealism by way of what Lenin described as a right critique of Kant.

Lenin accurately states, "Mach and Avernarius reproach Kant not because his conception of the thing-in-itself is not sufficiently realistic, i.e., not sufficiently materialistic, but because he admits its existence. That is, Kant is reproached not because he refuses to deduce causality and necessity from objective reality, but because he admits any causality and necessity in nature at all."[27]

A left critique, a materialist analysis (mechanical or dialectical), would have accentuated the opposite side, i.e., noumena, the objective, material side of Kant's philosophy. Hence, Holmes erred in assigning mechanistic materialism as the source of the incorrectness of Mach and Avernarius. Their position was at base idealist and their subsequent conception of space and time was rooted in a reactionary, rightist interpretation that went beyond Kant's dualism directly to idealism.

Holmes returns to the correct philosophical path when he emphatically supports Marx, Engels, and Lenin in their defense of materialism. Specialized sciences, physics, geometry, and mathematics, all confirmed the dialectical materialist thesis that the universe is matter in motion and that space and time are intrinsically tied to matter as its mode of existence. Thus, "space and time are objectively real forms of existence." Space and time are understood as existing in unity.[28]

Holmes argues, "before there could be any new contribution to the study of the physical nature of space, there had to come into being revised or new geometries. . . ."[29] This "new" geometry (or geometries) significantly altered the Euclidean conception of space. The fixed and seemingly immutable character of spatial relations in Euclidean geometry was in fact the basis for Kant's subjective and intuitive notion of mathematics. Holmes explains "the Euclidean geometry had become established as the Platonist philosophy of logical and mathematical harmony, with its emphasis on unswerving and invariant relations."[30] The advent of non-Euclidean geometries meant "geometrical axioms have value and retain validity only in the event that they mirror definite, actual properties of real space."[31] The new geometries along with field theory change the classical notion of physics regarding space and time.

Einstein's theory changed the classical notion of physics regarding space and time; Einstein's theory of relativity limited the applicability of Newtonian physics and erased absolute space and time. Instead, as Holmes stated, "Einstein referred to the absolute character of the space-time continuum."[32]

Space and time were inseparable and motion (velocities) were calculated relative to a relationship of different coordinate systems and not on the "perception of the observer or his subjective qualities."[33] Holmes correctly asserts that dialectical materialism is compatible with the objectivity of the theory of relativity, the eternality of time, and the infinity of space/time.

Holmes concludes his essay by explaining that the theory of relativity supports the Law of the Conservation of Mass and Energy, i.e., the indestructibility of matter and energy and their mutual transformation. Unfortunately, he does not elaborate on how this verifies dialectical materialism's demand that the unity of the world consist in its materiality. And, thus how the dialectical conception of matter denies the necessity for divine intervention by God or a first cause to explain the development of the nature. Such a summation would have cast in bold relief the revolutionary implication of dialectics for the emergence of a consistent materialist ontology in correspondence with the historical development of science. Yet, Holmes' contribution to the philosophy of science was his militant defense of materialist philosophical tradition. He stood as the only professionally trained Black philosopher, of this period, to apply dialectical materialism to an analysis of space and time.[34]

It may be asked, why was Holmes attracted to Marxist philosophy? Why did he stand apart from other Black philosophers of his time? Any substantive answer to these questions would of course demand an intellectual biography of Holmes and others, which is beyond the scope of this essay. However, it can be pointed out that Holmes' activist's scholar orientation led him to associate with like-minded thinkers, all of whom were deeply engaged in the Black liberation movement. Alpheus Hunton, a colleague of Holmes at Howard, for example, was one of the founders of the Council of African Affairs, an anti-imperialist organization seeking the independence of Africa from colonialism. Hunton worked with Paul Robeson and W. E. B. DuBois, both of whom were Marxist activist/scholars, as the executive committee of that organization. Holmes' close collaboration with such fighters for Black liberation allowed for cross fertilization in the study of dialectical materialism. For Holmes, the role of philosophical exposition was not a mere act of gaining professional recognition but more significantly philosophy was a weapon, an ideological armament in the battle for liberation. Moreover, Holmes attempted to bring philosophy into the orbit of Black intellectual inquiry, and as such, spoke to a broader audience than technically trained philosophers.[35]

Holmes gave an address before the American Philosophical Association in December 1965. His paper, "A General Theory of the Freedom Cause of the Negro People," was probably the best expression of his social philosophy. He began by defining freedom as a socio-historical category. Humanity's quest for freedom from nature, i.e., the transformation of nature, always took place

45

in the context of political and social relations. The objective of human emancipation from exploitation was a real possibility in the present historical epoch. Yet, there would be no true human liberation without the liberation of Black people.[36]

Holmes explained that the existence of slavery, both ancient and modern, was the material foundation for the struggle to attain freedom. The tradition of reactionary philosophers and philosophies could be traced historically to the persistence of the "master/slave relationship." He denounced the philosophies of Plato, Cicero, Paul, Augustine, Aquinas, and Calhoun as philosophies that either gave justification to slavery or had failed to condemn it. Of particular note, he described John C. Calhoun as the only philosopher produced by the antebellum South.[37]

Holmes has an historical materialist account of U.S. history and he castigated both conservative and liberal ideologists for their racism. He analyzed the collapse of Reconstruction and both post World Wars' blacklash. Central in Holmes' discussion was that Black progress was the result of the determined struggle of Black people. He welcomed the recent upsurge of the Black Power movement and supported the militant stand of S.N.C.C., and the Mississippi Freedom Democratic party. He caustically remarked that the South was a "wasteland of the denial of opportunity" and added "much of America is a wasteland because of the ghetto-like practices of educational segregation. . . ."[38] He observed that the Black community was not without a class structure and derided the Black middle class. Holmes saw in the Black arts movement of the 1960s a similarity in purpose as in the case of the Harlem Renaissance movement of the 1920s. Both gave to Black people the opportunity to be "active creators . . . in a new cultural development."[39] Thus, Dr. Eugene Clay Holmes was a philosopher who gained his intellectual insights from the persistent and militant struggle of Black people. Philosophy for Holmes was not an esoteric exercise or the juggling of words. As a philosopher, he belonged to the tradition of Marx, Engels, Lenin, DuBois, and Bernal.

His passing no doubt is a serious loss to our Black intellectual tradition and to the Black liberation movement. And although many are unaware of his death, the real tragedy is that even more are ignorant of the life he led in the cause for liberation and therefore, and few are committed to continuing his work.

Notes

1. For biographical data on Holmes see Jacques Cattell Press ed., *Directory of American Scholars* (New York: R. R. Bowker Co., 1974), p. 193. For an announcement of his death, see *Jet* (July 31, 1980).
2. Eugene C. Holmes, "Jean Toomer: Apostle of Beauty," *Opportunity,* vol. 10, no. 8 (August 1932), pp. 252–254. In the biographical sketches of contributors, Holmes is identified as "a graduate student in literary criticism at New York University;" however, the *Directory* indicated he was an undergraduate at New York University.

3. Locke was generally regarded as the mentor of the young Black writers of the Harlem Renaissance and the foremost critic of Black literary expression. See Eugene C. Holmes, "Alain Locke, Philosopher, Critic, Spokesman", *Journal of Philosophy*, vol. 54, no. 5 (February 28, 1957), pp. 113–118.

4. For a good account of some of the intellectual output during the 1930s at Howard, see Michael R. Winston "Through the Back Door: Academic Racism and the Negro Scholar in Historical Perspective," *Daedalus*, vol. 100, no. 3 (Summer 1971), pp. 699–701.

5. For a graphic example of Hook's attempt to reconcile Pragmatism with Marxism, see Sidney Hook, "Marxism—Dogma or Method?", *The Nation*, vol. 136, no. 3532 (March 15, 1933). Hook once remarked "The most outstanding figure in the world today in whom the best elements of Marx's thought are present is John Dewey. . . . They were independently developed by him and systematically elaborated beyond anything found in Marx." See Sidney Hook, *Reason, Social Myths and Democracy* (New York: John Day, 1940).

6. C. Wright Mills, *Sociology and Pragmatism* (New York: Oxford University Press, 1966), p. 317. Dale Riepe, in a criticism of American mainstream philosophy, once remarked, "the ruling class . . . has not hunted down either pragmatists or naturalists, while keeping a sharp nose in the wind for non-mechanical materialist, Marxists, and socialists who indicate a belief in the existence of a fairly sharply defined struggle, and who have chosen to emphasize worthy ends and goals for America. . . ." See his "Critique of Idealistic Naturalism: Methodological Pollution in the Mainstream of American Philosophy" in David DeGrood, Dale Riepe, and John Somerville, eds., *Radical Currents in Contemporary Philosophy* (St. Louis: Warren H. Green, Inc., 1967), p. 22.

7. Eugene C. Holmes, *Social Philosophy and Social Mind: A Study of the Genetic Methods of J. M. Baldwin, G. H. Mead, and G. E. Boodin* (New York: privately printed 1942), p. 73.

8. Consult the *Directory*, p. 193.

9. See Rayford W. Logan, *Howard University: The First Hundred Years* (New York: New York University Press, 1969), pp. 362–63, 490, 439–40, 485; Holmes was coeditor with Rayford W. Logan and G. Franklin Edwards of *The New Negro Thirty Years Afterwards: Papers Contributed to the Sixteenth Annual Spring Conference of the Division of the Social Sciences* (Washington, D.C.: Howard University Press, 1955); Holmes' paper in the *Proceedings* was "Alain Locke—Philosopher".

10. Holmes had cited this manuscript as a publication in the *Directory of American Scholars*. This writer is personally aware of the fact that it was under consideration by Howard University in 1974.

11. Eugene C. Holmes "The Legacy of Alain Locke", *Freedomways*, vol. 3, no. 3 (Summer 1963), p. 297.

12. Ibid., p. 301.

13. Eugene C. Holmes "W. E. B. DuBois—Philosopher", *Freedomways*, vol. 5, no. 1 (Winter 1965), pp. 43–44.

14. Ibid., pp. 44–45.

15. Eugene C. Holmes "Langston Hughes, Philosopher—Poet", *Freedomways*, vol. 8, no. 2 (Spring 1968), p. 146.

16. Ibid., pp. 148–51.

17. The most extensive exegesis of Holmes' space/time research has been done by a former student of Holmes, Percy E. Johnston, *Phenomenology of Space and Time* (New York: Dasein Literary Society, 1976). However, this work is flavored with esoteric and useless verbage and lacks a consistent dialectical materialist outlook; see Eugene C. Holmes, "The Main Philosophical Implications of Space and Time,

American Journal of Physics, vol. 18, no. 9 (December 1950), p. 560. For recent work on the relationship of Egyptian to Greek philosophy, see Henry Olela, "The African Foundation of Greek Philosophy" and Lanciany Keita "The African Philosophical Tradition," both in Richard A. Wright, ed., *African Philosophy: An Introduction* (Washington, D.C.: University Press of America, 1979). Additionally, consult Edward P. Philip's "Can Ancient Egyptian Thought be Regarded as the Basis of African Philosophy?" *Second Order,* vol. 3, 1974).

18. Ibid., p. 560.
19. Lenin's *Materialism and Empirio-Criticism* appears in Lenin, *Collected Works,* vol. 14. (Moscow: Progress Publishers, 1972); Maurice Cornforth, *Science versus Idealism* (New York: International Publishers, 1962).
20. Holmes, *Main Philosophical,* p. 561.
21. Theodore Oizerman, *Problems of the History of Philosophy* (Moscow: Progress Publishers, 1973), pp. 81–84.
22. Holmes, *Main Philosophical,* p. 561.
23. Ibid., pp. 561–62.
24. Karl Marx's and Frederick Engels' *The Holy Family* can be found in Marx/Engels, *Collected Works,* vol. 4 (New York: International Publishers, 1975). For Lenin's conspectus on *The Holy Family,* see Lenin, *Collected Works,* vol. 38 (Moscow: Progress Publishers, 1972), pp. 19–51. For a more recent Marxist discussion on the materialist critique of Descartes see Howard Selsam, *Philosophy in Revolution* (New York: International Publishers, 1957), pp. 94–95.
25. Holmes, *Main Philosophical,* pp. 563–64.
26. Ibid., p. 564; for Lenin's critique of Kant, see Lenin, vol. 38, pp. 91–92, 100, 108–09, 112–13.
27. Lenin, vol. 14, p. 197; his full exposition is section 1, chapter 4, (pp. 194–204), subtitled "The Criticism of Kantianism from the Left and from the Right."
28. Holmes, *Main Philosophical,* pp. 564–65.
29. Ibid., p. 565.
30. Ibid.
31. Ibid.
32. Ibid., p. 566.
33. Ibid., pp. 566–67; also, see Albert Einstein and Leopold Infeld, *The Evolution of Physics* (New York: Simon and Schuster, 1961), especially pp. 177–208. For more recent dialectical materialist philosophical critiques of classical physics and the "revolution" in physics, see V. Ia. Pakhomov, "Contemporary Physics," and Lenin's "Conception of Objective Truth," *Soviet Studies in Philosophy,* vol. 9, no. 1 (summer 1970), pp. 70–80; also, see M. E. Omel'ianovskii, "The Conception of Dialectical Contradiction in Quantum Physics" in John Somerville and Howard Parsons, eds., *Dialogues on the Philosophy of Marxism* (Westport, Conn.: Greenwood Press, 1974), pp. 116–139.
34. This is not to imply that white professional philosophers were any different in their attraction to Marxism-Leninism. Notable exceptions are John Somerville, Howard Selsam, and Howard L. Parsons.
35. Holmes' specific relationship to Hunton, DuBois, and Robeson necessarily involves more biographical research. But all of them were closely associated with *Freedomways.* On the relationship of Hunton and DuBois to *Freedomways,* see my remarks in Faustine C. Jones, *The Changing Mood in America* (Washington, D.C.: Howard University Press, 1977), pp. 164, 165, 167, 181; not mentioned in the text of this essay is that Holmes had published an essay in 1935 where he ostensibly identifies with a Marxist critique of literature. See Holmes' "The Negro in Recent American Literature," in Henry Hart, ed., *American Writers' Congress* (New York: International Publishers, 1935).

36. Eugene C. Holmes, "A General Theory of the Freedom Cause of the Negro People" in Percy E. Johnston, ed., *Afro-American Philosophies: Selected Readings from Jupiter Hammon to Eugene C. Holmes* (Upper Montclair, N.J.: Montclair State College Press, 1970), pp. 18–19.
37. Ibid., p. 20.
38. Ibid., p. 25.
39. Ibid., p. 28.

Eugene Clay Holmes

Books

1. *Social Philosophy and the Social Mind: A Study of Genetic Methods of J. M. Baldwin, George Herbert Mead, and J. E. Boodin.* New York: privately printed 1942 (Ph.D. dissertation).

Edited Works

1. *The New Negro Thirty Years Afterward: Papers Contributed to the Sixteenth Annual Spring Conference of the Division of the Social Sciences.* Coeditor with Rayford W. Logan and G. Franklin Edwards. Washington, D.C.: Howard University Press, 1955.
2. Also see "Alain Locke—Philosopher" in *The New Negro Thirty Years Afterward.* Washington, D.C.: Howard University Press, 1955.

Reviews

1. "Famine," by Liam O'Flaherty. *American Teacher,* March-April 1938.
2. "Guide of Philosophy of Morals and Politics," by C. E. M. Joad. *Science and Society,* Spring 1939.
3. "The Negro as Capitalist," by A. L. Harris. *Science and Society,* no. 2, 1937.
4. "Negro College Graduate," by C. S. Johnson. *New Masses,* November 1938.
5. "Origins of American Sociology," by Bernard. *Science and Society,* Summer 1944.
6. "Philosophy Takes a Holiday," by Irwin Edman. *American Teacher,* January 1939.
7. "Race Against Men and the Negro Immigrant," *Science and Society,* 1940.

Articles

1. "Alain LeRoy Locke: A Sketch," *Phylon,* 1st Quarter (Spring 1959), pp. 82–89.
2. "Alain Locke, Philosopher, Critic, Spokesman," *Journal of Philosophy,* vol. 54, no. 5 (February 28, 1957), pp. 113–118.
3. "Jean Toomer" Apostle of Beauty," *Opportunity,* vol. 10 (August 1932), pp. 252–54.
4. "The Kantian Views of Time and Space Evaluated," *Philosophy and Phenomenological Research* (September 1955–56).
5. "The Legacy of Alain Locke," *Freedomways,* vol. 3 (Summer 1963).
6. "The Main Philosophical Considerations of Space and Time," *American Journal of Physics,* vol. 18, no. 9 (December 1950), pp. 560–570.
7. "Mrs. James Crow: D.A.R." *New Masses,* vol. 30, no. 12 (March 14), 1939.
8. "Philosophical Problems of Space and Time," *Science and Society,* vol. 24 (1950), pp. 207–227.

Articles in Books

1. "The Negro in Recent American Literature." In Henry Hart, *American Writers' Congress.* New York: International Publishers, 1935.

Papers Presented at Scholarly Conferences
1. "A General Theory of the Freedom Cause of the Negro People," *American Philosophical Association,* December 1955. This paper was later published in Percy E. Johnston, *Afro-American Philosophies: Selected Readings from Jupiter Hammon to Eugene C. Holmes.* Upper Montclair, N.J.: Montclair State College Press, 1970.

Miscellaneous
1. "The American Negro Theatre." *Dictionary of the Fine Arts,* New York, 1944.
2. "Anti-Semitism." Series of articles in *The Chicago Defender,* 1944.
3. "Educators Fight for Federal Aid." *American Teacher,* May-June 1938.
4. "The Philosophy of Charles A. Beard." Columbia University, M.A. thesis, December 1936.
5. "Problems Facing the Negro Writer." *New Challenge,* Fall 1937.
6. "A Program for African Liberation." *The African,* vol. 2, no. 1, (September–October).
7. "Pushkin in America." *International Literature,* no. 6, 1937.
8. "Race Against Men and the Negro Immigrant," *Science and Society,* 1940.

Note on the Author

John H. McClendon teaches Afro-American Studies at the University of Illinois-Urbana. He authored "Afro-American Philosophers and Philosophy: A Selected Bibliography," *Afro Scholars Working Papers, University of Illinois-Urbana,* and published works on Eugene Clay Holmes in *Freedomways* and the history of Afro-American philosophy *Sage Race Relation Abstracts,* November 1982.

Philosophy, Politics, and Power: An Afro-American Perspective

Cornel West

Is it a mere coincidence that the major philosophical thinkers in the modern West—Marx, Kierkegaard, and Nietzsche in the nineteenth century and Wittgenstein, Heidegger, and Derrida in the twentieth century—call for an end to philosophy? What do these post-philosophical voices have to do with Afro-Americans engaged in the philosophical enterprise?

I suggest that the calls for an end to philosophy are symptomatic of fundamental cultural transformations in the modern West. These transformations primarily consist of three salient developments in modern Western culture. First, the demythologizing of the institution of science—still in its rudimentary stage—renders the status of philosophy problematic. This demythologizing is not a discrediting of the achievements of science, but an undermining of its legitimacy regarding its alleged monopoly on truth and reality. Second, the demystifying of the role of authority makes the function of philosophy suspect. This demystifying is not simply a revolt against intellectual, social, and political authority, it calls into question the very notion of and need for authority. Third, the disclosure of a deep sense of impotence tends to support the view that philosophy is superfluous. This disclosure is not only a recognition of dominant ironic forms of thinking and narcissistic forms of living, but a pervasive despair about the present and lack of hope for the future.

These three developments require that philosophy—both as a professional discipline and as a mode of thinking—either redefine itself or bring itself to an end. In this historical moment, Afro-Americans engaged in the philosophical enterprise can contribute to the redefining of philosophy principally by revealing why and showing how philosophy is inextricably linked to politics and power—to structures of domination and mechanisms of control. This important task does not call for an end to philosophy. Rather it situates philosophical activity in the midst of personal and collective struggles in the present.

Revaluations of the Philosophical Past

In order to understand the prevailing crisis of philosophy in the modern West, it is necessary to examine the beginnings of modern Western philosophy. Modern philosophy emerged alongside modern science. The basic aim of modern philosophy was to promote and encourage the legitimacy of modern science. Descartes, the famous mathematician and scientist, was the father of modern philosophy. He tried to show that modern science not merely provides more effective ways of coping with the world, but also yields objective, accurate, value-free copies of the world. Descartes attempted to do this by putting forward rational foundations for knowledge independent of theological grounds and moral concerns. For the first time, epistemological matters became the center around which philosophical reflection evolved. Henceforth, the principal thrust of modern philosophy would be toward the justification of and rationale for belief. Modern philosophy became a disinterested quest for certainty regulated by a conception of truth that stands outside the world of politics and power—a prop that undergirds the claims of modern science.

The emergence of the capitalist mode of production, with its atomistic individualism and profit-oriented dispositions toward nature and people, partly accounts for the way in which Descartes chose to defend modern science. This defense takes the form of a justification of knowledge that starts with the self-consciousness of the individual, the immediate awareness of the subject, the *cogitatio* of the ego. Descartes' methodological doubt, a search for certainty that begins in radical doubt, rests upon the only mental activity that cannot be doubted: the activity of doubt itself. In his view, such doubting presupposes an agent who doubts, that is, a thinking individual, subject, or ego. Only by validly inferring from this indubitable activity of doubting—the only certainty available—can claims about God, the world, and the bodily self be justified. Like the new literary genre of early capitalist culture—the novel—Descartes' viewpoint supports the notion that we have access to, arrive at, and acquire knowledge of the world through the autonomous individual. Therefore, the primacy of the individual, subject, or ego who accurately copies the world or validly makes inferences about the world serves as the foundation of knowledge, the philosophical basis of modern science.

The obsession of the early modern philosophers with science (especially Newton) partly explains the empiricist twist given to Descartes' subjectivist turn in philosophy. For Locke, Berkeley, and Hume, the primacy of the thinking individual, subject, or ego remained, but experience (understood as sensations and perceptions) became the major candidate for the foundation of knowledge. Yet this ambitious project faltered. When Berkeley rejected the substantial self—the subject to which attributes are attached—and called on God to ground it as spirit, philosophical havoc set in. Hume, who had little philosophical use for God, explicitly articulated the skeptical result: the idea that knowledge has no empirical foundation. Instead, knowledge is but the (philosophical unjustifiable) imaginative constructs enacted by thinking individuals, subjects, or egos. Yet these thinking individuals, subjects, or egos are but themselves bundles of sensations and perceptions. Hence the subject and object of knowledge is rendered problematic—and modern philosophy found itself in a quandary.

Kant, the first modern professional philosopher in the West, rescued modern philosophy by providing transcendental grounds for knowledge and science. He reenacted the quest for certainty—the situating of the grounds for truth outside of politics and power—by locating the justification of what we know in the conditions for the possibility of knowing. These conditions are neither deductively arrived at nor empirically grounded. Rather they are transcendental in that they consist of the universal and necessary conceptual scheme people employ in order to know and hence have experience. Although Kant rejected the rationalist inference-making activity of Descartes, he deepened Descartes' subjectivist turn by locating the universal and necessary conceptual scheme in the thinking activity of the subject. Although Kant criticized the empiricist perspectives of Locke, Berkeley, and especially Hume, he accepted Hume's skepticism by holding that the universal and necessary conceptual scheme constitutes an objective world, but not the real world. In addition, Kant's architectonic project tried to link science, morals and aesthetics—Truth, Goodness, and Beauty—while arguing for their different foundations.

With the appearance of Hegel, modern philosophy drifted into a deep crisis. This was so primarily because of the emergence of historical consciousness. This consciousness was threatening to modern philosophy because it acknowledged the historical character of philosophy itself. This acknowledgement presented a major challenge to modern philosophy because it implied that the very aim of modern philosophy—the quest for certainty and search for foundations of knowledge—was an ahistorical enterprise. Hegel's historicizing of Kant's universal and necessity conceptual scheme questioned the very content and character of modern philosophy.

It is no accident that the first modern calls for the end of philosophy were made by the two major thinkers who labored under the shadow of Hegel: Kierkegaard and Marx. Both accepted Hegel's historicizing of the subjectivist turn in philosophy, his emphasis on activity, development, and process, his dialectical approach to understanding and transforming the world, and his devastating critiques of Cartesian and Kantian notions of substance, subject, and the self. Kierkegaard rejected Hegel's intellectualist attempt to link thought to concrete, human existence and put forward a profound existential dialectic of the self. Marx discarded Hegel's idealistic project of resolving the dominant form of alienation in the existing order and presented a penetrating materialistic dialectic of capitalist society. Both Kierkegaard and Marx understood philosophy as an antiquated, outmoded form of thinking, a mere fetter that impeded their particular praxis-oriented projects of redemption. Kierkegaard noted that, "philosophy is life's dry nurse, it can stay with us but not give milk". And Marx stated that, "philosophy stands in the same relation to the study of the actual world as masturbation to sexual love".

Afro-American philosophers should take heed of the radical antiphilosophical stances of Kierkegaard and Marx, not because they are right but rather because of the concerns that motivate their viewpoints. Both stress the value-laden character of philosophical reflection; the way in which such reflection not only serves particular class and personal interest, but also how it refuses to see itself as a form of praxis-in-the-world-of-politics-and-power. This refusal conceals the complex linkages of philosophical reflection to politics and power by defining itself as above and outside politics and power. By viewing itself as the queen of the disciplines that oversee the knowledge-claims of other disciplines, modern philosophy elides its this-worldly character, its role and function in the world of politics and power.

Despite Hegel's historicizing efforts, academic philosophers managed to overthrow Hegelianism, ignore Kierkegaard and Marx (both nonacademics!), and replace Hegelianism either with the analytical realism of Bertrand Russell and G. E. Moore in England; the diverse forms of returns to Kant (neo-Kantianisms) and Descartes (phenomenology) in Germany; and the various modes of vitalism (Bergson) and religious-motivated conventionalism (Pierre Duhem) in France. The only kind of professional philosophizing that took Hegel seriously was Dewey's version of American pragmatism, yet even Dewey wrote as if Kierkegaard and Marx never lived. In short, the professionalization of modern philosophy in the West shielded the academy from the powerful antiphilosophical perspectives of post-Hegelian figures, especially that of Nietzsche.

Since Nietzsche is first and foremost a philosopher of power—who links philosophy to power, truth to strategic linguistic tropes, and thinking to coping techniques—he has never been welcomed in the philosophical academy. This is so primarily because—like Kierkegaard and Marx—his understanding of the power dimensions of knowledge and the political aspects of philosophy calls into question the very conception of philosophy that legitimates philosophical reflection in the academy. Ironically, the recent developments in philosophy and literary theory—antirealism in ontology, antifoundationalism in epistemology, and the detranscendentalizing of the subject—were prefigured by Nietzsche.[1] Yet the relation of these developments to politics and power is ignored.

Repetition in the Post-Philosophical Present

The contemporary philosophical scene can be viewed as a repetition of Hegel's historicizing efforts—but with a difference. This crucial difference primarily consists of retranslating Hegel's stress on History as an emphasis on Language. The Hegelian notions of origins and ends of history, of homogeneous continuities in and overarching totalizing frameworks for history, are replaced by beginnings and random play of differences within linguistic systems, heterogeneous discontinuities in and antitotalizing deconstructions of linguistic discourses. This repetition of Hegel—the replacement of history with language—is mediated by three central-European processes in this century: the nihilistic Death-of-God perspective conjoined with Saussurean linguistics, which radically questions the meaning and value of human life (best portrayed in contemporary literature); the rise of fascism and totalitarianism, which tempers efforts for social change; and the sexual revolution, which unleashes hedonistic and narcissistic sensibilities on an unprecedented scale. These three processes circumscribe the repetition of Hegel within the perimeters of philosophical nihilism, political impotence, and hedonistic fanfare. Professional philosophy finds itself either radically historicized and linguisticized hence vanishing or holding on to the Kantian tradition for dear life.[2]

On a philosophical plane, the repetition of Hegel takes the form of an antirealism in ontology, antifoundationalism in epistemology, and a detranscendentalizing of the Kantian subject. The antirealism in ontology leaves us with changing descriptions and versions of the world, which come from various communities as responses to problematics, as fallible attempts to overcome specific situations and as means to satisfy particular needs and interests. The antifoundationalism in epistemology precludes notions of privileged representations that correctly correspond to the world, hence ground our knowledge; it leaves us with sets of transient social practices that facilitate our survival as individuals and members of society. The detranscendentalizing of the Kantian subject—the historical and linguistic situating of ourselves as knowers and doers—focuses our attention no longer on the mental activity of thinking individuals, but rather on the values and norms of historical and linguistic groups. Kierkegaard and Marx, like their master Hegel, held such antirealist, antifoundationalist, detranscendentalist views, but they did so with a sense of engagement in the present and hope for the future. The repetition of Hegel holds similar post-philosophical views yet despairs of the present and has little hope, if any, for the future.

This post-philosophical despair and hopelessness—with its concomitant forms of ironic and apocalyptic thinking and narcissistic living—is inextricably linked to the fundamental cultural transformations I noted earlier: the demythologizing of the institution of science, the demystifying of the role of authority, and the disclosure of a deep sense of impotence. Since modern philosophy at its inception was the handmaiden to modern science, it is not surprising that the demythologizing of science occurs alongside the vanishing of modern philosophy. Just as the Enlightenment era witnessed the slow replacement of the authority of the church with that of science, so we are witnessing a displacement of science, but there is no replacement as of yet. The *philosophes* of the Enlightenment—the propagandists for science and ideologues for laissez-faire capitalism—had a vision of the future; whereas the professional avant-gardists—propagandists against 'bourgeois' science and ideologues against monopoly capitalism—rarely present a project for the future. The neo-Marxist Frankfurt School, including Max Horkheimer, Theodor Adorno, and Herbert Marcuse, along with creative followers like Stanley Aronowitz and Michel Foucault, are pioneers of this novel perspective of philosophy.[3] Yet, with the exception of Aronowitz and Marcuse at times, the hopelessness for the future is overwhelming. Nevertheless, these figures are much further along than their contemporaries, as illustrated by Quine's outdated neo-positivist veneration of physics or Rorty's nostalgic longing for preprofessional humanistic "conversation" among men and women of letters.

The demystifying of the role of authority—promoted by the 'hermeneutics of suspicion' of Marx, Nietzsche, and Freud and encouraged by the antifoundationalism in contemporary philosophy—can be traced to the more general problem of the deep crisis of legitimacy in postmodern capitalist civilization. Of course, the breakdown of scientific, technocratic culture also affects the socialist world, but the crisis of legitimacy is in many ways a phenomenon rooted in the processes of monopoly capitalist societies. By undermining traditional forms of authority—church, family, school—owing to the profit-motivated promotion of hedonistic sensibilities, capitalist societies can legitimate themselves principally by satisfying the very needs it helps activate. These societies keep the populace loyal to its authority primarily by "delivering the goods", often luxury consumer goods that are rendered attractive by means of ingenious advertising. These goods do not merely pacify the populace; they also come to be viewed as the basic reason, in contrast to moral, religious or political reasons, that people have for acquiescence to capitalist authority. Hence, the crisis of legitimacy—the undermining of the work ethic, the collapse of the family, anarchy in public schools, and the proliferation of sexually-oriented advertisements, commercials, movies, and television shows—becomes part and parcel of the very legitimizing processes of monopoly capitalist societies.

The disclosure of a deep sense of impotence sits at the center of the postphilosophical present: the sense of reaching an historical dead end with no foreseeable way out and no discernible liberating projects or even credible visions in the near future. This disclosure is related to the detranscendentalizing of the Kantian subject in the sense that the emergence of the transcendental subject—the creative and conquering romantic hero—signifies the sense of optimistic triumph of early modern capitalist civilization. The detranscendentalizing of the subject portrays the sense of pessimistic tragedy of postmodern capitalist civilization, with the primary redemptive hope for this civilization, Marx's collective subject, the proletariat, remaining relatively dormant and muted.

The dominant forms of intellectual activity, especially philosophical reflection, enact this sense of impotence: analytical philosophy makes a fetish of technical virtuosity and uses it as a measure to regulate the intense careerism in the profession; antiacademic professional avant-gardists fiercely assault fellow colleagues and fervently attack notions of epistemological privilege yet remain relatively silent about racial, sexual, and class privilege in society at large; and poststructuralists perennially decenter prevailing discourses and dismantle philosophical and literary texts yet valorize a barren, ironic disposition by deconstructing, hence disarming and discarding, any serious talk about praxis. In this way, the repetition of Hegel is, from an Afro-American perspective, meretricious: attractive on a first glance but much less substantive after careful examination.

Recommendations for a Revolutionary Future

The principal task of the Afro-American philosopher is to keep alive the idea of a revolutionary future, a better future different from the deplorable present, a state of affairs in which the multifaceted oppression of Afro-Americans (and others) is, if not eliminated, alleviated. Therefore the Afro-American philosopher must preserve the crucial Hegelian (and deeply Christian) notions of negation and transformation of what is in light of a revolutionary not-yet.[4] The notions of negation and transformation—the pillars of the Hegelian process of *Aufhebung*—promote the activity of resistance to what is and elevate the praxis of struggle against existing realities. In this way, Afro-American philosophers must wage an intense intellectual battle in the form of recovering the revolutionary potential of Hegel against the ironic repetition of Hegel, which dilutes and downplays this potential. The revolutionary potential of Hegel—indigenously grounded in the prophetic religious and progressive secular practices of Afro-Americans—can be promoted by a serious confrontation with the Marxist tradition and, among others, the recent work of Michel Foucault.

Foucault's exorbitant reaction to his former vulgar Marxism and past Communist allegiances often leads him to embody the worst of the repetition of Hegel: precluding any talk about a better future and downplaying the activity of resistance and struggle in the present. Despite these limitations, certain aspects of Foucault's work can contribute to a revolutionary future, notably his attempt to construct "a new politics of truth." For Foucault, the Western will to truth has not been truthful about itself. Only with the appearance of Hegel and later Kierkegaard, Marx, and Nietzsche, has the this-worldly character of truth—its rootedness in politics and power—been disclosed and dissected. Foucault, who views his own work as "philosophical fragments put to work in a historical field of problems," begins his philosophical reflections with two basic questions: How are the conditions for the possibility of knowledges—the rules, conventions, and operations that circumscribe fields of discourse wherein notions, metaphors, categories, and ideas are rendered intelligible and comprehensible—ensconced in particular sets of power-relations? How are these conditions articulated in discursive practices and elaborated (in the sense in which Antonio Gramsci defines this crucial term) in nondiscursive formations? These questions are answered neither by abstract philosophical arguments nor by systematic theoretical treatises, but rather by detailed analytical descriptions—containing arguments and explanations—that constitute a genealogy of moral and political technologies, a genealogy that lays bare the workings of structures of domination and mechanisms of control over human bodies. Foucault's genealogical approach eschews the philosophical past and shuns the ironic repetition of Hegel in the present; he writes a subversive history of this past and present by discerning and detaching "the power of truth from the forms of hegemony, social, economic, and cultural, within which it operates".[5]

Foucault's perspective can be valuable for Afro-American philosophers whose allegiance is to a revolutionary future. With the indispensable aid of sophisticated neo-Marxist analysis, Foucault's viewpoint can be creatively transformed and rendered fruitful for a genealogy of modern racism, in both its ideational and material forms. This genealogy would take the form of detailed, analytical descriptions of the battery of notions, categories, metaphors, and concepts that regulate the inception of modern discourse, a discourse that constituted the idea of white supremacy in a particular way (e.g. inaugurated the category of 'race') and excluded the idea of black equality in beauty, culture, and character from its discursive field.[6] Unlike Foucault, this Afro-American genealogical approach also would put forward an Afro-American counter-discourse, in all its complexity and diversity, to the modern European racist discourse and examine and evaluate how the Afro-American response promotes or precludes a revolutionary future.[7] In addition, a more refined effort would even delve into the political content of Afro-American everyday life and disclose the multivarious Afro-American cultural elements that debilitate or facilitate an Afro-American revolutionary future.

If Afro-American philosophers are to make a substantive contribution to the struggle for Afro-American freedom, it is imperative that we critically revaluate the grand achievements of the past philosophical figures in the West and avoid falling into their alluring ahistorical traps, traps that disarm Afro-American philosophers and render us mere colorful presences in the glass menagerie of the academy in monopoly capitalist USA. Afro-American philosophers must understand the repetition of Hegel in the present time as inescapable yet of highly limited value owing to its nihilistic outlooks; outlooks that implicitly presuppose luxury and explicitly preclude any serious talk about a future better than the inferno-like present. Lastly, Afro-American philosophers must articulate and elaborate recommendations for a revolutionary future. This articulation and elaboration requires a recovery of the revolutionary potential of Hegel, a deepening of the Marxist tradition, and a concrete grounding in the indigenous prophetic and progressive practices of Afro-Americans. This calling of Afro-American philosophers—this vocation of service—permits us to take our place alongside, not above, other committed Afro-Americans who continue to hold up the blood-stained banner, a banner that signifies the Afro-American struggle for freedom.

Notes

1. Cornel West, "Nietzsche's Prefiguration of Postmodern American Philosophy," *Boundary 2: A Journal of Postmodern Literature,* Special Nietzsche issue, vols. 9,10, nos. 1,3, (Fall-Winter 1980–81), pp. 241–270.
2. The most penetrating and provocative examination of these two options for contemporary philosophy is Richard Rorty's *Philosophy and the Mirror of Nature* (Princeton, 1979). For a sympathetic yet biting critique of this book, see my review in *Union Seminary Quarterly Review,* vol. 37, nos. 1,2, (Fall-Winter 1981–82).

3. The central works on this subject are Max Horkheimer and Theodor Adorno, *Dialectic of Enlightenment* (New York, 1972); Herbert Marcuse, *One-Dimensional Man: Studies in the Ideology of Advanced Industrial Society* (Boston, 1964); Stanley Aronowitz, *The Crisis in Historical Materialism: Class, Politics and Culture in Marxist Theory* (New York, 1981); Michel Foucault, *Discipline and Punish: The Birth of the Prison,* trans. Alan Sheridan (New York, 1977).

4. For a brief treatment of these two basic notions as a basis for prophetic Christian and progressive Marxist praxis, see Cornel West, *Prophesy Deliverance! An Afro-American Revolutionary Christianity* (Philadelphia, 1982), "Introduction: The Sources and Tasks of Afro-American Critical Thought."

5. Michel Foucault, *Power/Knowledge: Selected Interviews & Other Writings 1972–1977* (New York, 1980), p. 133.

6. For a rudimentary effort at such a genealogical approach, see Cornel West, *Prophesy Deliverance! An Afro-American Revolutionary Christianity* (Philadelphia, 1982), Chapter 2.

7. For a humble attempt at such a project, see Cornel West, "Philosophy and the Afro-American Experience", *The Philosophical Forum,* vol. IX, nos. 2–3 (Winter-Spring 1977–78), pp. 117–148, and, with additions and revisions, Cornel West, *Prophesy Deliverance! An Afro-American Revolutionary Christianity* (Philadelphia, 1982), Chapter 3.

Note on the Author

Cornel West, Assistant Professor of Philosophy of Religion, Union Theological Seminary, New York City. His work focuses on the compatibility of Christianity and Socialism and the interpretation of cultural phenomena. He is author of *Prophesy Deliverance! An Afro-American Revolutionary Christianity.*

Philosophy, Hermeneutics, Social-Political Theory: Critical Thought in the Interest of African-Americans

Lucius T. Outlaw

Speculative thought is hostile by its very nature to resignation and disintegration. To examine our most simple ideas systematically is to assert the claims of unity against disintegration and of the mind's authority over the world against resignation of the world's dark order. Hence, philosophy is revolutionary even when it appears conservative, and thought is the denial of fate even when it seems to be its defense. No one who has heard a whispered intimation of the power and greatness of theory will ever surrender to despair, nor will he doubt that this sound of thought will one day awaken the stones themselves.[1]

Roberto Mangabeira Unger

If the "stones" are the dispossessed and oppressed of the American social order, particularly if they are people of African descent, what will be the content and focus of the thought that "awakens" us to the needs and possibilities for critical, revolutionary thought and practices by which we, with others, will fashion a social order oriented to the liberated and viable existence, to the highest degree possible, for all who share this land? For all of us concerned with the revolutionary transformation of the American socio-political-economic order, this is a crucial question. It is so particularly for people of African descent in this country in light of our historical and continuing struggles against racism in addition to the other ills we suffer. And the history of aspirant "revolutionary" theories and practices, and their embodiment and institutionalization in various groups/organizations, has not been free of this same racism, at worst, paternalism at best.

Still, even within our own ranks all has not been well. For we black folk also have been guilty of many errors, in addition to our significant contributions, sacrifices, and gains. Not the least of these errors have been our limited, sometimes shallow, views of American society as is and as it might or should be. An important aspect of our situation has been—and continues to be—the difficulty of properly dealing with the appropriate place of blacks (i.e., people of African descent) within our theories and practices.[2]

This essay was drafted originally during my tenure as a 1976 Spencer Foundation Fellow at the Robert R. Moton Center for Independent Studies located, at the time, in Philadelphia, Pennsylvania. This revised version was prepared with support provided by a Morgan State University Faculty Research Grant during my tenure at Morgan as a member of the Department of Philosophy (1977–1981). Special thanks to both institutions for their support.

The way out of this difficulty requires the elaboration of a global theory (i.e., theoretical grasp of the social order as a whole, including its international connections and its history) within which the particularity of African-Americans is properly situated, that is to say, within which our true needs and interests, our values and contributions—in short, our life-world—are legitimatized. It is to this end that I wish to contribute in this essay.

I. 1.

The effort to elaborate a global, theoretical view of social life in general, and of a particular people within it, represents the endeavor of "philosophy" at its very best. But for those of us who are *not* of European descent, the effort to construct a critical, radical view of the whole that includes a respectful, legitimizing consideration of the life-worlds of others—in this case, people of African descent—is beset with serious difficulties. For, systematically, the institutionalized tradition of philosophy, thus even the guiding notions of what constitutes "philosophy" in form and content, has excluded almost wholly the philosophical contributions of non-European peoples. As an enterprise philosophy, like all else in the social order, suffers from racial/ethnic/class/sexual biases and deformations even while it claims to be the guardian of the most developed and progressive notions of "reason." In addition, the enterprise of philosophy suffers from the pervasiveness of the intensified historical tendency toward increasing specialization and the development of narrowness, over concern with method and discipline immanent matters, and, in some cases, has degenerated into scienticism.[3] Concretely, then, the enterprise of philosophy, its meaning, and possibilities in the West, is in need of clarification and redirection if the question of the transformation of the American social order is to be addressed.

Confronting this issue is a necessary first step for those of us of African descent. Recognition of this is, to some extent, reflected in the debates over the past half-decade or more regarding a "Black Philosophy" to the extent that the effort has been aimed at setting forth the life-worlds, in terms of structures and practices, of African peoples in our particularities as a corrective to the false universality of European and European-descendant world views, on the one hand; and, on the other, to the extent that the effort has been aimed at exploring critically and transforming and/or preserving where necessary the life-world of African people in America. These efforts, focused in our beginnings by the phrase "Black Philosophy," were necessary to avoid the deformations of both philosophy, in particular, and the West, in general. A rush to uncritical intellectual integration in a dangerously problematic situation would prove to be our undoing: in addition to reinforcing our self-denial, we would fail to be aware of historical tendencies and possibilities that we might struggle with others to realize and, in so doing, condition a line of historical development that could lead to enhanced conditions of life for all and, in particular, for the "marginal" peoples in the present order of life.

The concerns grounding the effort to elaborate the philosophical orientations of people of African descent have included one that is essential to the articulation of a critical theoretical overview of the American order, including a view of black people in it and our roles and responsibilities in its transformation: the need to be clear concerning our own being as a people historically, culturally, socio-politically, economically, and futuristically. The development of critical thought in the interest of African people must avoid a naive rush into traditions of thought/praxis on the assumption that 'reasonableness' has come to pervade the relations among different racial and ethnic groups and economic classes in this society or among the relations between nations.

The struggle of African-Americans continues to be that of seeking progressive liberation at a level capable of being shared given the level of development of the culture as a whole. It is also a continuing struggle for many who are nonblack, including many whites. It is, overall, the struggle to harness and direct the capabilities of the total society in the maximum utilization of resources, with minimum waste and environmental destruction, toward the satisfaction of essential human needs with minimum exploitation and oppression—the struggle for the realization of life based increasingly on reason democratically envisioned and realized. Toward this end, however, the concrete realities of the politics of the past, present, and foreseeable future demand that African people in America approach the struggle from the level of a group, i.e., ethnic (or nationalistic, as some would say) position, the only viable position in terms of which to achieve limited goals within the present order of things. In order to realize ends beyond the present order, however, it will be necessary to move beyond the important, yet limited, program of group-centered politics as the prime mode of political activity. The pursuit of progressive possibilities, which might lead to the radical transformation of the present order of life, thus, hopefully, to greater benefits for greater numbers of people, will require a social democracy based on pluralistic integration. Even so, we cannot be premature (i.e., unilateral) in this regard.

I. 2.

A very serious phase of preparation for the task of philosophizing critically in the interest of African people (and others) includes the need to come face to face with the history of the relationships of black thinkers to the historical thrusts of black people and, most importantly, with where this history leaves us today. We African-Americans involved in traditions of critical thought must, in other words, become transparent to ourselves as a class in terms of our history, our responsibilities, our possibilities.

Significant insights into the history of black thinkers are to be had in Harold Cruse's *Crisis of the Negro Intellectual*.[4] A controversial book, to say the least, but often a penetrating analysis harboring a very substantial core of truth. From the historical side there emerges from his analyses a picture of an essential failure on the part of black intellectuals (i.e., writers, social critics, artists, etc.) in not having forged a collective vision for African people in America based on an appropriate grasp of the realities of the socio-politico-economic and cultural schemes. For Cruse this failure rests fundamentally on the erroneous commitment on the part of black intellectuals to the unclarified ideal of integration. Even more, this failure of left-looking, 'radical' African-American thinkers, in his judgment, has been and continues to be, too often, an uncritical commitment to Marxism-Leninism and to the sufferance of intellectual apprenticeship to white, particularly Jewish, liberal, left-wing intellectuals. The pervasive reality of American life, says Cruse, is that its politics, cultural systems, and economics are group based: power resides in ethnic/ national groupings, primarily. The struggle for integration on the part of black people without having first developed, cultivated, and consolidated our own group solidarity has resulted in—and will continue to result in—the unsuccessful realization of the struggle for equality and freedom *within the present scheme of things*. The struggle, for the most part, has not been revolutionary, including separatist schemes (which, argues Cruse, seek to avoid the problem via escape) or those seeking systemic reform.

The arguments advanced by Cruse call for serious critique. However, a number of insights that emerge are immediately clear. Particularly important in the context of this essay is the need, Cruse stresses, for African-Americans to be clear of our grounding. That grounding is the historical struggle on the part of our people for an increasingly liberated existence. Out of this emerges a first task: the struggle to achieve a critical understanding of our situation, our real needs, and the means by which they might be met. In struggling to meet these responsibilities black thinkers must work against the tendencies leading to deformation, and must, particularly, be prepared to commit "class suicide" in order that energies be given unequivocally in service to the historical struggles of the masses of African people, here and elsewhere. In this regard there is a particular turn that must be made in our development, the importance of which is heightened by the debate regarding "Black Philosophy." That turn of development and its ground of necessity is clearly set out by Cruse:

> *Every other ethnic group in America, 'a nation of nations,' has*
> *accepted the fact of its separatedness and used it to its own social*
> *advantage. But the Negro's conditioning has steered him into that*
> *perpetual state of suspended tension wherein ninety-five percent of his*
> *time and energy is expended on fighting prejudice in whites. As a*
> *result, he has neither the time nor the inclination to realize that all of*
> *the effort spent fighting prejudice will not obviate those fundamental*
> *things an ethnic group must do for itself. This situation results from a*
> *psychology that is rooted in the Negro's symbolic 'blood-ties' to the*
> *white Anglo-Saxon. It is the culmination of that racial drama of love*
> *and hate between slave and master, bound together in the purgatory of*
> *plantations. Today the African foster child in the American racial*
> *equation must grow to manhood, break the psychological umbilical*
> *ties to intellectual paternalism. The American Negro has never yet*
> *been able to break entirely free of the ministration of his white masters*

to the extent that he is willing to exile himself, in search of wisdom,
into the wastelands of the American desert. That is what must be done,
if he is to deal with the Anglo-Saxon as the independent political
power that he, the Negro, potentially is.[5]

The insights of Cruse thus uncover the historically conditioned *vocation* of African intellectuals in America, which is fixed even more specifically by Vincent Harding:

> *. . . the fact still remains that for the life and work of the black*
> *scholar in search of vocation, the primary context is not to be found in*
> *the questionable freedom and relative affluence of the American*
> *university, nor in the ponderous uncertainties of "the scholarly*
> *community," nor even in the private joys of our highly prized,*
> *individual exceptionalisms. Rather, wherever we may happen to be*
> *physically based, our essential social, political, and spiritual context is*
> *the colonized situation of the masses of the black community in*
> *America.*[6]

The vocation of the black intellectual/scholar thus grounded structures, in Harding's words, our *calling:*

> *. . . to speak the truth to our people, to speak truth about our people,*
> *to speak truth about our enemies—all in order to free the mind, so*
> *that black men, women, and children may build beyond the banal,*
> *dangerous chaos of the American spirit, towards a new time.*[7]

Still, the struggle to hear our calling, to respond, in part by taking a pilgrimage through the desert in search of wisdom, in part by speaking the truth, all directed by the concern to contribute to the historical movement toward the realization of a more reasonable life, takes us beyond the limited goals that emerge from group consciousness (i.e., nationalism, ethnicity). It will, in fact, drive us beyond the boundaries of the present order of life, and, necessarily, bring us into serious conflict with it. Again, many of the more fundamental needs of black people are shared by many others. And these are, on the other hand, needs to be met in the lives of others which, while black people might not suffer them either at all or in the same intensity, do require the concern and attention of blacks in the struggle to realize a life of progressive liberation. This world historical struggle thus draws us beyond limited peoplehood to a generalized peoplehood that recognizes peoples in their diversities. It makes for toil to achieve unity in diversity: reasonableness in life as a unity based on democratically agreed upon notions of 'reasonableness' in a diverse, pluralistic, finite world.

Judged against these goals, limited and generalized, the vocation of philosophizing, for those who would choose it, takes on decisive meaning: *it is to share in the refinement and perpetuation of critical intelligence as a practice of life that has as its goal raising to consciousness the conditions of life, historical practices, and blocked alternatives which, if freed, might lead to life experienced as qualitatively-progressively-different.* As conceived by Stojanović:

> *Philosophy explores and evaluates the* totality *of the human condition in society. It represents society's most general and most fundamental theoretical-critical self-consciousness. No other form of human intellect is as condemned to aspire to totality as is philosophy.*[8]

And according to Max Horkheimer, the *social* function of philosophy is to develop critical, dialectical thought: "Philosophy is the methodical and steadfast attempt to bring reason into the world."[9] A crucial moment of this process, according to Horkheimer, is the radical critique of what is, at a given time, prevalent:

> *By criticism, we mean that intellectual, and eventually practical, effort which is not satisfied to accept the prevailing ideas, actions, and social conditions unthinkingly and from mere habit; effort which aims to coordinate the individual sides of social life with each other and with the general ideas and aims of the epoch, to deduce them genetically, to distinguish the appearance from the essence, to examine the foundations of things, in short, really to know them.*[10]

And the 'dialectical' aspect of critical thought? As Marcuse has characterized it:

> *Dialectical thought starts with the experience that the world is unfree; . . . man and nature exist in conditions of alienation, exist as 'other than they are.' . . . Dialectical thought thus becomes negative in itself. Its function is to break down the self-assurance and self-contentment of common sense, to undermine the sinister confidence in the power and language of facts, to demonstrate that unfreedom is so much at the core of things that the development of their internal contradictions leads necessarily to qualitative change: the explosion and catastrophe of the established state of affairs.*[11]

For African-Americans involved in the practices of philosophy, who would live a life conditioned primarily by the activity of critical, dialectical thought, a very first task involves bringing this activity to bear on the practice of 'philosophy' in the academy. Beyond this, however, the need to be grounded in the historical struggles of African peoples, in particular, and in the wider struggles of peoples for more reasonable forms of existence, in general, sets the tasks we must be about.

II
Hermeneutical Understanding

Having established that critical, dialectical thought, guided by the interest (i.e., the *value commitment*) to serve the emancipatory efforts of people of African descent, in particular, is the appropriate orientation and form of philosophizing required as part of the project to achieve the revolutionary transformation of the American order, it is necessary to specify further the way to a grounding of this philosophical praxis in the concrete needs and aspirations of black people. Here, too, the justification for this move rests firmly and explicitly on a set of value judgments and hopes: a positive judgment concerning the importance of the continued existence and viability of African peoples as a distinct group enjoying the practices of life at a level possible given the most advanced and "progressive" developments of human cultures and capabilities, to the extent that they are compatible with those interests and values that are essential to our *continued* survival and viability as a people into an extended, indefinite future; and the hope that we, an African people, and those who join with us in our struggles, will be successful. There is a foundational commitment to the value of the life-world, the contributions and possibilities, of African-American people at our most progressive best, co-equal with those of other peoples. Explicitly rejected are the ideas and ideals of an American "melting pot" and assimilation *qua* "integration" functioning as the covers for the cultural (and political and economic) imperialism and domination of other nationalities and ethnic groups by people of European descent.

The turn must be made to the life-world of African-American people, in all of its ambiguities, complexities, contradictions, and clarities; to our concrete life-praxis, in search of our distinct orientation with regard to the matters to be addressed in a revolutionary transformation of the American order. Such orientations are given, for example, in the mediated folk tales; in religious practices; in political language and practices prevalent during various times under various conditions; in forms of music, poetry, language of common currency, etc. As these forms of expression, in their concreteness as life-praxes, are constitutive elements of the *life-world* of African-American people, then the meanings they hold, in symbolic and/or explicit form, contain fundamental orientations. Reclaiming them through acts of reflection will provide understandings of the historically conditioned concerns of black people. Such acts of reclamation or interpretive understanding constitute the practice of philosophical hermeneutics. As such they are fundamental, for they must provide the clarified historical grounds for the orientation of present and future philosophical and practical activities in the interest of African-American people.

II. 1. Hermeneutical Understanding in General

Having identified some of the various *life-world* praxes and forms of expression constitutive of the *life-world* of black people, how are they to be interpreted? In general, notes Aron Gürwitsch, the task is to:

find and lay bare the acts of consciousness which in their systematic concatenation and intertexture make this specific world possible as their correlate. Answering this question for a particular cultural world amounts to understanding that world from within by referring it to the mental life in which it originates.[12]

Even more, we are to grasp not only the 'mental life' in which the life-praxis/ forms of expression have their origin, but also the relevant historical circumstances that provide the ground and context of their development. For blacks who would philosophize, this task should be one that can be met easily, for doing so constitutes self-understanding: we seek to understand our *own* life-world.

Yet the process of hermeneutical understanding, if it is to be appropriately carried out, must first be understood. We are assisted in the achievement of this understanding by the work of Richard Palmer.[13] In general, hermeneutical understanding is an *experiential encounter* with a *heritage,* a tradition, which *speaks* through the work (say a text) or life-praxis/form of expression. The nature of this "experiential encounter" is complex but involves, among other things, first, *hearing* the questions (and/or issues) that give rise to the work/praxis/form of expression. The process of achieving hermeneutical understanding is thus a dialogue between interpreter and object to be understood: the interpreter must be oriented by a fundamental questioning that seeks to hear the question of the work. This is the first canon to be met if hermeneutical understanding is to be authentic, that is, if the understanding achieved is to involve a grasp of the text/practice/expression for what it says. Doing so requires that the interpreter effect a merger of horizons (of meaning/being): the horizon of the question of the work/practice/expression and the horizon of the interpreter, constituted by the questions asked. Thus, "hearing" the work requires that one, as interpreter, come to share, by way of the appropriation of meaning, the *world* that the work in its language/ praxis reveals. Such revelations manifest, say, the time and space conditions of the person or people who ground the *world* of the work: for example, the relative degree of their freedom or oppression; how their *world* is conditioned—the nature, forms, and perpetuators of their oppressions—and, in short, how life in their world goes, or fails to go. It reveals, then, a heritage, a tradition; or, a break in tradition: revolution or decline.

The creation then of a common horizon between the work and the interpreter is both a condition and an achievement of hermeneutical understanding. This is made possible by each—both interpreter and work—belonging to a language and a heritage. The more closely the horizons encompassing the worlds of both can be fused, the greater the achievement of hermeneutical understanding.

II. 2. Hermeneutical Understanding in Particular

In a social order complicated by, among other things, a plurality of life-worlds of different racial, ethnic, national, and class groupings of people, and a continuing heritage of various forms and degrees of discrimination and oppression, the achievement of hermeneutical understanding across the fluid boundaries of these various life-worlds is a serious and difficult task. This is especially the case when the horizon of understanding of the interpreter is conditioned by the assumed superiority of his or her heritage, of the heritage mediated in the frameworks of understandings of a given people, or group of peoples, who may be socially dominant, and who thus attempt to generalize these frameworks as the only valid and authentic modes of understanding. We are painfully aware of the degree to which the notion of an "American Culture" has served as the ideological cover for the imperialistic domination of the cultures of other peoples in this country and elsewhere in the world.

On the other hand, the situation is equally problematic when the interpreter is objectively a member of the life-world he or she seeks to explicate, but, in terms of frameworks of understandings, share those of other people(s) including the implicit or explicit value/reality assumptions. Such is the case when, say, a black thinker, having not yet broken through the intellectual chains resulting from the colonization of his or her mind, carries through a hermeneutic of works emerging from the life-world of black people and denies the claims which are advanced—in short, does not *hear* the work or negates the authenticity of the questions put by the work. Such would be the case if, say, black spiritual music were to be denounced as the product of a misguided people who wrongly appeal to a "white man's God" and to another world ("heaven") rather than deal with their own affairs in a concrete fashion. Such a hermeneutic is itself inauthentic: it has not fully heard the question put by the experiences that ground spirituals, nor has it fully grasped the answer the music seeks to be. The struggle to achieve an authentic hermeneutical understanding of the life-world of African peoples cannot be unmindful of frameworks and traditions of understanding that, implicitly or explicitly, rationalize and thus contribute to the stabilization and perpetuation of our oppression, our blocked progressive development, or contribute to our liberation.

The idea of an 'authentic hermeneutic' is actualized in the dialogical encounter with the work, in a probing beyond the work to see, hear, question, what the work itself may not see, hear, question, but which conditions and grounds it. Hearing black spirituals, for example, would entail moves into and through the music and lyrics to the conditions of life that ground them, to the responses of African-American people to these conditions, and to the modes of being that the spirituals carry: not resignation in the face of oppression, perhaps, but a form of struggle against oppression, which, even though symbolic, becomes a source of strength to endure, to survive, to provide the foundations for future viability here and in the "other world." The struggle to achieve authentic hermeneutical understanding is a struggle to place the work, in its horizon of meaning, within the horizon of the heritage, needs, and aspirations of a living people, within their tradition or their break with tradition—within the revolution they struggle to realize, or the decline which intends their death.

If the context of authentic hermeneutical understanding is structured by these orientations, what is to be achieved by it? The end, in short, is enlightenment, growth, and, as a consequence, progressively liberating existence. As noted by Palmer:

> *When the author of a great work* [expressions of various forms, we might add] *opens up a possibility of being, we are interested in it not because he experienced it nor for anything it shows about himself (generally speaking) but because of our rootedness in existence, which furnished the deeper reference point for the assertion and the ground for its significance.*[14]

More specifically, the goal of hermeneutical understanding in the interest of African-Americans is increased self-transparency—a broadening and intensification of our personal and collective self-understanding—as a condition necessary for structuring present and future projects.

Critical decisions regarding where we must or should go, as persons, as a people, and what it is we must be about in the context of reasonable, concrete possibilities, require that we know whence we have come. What forms of life-praxes are liberating can, to a great extent, be decided reasonably only to the extent that we have understood well the range of forms of oppression suffered by African peoples and the conditions within which they did and continue to do so. Likewise, our stability and viability as a people require that the various joys and forms of happiness which have sustained us be grasped and preserved as guides to future endeavors, particularly in the context of a social world administering forms of entertainment serving to pacify us in a situation of administered unfreedom. The achievement of hermeneutical understanding is thus enrichment through an encounter with the sedimentation of tradition resulting in an enlargement of possibilities of existence on the personal level, and, on a social level, with the communication and affirmation of the revealed possibilities.

As a form of understanding, hermeneutics is grounded in a *practical interest:* a value grounding cognition as a commitment to the restoration and refinement of human concensus by way of the mediation of tradition.[15] Such an interest has at times served to ground the human or cultural sciences. In the words of Radnitzsky:

> *Hermeneutic human sciences study the objectivations of human cultural activity . . . with a view to interpreting them, to find out the intended or at least the expressed meaning, in order to establish the co-understanding or possibly even consent which has not (yet) been obtained or repairing the same-such which has been disturbed; and, in general, to mediate traditions so that the historical dialogue of mankind may be continued or resumed, and also deepened.*[16]

It should be noted that the view of hermeneutics as an endeavor grounded in a practical interest involves the commitment, by virtue of that interest, to struggle against the tendencies that might lead to group-centered theorizings and practices as an end. The ideal is the realization in history of reasonable forms of life that condition progressively liberated existence for *all* peoples. Thus endeavors in hermeneutics in the interest of African people are to be understood as a necessary moment in the world-wide struggle for generalized, emancipated human existence.

The practice of psychoanalysis, for example, stands out as a critical endeavor in hermeneutics that serves the interest of emancipation: by way of the dialogue of the psychoanalytic situation, the patient is assisted in the achievement of liberation, in terms of increased self-transparency, from unconscious motives and various repressions that lead to illness, i.e., an imbalance among the dynamic structures of the ego. Psychoanalysis has thus become a model of the development of knowledge as hermeneutics.[17] Much of the work of the revolutionary black psychiatrist Frantz Fanon [18] is striking confirmation of the emancipatory thrusts of hermeneutical understanding. This is particularly the case in the chapter "The Negro and Language," wherein Fanon probes the grounds of personality changes experienced by African people of colonized countries who visit the "Mother Country." Fanon focused on the strenuous efforts of some African people—in this case of the Antilles—to learn the French language, the language of the "master," as the completion of their (the "Natives' ") being:

> The Negro of the Antilles will be proportionately whiter—that is, he will come closer to being a real human being—in direct ratio to his mastery of the French language. I am not unaware that this is one of man's attitudes face to face with being. A man who has a language consequently possesses the world expressed and implied by that language.[19]

For Fanon, this struggle to master the French language was at base an attempt thereby to achieve acceptance and, supposedly, liberation within and in terms of the world of the French oppressors. It was a struggle to *be* by being like the oppressor. The uncovering of this as the true motive for the activity of the "native," the effort to bring it into full view that it might be confronted and affirmed as one's own motive in the process of being overcome via negation—the raising of it to the level of critically reflective consciousness so that it could be grasped for what it was as a process of radical self-denial, a struggle towards inauthenticity of person and people, from which we must be freed—this was an act of understanding in full service to the interest in emancipation: enlightenment as a necessary condition for correct praxis.

This hermeneutic of the passage of African peoples through the language forms, hence, all too often, the life-forms of other peoples in a way that denies who we are, that prevents us from becoming what we must be, is but part of a wider endeavor called for if African peoples are to enjoy progressive enlightenment as a condition for the revolutionary moves we must be about.

Such a wider endeavor I would term cultural hermeneutics, in general. For without question one of the most significant aspects of the multifaceted struggle on the part of African peoples for liberated existences has been, and is, the endeavor to achieve cultural integrity: i.e., to embrace where available, to construct where unavailable, those productions and expressions of meaning that serve to reflect the self-affirmations of black people, our views of the world, in concepts and life-forms that have been projected for these purposes.[20]

This is decisive. What is at issue is the meaning (and meaningfulness) of the existence of African-Americans and, subsequently, the nature of our being in terms of how that existence is described. The struggle, then, for cultural integrity (for a level of cultural development, and an understanding of it, which affirms and reflects our history, our present, and our future possibilities *as a people,* as a people among others), given the history of the various forms of oppression that have been, and are being, directed against us, involves, in the words of James Turner ". . . a counter-movement away from subordination to independence, from alienation through refutation, to self-affirmation . . ." by way of a process of "reflection" that ". . . creates a different (and opposing) constellation of symbols and assumptions."[21] Thus the cultural struggle calls for endeavors in *symbolic reversal* whereby one moves, on the level of symbolic meaning (and on the level of concrete existence) from imposed determinations of a people's existence to those generated by the people themselves in the process of living as affirmations of that existence in its authenticity.[22]

Hermeneutics, grounded, as we understand it, in an interest in enlightenment and emancipation, is a continuous task to be performed within the context of a number of African peoples' forms of expression: the various musics of jazz, blues, pop, spirituals; literature, poetry, and art; religious language; folklore, etc. The understanding achieved, when joined with that coming out of direct, distortion-free, democratic discussions[23] which focus on what people of African descent would have out of life, should thus provide an agenda for *further* critical discussions, theorizings, and planning of practical activities to guide both the transformation of the social order and historical evolution.

Yet the needs, wishes, desires, hopes, fears, denials, affirmations—the orientation and commitments to, the withdrawals from, life—which the hermeneutical effort reveals will not be pure and innocent positive representations of our "blackness," our "Africanness." Nor will they be immediately sufficient to establish an agenda for revolutionary transformation in the interest of African people. Oppressed people come to embody in their very being the negations imposed upon them and thus, in the reproduction of their lives, perpetuate their own enslavement.

The question, then, whether hermeneutics serves an emancipatory interest is a crucial one. In part it is a matter of the self-understanding of the interpreter given his/her historical situation. Additionally it is a matter of the concrete historical situation—past, present, and possible futures—of the social order as a whole and the particular situation of people of African descent.

71

Whether *in fact* the hermeneutical endeavor serves the interests of critical enlightenment and emancipation, rather than serving the interests that would work to secure continued oppression, will, in large part, be determined by the extent to which it is grounded on an *explicit* commitment to emancipation and revolutionary transformation. For the only sure way that African people in America can act in accord with an interest in emancipation is to be self-conscious about our own liberation: praxis, even as an act of critical understanding, as in hermeneutics, must be guided by global theoretical-critical understanding, which has as its primary interest the liberation of black folk, and others, from domination, to the greatest extent possible.

III Critical Thought in the Interest of African-Americans

The elaboration of a global, critical socio-political-economic-cultural theory, which acknowledges and serves the legitimate needs and interests of people of African descent and others, is a serious and yet-to-be-completed task. A review of the history of our struggles in this country, as well as the struggles of African people in other parts of the world, reveals, in addition to our substantial successes, obvious mistakes, weaknesses, and wrong turns in our modes of organization, patterns of leadership, and forms of praxis as a result of serious deficiencies in understanding our situation. This has led to deficiencies in theories of struggle.[24] Throughout the history of the presence of African people in this country, the dominant theoretical framework out of which we have struggled has been that provided by the Declaration of Independence, the Constitution, and the Bill of Rights. Although progressive achievements have been realized as a result of efforts conditioned by a commitment to the utopian vision of this framework, particularly in the areas of civil and political rights, it provides the ideological cover for a nondemocratic economic order and the concentration of political and economic power and socially produced wealth in the hands of few. Particularly, this framework and its supporting beliefs, especially the commitment to reasoned persuasion and evolutionary reform—and occasionally nonviolent direct action—as the only acceptable forms of contention, have conditioned our endeavors to such an extent that rarely have we broken through the veil of this cover to focus our energies on the centers of power which will have to be transformed if progressively liberated existence is to be realized.

African-Americans have been slow to learn from mistakes along these lines. The moves during the sixties from the struggle to achieve civil rights to the struggle to consolidate "black power" reflect the incorporation of understandings that were achieved as a result of concrete experiences. Still, the theoretical weaknesses, hence, misguided political praxes, in terms of strategies and tactics, were evident. And, again, the critical insights of Cruse[25] are to the point. For certainly, among other things, there was the now obvious *failure of historical continuity:* the under-development of historical understanding, of ourselves and the world, led to the premature acclamation that the struggles

72

at that point (i.e., the 1960s) were in fact "the revolution." We entertained, generally, a rather naive, nondialectical conception of historical change. In the face of the countermoves by the established powers, many of us were left convinced of the impossibility of revolutionary change in America. Conditioned by the "Pepsi generation" mentality of youthful America, we had wrongly expected "instant revolution."

On the other hand, there were many positives gained during this same period, not the least of them being the intensification of the consciousness of blacks in America as an African people with subsequent developments in educational, political, and social dimensions. There were, even more, some recognitions of limitations in our theoretical understanding, though to a large extent the result was a quick scramble to embrace uncritically the theoretical/ideological developments of other peoples developed in other times and places. But we imported the theories without being able to import the historical conditions within which they were developed, within which they served as the guides to praxis.

The present lull, in this country at least, in the activities of organized mass struggle provides the much needed opportunity to correct this deficiency in the theoretical understanding of American society and of historical change. A fair share of attention must be given to the development of critical understanding that is *global,* that is, that encompasses the totality of dimensions of life in their interconnection: political, economic, socio-cultural. We need, in short, a *critical* theoretical overview of the social order and of the prospects for change.

III. 1. *Critical Theory, in General*

The essay "Traditional and Critical Theory" by Max Horkheimer is a classic statement regarding the difference between critical and traditional conceptions of theory and science:

> *Theory for most researchers is the sum-total of propositions about a subject, the propositions being so linked with each other that a few are basic and the rest derive from these. The smaller the number of primary principles in comparison with the derivations, the more perfect the theory. The real validity of the theory depends on the derived propositions being consonant with the actual facts. If experience and theory contradict each other, one of the two must be re-examined. . . . In relation to facts, therefore, a theory always remains a hypothesis. . . . The general goal of all theory is a universal systematic science, not limited to any particular subject matter but embracing all possible objects.*[26]

However, this theoretical activity is effected within a divided labor force as a scientific activity, alongside all other activities of a society, but with no clear relationship to them. According to Horkheimer:

> *In this view of theory, therefore, the real social function of science is not made manifest; it speaks not of what theory means in human life,*

but only of what it means in the isolated sphere in which for historical reasons it comes into existence.[27]

Yet, for Horkheimer, even theoretical activity is but one moment of a whole, another aspect of the division of labor that has developed historically. The purpose it serves can only be determined by viewing it in relation to other activities in the social totality and to the historical development of the social whole.

Critical theory, in contrast, has as its object society *as a whole,* not some isolated, delimited realm of 'objects'. And it understands any given stage of the historical development of society to be the result of human activity acting upon nature and in response to it. Thus, a critical theory of society seeks to reconstruct, through reflective understanding, the development of historical forms of understanding, and their groundings in the social order, in order to reveal how they misrepresent actual social relations and thus justify forms of oppression that are in reality historical. In the words of Schroyer,[28] critical theorists actualize dialectical reason and, by way of their reflective critiques of the basic categories of historical consciousness and social conditions, seek to reconcile men and women to the actualities of their historical conditions and possibilities.

Again, the development of a critical theory of society is governed, according to Schroyer, among other things, by the principle of "immanent critique:"

By first expressing what a social totality holds itself to be, and then confronting it with what it is in fact becoming [and has become] a critical theory is able to restore the actuality to a false appearance . . .[29]

Critical theory thus seeks to cut through the veil of socially unnecessary domination by socially unnecessary systems of authority and control via the praxis of critical reflection, which restores missing parts of the process of the historical self-formation of men and women and of a social whole. The expectation[30] is that this reclamation of lost collective and individual past experiential dimensions will release emancipatory reflections and lead to changed social praxis, which aims at the transformation of a social order. Thus, a theory of society that is critical is grounded in a practical interest: to achieve, in the words of Thomas McCarthy,[31] the self-emancipation of men and women from the constraints of unnecessary domination in all its forms. Its task, according to Marković,[32] is to build the outlines of a *historically optimal society* proceeding from a grasp of the historical *conditions* and historical *possibilities* of a given social order.

Contemporary efforts to develop a critical theory of modern capitalistic-technological societies have been conditioned substantially by the collaborative endeavors of a group of thinkers who comprised what has come to be known as the "Frankfurt School."[33] Although successful in their struggles to integrate philosophy and materialistic social analysis by way of Hegelian dialectics, giving particular focus to the exploration of possibilities of social transformation through human praxis, still these thinkers (Horkheimer, Theodore Adorno, and Marcuse, to a lesser extent, et al.) were opposed to closed philosophical systems. Instead, the labors of critical theory were for them best expressed through a series of critiques of various situations, tendencies, and modes of thought of still changing advanced technological-bureaucratic capitalistic and socialistic social orders. The writings of Marcuse[34] are distinctive, to some extent, as efforts tending more toward a global theory. A more developed effort is to be found, however, in Marković[35] wherein he sets out the key elements of a critical social philosophy.

III. 2. *Elements of a Critical Social Philosophy, in Particular*[36]

A developed critical social theory is grounded in a complex of assumptions, hence commitments, that are critically appropriated as its orienting *interests*. These may be grouped as ontological, epistemological, and axiological assumptions.

III. 2.1 *Ontological Assumptions*

A critical social philosophy understands (assumes) that social institutions and historical processes, though they may be studied objectively as entities and processes that exhibit various structural arrangements, continuity, and immobility, are, ultimately, composed of and created by conscious persons who are *potentially* free hence are not fully predictable. Social "laws" are thus statistical expressions of certain regularities of human behavior that are characterized, potentially at least, by freedom and universality. This freedom and universality is evidenced by the ability of men and women to remove numerous limitations imposed by nature and the human past; by the ability to change the conditions under which the laws of social behavior operate; and to broaden—radically so today—the framework of possibilities from which to choose. Humans, in addition, learn from others; we can share the accomplishments of other nations and civilizations. On the other hand, we fail to learn and thus suffer the consequences: the repetition of adverse historical development.

Conscious of these conditions of human existence, a critical social philosophy avoids reducing men and women to their existence as it may be at a given moment or period, for time in human history (in contrast to natural history) is understood to have a different meaning and structure: it is, within certain cosmic, biophysical, and psychological limits, open, contingent. The future is not something that will emerge without human intervention. Given this relative openness of history, a number of futures are *possible,* others *probable.* Which prevails, is, in large measure, a function of human choice, leading either to action or inaction and/or a combination of both. And the choices made condition the perspectives from which we view things as well as other choices we make and preferences we share.

Laws regarding human behavior are thus *inherently* flexible and open, given their conditioning by the human capacity to learn, which leads to possibilities of transcending the past and projecting futures in tune with actual needs. This understanding leads to the necessary distinction between what men and women are or appear to be and what we can be: actuality and potentiality. For Marković, "A social philosophy which fails to make this distinction, which assumes that man *is what prevails in his actual existence,* is condemned to end as an ultimate ideological justification of the existing social order."[37] What men and women are, in large measure, is a function of which of our potentialities, individual or collective, have been allowed the freedom to develop. And the nature of this freedom is determined by the technological, economic, political, and cultural conditions of the social order within which we live, by the levels of development of each of these dimensions, and their interactions. Conditions of relative abundance, security, freedom, and social solidarity are those within which human capacities develop creatively and progressively and contribute to individual and social life-enhancing historical development.

Humans are capable of much: of evil as well as good; of retrogression and stagnation as well as progressive development.[38] Which capacities are fundamental to progressive development? They are, according to Marković: unlimited development of the senses; reason; imagination; communication; creative activity; the ability to harmonize interests, drives, and aspirations with those of others; the ability to discriminate, assess, and choose among alternative possibilities; and, most importantly, our ability to develop a clear, critical consciousness about ourselves. To the extent that these capacities are regarded as fundamental to progressive human development, they serve as the *foundational criteria of all critical evaluation.* They are the result of explicit value judgments based on studies of human development and a grasp of sociohistorical possibilities for further development into what we project as an ideally optimal world. In the words of Marković: *The Standpoint of All Philosophical Criticism is Man's Self-Realization in History and the Transformation of an Alien, Reified World into a Humane One.*[39]

III. 2.2 *Epistemological Assumptions of a Critical Social Philosophy*

Assumptions regarding the possibilities and conditions of knowing social, historical phenomena are, and must be, different from those that ground knowing in the natural sciences.[40] For the latter are concerned, primarily, with knowledge of objects and processes void of the openness that characterizes human existence. It is not possible to reduce human subjectivity to structures of overt behavior, granted the range of legitimacy of the behavioral approach. Nor can social knowledge be reduced to descriptions and explanations of these structures; or all valuable explanations reduced to casual and functional explanations. For a great deal of history is teleologically determined: it is a function of human praxis based on an awareness of goals and intentions to realize them. An appropriately developed critical social philosophy must thus be a

76

synthesis of descriptive-explanatory knowings that focus on "objectivities," and interpretive knowings that concentrate on the grasp of the meaningfulness of existence as experienced by human subjects. In the words of Marković:

> *The former provides analytical information about the facts and external, objective, structural characteristics of certain isolated social phenomena. The latter supplements these informations by a concrete, qualitative, historical understanding of the subjective dimensions of a social whole.*[41]

For Marković, the complex method that achieves this synthesis is "dialectic," a concept that must be understood nondogmatically, that is to say, not only as a general theory and method of acquiring positive knowledge, but also as a theory and method of revolutionary negation and transcendence of existing reality in terms of its limitations to progressive human development. To understand dialectics as a universal ontological theory which, supposedly, grasps the permanent patterns of change in the world and the fixed number of "laws" that govern them, is to make a principle of change not itself subject to change and development based on our increased understanding. It is to make the principle dogma and, when joined to political praxis, an instrument of ideology. On the other hand, dialectics, as a general philosophical method, proceed on the understanding (the ontological assumption of critical social philosophy) that social phenomena are not simply given but are the result of human action based on conscious choice (and/or lack of conscious choice) from among various possibilities.

The concept "dialectic" thus denotes a complex process that, notes Lonergan[42], combines the concrete, the dynamic, and the contradictory. In his words, a dialectic is a ". . . concrete unfolding of linked but opposed principles of change;" we have a dialectic if:

(1) there is an aggregate of events of a determined character,
(2) the events may be traced to either or both of two principles,
(3) the principles are opposed yet bound together, and
(4) they are modified by the changes that successfully result from them.

So conceived, a dialectic may be seen in a dialogue, in a history of philosophical, or other, opinions, or in historical process in general. As a method of social philosophy, however, Marković[43] points out that dialectics is unique in that it is particularly useful for discovering, on the one hand, the *essential limits* of a given social system, (i.e., those structural features that prevent the system's evolution toward a more desirable state), and, on the other hand, for identifying the concrete possibilities and means for *superseding* such limits. As such dialectics is a method of criticism—the negation of negation—of real social relationships.

77

III. 2.3 *Axiological Assumptions of Critical Social Philosophy*

Critical social philosophy presupposes, as does all thought, some value considerations. The assumptions are visible even in its ontological and epistemological assumptions. One such value judgment is revealed in the commitment to the necessity to study phenomena, not in isolation, but in their structural and historical contexts. Hence, the normative judgment: critical social philosophy must be concerned with *meaningful wholes*. However, a 'meaningful whole' is not an arbitrary collection of phenomena. It is, as Marković puts it, a "historically conceived totality which is practically relevant to some of our goals and which meets some of our important needs."[44] Relative to the whole, which is our object of concern, our prevailing values (which themselves are socio-culturally, historically grounded) constitute the criteria for evaluating the whole, its parts, the history of its development, our notions of what *should* be its future.

Again, the dialectical viewpoint sees phenomena as dynamic totalities, in themselves, and as parts of larger wholes. Moreover, this process of development, this dynamism, particularly in the social world, is understood to be open: historical development is not a fixed pattern within a closed system leading to eternal repetition. To the extent that developmental changes of a social system contribute to its greater well-being, as experienced in the lives of the peoples and institutions that comprise it, such changes are regarded as *progressive*. *Retrogressive* changes, on the other hand, are those that are counterproductive to the progressive evolution of a social totality. However, as is the case with systems in general, social systems have ideal developmental limits beyond which changes alter their identity, stability, and continuity. When a system has developed to such a point it has reached a situation of *crisis*.[45]

Such notions—the ontological, epistemological, and axiological assumptions—are key for a critical social philosophy. They are central to the historical analysis and evaluation of a social totality in terms of weighing the cumulative impact of qualitative and quantitative changes in the social system that may, singularly, seem unimportant. Even more, these evaluative, normative concepts are foundational to the process of determining the necessity, conditions, possibilities, and means for radical change in the social system, i.e., changes that alter the basic structure of the system, its organization of life, hence the system's identity. To quote Marković:

> In each historical epoch there is a general structure which is a
> crystalization of the whole past history of human praxis. This
> structure is a concrete dynamic totality which underlies all more
> specific determinants—those of class, race, nation, religion, profession,
> and individual character. It is constituted by the opposite general
> features and tendencies of human behavior and therefore is dynamic
> and open for further change. We have to move within these natural,
> social and cultural limits. But within these limits a process of self-
> determination takes place. We choose among possibilities, we create

new possibilities. As there is more than one possibility, self-determination could obviously take place in various directions. The problem, therefore, arises: which is the optimal historical possibility in the given historical conditions?[46]

For a critical social philosophy, answering this question—even its formulation—presupposes a commitment to the potentiality, actuality, and responsibility of human freedom within limits to determine a desirable existence and to work for its realization. Value commitments—axiological assumptions—are thus involved in critical social theory in two ways: first, as goals of human behavior which the history projects as transgressions of limited situations in the social totality; secondly, as grounding assumptions of the theory itself. In the latter case, recognition of this grounding constitutes a vital distinction between critical and traditional theory where the latter has, naively, ideologically, attempted to be *value free.*

The three complexes of assumptions together make for a coherent unity of principles of critical social philosophy. Together they provide what Marković terms:

A conception about man that distinguishes between his limited actual existence and a totality of man's potential capacities and true needs, a method of inquiry that is radically critical, aiming at the transcendence of given limitations both in theory and in reality, and a theory of value that has human self-realization as its ultimate criterion. . . .[47]

Such a criterion—human self-realization, personal and collective, to the highest degree possible that is consonant with the well-being of others in the social totality—remains a vital concern of people of African descent in this country. The notion of a social philosophy summarized above is thus intended as a programmatic, critical framework out of which issues regarding the historical evolution of African-Americans within the context of the evolution of American society may be addressed. Intentionally the discussion is abstract, theoretical, at this point. The focus is not on concrete issues but on theoretical understanding as a possible guide to the resolution of such issues.

Significant in this regard is a much-needed cleared understanding of social totalities in a global sense and of their limits, in structures and processes, to particular kinds of historical development. For the key to the articulation of strategies and tactics seeking social change is an understanding of the limits to be faced. Not all revolutions are successful, nor are all attempts at reform. The projection of courses of action inappropriate to particular limit situations is a particular source of setbacks and failures. Limit situations must be well understood, in their general nature at the very least.

IV
Crises: Limit Situations to Be Transcended[48]

What are the limitations within social reality that prevent human evolution to a more progressive level so that human needs and potentialities can enjoy greater satisfaction and realization? Only a concrete analysis of a social order at a given historical juncture will provide the answers. Still, the tradition of critical social thought, as the theoretical moment of the process seeking the resolution of contradictory historical (social, political, economic) situations, has evolved as a refined perspective by which to detect blockages to progressive historical development. A central concept in this aspect of critical theory is that of "crises." It refers to decisively problematic situations within the social order wherein the normal recipes for action conditioning historical evolution are inadequate for the resolution of the situation. Such situations become critical—points of *crises*—in that failure to resolve them threatens the "normal flow" of historical development.

This 'normal flow' of social evolution is conditioned, in complex, highly rationalized societies, by the basic organizational principles of the society, which, among other things, determine the standards of adequacy of procedures for action adopted by various groups and subsystems in the society. The political subsystem is the principle arena within which such action schemes are developed. Or, at the very least, within the political subsystem they receive their legitimations as principles by which the historical development of the social order is directed, to the extent that it is. Thus crises, as blockages to historical development, call for new action programs from the political dimension in order to guide social evolution through the problematic situation.

When we deal with crises in social reality, there are two levels of analysis from which the concept and reality of crises must be understood. On the one hand, we must speak of crisis from the level of the social totality as a whole. From this level a crisis emerges when the *structures* of the social system, in terms of its principles of organization, provide fewer possibilities for resolving problems than are necessary if the system is to continue to function. Here a crisis is a *disturbance of system integration.* More precisely, crises in social systems are based on structurally inherent imperatives of the system that are incompatible and cannot be integrated hierarchically. We speak of such "structurally inherent contradictions" only when we have identified structures that are important to the continued existence of a social system in contrast to others that could change or be eliminated without the system losing its identity. On the other hand, only human subjects actually *experience* a crisis; a social system is *meaningful* only in terms of the experiences of its members. Thus, only when the people of a social system experience change, or the failure to realize change, as critical for existence and thus feel their individual and social identities threatened, can we really speak of a crisis. We have a crisis when a disturbance of system integration endangers social integration. Put differently, we have a crisis when the consensus that serves as the foundation of the *normative structures* of society is disturbed.

An adequate grasp of crisis situations in the area of social reality requires that we distinguish the poles of individual/social identity/integration and system (the totality) integration. When speaking of the former we have in mind the systems of institutions (schools, social service agencies, churches, etc.) through which people are socially related. Such subsystems are symbolically structured and are the principle means through which we orient ourselves and go about our life-practices in a meaningful fashion. Reference to system integration, on the other hand, is made from a perspective that looks at the "steering performances" of a self-regulated system, that is, the ability of a social order, through its subunits responsible for making and effecting decisions, to guide or "steer" the various dimensions of life of the social unit, hence guide or steer social development. A critical analysis of a social system achieved through the dialectics of these two levels of analysis thus seeks to evaluate a social order's ability to master the complexities of an inconstant environment and its ability to maintain itself.

However, crucial questions emerge at this point: Should the system attempt to maintain itself by resolving the crises experienced by its peoples and thus itself evolve to a higher level of integration by way of a higher level of social integration? Or, should it attempt to maintain itself at a given level of development by "managing" or covering over the crises?

A critical theory of society commits itself to the line of development indicated by the first question. This struggle is assisted by the dialectic of perspectives on social integration, on the one side, which is achieved by the coming together of the ordered worlds of meaningful experiences of human subjects; and of system integration—achieved by way of the ordering of various elements and structures of social reality into an integrated whole—on the other. In terms of the former we focus on the *normative structures* (values and institutions) of a society, viewing situations from the point of view of their either contributing or failing to contribute to social integration and, reciprocally, to the sense of well-being of those affected. In terms of the latter, we focus on the ways in which a system functions to achieve integration through its steering activities. These activities we judge by comparing them, as they unfold historically, to the goal *values* of the system, i.e., the *survival imperatives* (the minimum conditions that must be met if the system is to survive) of the system, which reveal the cultural definitions of social life as expressed by its inhabitants, or by some of them. We can, then, study crisis situations in social reality from the point of view of the possible failure of the steering unit to fulfill the imperatives of goal values that establish where we should be going as a society, or as a failure of the steering unit to integrate into its goal values other goals—or a rearrangement of goals and priorities—expressing the genuine human needs of people in the social order that are not being met.

In order to make greater critical use of the concept of crisis in a discussion of social theory, the concept of social totality must be developed further. This development is made possible by the incorporation of insights from the framework of systems theory, i.e., the latter's grasp of systematic wholes.

A social totality is comprised of three basic subsystems. There is, on the other hand, the *socio-cultural* subsystem that serves the normative function of establishing the various ordering principles of social life and the forms of cultural life. It provides for the distribution of rewards and dispositions that hold socio-cultural life intact: it provides for social integration. The *political-administrative* subsystem (government, at all levels) is made up by the various political institutions and functions to distribute "legitimate" power as well as to serve as the repository and dispenser of organizational rationality. Finally, the *economic* subsystem, comprised by the various economic institutions (relations of distribution and production), distributes economic power.

According to this model, these three subsystems have the following interrelations: the political-administrative subsystem skims fiscal resources, via taxation, from the economic subsystem to provide for citizens the social-welfare services that they cannot provide for themselves individually; it also fills in gaps resulting from structurally inherent system contradictions. Citizens live in and by means of the meaning-orders of the socio-cultural subsystem; they (the citizens) provide legitimations for the political-administrative and, subsequently, the economic subsystems. The political-administrative subsystem provides guidance, hence steers, the production and distribution of goods in the economic subsystem and, to some extent, the unfolding of life in the socio-cultural subsystem. And the economic subsystem, through its production and distribution of goods in exchange for capital, serves both the political-administrative and socio-cultural subsystems.

Each of the subsystems is subject to a particular form of crisis. In the socio-cultural dimension *legitimation* and/or *motivation* crises emerge when the consensual basis of government is destroyed through a breakdown of the normative structures of socio-cultural life. A *crisis* of *rationality* emerges in the political-administrative order when the government's ability to meet the demands placed upon it to achieve a rational integration of various demands and secure system integration becomes overloaded: the demands are greater in quantity and/or substance than can be accommodated by the order of rationality of the political-administrative structure. And, finally, economic crises erupt in the economic subsystem, in the forms of recessions, depressions, inflation, deflation, combinations of these, when the organization of production and distribution is in conflict with itself and demands arising in the political-administrative and socio-cultural subsystems.

This brief sketch, joining insights from a systems' theoretical approach to social realities and crisis theory, makes for a creative evolution of critical social philosophy in a way that expands its range and critical power. This development is well in line with the guiding principle of critical social theory, namely, to be able to detect the points of blockage to social evolution in order that praxis can be directed toward their resolution. For understanding crises requires understanding the conditions that give rise to them. When this knowledge is combined with the projections of concrete possibilities for realizing higher levels of human existence, the ground is then laid for liberating, revolutionary/evolutionary praxis.

V
Critical Social Thought and African-Americans

The framework of critical social theory, joined with praxis aimed at revolutionary/evolutionary socio-historical development, provides, therefore, a context within which we people of African descent (and others) can assess our situation and achieve clarity regarding which concrete historical possibilities are in our best interest. To the extent that we do so within this context of understanding, conditioned by a commitment to generalized progressive human development, then it is clear that our interest in our own well-being cannot be limited to narrow self-interest. For example, if we come to understand the crisis tendencies, which in part condition the historical development of advanced capitalism, we will see that the resolution of these contradictions cannot be accomplished by African people alone, nor would their resolution serve us alone.

As the analysis by Habermas[49] goes, in contrast to the liberal period of the development of capitalist social orders, conditions now require the intervention of the state more and more in order to steer the system to avoid crises and to insure system integration by maintaining social integration. This intervention involves various endeavors that work to realize the prerequisites constituting and maintaining the capitalist mode of production (i.e., the system of civil law, particularly property and the freedom of contract; alleviation of the negative side effects of the market, etc.). Again, intervention also assumes the form of "market-complementing" adaptations of capital accumulation. On the other hand, "market-replacing" activities are undertaken by the state (e.g., government demand for the production of commodities as a way of creating jobs; public works programs to alleviate unemployment) as reactions to weaknesses of the structural dynamics of a capitalistic economy. Intervention is also at work in the compensatory activities of the state for consequences of dysfunction in the process of accumulation, particularly in response to the effective political reactions of those affected. We see this in state assumption of the responsibilities for ecological damage resulting from the activities of private enterprise; in various regulations aimed at protecting and improving the conditions of various workers; in "welfare" programs; support of education, housing, health care, and others.

Such a pattern of intervention, it can be argued, reveals a unique historical development in advanced capitalistic social orders: the displacement of relations of production. The state is now a major participant in the process of production and distribution. To the extent, however, that, in a liberal democracy, the state requires for its stability the legitimations of civil subjects, then the form of struggle required to transform the structures of economic and political life is different from one that would be required in a historical situation wherein race/class/sex dominations are not mediated by state interventions and thus leave unaffected the fundamental principles of social organization that gave rise to these dominations. Instead, this source gets covered over by the ideology of liberal democracy and free enterprise when, in reality, the private appropriation of socially produced surplus wealth is secured by the state. The once unpolitical race/class/sex struggles are now fully a part of the political realm.

The struggle to realize genuine human needs (i.e., racial/ethnic liberation; freedom from sex discrimination, etc.) raises demands directed at the political order, as the steering unit of the social order as a whole, given the history of liberal democracy, which can only be satisfied by more or less radical change in the organizational principles of the social totality. Our struggle for liberation as a people is but a part, a moment, of a wider struggle that embraces other peoples, groups, and classes within the social order. Even more, given the international prerequisites for the production and reproduction of economic life in this country, our struggle becomes part of a wider global effort on the part of those who would be free of the forms of domination imposed by the global effects of advanced capitalism as it seeks to secure its continued existence. Our self-centered, "nationalistic" endeavors are thus a necessary moment in the praxis of human evolution; they are not, however, sufficient. Narrow self-interest alone is thus not in our interest. Only a well developed, critical understanding of human history, global in its reach, is.

This understanding—the point of view of a critical socio-political philosophy—must be reflected then, in the political praxes of African-Americans. As a people we must be critically aware of our genuine human needs (food, clothing, shelter, social solidarity, nonrepressive happiness) and of how they can be fulfilled, given the level of cultural development of the social order, with a minimum of socially necessary domination, decided in the most democratic fashion possible, among ourselves and with others. Our projection of this "historically optimal society" must be followed by the articulation of forms of praxis intending its realization. In some cases these activities will involve only African-American people. In others, we must join forces with others who struggle for progressive changes. And our joining with them must be conditioned, first and foremost, by the shared commitment to a projected future and to the strategies and tactics for realizing it. Although the forming of coalitions with others will require compromises, they must not be compromises of fundamental principles that will result in our compromising our well-being within the wider context of progressive human development.

Such an approach to our historical development necessitates a number of things: that we understand the necessity, though *in itself* insufficiency, of narrow self-interest articulated as a "nationalism," that we be critically aware of the degrees to which our needs, as well as those of others, can be met through the 'legitimate' politics of the present order, the degrees to which the struggle to meet our needs will bring us into radical conflict with this order and with

84

those who seek to maintain it. Given present social realities, and the dominate tendencies that condition their evolution, the formation of a historically optimal future for this country is a serious and complex task that will require the labors of others. So too will the struggle to realize it. We can be for ourselves only, then, if we are for others; these others can be for themselves only if they are for us—as long as we all share the understanding of the need for and vision of a shared world of the highest levels of progressive existence that are humanly possible.

Humans do not control historical development totally. But we, especially, as a people of African descent, must be about exerting greater conscious, rational, progressive influence if we are to insure as best we can, our well-being. There is no other task for critical understanding in the interest of African peoples that is conscious of its mission.

Notes

1. Unger, R. M. *Knowledge and Politics*. New York: The Free Press, 1976, p. 28.
2. Reed (1979) for a critical review of this matter of "black particularity" relative to theoretical and practical activities of the 1960s. Reed, A. Jr. "Black Particularity Revisited." *Telos,* No. 30 (Spring 1979), pp. 71–93.
3. Barrett (1962), especially pages 4–5, for a characterization of the existence of philosophers in the modern world; and Outlaw (1976). Barrett, W. *Irrational Man.* Garden City, New York: Doubleday, 1962. Outlaw, L. "Blacks and the Struggle in Philosophy." *Radical Philosophers' News Journal,* 1976, VI, pp. 21–30.
4. Crus, H. *The Crisis of the Negro Intellectual.* New York: William Morrow, 1967.
5. Ibid., p. 364.
6. Harding, V. "The Vocation of the Black Scholar and the Struggles of the Black Community." *Harvard Educational* Review, 1974, Monograph No. 2, (3–29), p. 6.
7. Ibid., p. 8.
8. Stojanović, S. *Between Ideals and Reality: A Critique of Socialism and Its Future* (G. Sher, trans.). New York: Oxford University Press, 1973, p. 12.
9. Horkheimer, M. "The Social Function of Philosophy." In M. Horkheimer, *Critical Theory: Selected Essays* (M. O'Connell, et al., trans.). New York: Herder & Herder, 1972, p. 263.
10. Ibid., p. 270.
11. Marcuse, H., 1968, p. ix.
12. Gurwitsch, A. "Problems of the Life-World." In M. Natanson (ed.), *Phenomenology and Social Reality*. The Hague: Martinus Nijhoff, 1977, p. 53–54.
13. Palmer, R. *Hermeneutics: Interpretation Theory in Schleiermacher, Dilthey, Heidegger, and Gadamer.* Evanston, Ill.: Northwestern University Press, 1969.
14. Palmer, R. "Phenomenology and Literary Interpretation." *Cultural Hermeneutics,* 1973, 1, pp. 207–223.
15. Habermas, J. *Knowledge and Human Interests* (J. Shapiro, trans.). Boston: Beacon Press, 1971.
16. Radnitzsky, G. *Contemporary Schools of Metascience*. Chicago, Ill.: Regnery, 1973, p. 214.
17. Op. cit., Radnitzsky (1973, Chpt. IVF 4, pp. 233ff) and Ricoeur (1970) for discussions of psychoanalysis as an effort in hermeneutics. Ricoeur, P. *Freud and Philosophy: An Essay on Interpretation* (D. Savage, trans.). New Haven, Conn.: Yale University Press, 1970.
18. Fanon, F. *Black Skin, White Masks* (C. van Markmann, Trans.) New York: Grove Press, 1967.

19. Ibid., p. 18.
20. Outlaw, L. "Language and Consciousness: Toward a Hermeneutic of Black Culture." *Cultural Hermeneutics,* 1974, 1, pp. 403–413.
21. Turner, J. "The Sociology of Black Nationalism." *The Black Scholar,* 1969, I, pp. 18–27.
22. Gerald (1971) for a discussion of a reversal of symbolism as one of the responsibilities of the black writer. Gerald, C. "The Black Writer and His Role," In A. Gayle, Jr. (ed.), *The Black Aesthetic.* Garden City, New York: Doubleday, 1971, pp. 370–378.
23. Habermas, J. "On Systematically Distorted Communication." *Inquiry,* 1970, pp. 205–218.
24. See Allen (1976); Boggs (1970); Brisbane (1970, 1974); Cruse (1967); Meier (1963); Pinkney (1976) and Sochen (1972) for critical discussions of various thought-praxis complexes which have guided black struggles. Allen, R. "Racism and the Black Nation Thesis." *Socialist Revolution,* 1976, 8, pp. 145–150. Boggs, J. *Racism and the Class Struggle.* New York: Monthly Review, 1970. Brisbane, R. *The Black Vanguard.* Valley Forge, Pennsylvania: Judson Press, 1970. Brisbane, R. *Black Activism.* Valley Forge, Pennsylvania: Judson Press, 1974. Cruse, H. *Rebellion or Revolution?* New York: William Morrow, Apollo Edition, 1969. Meier, A. *Negro Thought in America:* 1880–1915. Ann Arbor, Michigan: University of Michigan Press, 1966. Pinkney, A. *Red, Black, and Green: Black Nationalism in the United States.* New York: Cambridge University Press, 1976. Sochen, J. *The Unbridgeable Gap: Blacks and Their Quest for the American Dream, 1900–1930.* Chicago, Ill.: Rand McNally, 1972.
25. Op. cit., Cruse, H., *Crisis of the Negro Intellectual.*
26. Op. cit., Horkheimer (1972), pp. 188–189.
27. Ibid., p. 197.
28. Schroyer, T. "Forward." In T. Adorno, *The Jargon of Authenticity* (K. Tarnowski & F. Will, trans.). Evanston, Ill.: Northwestern University Press, 1973, pp. viii–ix.
29. Schroyer, T. *The Critique of Domination: The Origins and Development of Critical Theory.* Boston: Beacon Press, 1975, pp. 30–31.
30. Ibid., p. 31.
31. McCarthy, T. "Translator's Introduction" In J. Habermas, *Legitimation Crisis.* Boston: Beacon Press, 1975.
32. Marković, M. *From Affluence to Praxis: Philosophy and Social Criticism.* Ann Arbor: University of Michigan Press, 1974.
33. For historical and critical discussions of the Frankfurt School, see Jay, M. *The Dialectical Imagination: A History of the Frankfurt School and the Institute of Social Research,* 1923–1950. Boston: Little Brown, 1973. O'Neill, J. (ed.). *On Critical Theory.* New York: Seabury, 1976. Slater, P. *Origin and Significance of the Frankfurt School: A Marxist Perspective.* Boston: Routledge & Kegan Paul, 1977. Tar, Z. *The Frankfurt School: The Critical Theories of Max Horkheimer and Theodore Adorno.* New York: John Wiley & Sons, 1977. Wellmer, A. *Critical Theory of Society* (J. Cumming, trans.). New York: Herder & Herder, 1971.
34. Marcuse, H. "A Note on Dialect." In H. Marcuse, *Reason and Revolution; Hegel and the Rise of Social Theory.* Boston: Beacon Press, 1960, pp. vii–xiv. Marcuse, H. *One-Dimensional Man.* Boston: Beacon Press, 1966.
35. Op. cit., Markovic, M., *From Affluence to Praxis.*
36. This section is a summary of Marković (1974, pp. 1–45). I am especially indebted to Professor Marković for amplifications of his views which he shared with me during an interview/discussion in his office on 28 May, 1976, at the Woodrow Wilson Center for International Scholars, Smithsonian Institute Building, Washington, D.C.
37. Ibid., p. 12, emphasis in original.

38. For a critical analysis of historical development in terms of rationality and irrationality, see Lonerman, B. *Insight: A Study of Human Understanding.* New York: Philosophical Library, 1967.
39. Op. cit., Markovic, M., *From Affluence to Praxis,* p. 16, emphasis in original.
40. For a critical discussion of this difference, its ground and implications, see op. cit., Habermas (1971) and Radnitzsky (1973).
41. Op. cit., Marković, M., *From Affluence to Praxis,* p. 20.
42. Op. cit., Lonerman, B., Insight: *A Study of Human Understanding,* p. 217.
43. Op. cit., Marković, M., *From Affluence to Praxis,* p. 24.
44. Ibid., p. 38.
45. The matter of a *crisis* in socio-historical life is discussed below, Part IV.
46. Op. cit., Markovic, M., *From Affluence to Praxis,* p. 35.
47. Ibid., p. 47.
48. This section is based on the discussions of Habermas (1975). I am indebted to Professor Habermas for an elaboration of his views and, in particular, for his critical reactions to my notion of a critical theory in the interest of African-Americans, during conversations we shared in Philadelphia, Pennsylvania in the fall of 1976.
49. Habermas, J. *Legitimation Crisis* (T. McCarthy, trans.). Boston: Beacon Press, 1975.

Note on the Author

Lucius T. Outlaw, Jr., is well known for his work in hermeneutics and critical theory. He is Associate Professor of Philosophy, Haverford College, having previously taught at Morgan State University and Fisk University. His professional activities include Managing Editor, *Praxis International,* and Consulting Editor, *Philosophy and Social Criticism.* His published works include "Black Folks and the Struggle in 'Philosophy'," *Radical Philosophers Newsjournal,* April, 1976.

V

William Thomas Fontaine
1909–1968
c. 1962

II
Experience Explained

A. Explanatory Theory

"Social Determination" in the Writings of Negro Scholars [1944]

William T. Fontaine

Abstract

Absolute truth is, at best, a regulative ideal, a goal infinitely remote that man would approach with ever increasing hope. All knowledge is conditioned by incompleteness of development and by perspectives which the plastic human organism acquires in interaction with environment. Negro scholars propound a knowledge reflecting resentment of the caste-like status forced upon their group. Bias is not deliberate, but there exists an unconscious attitude of immediate group defense. This narrows the scholar's angle of vision. His knowledge is affected in "form" and in "content." Analytical categories are preferred to morphological, environment to heredity. Exceptions have logical priority over quantitative majorities. Range of validity is narrowed, since the mentality of the opponent is not understood through sympathetic interchange of attitudes.

During the 1930's scholarly literature came to the forefront as a form of expression of the Negro of the United States. The place once momopolized by poets and novelists such as Claude McKay, Countee Cullen, Langston Hughes, and Walter White must now be shared with the men of the schools. Sociologists, anthropologists, educators and psychologists, historians, editors of scholarly journals, and scientists of the past decade have produced a literature which, for quality as well as bulk, is unmatched in the intellectual history of the Negro.

Factors accounting for this emergence of the Negro scholar include (1) the great increase in the number of Negro college graduates, a fact fully appreciated only when it is realized that Negroes earned college degrees in greater numbers during the eleven-year span 1926–36 than for the entire hundred-year period from 1826 to 1926;[1] (2) the doctoral and post-doctoral study by Negroes in the universities of Europe and America; and (3) the establishment of the Negro as a fruitful subject of research by recognized scholars. It is interesting also to note with Charles Beard that during the "Midpassage" the American people generally turned to "brain-trusters," the debacle caused by the depression obliging pragmatic Americans to intrust recovery to speculations of "the man of knowledge."

The Negro scholar has arrived. But what of his knowledge? Does he seek truth disinterestedly or does he have an ax to grind? Is there any correlation between his knowledge and the position occupied by the Negro in the Americn social order? Is his knowledge "socially determined"?[2] Is it possible that sociopsychological factors such as resentment, aggression, rage, and the desire for equality make the mental set of the Negro scholar one of immediate group defense?

This paper proposes to answer the foregoing questions by analysis of the more outstanding works in fields of greatest interest: sociology, anthropology, educational psychology, history and historiography, and biology.[3] Attempt will be made to show a relation of functional dependence between the social situation confronting the Negro group and much of the knowledge cultivated by its scholars. It is contended that such a relation is revealed in (a) categorical apparatus, that is, the scholar frequently employs *analysis*, since in this way he can break up such morphological conceptions as a "race" "race soul," "Negro," and "white" and recombine the resulting data in a manner precluding racial distinctions and inequality; (b) the selection of certain data as logically prior, as, for example, the citation of the abilities of the few "exceptional" Negroes as of greater significance for the problem of racial equality than the evidence presented by the shortcomings of the many; (c) the selection of theories obviously supporting group interests, viz., environment in preference to heredity; and (d) the narrow scope of observation and the consequent effect upon range of validity.

The mind of the Negro scholar is fundamentally the same as any other. It is a historical phenomenon, existent in and subject to the influences of its epoch. It both conditions and is conditioned by its social position. As a Negro, the scholar has faced discrimination against his race, and his experiences consciously and unconsciously have engendered psychoses centering around fear, rage, repression, aggression, security, status, and equality. As undergraduate and graduate student, he learns that certain kinds of knowledge lend support to race discrimination. Before attempting to place himself in the position and attitude of those who subscribe to this knowledge, he brands it as inimical to the interests of himself and his group, and he launches forthwith into its refutation. The scholar thus becomes "defensive" before he has understood that his attitude is but one of several from which knowledge relevant to the problem might be propagated. If he would assume the attitude of his opponent and view the question from that side, both his and the opponent's conclusion would appear in broader perspective. The fact that the majority of scholars have been trained in a psychological tradition that casts mind in the role of supratemporal judge pronouncing universal truth with every utterance prompts them all the more to confer absolute truth upon their immediate "defensive" knowledge. When it is considered, too, that the vast majority of Negro scholars are forced to seek employment in the South, the sociopsychological significance of the above facts becomes even greater. Upon the soil of ancestral slave generations, some of whom are still alive, they face a social situation of inferior status, of economic, political, and civil discrimination, of sexual repression, of insult to self and Negro womanhood, and, above all, of the threat of mob murder without recourse. In the South and, with some reservation, in the North the Negro is considered an out-group, a counterrace. The knowledge of the Negro scholar, in the larger number of cases, is a counterknowledge propagated from an immediate "defense" perspective; it is a particularized knowledge reflecting the angle of vision from which it has been generated. Nevertheless, it is not unique in this respect. All knowledge contains a measure of perspective. Every generation is limited, first, by the necessarily incomplete development of knowledge up to that time; second, by the plastic nature of mind itself; and, third, by the inseparable connection of feelings, emotions, moods, interests, and beliefs with the so-called purely logical processes of thought. In the activity of knowing, no *pure* reason or transcendental self remains poised in passionless objectivity while recording an external world in itself. Such a view fails to take into account the interactional theory of personality. It fails to consider, too, the perseveration of unexpressed wishes and the causative significance of these unconscious forces in the activity of thought. Moreover, in those sciences dealing with the action of human beings, neutrality and disinterested curiosity are for the investigator a psychological impossibility. Says Lynn in *Knowledge for What*:

> "Pure scientific curiosity" is a term to which students of semantics
> should turn their attention. There is "idle" curiosity and "focused"
> curiosity but in the world of science no such thing as "pure curiosity"
> [pp. 182–83].

The analysis set forth here is, therefore, for purposes of revelation, not ridicule. Negro scholars have wrought well. The question is not whether it is right or wrong for them to plead the cause of their group but to what extent there is a correlation between the group wish for equality and the knowledge produced by its scholars. It may be contended that the scholars occupy different social positions. Within the Negro community this is unquestionably true, but the range of variation within the nation at large is slight. Before the bar of American public opinion a Negro is a Negro. Regardless of complexion, education, wealth, achievement, refinement, whether he is northern or southern, urban or rural, his social position is restricted to a caste-like condition. It may be contended that Negro scholars react differently to this caste-like status imposed upon themselves and their brethren, that there may be some who, instead of propounding knowledge consistent with group interests, consider themselves above the herd and proclaim the justice of the Negro's plight. No outstanding scholar holding such a view appeared in the 1930's. If, on the contrary, variation in reaction be cited on the ground that some reveal less emotion and consequently a broader perspective than others in their writings, then this is indeed true. As the discussion proceeds, certain authors will be singled out to show how the influence of existential factors upon their writings has been more or less peripheral, while for others significant penetration into both "form" and "content" will be uncovered.

Social Determination and Categorical Apparatus

After investigating the programs and apologetics of divers social groups, Karl Mannheim concluded that there was a correspondence between the social position of a group and the method employed in its supporting body of knowledge.[4] The thought style of the conservative Rightists made use of such categories as race, race soul, and race morality. Its categories were most frequently "morphological," seeking rather to preserve the data of experience in all its uniqueness rather than to break them up so as to render the possibility of contrary interpretation. On the contrary, the thought style of the parties of the Left was most frequently analytical. These parties sought by a counter-thought to break down the morphological classifications into units so as to recombine the units in a manner affording intellectual support for its social goals.

The analytical attack of Negro scholars is directed against such morphological concepts as race, race morality, race ability, and superior races and the concept of "genes" as immutable sources of characteristics distinguishing racial types. While numerous examples of morphological thought occur in the writing of Negrophobes such as Madison Grant and Stoddard, it is in Spengler that the classic example is found; for example, Spengler's conception of "a morphology of world history" in terms of race souls: Apollonian, Magian, Faustian. It is this habit of the morphological thought style to lump the entire Negro group into an "undifferentiated mass" that riles Frazier in his *The Negro Family in Chicago*. Therefore, just as Mannheim's hypothesis would lead one to expect, Frazier's thought *breaks up* this "undifferentiated mass" into seven zones; the morality of those in each zone is then related by means of the category of causality or functional integration to environment rather than to the morphological category, race. So likewise the anthropologist, Allison Davis, in his article on "Race and Blood Groups" *breaks up* the classifications of peoples in terms of morphological characteristics by showing the inconsistency of these characteristics, first, with the data of the isoagglutination blood group reactions and, second, within themselves. He analyzes the several methods employed throughout the history of taxonomy and shows how they fail to account for all members of the hypothetical type. He analyzes and uncovers the variegated character of so-called "distinct races" and shows how the possible appearance even of a future pure race is now precluded by the principle of genetic segregation. This breaking-up of the morphological category of race is followed by recombining the data in such a way as to bring out the functional relation of different types to such environmental factors as ocean barriers, mountain ranges, and social prohibitions. Similarly, the psychologists, Bond and Jenkins, analyze the test scores of the Negro group and the white so as to break each up into intragroup data; the rank of each individual is then functionally related to factors in his social environment. The historiographers, Wesley and Reddick, analyze history as conceived under the form of Nordocentrism;[5] the data of world history are then recombined so as to include the facts and role of the Negro. Cobb, the physical anthropologist, contends that morphological differences in peoples do not constitute functional disadvantages. Differences are explained by relating them to the different environments in the original habitats of the people. The physician, Lewis, breaks down the concept "Negro" into intragroup units.[6] He then shows the variation in the incidence of tuberculosis and other diseases upon each unit. Lewis is a very cautious scholar and never hesitates to present both sides of the question, but that the variant reactions of different Negroes are functionally related to socioeconomic factors is unmistakably the author's conclusion. The biologist, Just, *analyzes* "genetic continuity" and the socalled "individuality" of the gene in the light of cell division. His conclusion is that each division proportionally destroys "individuality" and continuity. The determinative forces of heredity are then located in the ectoplasm, the outermost layer of the cell surface, a habitat closest to environment and the influence of forces in the external world.

"Social Determination" and Logical Priority of the "Exception"

Those who contend that the Negro is immoral, criminal, or intellectually inferior usually support their claims with abundant statistics. What is true of the majority they ascribe to the group as a whole; their actions are functions of the biological type, of "natural impulses." While this manner of thinking stresses the failings of the rank and file of Negroes, the counterthought of the Negro scholar emphasizes the accomplishments of exceptional Negroes. In the one case, these latter are relegated to incidental value or explained where possible in terms of admixture of "white blood"; in the other, they are the actualized potentialities of each member of the group. Again, on the one hand, the majority of Negroes are socially disorganized and are said merely to be living out their brutish nature; on the other, the Negro scholar declares these same Negroes to be hampered by great environmental disadvantages, despite which considerable numbers achieve the fuller life. Each looks at the data from his own position and selects from them the type affording an explanation consistent with his interests.

Bond and Jenkins bear out the above conclusions in their stress upon the achievements of the few exceptional Negroes making high scores on the intelligence tests. Lewis, in refuting the contentions of Casper and Pinner that there exists a genotypic difference between the high resistance of the whites to tuberculosis and the low resistance of Negroes, cites as evidence the presence of fibrotic reactions which, though exceptional, are yet found in Negroes. However, it is in Frazier that the emphasis upon the exceptional Negro is most pronounced. Frazier says definitely that he seeks to ascertain the causes and conditions enabling a small element of Negroes of Chicago to make favorable adjustments to urban civilization.[7] When he has uncovered such factors as occupational level, length of residence in Chicago, free or slave ancestry, he then interprets the relative progress or disorganization of the entire seven zones of the Negro community in terms of these alterable environmental factors. Thus all the data of every zone are seen as in a flux tending toward the higher zones. Favorable or unfavorable environment speeds or retards the process. The Negro scholar does not look upon the exceptional Negro as a sporadic incident; he is rather a sort of terminus toward which all Negroes are moving, some more retarded than others by environmental handicaps.

Social Determination and Theories Selected

Without exception, Negro scholars prefer "environment" to "heredity" to explain such phenomena as racial types, comparative incidence of diseases, differences in levels of social organizations, personality, and intelligence. The relation of environment to "defense" of race is made obvious by the fact that it enables ascription of the shortcomings of Negroes to external handicaps, and it counterattacks the arguments of those who point to innate incapacity.

Biologists and scientists of closely related fields take the lead in this matter. Cobb contends that Mendelian principles fail to give adequate explanation of the American Negro as a phenomenon of hereditary processes. He is interested in refuting the contentions of Hrdlička, Steggerda, and Davenport that Negro-white crossings are undesirable, since the products are disharmonic combinations. These latter contend that in accordance with Mendel the traits of whites tend to be inherited as a whole and the race traits of the Negro likewise. The specificities of one group do not fit in with those of the other so as to produce desirable types. Thus the offspring suffer such physical handicaps as short arms and long trunk and legs; or the brown crosses are frequently "wuzzleheaded." Obviously, such a principle supports laws forbidding intermarriage as well as social segregation of the opposite sexes of the two races. It also carries implications of inequality. Cobb answers by challenging the validity of the Mendelian theory. His attack, however, is confined to citation of contrary theories—the argument of Castle that Mendelism does not account for the inheritance of "the more general and fundamental characters."[8] Cobb's opposition to Mendelism is, in truth, twofold: (1) the observation that the measurements of Davenport and Steggerda refute rather than validate the principle, since there is not a high variability among Jamaica browns in those traits which are marked differentials between whites and blacks, and (2) the citation of authorities opposing a strict, Mendelian interpretation of the physical traits of the American Negro.[9]

94

Consciously or unconsciously, the Negro biologist just completes this "defensive" attack upon the Mendelian theory of inheritance. The contempt of Just for race prejudice has been attested to by those who knew him best.[10] It is not meant that he deliberately sought to destroy Mendelism because of a desire to defend the Negro. Deliberation itself never brings into the focus of attention all the forces sustaining it. Deeper-rooted experiences arising out of collective living and funded in the organism, though unconscious, are powerful determiners of thought. As for practical interests influencing the truths of the scientist, witness the statement of the biologist, Dr. Francis Sumner, who cites his confreres as having "too much sense to believe in a disinterested love of some abstraction called Truth or Science."[11]

Just attacks Mendelism at its basis. It is for him a problem of cytology. He asks: "Is heredity explicable by unit characters, genes, archtypal units, self-sustaining and passed down in holistic, immutable state from generation to generation?"

In the place of Mendelian explanations of heredity, Just proposes a theory of "genetic restriction." The determinative factors of heredity are located not within the sequestered nucleus but in the outer cell surface. Cytoplasm and, specifically, the ectoplasm take precedence over the inner chromosomes and genes. To support this theory, Just advances the following evidence: (1) the nucleus of the cell (in which reside the gene and chromosomes) may be removed from the egg at the onset of the fertilizable condition and embryos produced from the cytoplasm alone; (2) the so-called "genetic continuity" and "individuality" of the gene and chromosome are not consistent with the facts of cell division; (3) experiment reveals the function of genes to be to "act only through binding of potencies in such wise as to free the cytoplasm-located factors of heredity; and (4) such phenomena as polyembryony, merogony, haploid parthenogenesis, experimental and natural polyploidy, asexual reproduction by budding and fragmentation, regeneration of lost parts, and sex and hermaphroditism are better explained by "genetic restriction." His attitude toward the gene theory is best expressed in the following statement: "Untutored savage man made his god as big as possible because his god could do everything. It remained for the geneticist to make one of molecular size, the gene."

The Weltanschauung of Just is environmentalistic. Time, the rate and rhythm of change, contains the very secret of life. Life arose originally as an emergent from the nonliving environment. Mind, too, knows its environment because it sprang from that source.[12]

Lewis, who is always meticulous in giving due weight to both sides of a question, has a decided preference for environment. In the first place, he defines hereditary factors in such a way as to reveal their natural and environmental origin.[13] Differences between races that are inheritable are biological, anatomical, physiological, and chemical; all these are probably the result of adaptation to environment. Second, he includes under the category "environmental" not only "living conditions" but also "the habits and effects reflecting the mentality of races." Notation of the significance of environment for the mentality of races in subsumption under that category of one of the crucial factors employed by those who argue for the hereditary character of racial abilities and disabilities. Third, Lewis observes that the immunity of certain races to certain diseases is "an acquired racial immunity." The implication is that in time other races will build a similar immunity. At the basis of these thoughts lies a Weltanschauung similar to that of Just: Reality is time, change, the mobile interplay of environment-produced organism with its environment in an increasingly favorable adaptation. Lastly, Lewis announces as his purpose not only to point out differences but to *explain* them. The implication is that existing explanations based upon racial types are inadequate and that explanations are needed that will enable eventual eradication of the disease and *ipso facto* of the supposed racial differences. Finally, the significance of environment for the question of differences in the reactions of races to diseases is revealed in the statement that "one must determine first of all in each case if the disease behavior cannot be accounted for by the kind of houses people live in or the kind of work they do or the food they eat."[14]

As with the biologist, so with the sociologist, anthropologist, educational psychologist, and historian, environmentalism holds sway. Frazier accounts for the social disorganization of the Negro community by pointing to such determining factors as the economic struggle, recency of migration to Chicago, difference in the social controls of the Deep South and those of the new urban environment, and disparity in the cultural heritage of various groups of Negroes. In his later work, *The Negro Family in the United States*, the division of contemporary Negro society into a "brown middle class" and a "black proletariat" is based upon class rather than upon race. It is not approximation to the white type that has placed the browns in the middle class and the blacks in the lowest class. Both classes have emerged as a result of historical and socioeconomic factors. The ideals of the brown middle class are not "Negro" ideals; they reflect the diverse background of the components and much borrowing from the white leisure class as well. The ideals of the white leisure class are largely a function of the economic substructure. The outlook of the black proletariat is beginning to approximate that of white industrial workers; the fundamental basis of the latter is economic. Ultimate reality is concrete and empirical rather than a mysterious biological essence. In his *Negro Youth at the Crossways*, Frazier, so to speak, takes the bull by the horns. He devotes an entire section of the Appendix to the question of heredity versus environment. His counterattack is directed against McDougall's "unwarranted assumption that the Negro has a strong instinct of submission."[15] He replies that physique, temperament, and intelligence are modified and influenced by social interaction. The original nature of the individual does not enter into the organization of his personality as a fixed quantity determining his responses to the culture. Motives, wishes, attitudes, and traits are emotions and impulses which "have been organized and directed toward goals in the course of social interaction."

Johnson's *Growing Up in the Black Belt* is also environmentalistic in perspective. In speaking of the personalities of Negroes of the Deep South, the author says:

> The racial position of Negroes in the South is a part of the institutional organization of the South and reflects a long history of racial conflicts and accommodations. The attitudes and the behavior prompted by them may be said, in turn, to be a reflection of general economic and cultural factors.[16]

The fears, wishes, and emotional tensions centering about survival, security, and status are environmentally, not biologically, determined. Johnson relates personality to the will not only "to survive" but to "achieve a career." The achieving of a career definitely attaches the plastic tendencies of original nature to the conditioning influences of social goals.

The educational psychologists, Bond and Jenkins, emphasize environmental handicaps as determining factors in the low test scores of southern Negroes and southern whites. The anthropologist, Davis, cites from Hogben a passage supporting his contention that human conduct is to a considerable degree a function of environmental factors.[17] Davis also gives prominence to geography as a factor significant for the development of physical differences among human beings. Cobb points out a functional connection between certain differential characteristics of Negroes and development of the group in a previous habitat.

With some reservations the story is the same with the historians. Woodson clings to the idea of an immutable "African background"[18] or folk soul; but, when it is of advantage to his counterknowledge (and this is frequent), he appeals to environment as an explanation of the shortcomings of Negroes.[19] Du Bois' *Black Reconstruction* envisioned in the Marxist dialectic a principle whereby the racial interpretation of the events of that era might be supplanted by one that did less violence to the capabilities of Negroes. Negroes were not naturally timid; they fled to the Union armies; they initiated a general strike. The excesses of the Reconstruction were not confined to Negroes or to the South; they were nationwide, world wide. They were a part of the Gilded Age, the noontide of capitalism and imperialism. The Negro was a pawn in the game of exploitation, not a people doomed innately to timidity, ignorance, and shiftlessness. Wesley's monograph on *The Reconstruction of History* contains much that is indicative of an environmentalist perspective. The contention that history should not be "narrow," "tribal," or "nationalist" but a "concept for which world history is as important as the history of a nation or a group" obviously opposes the "race-soul" point of view. Wesley desires a history that is "the study of the past as it is," history-as-actuality, concrete, empirical phenomena, not the recasting of these pheonomena in the form of some fantastic racial or national prototype. Wesley says it is in keeping with fact to demand that history be reconstructed "so that Negroes shall be known on a higher level than jokes and minstrels," for from the earliest periods of American history Negroes have been associated with all forward trends. The argument counterattacks the conception of the Negro as innately humorous by appealing to external fact. He further contends that Negroes should be looked upon as Americans rather than as Negroes, an idea that supplants biological classification with cultural. In his *Collapse of the Confederacy* Wesley cites, among others, the importance of the decline of morale as a factor contributing toward the defeat of the South. It must not be supposed that an innate desuetude of spirit determined this decline. Rather was it the deterrent effect of the oligarchic slave system itself. Hinton Helper and many of the apologists of the poor whites had nothing to fight for. Reddick's article, "A New Interpretation for Negro History," contends that economics should be the basic frame of reference for construction of the history of the Negro in the United States. Thus the movement toward emancipation during the Revolution ought to be attributed to the decline of demand over against the supply of the colonial staples in a world market; the North-South conflict of opposed economic systems; the political parties to the economic interests represented by them, and the Negro as a pawn for consolidating Civil War gains; the post-Civil War history of the Negro to a "rather blatantly aggressive industrialism conditioned by the interplay of population movements, the resistances of public opinion and the unchannelized labor protests, plus the rise in southern life and politics of the yeoman white leadership with its appeals to tradition and sympathy."[20] The major contribution of Reddick is his criticism of the Negro historian and the uncovering of biases emanating from theology and the ideology of liberalism. Similarly some few Negro scholars—Abram Harris,[21] the economist; Ralph Bunche,[22] the political scientist; and Frazier, the sociologist[23]— have adopted the perspective that views the race problem as a class problem. Thus they tend to rise above the narrow "defense" perspective and, from the broader view afforded by the transracial position, are able to see the angle of vision accruing to much race scholarship. The term "class," however, is conceived environmentally and not biologically.

Range of Validity

It is perhaps clear by now that there is a correlation between the practical interest in group status and the knowledge propounded by Negro scholars. Analysis is used frequently because it breaks up such morphological conceptions as "race" and enables reclassification of data in terms of meanings more favorable to the Negro. This intellectual phenomenon has its parallel in social action which aims to break up the status quo. Logical priority is conferred upon "exceptions" rather than the quantitative majority, for the exceptional Negro is living evidence of the ability of the Negro to take his place in Western civilization. He is an example of what all Negroes might become. Environmentalism is preferable to geneticism, since the former ascribes the shortcomings of Negroes to a nonracial factor and, simultaneously, implies demand for social reforms. It remains to discuss the epistemological significance of this correlation and its bearing upon the validity and truth of the knowledge.

As related above, social forces habituate the scholar to an immediate, "defense" reaction. Since this is his mental set, he fails to assume ideationally the attitude and mentality of the opposite group.[24] Thus he does not see the problem as the others see it, and their perspective is excluded from his purview. His "defense complex" frustrates his very aim (a firmer, more inclusive truth than that of his opponent), for the comprehensiveness of experience and the range of validity of knowledge are directly related to breadth of perspective. If one knows a problem from only one angle of vision when there are many, one's knowledge is obviously limited. The epistemological consequences of this for the knowledge of Negro scholars are: (1) absence of the awareness and, consequently, of the analysis of certain aspects of the problems that arise when experience is extended to comprehend the mentality of the opposite group; (2) an instantaneous and aggressive "drive" to reject the opponent's knowledge even before considering its implications as support for the position of his own group; (3) failure to evaluate his conclusions critically and systematically from the perspective of the opponent, a condition that renders him blind to the implications his own knowledge may have as support for the position of the opponent; and (4) preclusion from experience of a great vista of relevant data which, if not obtained by conscious, systematic role-taking, may come into experience only through laborious, random thinking. The discussion immediately following illustrates this "particularity."

Cobb's *Physical Constitution of the American Negro* is a good example of a counter-knowledge which, because it is ideationally bound to its own role of group defense, fails to turn the knowledge of the opponent to its own advantage. It also shuts out of its experience the wide variety of data likewise accruing to the broader perspective.

A major interest of Dr. Cobb is to show that race-crossing is not dysgenic. In reply to the contention of the Jamaica study that crosses between whites and blacks are frequently "wuzzleheaded" or disharmonious combinations, he responds, inconsequentially, that insufficient examples are given. He adds also that individuals with long arms and short legs suffer no functional disadvantage. Such thinking may be styled "fortuitous refutation"; it is catch-as-catch-can, void of a definite locus from which it may generate and anticipate systematically arranged objections to its own knowledge. Hence it seizes now upon this thought, now upon that, and very often misses the thought most vital to its argument. Had Cobb assumed ideationally the attitude of the scholars of the Jamaica group looking upon their own knowledge as well as at his criticism, instead of the particularized attitude of defense by direct refutation, his thought would have been broader and of greater effect than a mere tit for tat.

99

Since Cobb's article is dominated by environmentalism as opposed to genetic determination, it is not surprising that consideration of the possibility of genetic factors as determining the "wuzzleheadedness" of the brown does not enter his experience. Inclusion of that factor would have admitted of an explanation in terms of both heredity and environment and still along lines favorable to his social position. In a society in which race-crossing is frowned upon, sexual relations between the groups, for the most part, do not take place under eugenic conditions. The participants are frequently the sexually abnormal, the venereally diseased, and in many instances blood relatives (e.g., mating of the sons of planters with their half-sisters by plantation concubines). This opens up the significant question of correlating the subnormal intelligence of black-white crosses with intelligence, health, and blood relationship of the parental stocks. It is to the merit of the biologist Lewis that, in discussing the comparative reactions of Negroes and whites to diseases, he enters sympathetically into the evidence presented from both sides. He cites evidence that favors the Negro and that against. Where scientific basis is lacking, he merely states facts and suspends judgment.

Ideational assumption of the attitude of the opposite group would have brought within the experience of the educational psychologist such considerations as the following: Does not overstressing of environment as determinative of human conduct unduly minimize the creative power of mankind in general and of the Negro in particular? Granted that the low scores of Negroes are indicative of poor support and prejudice on the part of the whites, do they not also indicate the inability of the Negro to master adverse conditions? In fact, many examples show that the immediate environment of the Negro is more directly his creation than that of the white man. It is conceivable that other races under identical or even more severe conditions might attain a greater degree of internal organization and improvement than the Negro. Preoccupation with the mentality of his own, as it opposes the genetic explanations of the other, group delimits the data and range of possible explanations.

The historiographer who would reconstruct history so as to change the stereotyped opinion the world has of the Negro might pause to consider whether the mentality of the opposite group might not consider his task presumptuous. Stolberg's article on "Minority Jingo" suggested this very thing.[25] Undeniably, the achievements of Negroes have not been given their place in world history; but to set up the social demands of a race (though ever so noble) as axioms according to which history is to be interpreted (Wesley) is to predetermine the historian to selection of certain events and suppression or distortion of others. Preoccupation with a racially pointed "reconstruction of history" blinds the historian to the fact that his extravagant praise of the trivial makes his knowledge as well as his group the easy target of the "debunker." Interchange of his immediate, defense attitude with that of the opposite mentality would afford acquaintance with and anticipation of the reply of the "debunker," with consequent repudiation of the knowledge that would make his a target, or inclusion of it with adequate protection. The historian would do better to "paint his gray in gray" rather than in a false gold easily tarnished by the heat of satire.

In the work of Frazier, absence of thorough explanation of the numerous mulatoes in the more advanced "zones" as well as their prominence as leaders in the lesser "zones" leaves openings for objections by the Nordicist. Is it possible that *analysis* has consciously or unconsciously halted here? Is it possible that analysis is functionally dependent upon group interest to the extent that it is a noetic instrument breaking up the data only to the point at which they may be conveniently recombined in a manner consistent with social objectives? The major argument of Dr. Frazier's book is that the social organization or disorganization of the Negro group is not determined by genetic or racial factors. The obvious question posed by the opposite social group to Dr. Frazier would be: Granted that there are varying "zones" of social disorganization within the Negro community, is it not true that those individuals most closely approximating the Nordic type are culturally superior? Is this not a correlation between racial characteristics and degree of social organization? Dr. Frazier states that in some cases the mulatto is vocationally preferable and that this gives him an advantage. But he also says that the inhabitants of the higher "zones" are more ambitious and energetic, just as are certain individuals in any community. The question hinges, then, upon relation of environment to ambition, industry, etc., a problem scarcely touched upon.

If it be assumed that group welfare has consciously or unconsciously motivated the biological hypotheses of Dr. Just (and the Nordophile would so assume, witness Spengler's distinction between Faustian and Magian nature knowledge), then his minimizing of the strictly genetic factors of heredity might provoke the following question: Granted that the gene may lose individuality with each cell division, still the portion remaining may have the power of approximate regeneration—a phenomenon as feasible as regeneration of lost parts by the total organism. Cell division need not destroy the "individuality" or "genetic continuity" of genes and chromosomes. The sources of the morphological characters distinguishing human races are genetic units, passed down holistically from generation to generation.

The following question arises in connection with Davis' article on blood groups. Is it not possible to analyze the isoagglutination blood reactions themselves and find criteria for racial difference? Perhaps the reaction for members of one race differ from another? Speed of clumping, stability, or other factors may constitute differentials. While such suggestions often border upon the absurd, their mention must be considered relevant, since the mentality of the Nordophile, as most race-thinking, abounds in absurdity.

In the far greater number of cases studied the Negro scholar has risen above the narrow racist perspective such as was characteristic of the imaginative writers of the "Negro Renaissance."[26] He no longer overtly postulates a separate group of race values according to which all things Negro are apotheosized. He attempts to follow scientific procedure and keeps before him the ideal of truth independent of perspective. But he is unaware of the determinative significance of social forces especially for the historiocultural sciences, the sphere of knowledge in which discussion of the race problem, for the most part, falls. Born and confined to a milieu within which struggle against outgroup and counterrace status has been waged for generations, his action and thought have become interwoven with "defense mechanisms." The defense has become a "fixed response." As a result, though his analyses propose to observe scientific method and fact, still they too readily oppose before they have understood, or they halt the analytical attack consciously or unconsciously at those points most convenient for recombination of the data in accordance with group interest. The ruling group cites the failures of the masses of Negroes; the scholar retaliates with the achievements of the exceptions as indicative of the potentialities of these masses. The former again stresses inborn, racial inequalities; the latter replies with environmentalism. Both have failed to recognize that their knowledge is part of the knowledge of a "public," that such knowledge is dialectical in nature, and that its range of validity is directly proportional to the breadth of its role-taking in an "interchange of attitudes." Recognition of this will not only prove a logical technique for systematic anticipation of objections thereby promoting cogency of argument; it will be an instrument for improvement of racial understanding. Sheer, empathetic assumption of the attitude and mentality of one race by the other is creative overcoming of culturally rooted complexes and prejudices. "Talking past one another" will be reduced and bases established for community of meaning and actual living.

University of Pennsylania
Philadelphia, Pa.

"Social Determination" in the Writings of Negro Scholars Commentary

I
E. Franklin Frazier

It would not be difficult to show that the research interests of many Negro scholars have been "socially determined." For example, in his autobiography, *Dusk of Dawn*, DuBois shows how, because of his racial identity, he was led first to study the Philadelphia Negro and later to inaugurate the Atlanta University studies of Negro life. In the graduate schools of the country the Negro is often expected and encouraged to devote his time to the study of the Negro. However, Mr. Fontaine is not concerned with these more or less obvious phases of "social determination" but rather with the more subtle aspects of the intellectual outlook of Negro scholars and the conceptual tools which they employ. Armed with the concepts of the sociology of knowledge he undertakes to show that the "mental set" of the Negro scholar is determined by "such psychosocial factors as resentment, aggression, rage, and the desire for equality."

In order to prove his thesis, the author does not utilize social-psychological data such as could be found in the printed works of Du Bois or might have been secured from the other scholars whose works he examined. Perhaps, he failed to use such empirical data because, as he asserts, the Negro scholar may be unconscious of the "social determination" of his scientific conceptions. If Mr. Fontaine is correct, I am sure that this was true of the late Dr. Ernest Just, who would have been surprised to learn that his work in cytology, some of which was done in collaboration with Professor Lillie, was due to an unconscious attempt to locate the hereditary forces in the ectoplasm because it was closest to the influence of the environment! Dispensing with psychosocial data, the author attempts to establish his thesis by showing "the functional dependence between the social situation confronting the Negro group and much of the knowledge cultivated by its scholars." This is shown, according to the author, by the "categorical apparatus" employed; "the selection of certain data as logically prior"; the selection of theories obviously supporting group interests"; and the narrow scope of observation. No one can deny that Mr. Fontaine has exhibited considerable ingenuity in showing that the works of certain Negro scholars possess these characteristics. But the ingenuity which he exhibits is on a purely verbal level, for his analyses fail to meet the requirements of even a formal analysis of the works which he considers. The mechanical manner in which he utilizes the concepts of the sociology of knowledge makes his analysis appear at times as a logomachy. In fact, he may object to my using the word "analysis" to describe his treatment of the works of Negro scholars, since the use of *analysis* by Negro scholars is one of the evidences of the "social determination" of their thinking. However, since Mr. Fontaine (I presume) is a Negro, he, too, is subject to "social determination."

It is unnecessary to show the futility of the author's speculations concerning why Just became interested in cytology. Probably if he had known of the work of the late Dr. Imes in physics, he could have worked out some ingenious reason to explain the interest of the former in the infra-red rays. I shall limit myself here to some remarks on what the author has said concerning the work of Negroes in the field of the social sciences and psychology. It is not difficult to explain the scientific outlook of the Negro scholar and the conceptual tools which he utilizes. If, as the author states, the Negro scholar has arrived, he has only become a competent thinker and craftsman. The techniques and conceptual tools which he uses have been acquired during the course of his education. Doubtless, he has made some worth-while contributions in the various fields, but so far he has not broadened our own intellectual vistas or forged new conceptual tools. That the majority of Negro psychologists and social scientists are environmentalists simply means that they have taken over the viewpoint prevailing today. I say "the majority of Negro psychologists and social scientists" because there are some who believe in biological determinism. However, it seems that the author is not concerned with material which he cannot use to prove his thesis.

Since the author has singled out my two books on the Negro family for study, it will not be considered out of place for me to make some comments concerning these works. My interest in the study of the Negro family began while I was the director of the Atlanta School of Social Work. Through the reading of the works of Burgess and Mowrer, I developed the idea that a more fundamental knowledge of the processes of disorganization and reorganization of Negro family life than was in existence at that time should be made available for social workers. Subsequently, when I entered the University of Chicago, I was very much impressed by the ecological approach to the study of social phenomena. One day in "The Temple," as the old social research laboratory was called, I separated the data on Negro homeownership from similar data for whites according to zones of urban expansion in order to find out if the rates for Negroes showed a gradient as did the figures for the total population. Thus I discovered the zones in the Negro community which became a frame of reference for my other data on the family. Somewhere in my unconscious I may have been trying to break up a "morphological category," but, as far as my conscious self was concerned, I was engaged in what Lin Yutang has called "playful curiosity." Moreover, instead of building a defense for the disorganization of Negro family life, I accepted it as a fact and documented it, with the result that I was attacked as a "prejudiced Texas cracker." In my later work, *The Negro Family in the United States*, I attempted only to show how the Negro family had developed in the environment of the United States. I was criticized by Negroes because I did not represent Negro women as martyrs in their relations with southern white men, and I was criticized by some whites for being "too damned objective." But Mr. Fontaine wants to know why I did not study the influence of genetic or biological factors on the organization and disorganization of Negro family life. The answer is simple. I did study the racial or biological factor, color, where it was relevant in a sociological and cultural analysis. Then there was the prosaic fact that I found mulatto and pure black families that were well organized and mulatto and pure black families that were completely disorganized. Therefore, my "playful curiosity" was stopped when I began to speculate on the role of white and black genes in family organization.

This negative criticism of the article by Mr. Fontaine does not mean that the contributions of Negro scholars could not be studied profitably from the standpoint of the sociology of knowledge. Such a study would require, first, a more fundamental knowledge of the "social position" of the various Negro scholars than the author of this article possesses. To assume that the "social position" of all Negro scholars is identical indicates a lack of an understanding of the viewpoint of the sociology of knowledge. A study of this type would require a better understanding of the works of Negro scholars than the author has exhibited. It is misleading to lump together, as the author has done, objective studies which simply reveal variations in the intellectual and cultural

104

development of Negroes and those which are obviously defensive and chauvinistic and emphasize achievements that have no meaning except within the black ghetto. For example, to say that both Professor Bond and Dr. Woodson emphasize the *achievements* of the Negro is a complete misrepresentation and confusion of the viewpoints of these two scholars. Finally, such a study would explain a writer like William H. Thomas, a mulatto, who did not *analyze* the "morphological category," Negro race, but found in it an adequate explanation of the immorality and the degradation of the Negro. Such a study may even explain the mixed-blood's "wuzzleheadedness," a term which was not clear to me when I read the work by Staggerda and Davenport but which now is beginning to have a meaningful content.

Howard University

Notes

1. Charles S. Johnson, *The Negro College Graduate* (Chapel Hill: University of North Carolina Press, 1938), p. 10.
2. "Social determination: as used here means that there is a correlation between the knowledge propounded by Negro scholars and the social situations confronting the Negro group. This correlation amounts to functional dependence. Mechanical, cause-effect sequence, however, is not meant. The extent to which a body of knowledge is affected by social interests or any extra-theoretic factors is a matter of empirical investigation (see Karl Mannheim, *Ideology and Utopia,* trans. L. Wirth and E. Shils [New York: Harcourt, Brace & Co., 1936], p. 239).
3. Specifically, the studies analyzed and considered are the following: E. Franklin Frazier, *The Negro Family in Chicago, The Negro Family in the United States,* and *Negro Youth at the Crossways; Charles S. Johnson, Growing Up in the Black Belt;* Allison Davis, "The Distribution of the Blood Groups and Its Bearing on the Concept of Race," *Sociological Review,* January , 1935; W. M. Cobb, "The Physical Constitution of the American Negro," *Journal of Negro Education,* Vol. III (1934); Horace M. Bond, *Education of the Negro in the American Social Order;* Martin Jenkins, "The Mental Ability of the American Negro," *Journal of Negro Education,* Vol. VIII (1939); Carter G. Woodson, *The Negro in Our History* and *The African Background Outlined;* Charles H. Wesley, *The Collapse of the Confederacy* and "The Reconstruction of History," *Journal of Negro History,* Vol. XX (1935); W. E. B. Du Bois, *Black Reconstruction;* L. D. Reddick, "A New Interpretation for Negro History," *Journal of Negro History,* Vol. XXII (1937); Ernest E. Just, *Biology of the Cell Surface;* and Julian Lewis, *The Biology of the American Negro.*
4. *Op. Cit.,* pp. 264ff.
5. The Nordocentric history picture looks upon all history as revolving about Europe as the home of the white races (see Oswald Spengler, *The Decline of the West*).
6. Julian Lewis, *The Biology of the Negro* (Chicago: University of Chicago Press, 1942), p. 19.
7. E. Franklin Frazier, *The Negro Family in Chicago* (Chicago: University of Chicago Press, 1932), p. 247.
8. W. M. Cobb, "Physical Constitution of the American Negro," *Journal of Negro Education,* Vol. III (1934).
9. *Ibid.,* p. 355.
10. F. R. Lillie, "Ernest Everett Just," *Science,* January, 1942.

11. *Biological Symposia,* II, 18.
12. Ernest E. Just, *Biology of the Cell Surface* (Philadelphia: P. Blakiston's Sons & Co., Inc., 1938), p. 307.
13. *Op. cit.,* p. ix.
14. *Ibid.,* p. x.
15. E. Franklin Frazier, *Negro Youth at the Crossways* (Washington, D.C.: American Council on Education, 1941), p. 276.
16. Charles S. Johnson, *Growing Up in the Black Belt* (Washington, D.C.: American Council on Education, 1941), p. 276.
17. Allison Davis, "The Socialization of the American Negro Child and Adolescent," *Journal of Negro Education,* VIII (1939), 266 n.
18. C. Woodson, *The African Background Outlined—African Survivals* (Washington, D.C.: Association for the Study of Negro Life and History, Inc., 1936), p. 478.
19. Carter G. Woodson, *The Negro in Our History* (New York: Association Publishers, 1941), p. 9.
20. L. D. Reddick, "A New Interpretation for Negro History," *Journal of Negro History,* Vol. XXII (1937).
21. Abram Harris and Sterling D. Spero, *The Black Worker* (New York: Columbia University Press, 1931); Abram Harris, *The Negro as Capitalist* (Philadelphia: American Academy of Political and Social Science, 1936).
22. Ralph Bunche, *A World View of Race* (Washington, D.C.: Associates in Negro Folk Education, 1930).
23. E. Franklin Frazier, *The Negro Family in the United States* (Chicago: University of Chicago Press, 1940).
24. For the conception of "immediate" knowledge as narrow in contrast to the wider knowledge derived from the "delayed response" see George H. Mead, *Mind, Self, and Society*, ed. Charles W. Morris (Chicago: University of Chicago Press, 1934), pp. 98, 109,177 (n. 254).
25. Benjamin Stolberg, "Minority Jingo," *Nation,* July, 1931, 1937.
26. For the race-centered thought of the "Negro Renaissance" see Charles S. Johnson, "The Possibilities of a Separate Black Culture," in *Race Relations;* cf. also Alain Locke, "The Negro—New or Newer," *Opportunity,* January, 1939.

Note on the Author

William T. Fontaine (1909–1968) authored numerous articles on the issues of segregation and desegregation and was renowned for his teaching and theoretical efforts of forging compatibility between the sociology of knowledge and an emotive theory of ethics. He was a member of the Executive Council of the American Society of African Culture and author of *Reflections on Segregation, Desegregation, Power and Morals,* 1967. At his death, he was Professor of Philosophy, University of Pennsylvania, having previously taught at Lincoln University, Southern University, and Morgan State College.

The Race-Class Questions

Bernard R. Boxill

Few questions have troubled and divided black Marxists more than the question of the relation of race to class. Some have been moved to reject Marxism as it is commonly understood. Harold Cruse, for example, claiming to discard orthodox Marxism while retaining the Marxian *method* of dialectics, writes that orthodox "Marxian ideas about capitalism in advanced countries are not to be taken seriously"[1] and that "white capitalist nations, including all the different classes within these nations from upper bourgeoisie to lower proletariat, have become, in fact, bourgeois and, relative middle-class strata, vis-a-vis the nonwhite peoples who have in fact become the world proletarians".[2]

Others have been only slightly more generous. According to the famous Pan-Africanist George Padmore, for example, "Pan-Africanism recognizes much that is true in the Marxist interpretation of history . . . but . . . nevertheless refuses to accept the pretentious claims of doctrinaire Communism, that it alone has the solution to all the complex racial, tribal, and socio-economic problems facing Africa."[3] And writing in 1933 W. E. B. DuBois maintained that although "the Marxian philosophy is a true diagnosis of the situation in Europe in the middle of the 19th Century . . . it must be modified in the United States and especially so far as the Negro group is concerned."[4]

Finally, even those who adhere closest to classical Marxian theories insist that the racial factor introduces complications into the Marxian scheme that cannot be ignored. Thus, C. L. R. James, perhaps the most thoroughgoing Marxist among the writers I have cited, although noting that "The race question is subsidiary to the class question in politics, and to think of imperialism in terms of race is disastrous," maintains that "to neglect the racial factor as merely incidental is an error only less grave than to make it fundamental."[5]

It would be a mistake to see the controversy over the race-class issue as merely a controversy over what *strategies* to use to mobilise the proletariat in a multiracial and racist society. Controversy over strategies, of course, there are. DuBois, for example, indignantly repudiated the Communist party's strategy of what he called using blacks as the "shock troops of the Communist Revolution." Blacks, he declared, have no intention to be made the "sacrificial goat."[6] Perhaps in response to this, C. L. R. James once proposed the strategy that black people wait till the white working class is ready to rise and seeks their assistance.

Still the disagreements are not merely over *strategies*. This is explicit in the claims of Padmore and DuBois that the orthodox Marxian theory of class struggle is not sufficient to explain what happens in a multiracial society. This implies that race is in a sense "irreducible" to class and that class analysis must be either scrapped altogether, or amended with a qualitatively new and theoretically independent conception of race, if it is to be of any use in understanding multiracial societies. In this essay I will endorse this view. Further, I will argue that a theory of race cannot simply be grafted on to Marx's theory of class struggle. If I am right, any such attempt ends up casting doubt on the materialist conception of history.

First, it is perhaps necessary to emphasize what is *not* at issue. All are agreed, for example, that class *is* an important factor influencing behavior in society and cannot be ignored in any adequate social theory. Thus, there is no question of following Marcus M. Garvey in his view that all social divisions pale into utter insignificance before racial divisions. Clearly this is inadequate for understanding society. It is as implausible as the view that all divisions in society pale into insignificance before *class* divisions. The problem is to find a theory that *explains*, not denies, the patent fact that both racial and class divisions are *significant* influences in most multiracial, class societies. At the same time, however, it is perfectly consistent for such a theory to be so formulated that a theory of class struggle is more fundamental than a theory of races, or vice-versa.

C. L. R. James's claim that race is subsidiary to class is therefore perfectly consistent with both race and class being significant and important divisions. But what does it *mean* to say that race is subsidiary to class? First what it does *not* mean: It does *not* mean that race prejudice is any less objectionable, in itself, than class prejudice. A Marxist who held that race is subsidiary to class could consistently hold that racism is a far nastier phenomenon than class prejudice. Nor does it mean that racial divisions are less *visible* than class divisions. A Marxist can consistently allow that the members of a multiracial society mark a person's race more carefully than his class, and that social intermingling is more common between different classes than between different races. Only if it is taken in a certain sense is Frantz Fanon's claim that "what parcels out the world is to begin with the fact of belonging to, or not belonging to a given race" necessarily un-Marxian.[7] Neither, similarly, does the position that race is subsidiary to class entail that when violence erupts between antagonistic races it is any less virulent than the violence which the Marxists expect to erupt between classes. It is consistent for a Marxist to hope that socialism will come about in relatively peaceful ways, while allowing that racial conflicts have been, and will be, violent. Finally, the claim that race is subsidiary to class does not mean that racial antagonisms are really deep-down class antagonisms. If that claim is to be plausible at all, it must allow what is in any case obvious—racial lines need not coincide with class lines, races in conflict need not identify each other as classes, and the suppression or disappearance of one of the races may leave the class conflict relatively unaffected. What then does the claim that race is subsidiary to class mean? As I shall understand it, the claim that race is subsidiary to class means that it is the class struggle that is the cause, condition, or explanation of racial antagonisms, and not racial antagonisms that are the cause, condition, or explanation of class struggle. How plausible is this claim?

A skeptic may begin by citing how qualitatively different are the motives, attitudes, and sentiments of the antagonists in the race struggle and the antagonists in the class struggle. In the first place, the *concepts* of race and class are utterly different despite the considerable ambiguity and elasticity of Marx's concept of class. For, however many classes Marx counted, and he came up with many different sums, class was for him always a group a person belonged to by virtue of his economic position. Thus when he identified bourgeoisie and proletariat as the two main classes, the principle of division is whether or not one owns means of production—an economic criteria. Similarly, slaves, freemen, landowners, peasants, and the new "middle class" are all defined in virtue of some economic factor.

On the other hand, despite a similar or greater ambiguity in the concept of race, races are *never* distinguished in virtue of their economic position. This is not to deny, of course, that *often* (though not always) racial lines coincide with class lines. The concepts of race and class may be quite different though their extensions coincide. The point is that, in whatever sense, the concept of race differs from the concept of class.

This, however, presents no difficulty for the Marxist. That race cannot be *defined* in terms of class is a claim he can freely admit. For it says nothing against the claim he *does* want to maintain, that is that class divisions are the cause, condition, or explanation of racial antagonisms.

Now, of course, when he says this he does not mean that class divisions cause racial divisions when race is taken in a purely physical sense. In that sense race does not imply that any particular social relations exist between races. When the Marxist says that class divisions are the cause, condition or explanation of racial divisions, what he means is that the class divisions are the cause, condition, or explanation of racial *antagonisms*, and in particular, of racism. This is compatible with the subjective attitudes of the racist being quite dissimilar from the subjective attitudes of the class conscious person; and compatible with racist ideologies being qualitatively different and irreducible to class ideologies. I take it that we can perhaps summarize the Marxist position that race is subsidiary to class as holding that a theory of racial antagonisms can be deduced, with the help of bridge connections, from a theory of class struggle. On this account the subject of race-relations and of racism can be a self-contained theory. All it claims is that this theory is deducible from a theory of classes, much as a theory of thermodynamics, though self-contained, is deducible from a theory of statistical mechanics.[8]

If this were all that the Marxian theory claimed, it would be plausible. But it says much more: According to Marx, his theory of class struggle did not merely explain other conflicts. According to Marx, the distinctive aspect of his theory is that: "(1) The existence of classes is only bound up with particular historical phases in the development of production. (2) The class struggle necessarily leads to the dictatorship of the proletariat. (3) This dictatorship itself only constitutes the transition to the abolition of all classes and to a classless society."[9]

In accordance with this position Marx maintained that the class struggle was simplified and the working class united by late capitalism.[10] This is moreover *necessary* if the revolt and victory of the proletariat are to be plausible. Thus, according to Marx, it is not merely that class conflict is the cause, condition or explanation of race conflict. It is also the cause, condition, or explanation of the *transcendence* of race conflict. The difficulty is only accentuated when we notice that Marxists often say that it is late or mature capitalism that engenders racism. For, on Marx's own view, it is late or mature capitalism that brings about the transcendence of racism. This is clearly implied by the talk of the unity of the proletariat.

It might be objected that there is no difficulty here: All that it is necessary to see is that although late capitalism in a multiracial society will cause racial antagonisms to arise in the proletariat, this must be, and can be, successfully combated by the Communist party. It will, as Marx said, point out to the proletariat what their true interests are, thus overcoming racism and creating that unity in the working class that is necessary for their victory. Marx himself suggested this policy. Thus, commenting on the Irish Question, Marx wrote to Meyer and Vogt that England is "divided into two hostile camps, English proletarians and Irish proletarians. The ordinary English worker hates the Irish worker as a competitor who lowers his standard of life. In relation to the Irish worker he feels himself a member of the ruling nation". The attitude of the English worker to the Irish worker "is much the same as that of the 'poor whites' to the 'niggers' in the former slave states of the U.S.A. The Irishman pays him back with interest. . . ."[11] Despite this, Marx felt that a union of English and Irish workers was not only necessary but possible. Moreover, it was the task of the party to educate the workers. "It is the special task of the Central Council in London" he wrote, "to awaken a consciousness in the English workers."[12]

This does not altogether overcome the difficulty, however. A basic principle of Marx's materialist conception of history is that our ideas are determined by how we produce the material conditions of our existence. "We begin with real active men" he wrote in *The German Ideology*, "and from their real life process show the ideological reflexes and echoes of this life process."[13] Further, Marx often writes of the growing unity of the working class in terms that follow from this view. In *Capital Vol. I* he writes, for example, that the working class becomes, "disciplined, united, organized by the very mechanism of the process of capitalist production itself."[14] Now we are told, it appears, that unity grows among the black and white working class, not because of the "very mechanisms of the process of capitalist production" but because of the intervention of the Communist party.

Perhaps this objection can be countered by a more precise account of the relation of ideas to the manner of the production of the material conditions of life. Thus, it may be pointed out that racism does not spontaneously arise in the ranks of the proletariat because of the mechanisms of capitalist production. That is, according to Marx, the races among the proletariat do not simply begin tearing at each other in a kind of dog-eat-dog frenzy when their conditions deteriorate, as Garvey believed. Rather, racism is deliberately *fostered* by the capitalists because they see that it is in their interest that the workers *not* unite. Marx himself saw it this way: The "antagonism" between English and Irish workers, he wrote, is "artifically kept alive and intensified . . . by all the means at the disposal of the ruling classes. This antagonism is the secret of the impotence of the English working class. . . . It is the secret by which the capitalist class maintains its power. And that class is fully aware of it."[15]

With this in mind we can try to understand the determination of ideas by the method of material production in a more flexible and plausible way. It is not that our ideas are those we need to function and survive given our method of material production as Marx sometimes seems to suggest. Rather, it is that our ideas are designed to *justify*, excuse, or console us for our position in the given mode of production or to secure our interests. Thus religion is a consolation for misery, and racism a justification for racial exploitation and a strategy the capitalists use to secure their advantage. If this is correct, the fact that the Communist party may have to intervene to educate the white and black workers to unite constitutes no deviation from the materialist conception of history. For we can explain the success of its educational program by the affinity of the working classes for what it teaches.

This last point perhaps needs elaboration. Though Marx allowed that the Communist pary take the lead and educate the workers, he certainly thought that workers would not need much leading. Advanced capitalism, he often insisted, simplifies the issues. The democratic nature of the revolution he anticipated is incompatible with the idea of a mass of workers being led by a highly educated clique of leaders making a revolution on principles not clear to the workers.

Moreover, Marx had to believe in the affinity of the workers for unity and socialism for other reasons as well. We may allow that the materialist conception of history is compatible with the Communist party teaching the workers their interests. But if that conception of history implies that people think what justifies or secures their interests in an economic system, then given that the system makes their interests patent, the least we can expect is that the workers have an affinity for ideas of interracial unity. Otherwise, the materialist conception of history must again be placed under scrutiny.

But the efforts of the Communist party to educate black and white workers to the commonality of their interests has been far from successful. Not only that, the largest and most popular mass movement among black Americans—the Garvey movement—was openly and virulently anti-Communist and was to no avail roundly denounced by the Communist party.

The Marxist will begin saying, of course, that it is in the "true" interests of the white and black proletariat to unite—by which he means that it is the true interests of the proletariat to become socialists. This path was first taken by Marx himself. Thus he maintained that it was in the interests of the English workers to combine with the Irish workers to secure the national emancipation of Ireland, and that this was "no question of abstract justice or humanitarian sentiment but the first condition of their own social emancipation."[16]

Now I do not deny that it is in the true interests of the working class to combine to set up a socialist society. The difficulty is that according to the materialist conception of history—even according to the broader interpretation I have given to it—it is not the case that persons always acquire ideas that tend to secure and justify their *true* interests. If that were so, we should have had socialism from the start. In particular, at the bourgeois revolution, the bourgeoisie would have set up socialism, not capitalism, and even now we would not find the bourgeoisie making up ideologies to proect their narrow, bourgeois, "untrue" interests. We should find them striving as strongly as the proletariat, for a socialist society. For make no mistake about it, on the Marxist account, it is in the true interests of the bourgeoisie to set up socialism as much as it is in the true interests of the proletariat to set up socialism. As Marx put it in a famous sentence in *The Holy Family*, "The possessing class and the proletarian class represent one and the same human self-alienation."[17]

Accordingly, the doctrine of the materialist conception of history is that people acquire ideas that secure, protect, or further their interests, as they perceive them, or their interests, given the sorts of persons they are. On that account, the bourgeoisie set up a capitalist society when they overcame feudalism, not because it was in their "true" interests, but because given what they were, it was in their interests to do so.

This line suggests the following objection: Though it is in the true interests of both the bourgeoisie and proletariat to set up socialism, given what the bourgeoisie are, they will not recognize it as in their true interests, but given what they are the *proletariat* will. Thus, Marx continues the sentence from *The Holy Family* with the following comment: the bourgeoisie "feels satisfied and affirmed in this self-alienation, experiences the alienation as a sign of its own power, and passes in it the appearance of a human existence. The latter (proletariat), however, feels destroyed in this alienation seeing in it its own impotence and the reality of an inhuman existence."[18]

The implication is that at last, in the long history of the human race, the time has arrived when the *true* interests of a rising class coincides with their interests *as they perceive them*, given the sorts of persons they are. That is, given what they are, the proletariat will *feel* it in their interests to dispossess the bourgeoisie and set up socialism, and moreover, this will be in their true interests.

Unfortunately, however, this line is implausible. If it were in the *perceived* interests of the proletariat to unite to crush the capitalists, why are the proletariat of advanced capitalist countries so slow in becoming Communists?

It is dangerous to protest that the capitalist propaganda deceives the proletariat to an extent unanticipated by Marx. For to the extent that we press this point, to the same extent we call the materialist conception of history into question. That is, to the extent that we say that the capitalists successfully dupe the proletariat, to that same extent we cast doubt on the doctrine that people are strongly disposed to acquire or accept ideas that secure or further their clearly perceived interests.

The probable fact is that, to use a term Engels and Lenin made popular, the white working class has become "embourgeoisified". They have become just the sorts of persons the bourgeoisie are. Engels saw this long ago. In a letter to Kautsky he wrote, "You ask me what the English workers think about colonial policy. Well, exactly the same as they think about politics in general: the same as the bourgeois think . . . the workers gaily share the feast of England's monopoly of the world market and the colonies."[19]

Marx was aware of this difficulty. In a letter to Engels he wrote, ". . . quite apart from all phrases about international and humane justice for Ireland . . . it is in the direct and absolute interest of the English working class to get rid of their connection with Ireland. And this is my fullest conviction and for reasons which in part I can *not* tell the English workers themselves."[20] Talk of "direct and absolute interest" has an egoistic, empirical ring to it. We are led to believe that no unreasonable transformation of the English workers is envisaged or required. They will remain basically what they are—self-interested—and that this alone will be sufficient for their mobilization. But if so, why conceal from them the real reasons why they must collaborate with the Irish? The answer surely is that though it is in their "true" interest, it is not in their interest as they perceive it. Their true interest lies in the liberation of Ireland, but Marx cannot tell them this with any hope of moving them, for what moves them is their interest *as they perceive it*, and their interest as they perceive it lies in having a subservient class in Ireland, which is the condition of their enrichment.

Now these difficulties are, of course, exactly the difficulties that plague the Marxist solution of the race-class issue. For the Irish merely substitute the blacks and the Third World proletariat. The white proletariat of advanced capitalist societies is enriched and embourgeoisified as a result of the exploitation of black and third World proletariat. The true interest of the white proletariat lies in the liberation of the black and Third World proletariat. But Marxists cannot tell the white proletariat this with any hope of moving them, for what moves them is their interest as they perceive it, and their interest as they perceive it lies in having a subservient black and Third World proletariat.

The Marxist can respond to this in several different ways, which, however, all raise fundamental difficulties for the materialist conception of history. The first depends on the liberation of the Third World: The Third World will liberate itself, with or without the help of the white proletariat of the capitalist countries; when this happens, the capitalists of the industrialized countries will be compelled to step up the exploitation of their domestic proletariat; this will cause the emiseration of the white proletariat and bring their perceived interest into line with their true interests. One problem with this line is that it rests on the controversial claim that the embourgeoisification of the white proletariat depends on the exploitation of the Third World. It is far from clear that Marx proved this. A key step in proving the claim, the "law of the falling tendency of the rate of profit" is, as Paul M. Sweezy admits, "not very convincing."[21] For this reason many Marxists, including Marx himself, substituted the idea of a widening gap between capitalists and proletariat for the idea of an absolute emiseration of the proletariat.[22] But if so, the Marxist must live with the possibility that the white proletariat will remain embourgeoisified even after the liberation of the Third World, and correspondingly that its perceived interest will not come into line with its true interest.

It may be objected that the widening gap theory of the increasing misery doctrine is enough to bring the perceived interest of the white proletariat into line with its true interest, for confronted with the immense wealth of the capitalists, the proletariat cannot fail to see that it is in its interest to topple the capitalists in order to share in their wealth. But this argument is not very convincing. It is one thing, and plausible, that desperate people, who have "nothing to lose but their chains", will risk all for socialism. It is another thing, and implausible, that comfortable people who have much to lose will risk all for socialism.

Further, the assumption that the workers will be moved to revolution by self-interest or class-interest runs into the problem which arises from the fact, as Allen Buchanan put it, "concerted revolutionary action is for the proletariat a public good."[23] A public good has the following five features: (1) Action by some but not all is sufficient to produce the good, (2) if the good is produced it will be available to all, (3) there is no practical way to prevent those who did not contribute from enjoying the goood, (4) the individual's contribution is a cost to the individual, (5) the value of what each individual would gain from the good outweighs his share of the costs of producing it. If concerted revolutionary action is a public good in this sense, then each proletariat, if he is rational will conclude that he should not join in the revolution and consequently the revolution will not occur. For whether he joins or not either enough others will, or they will not. If the former then the revolution will succeed anyway and his effort will be wasted. If the latter then again his effort will be wasted. Moreover, as Buchanan demonstrates, the problem remains even if the individuals of the group are concerned to maximize the advantage of the group.[24]

It may be objected that the proletariat does not engage in such nice calculations as the Buchanan's argument requires, but I do not agree. The argument may well explain, for example, the passivity of the white proletariat compared to the black lower class. For the public goods problem does not apply to that class. In particular, the fourth condition is not satisfied since the members of the black lower class are typically in such desperate straits that they do not count revolutionary effort as a cost. Consequently, they have, despite

DuBois, tended to act as the "shock troops" against the established order with the white proletariat waiting safely to take the lions share of the concessions the blacks have won.[25]

Perhaps the Communist party can spur white workers to act with the black lower class by persuading them of the idea of interracial justice. But this raises difficulties. On the one hand, it seems to conflict with Marx's scornful dismissals of appeals to morality as a way of moving the proletariat.[26] Further, some writers have urged that Marx repudiated justice as a bourgeois ideal.[27] If they are right, and the Communist party preaches interracial justice to achieve concerted revolutionary action, it would be duping the workers, and although it could be said to be doing so in their interests, this would suggest that it was paternalistic and raises doubts about the democratic nature of the revolution and of communism itself. For my part I do not believe that Marx repudiated justice, and consequently I concede that the Communist party can, without dishonesty, preach interracial justice.[28]

But a difficulty yet remains. Marx laid no store on appeals to morality, not because he thought such appeals necessarily dishonest, but because he thought them ineffective. He believed that, in the thrall of bourgeois society the workers would be effectively moved only by appeal to their self-interest. Thus, he held that the decisive advantage of his own scientific socialism over other socialisms was that he could demonstrate to the workers that socialism was in their self-interest.

Now I agree with Marx that appeals to morality are generally ineffective and I believe that they are especially ineffective as a means of moving black and white workers to act together. As I have argued elsewhere, it is the sentiments associated with the sense of justice that ensure that persons are reliably moved to act justly, and these sentiments cannot bind the whole human race or those of a large and diverse society.[29] In particular they do not bind the black and white proletariat.[30] This does not mean that persons cannot learn to be "color-blind". It only means that until communal ties are established between the races, and until *de facto* segregation is overcome, black and white people are not generally likely to be reliably moved to act justly to each other. This suggests that justice and joint action by the black and white proletariat will only be won at the cost of some coercion, and since white coercion of black workers will only make the blacks the "shock troops" of the revolution, black workers must achieve black power.

Notes

1. Harold Cruse, *Rebellion or Revolution*, (New York: William Morrow & Company, 1968), p. 144.
2. Ibid, p. 155.
3. George Padimore, *Pan-Africanism or Communism*, (New York: Doubleday-Anchor, 1972), p. xvi.
4. W. E. B. DuBois, *W. E. B. DuBois*, ed. William M. Tuttle, (Englewood Cliffs, N.J.: Prentice-Hall 1973), p. 92.
5. C. L. R. James, *The Black Jacobins*.

6. DuBois, p. 92.
7. Frantz Fanon, *The Wretched Of The Earth,* (New York: Grove Press, 1963), p. 40.
8. Ernest Nagel, *The Structure of Science,* (New York: Harcourt-Brace, 1961), pp. 338–342.
9. Karl Marx, "Marx to Weydemeyer" in *The Thought of Karl Marx,* ed. David McLellan, (New York: Harper and Row, 1971), p. 164.
10. Karl Marx, "The Communist Manifesto" in *Karl Marx: Selected Writings,* ed. David McLellan, (Oxford: Oxford University Press, 1977), p. 222.
11. Karl Marx, "Marx to S. Meyer and A. Vogt" in *On Colonialism,* (New York: International Publishers, 1972), p. 337.
12. Ibid., p. 338.
13. Karl Marx, "The German Ideology" in McLellan, ed., *Karl Marx: Selected Writings,* p. 164.
14. Karl Marx from Capital Vol. 1, McLellan, ed., *Karl Marx: Selected Writings,* p. 487.
15. Karl Marx in *On Colonialism,* p. 337.
16. Ibid., p. 338.
17. Karl Marx, "The Holy Family" in *The Marx-Engels Reader,* (New York: W. W. Norton & Company, 1978), p. 133.
18. Ibid.
19. Frederick Engels "Engels to K. Kautsky" in *On Colonialism,* p. 341.
20. Karl Marx, "Marx to Engels" in *On Colonialism,* p. 332.
21. Paul M. Sweezy, *The Theory of Capitalist Development,* (New York: Modern Reader Paperbacks, 1942), p. 104.
22. On this see eg. Thomas Sowell "Marx's Increasing Misery" doctrine, *American Economic Review,* vol. 50 (March 1960), pp. 111–120.
23. Allen Buchanan, "Revolutionary Motivation and Rationality" in *Marx, Justice and History,* ed. Marshall Cohen, Thomas Nagel and Thomas Scanlon (Princeton: Princeton University Press, 1980), pp. 268.
24. Ibid., p. 269.
25. See Derrick Bell, "Brown v Board of Education and the Interest-Convergence Dilemma", *Harvard Law Review,* vol. 93, 1980, pp. 518–533.
26. Karl Marx, "Critique of the Gotha Program," *Karl Marx: Selected Writings,* p. 569.
27. For example, Robert C. Tucker in "Marx and Distributive Justice" in *The Marxian Revolutionary Idea,* (New York: Norton, 1969).
28. The literature on this is extensive. For a review see *Karl Marx* by Allen Wood, Boston: Routledge and Kegan Paul, 1981), pp. 140–150.
29. Bernard R. Boxill, "How Injustice Pays," *Philosophy and Public Affairs,* vol. 9, no. 4, 1980.
30. According to Robert Heilbroner white Americans often object to social reforms because they think such reforms will help undeserving blacks. R. Heilbroner, "The Roots of Social Neglect in the United States," in *Is Law Dead,* edited by E. Rostow.

Note on the Author

Bernard R. Boxill is an Associate Professor in the Department of Philosophy, University of South Florida. He has previously taught at the University of Kentucky, University of California, Los Angeles and Santa Barbara, and California State University. Boxill is well known for his works on interest theory and justice, represented by such works as "Morality of Reparations," *Social Theory and Practice,* Spring, 1972, and "How Injustice Pays," *Philosophy and Public Affairs,* Summer, 1980. His forthcoming book is entitled *Blacks and Social Justice.*

Race and Class in the Theory and Practice of Emancipatory Social Transformation

Lucius T. Outlaw

1. The Forcing of the Issue

The questions of how best to understand, and on the basis of that understanding how to deal practically, in an emancipatory fashion, with the various forms of oppression suffered by particular groups of people in the social order, are no longer questions of whose debate is restricted to theoreticians and practitioners of social transformation. Today the argument that the oppression of women should be viewed as a distinct form of subjugation, which cannot—and must not—be lost in the reduction of all forms of oppression in capitalist social formations to class exploitation, enjoys generalized support in various publics with varying interests and commitments. Likewise, the continuing historic struggles of people of African descent, in almost all forms and instances except those most assimilationist, have provoked intense debates regarding the most correct theory and praxis to achieve "liberation," particularly when the nationalist orientation is both theoretically and practically ascendent as was the case during the period of Black Power (mid-1960s to early 1970s). Conditioned, in part, by these developments and by significant economic, political, and social changes in the country (and world), which together result in a specific articulation, in the case of people of African descent, of a larger, equally specific conjuncture of the structural processes of the world capitalist system, the question of how best to understand and confront the problems of black Americans has again become a matter of generalized debate. The *New York Times Magazine* (5 October 1980) gave cover story prominence to the issue with a discussion focused on the question "The Black Plight: Race or Class?"

Though long debated by radicals both black and white, the joining of the issue in a wider public sphere is initially very significant, and may well become more so (though one should not expect either a ready resolution of the matter, or even a well-grounded discussion of it, as a reading of the presentations in the *New York Times Magazine* discloses). For the question is posed in the face of the glaring realities of the continuing and worsening situation of millions of black people, and others, following a quarter-century of intense agitation (the Freedom and Black Power movements) and significant economic expansion with rising standards of living. Both developments were guided by liberal philosophies of economic and social development that called for sustained economic growth steered by State intervention, including some

117

redistribution of social wealth to guarantee minimum social welfare, and for the realization of racial justice likewise architected, implemented, and enforced by the State. Together these developments (along with others) were to result in the "good life" for all.

The realities, however, have turned out quite differently. The good life has not been forthcoming for all. And, in the present period, the economic and social policies of President Ronald Reagan are explicitly designed to redistribute wealth into the hands of those most well-off in the social order on the claim that they will utilize it in ways that will give rise to economic expansion and prosperity that will eventually trickle down to the lower levels of the society. Such policies are having devastating effects on those at the lowest levels of the economic order, particularly members of the black "underclass." This return to nineteenth century classical liberalism, discredited by its own history, is transforming a bad situation into a system-threatening crisis. Consequently a debate regarding race and class takes on added weight in the present historical period if there is to be a serious effort to effect emancipatory social transformation guided by a radical, critical understanding of the present society that speaks to the conditions for and elements of a vision of a liberated future society. And to the extent that the debate is now being posed within and among larger publics in terms that are drawn from both the critical theoretical tradition of Marxism and from the tradition of Black Nationalism, opens possibly to those publics, to a degree seldom before realized, the critical resources of both traditions in a way that makes possible the revision of emancipatory theory and praxis in light of fuller recognition of the matters of racial/ethnic and class oppression (and of other forms of oppression) in contemporary American society. On the way to such a revised theory, it will be worthwhile to begin with a brief review of the terms of the debate.

Some participants in the Marxian (i.e., critical theoretical, emancipatory) tradition have long been convinced, for the most part, that a class analysis of the American social formation provides a necessary and sufficient understanding of it, even of its racism, to ground revolutionizing praxis. In general this has not been convincing to people of African descent who have dealt with such matters, even for some who have been—and are—active participants in various currents of the Marxist tradition. Certainly for many Black Nationalists the supposed sufficiency *and* necessity of Marxian class analysis, with particular additions of forms of race analysis, have been hotly contested, if not rejected. Such debates have a long and continuing history. And the matter was recently rekindled with the publication of William J. Wilson's *The Declining Significance of Race: Blacks and Changing American Institutions*, in which he argues that, in the economic order, class position, not race, is the most important determinant of the life-chances of individual blacks; racial antagonisms have, instead, been transferred, in the present period, to the political arena.[1]

Wilson's arguments have met with a veritable storm of debate and controversy and continue to be the subject of critical discussions. In addition to criticism and counterarguments that stress the insufficiency of class analysis, or even its irrelevance, others have argued the inadequacy of Wilson's analysis in class terms: he employs a Weberian, not a Marxian, concept of class, one based on income stratifications, not on relationships to the means of production, which is subsequently significantly weaker in critical, explanatory power.

On the other hand, other analyses of contemporary tendencies in the economic order (and in political and ideological relations) draw conclusions different from those of Wilson. Harold Baron, for example, argues that the American economic order is now characterized by a conjuncture of invidious racial discrimination and economic exploitation—both of which are suffered disproportionately by blacks—manifested in the virtually monopolistic relegation of people of African descent to the secondary (low-paying, insecure, dirty, dangerous) divisions of a segmented labor market.[2]

The positions of Wilson and Baron are only provisionally indicative of the lack of consensus at the level of theory with regard to the absolute and/or relative importance of race and/or class as constitutive of the objective and subjective realities of life in capitalist America. Social praxis is even more telling with the glaring absence of a multiracial/ethnic organized effort to transform the social order guided by appropriate understanding and commitments. This lack of consensus has deep roots in emancipatory theory itself.

The critical theory of society sets itself the task of achieving a radical, critical understanding of the total society: of its "laws" of operation, its history, its possibilities for continued existence, and the tendencies within it for its transformation into a better (or worst) society. Given this self-imposed agenda, the theory must itself be reviewed critically to determine why, as both theory and praxis, it has dealt so inadequately with the matter of race/ethnicity and racism in the American social order. Among other things, an answer must be given to the questions whether, and to what extent, racial oppression can be accommodated by the theory (and whether democratic, multiracial/ethnic organizations can be formed by those committed to the theory), or to what extent must the theory be changed if it is to confront adequately the problematics of racism (and other forms of group oppression), while, at the same time, taking due account of the integrity of the *national* character of people of African descent.

This concern on my part for the "race or class?" debate is grounded on a number of commitments. The first is to a historical project: the achievement of concrete (i.e., historically realized) unity-in-diversity of the various peoples in the American social order under democratic social principles and arrangements that ensure the existence and well-being of people of African descent in our cultural, ethnic (relative) autonomy and authenticity to the extent that this can be realized under conditions free from domination. A second commitment grows out of the first: to share in the theoretical (philosophical) project to set forth the principles and values, and to identify the means, which, if realized, might lead to the achievement of the historical project.

The commitment to the emancipatory historical project, and, therefore, to the philosophical project that grows out of it, reflects a choice based on an understanding of the historical situation of people of African descent in this country, a situation that can only be judged inadequate, oppressive, and unjust when it is measured by the yardsick of the progessive ideals of the liberal bourgeois revolution that continue to provide the expressed ideological foundation for the American social order. Any effort to significantly transform this situation requires an understanding of the society as a whole, structurally/ dynamically and historically, in a way that gets to its very foundations. Toward this end, the point of departure for the following argument is that the debate, when framed as "race or class?", is a false disjunction that grounds incorrect praxis. Rather, the matter is one of *both*, race *and* class, properly understood.

II. 'Race' and 'Class' in Critical Social Theory

By "critical and social theory," or "the critical theory of society," I have reference to the tradition of radical critique of society, a critique that is to be realized (and can only be realized) in the practical activity that follows from and is guided by it, that was articulated programmatically and demonstratively by Marx and Engels with subsequent contributions by a number of key figures (Lenin, Stalin, Lukacs, Gramsci, Mao Tse-Tung, etc.).[3] In the early writings of Marx, the "Economic and Philosophical Manuscripts of 1844" and "The German Ideology (Part I)" in particular, we find the demonstrative articulation of the critical manifesto along with a historical grounding of classes within social formations constituted by a capitalist mode of production.[4] In no way, of course, can these early writings be taken as the definitive contributions of Marx, nor can they be fully appreciated without serious study of his later, more mature writings, which involve carrying out the radical manifesto in terms of analyses of capitalist society in its most developed form at the time. On the other hand, however, the early works are not discontinuous with the later writings. It is not my reading of Marx that the early writings reflect his "Hegelian," philosophical period, which was transcended in the materialist political economy of *Capital* and the *Grundrisse*. Instead, as I read Marx, the latter writings are fulfillments of a project the grounds of which were in part laid out in the early works. It is on this reading that I thus turn to the early writings to review some of the foundational (indeed philosophical) notions that ground the Marxian project, notions that, I shall argue, continue to condition theoretical efforts, including the "race or class?" debate.

We can characterize the radical critique of society as "the reflective critique of socially unnecessary constraints of human freedom," a characterization that is embodied in the writings of Marx and Engels.[5] Such a characterization, once explicated, implies a number of distinct moments that structure the Marxian project: (a) a philosophical anthropology (i.e., a generalized description/articulation of the "human") wherein "freedom" is constitutive, which sets the stage for (b) evaluative judgments, of (c) an historical (i.e., empirical) determination, that particular constraints are "socially unnecessary," all of which then lead to (d) the theory of emancipatory activity, and its realization, which will remove the constraints and usher in a new social formation in which human "free, conscious, creative activity" will be maximized.

It is to Marx's philosophical anthropology that we must turn to locate a principal source for the difficulty the Marxian tradition has had in coming to terms with race/ethnicity, racism, and nationalism. For it is his view of human "being" in its essence, in its species being, that grounds the critique of capitalist social formations and subsequently grounds the revolutionary project in behalf of a society free of (class) oppression. And it is this view of humanity that implicitly and explicitly conditions the thinking of many Marxist such that they give primacy to class oppression as *the* condition to be overcome.

Marx's view of human being is expounded, particularly, in "The 1844 Manuscripts." Man, according to Marx, is an animal distinguished as a species by the fact that he produces the means for his own existence, hence reproduces his life, beyond the satisfaction of immediate needs, to the satisfaction of needs he himself has created, possibly in tune to a sense of beauty, out of his own free (because universal, as a *species being*), conscious, creative activity, within an environ of all of nature (which is man's *inorganic* body). All of man's activity, since he is, first and foremost, a *species* being, is constitutively *social*.

Now since it is the case that, within this ensemble of features constitutive of human existence, the reproduction of the means of existence is, for Marx, the *determining* aspect, then it follows that the means of production (the means of reproducing life) are determinative in social life, so much so that all of social life is conditioned by that sector of society in which this reproductive process is structured and becomes operative. Society is thus formed around (structured by) its economic order. Social classes arise when we get the historical situation in which the social means of production come under the control of private individuals (hence private property) who collectively act in concert to secure their dominant position from which they extract surplus value from those who labor to produce what is exchanged for profits; when, on the other side, those who labor have only their labor power (capacity to work) to sell for wages and have only an estranged (alienated) relation to the process of production, to the product, to other persons in the labor process, to the society as a whole, and to him/her self, to his/her own species being. Collectively laborers form the working class and are opposed to the class of owners. The relations between the two groups are thus contradictory (sometimes antagonistically, sometimes nonantagonistically); their relations are, thereby, relations of class struggle. Alienated labor, in all its forms, grounded in private property and the division of labor, is a constraint upon human activity in its

121

most fundamental mode: the reproduction of the means of existence as free, conscious, creative activity as a *species* act. The correction of this situation, the theory holds, will only be properly achieved when the working class, as the embodiment of the universal social (i.e., species) interests, successfully concludes the class struggle and frees itself, and thereby all of society, by abolishing private property (private ownership of the means of production) and the state (which heretofore has functioned as the "executive committee" of the class of rulers) and brings into historical realization a society of free producers/owners who produce and consume, first, in accord with *genuine* need, and beyond that in accord with creative freedom and beauty. Such a society will be classless. And this is the goal of emancipatory, revolutionary praxis.

Given this brief recapitulation of Marx, let us look more closely at what is meant by "class," both the concept and the reality it seeks to grasp. To the degree that a class analysis of capitalist social formations is one of the key elements of Marxian critical theory (since, in the theory, class struggle is the driving force of history), we must see to what extent the theory can account for the socially unnecessary constraints of racial/ethnic oppression and for its amelioration in a liberated society in a way that does justice to racial/ethnic national groupings of peoples.

With Marx, the concept of class is intended to capture and account for *"the effects of the ensemble of structures, of the matrix of a mode of production or of a social formation on the agents which constitute its supports: this concept reveals the effects of the global structure in the field of social relations.*[6] Classes, on this interpretation, are effects of *"an ensemble of the structures* of a mode of production and social formation . . . and of their relations, first at the economic level, second, at the political level, and third, at the ideological level."[7] Classes are thus constituted by a structural (economic, i.e., *place* in the production process; relations of production) and relational (political and ideological) ensemble, thus have their ground in a historically specific conjuncture (in its general or structural/relational features) of a mode of production and social formation. This is the "objective" nature of classes, that is, the historical, sociological places of social agents that are independent of their will (though this structure is amenable to willful transformative praxis). And with this we have the "structural determination" of classes that is manifested in class struggle.

But this structural determination is to be distinguished from the *position* of a class: the concrete situation of classes in the class struggle in the "always unique historic individuality" of social formations. The concept of "classes" thus refers to groupings of social agents defined principally, though not exclusively, by their places in the production process, though more specifically they are constituted by the (social) relations of production.[8] And within these relations (of production) political and ideological relations are constitutive:

The relations of production and the relationships which comprise them (economic ownership/possession) are expressed in the form of powers which derive from them, in other words class powers; these powers are constitutively tied to the political and ideological relations which sanction and legitimize them. Those relations are not simply added on to relations of production that are 'already there', but are themselves present, in the form specific to each mode of production, in the constitution of the relation of production. The process of production and exploitation is at the same time a process of reproduction of the relations of political and ideological domination and subordination.[9]

However, classes can be further distinguished by subgroupings. There can be "fractions" and "strata" that have their bases in differentiations within the relations of production and in differing political and ideological commitments/relations of various groupings of people. And there are "social categories," i.e., groupings of agents defined principally by their place in political and ideological relations such as intellectuals or a state bureaucracy.[10] These class fractions, strata, and social categories may, in fact, take up positions that are contrary to their class interests: a fraction of the working class, for example, may assume a position that coincides with that of the class (or a stratum of the class) of owners. In such cases political and ideological relations assume greater relative significance. Furthermore, under particular historical conditions, relative to a specific social formation, ideological and political relations may "assume the rule of relatively autonomous social forces."[11] Consequently, though it is the case that the economic order plays a *principal* role in the structural determination of a social formation, hence in the determination of social classes, it is also the case that (a) political and ideological relations are co-constitutive of social classes; (b) these latter relations have their base in other (noneconomic) spheres of the social formation (in political and civil/cultural realms); (c) these other realms have their own relatively autonomous structural and dynamic principles which constitute them; therefore (d) they may, at a specific historical conjuncture, function as more or less (relatively) autonomous dimensions. It is under these conditions that there can be fractions, strata, and social categories assuming various positions conditioned principally by political and ideological relations and orientations.

Even though Marx was not concerned about racial/ethnic oppression when he elaborated his critique of capitalism, still, a critical theory of society that claims to provide a global understanding of the American social order must offer a radical account of this form of oppression, and prospects for its elimination, if it is to serve as a guide to emancipatory praxis. We must, then, determine the extent to which it is possible to account for the oppression of racial/ethnic nationalities within the context of class analysis.

On the basis of what has been sketched out above regarding the nature of classes, we can understand racial/ethnic oppression as a set of invidious material practices/relations that have their foundation in ideological and political commitments/relations which play a principle role in the constitution of class fractions, strata, or categories. Such commitments/relations are the value, interest orientations/concrete practices ensemble that we refer to as *racism*, i.e., the complex of invidious, race defined orientation/practices of one racial or ethnic nationality toward another. Moreover, at specific historical conjunctures, these invidious ideological/political commitments/relations may be diffused throughout the whole of society and be taken up by (that is, become constitutive of, which is the same thing) all classes and their fractions, strata, and categories, including those which are the objects of the oppression (as is the case, for example, when blacks define themselves in the invidious terms advanced in their subordination). This is the situation when we have a more or less successful realization of a period referred to by Marx when "The ideas of the ruling class are in every epoch the ruling ideas: i.e., the class which is the ruling *material* force of society, is at the same time its ruling intellectual force."[12] Thus racism against blacks, as an orientation/practices ensemble, is taken up by virtually all persons of European descent, in all sectors of American society, and becomes universalized across class lines. We see this in the history of racism within the working class and within organizations seeking to bring about the revolutionary transformation of multiracial, multiethnic class societies.

Yet the ability to account for the affirmation of racial/ethnic nationalities with Marxian critical social theory is partial and, thereby, dangerous. It is partial in that the theory, as it is grounded in Marx's philosophical anthropology, does not appreciate the (always historically conditioned) absolute and relative *autonomy* of the racial/ethnic *national* character of humans in their particularity.[13] Marx's explicit commitments to "science" (the practice of explicating universal "laws" by way of empirical investigation) and to historical materialism notwithstanding, his critical social theory is grounded in a view of humanity that is achieved by abstracting from empirical, historical particularities. As has been noted, Marx is very much a German philosopher (among other things).[14] He is the heir to a mode of conceptualizing that is particularly characteristic of European thought (though it is not restricted to Western thought): a search for the *essential, determining* feature of any phenomenon in terms of which it is what it is. This feature, as it is constitutive of the object(s) of investigation, is the always present, typifying, class (understood, in this case, typologically), genus, or species-determining, hence *universal* (for *all* humans, say), element. The universal becomes the defining feature; in terms of it one can frame "laws," i.e., either empirically verifiable propositions that must hold true for all the elements of a grouping covered by it, or propositions that are universally and necessarily true by virtue of their having been deduced from more general propositions (laws) that satisfy these conditions.[15] Marx's philosophical anthropology is composed of statements passing as laws that are inductively achieved (we must say if we are to take him at his word in terms of his articulating an empirical *science* of society) as opposed to statements of an idealistic philosophy. It is my contention, however, that the notion of science, which structures Marx's theoretical efforts, is made problematic by two different tendencies: one that values the universal, the necessary, the unchanging—not the particular and changing—as the proper object of a true science, on the one hand; and one that values the historical and changing, on the other. It is his commitment to the former tendency that conditions Marx's early efforts and leads him, by way of abstractions, from contingent particularities (race, ethnicity, etc.) to "reproduction of the means of existence" as the species-distinguishing feature of the human animal.

But there are no such humans as real persons. The category is thus historically empty. *Real* humans exist in the concrete, historical fullness of an ensemble of shared *particularities* (race/ethnicity, sex), which must be appropriated if a theory of a historically concrete society is to be joined with concrete revolutionary praxis. Marx's philosophical anthropology is, in a sense, idealist in much the same fashion as are the notions of others he criticizes (Hegel, the Young Hegelians): it is historically empty. Thus when class analysis is offered as the only appropriate way to understand class-structured social formations, it is no long step to the attempted reduction of other forms of oppression to class exploitation. Race and ethnicity, or sexual identity, then take on secondary importance, at best. The danger, of which there is a long and continuing history of manifestation, is that beyond this secondary, temporary significance they will be thought to have no importance and be cast off as "epiphenomena" of the superstructure. One significant consequence of this orientation has been the disregard of the national integrity of various peoples in the attempt to fashion a liberated, socialist future. A corrective of this tendency requires a reworking of the philosophical anthropology of Marxian critical theory, at the very least.

III. Toward a Revised Critical Theory of Society

Race and ethnicity, constitutive as they are of the *nationality* of groupings of persons, are not secondary, unessential matters. They have both absolute (i.e., in themselves) and relative (i.e., in relation to other racial/ethnic groups) value *to the extent that, and for as long as,* persons comprising the group *take* them to be constitutive of who they are, that is, form a part of their personal and collective identity. A truly empirical science of society must note this as one of the *irreducible* features of its object. Consequently, a process of *impoverishing* abstraction that disregards these basic "social facts" on its way to a conception of the "species being" of humans is seriously deficient. And a revolutionary social praxis, grounded on such a conception, will be guilty of a tyrannical subjugation of the rich, concrete diversity of human social life, as all are regarded only as members of one or the other classes as though this constitutes a full articulation of historical existence. Or, in the face of the facticity of diverse races and nationalities, there emerges the *ad hoc*, tactical, often condescending and paternalistic efforts to deal with them as temporary carry-overs from the bourgeois-capitalist (or even feudal) social formation that will disappear with the transition to socialism-communism.

Both approaches are inadequate and incorrect. They may be (have been) used to justify crimes ranging from genocide to invidious discrimination while masking racism and ethnocentricism—all in the name of the revolutionary transformation of society. Instead, a critical theory of society must be grounded in a philosophical anthropology, *achieved by way of a full appropriation of particularities*, which gives due regard to human diversity as an irreducible facticity to be appreciated. Difference, as well as identity, must be fully embraced. Such a philosophical anthropology would take us beyond the abstract and empty humanitarianism of the old concept of the human and would posit the *necessity* of every people's appropriating the critical tradition, and of making its own revolution, from the context of its own life-world, *providing they wish to do so.*

That has, in fact, been the practice of a number of peoples (African, Chinese, Cuban). But the theory has been slow to catch up with historical developments, particularly in the United States. Often these developments have been perjoratively labeled as "deviations." Seldom has there been a recognition of racial/ethnic national diversities in a way that has resulted in a democratization of the theory, so to speak, and, subsequently, of the praxis it seeks to guide. The evidence of this is the prevailing situation in this country: the absence of any broad-based social movement, guided by revolutionary theory, that is organically, democratically plural where the plurality is composed of different racial, ethnic, and sexual groups. Nor is the situation much better at the level of theory as the "race of class?" question continues to be advanced and debated.

Theory must reflect the reality of the (relative) independence of race and ethnicity as positive determinants of historical human existence, along with other factors. Too many leftists, like so very many liberals, have become entrapped by an extreme reaction to racism that views the correction to racism as involving *no* reference whatsoever to national character. They are, in this respect, no different from confused liberal, bourgeois assimilationists: a society free of racism involves no racial or ethnic distinctions. Some vulgar Marxist, for example, find it hard to understand—and even argue against, other than as a short-term tactic—arrangements in support of racially or ethnically identifiable institutions, neighborhoods, etc., in a socialist-communist society.

A class analysis of American society is necessary if we are to understand the nature and the foundations of some of the constraints upon human freedom in terms of economic exploitation and other forms of oppression. Still, such an analysis is not sufficient. It must be complemented by analyses grounded in an appreciation of the value of racial/ethnic nationality. And praxes, in themselves and in terms of their goals and objectives, must be acts that are structured by an understanding that is the appropriate achievement of both modes of analysis. Only then will some of the necessary conditions exist for the development of a multinational movement, which has as its goal an economically, politically, socially, and culturally democratic social order.

Obviously such an achievement will, in no way, be easy. Nor will working out and having widely accepted a revised critical theory of society. Both efforts are made more difficult by a number of factors tending toward conjuncture: racism and a split labor market; the resurgence of various groups articulating positions of racial and ethnic purity and superiority (the Ku Klux Klan and American Nazi Party, for example); the economic and social consequences of the policies of conservative governments; global strife and political realignment prompted, in significant measure, by the various struggles, in numerous forms and levels of intensity, for national liberation on the part of peoples of color around the world; the increasing frequency and intensity of economic (an other) crises in the world capitalist system, in general, and in the advanced capitalist countries, in particular. The historical conjuncture of these and other tendencies make for a situation of significant complexity and danger. But this situation—and its possible, probable, likely consequences—are not insignificant for a transformative, emancipatory praxis that must come to terms with the problematics of race/ethnicity and class. And the responsibility for this situation must be borne by critical revolutionaries of both European and African descent.

For those of us of African descent who are both leftist and nationalist, the task is large. On both counts we are in the minority, more so in terms of the former than if we were simply nationalists or "race" men/women. And in the present historical moment, the theory and praxes of left-nationalists certainly are not dominant among the various manifestations of African-American politics.[16] Yet, given our commitments to both traditions (Marxism and Black Nationalism), we must successfully carry out analyses of the situation of people of African descent in the U.S. (and elsewhere) wherein we take due account of racism, in its structural/relational, dynamic manifestations, and of class and subclass stratifications, their sources, and their consequences.[17] In spite of the weaknesses of Wilson's *The Declining Significance of Race*, it offers important truths to be dealt with, not the least of which is its focus on the continuing neglect of the black underclass given a distorted concern with racism by many whose thinking is fundamentally shaped by commitments to one half of the false "race or class?" disjunctive, and who, thus, are on the wrong side of the nationalist question. The elimination of racism will not, in and of itself, lead to the eradication of the economic exploitation of people of African descent. Economic exploitation will only be eliminated with the elimination of the social formation that engenders it.

However, success along this line will still leave unanswered the questions regarding the practical living arrangements of the various racial/ethnic nationalities. Not after the revolution, but before, and in the very process of theorizing and realizing an emancipated society, these questions must be addressed. For the answers will in large measure determine how the struggle will be conducted and to what ends. Is the goal an open, democratic, pluralistic society? A federation of semiautonomous republics of nationalities? Or separate sovereign states of nationalities? A serious understanding of the history of the struggles of oppressed racial/ethnic nationalities and of pluralistic societies should lead us to conclude that these are not idle questions, nor matters of "fantasy."[18] The Black Nationalist tradition, with its long history, is still manifested in numerous concrete forms including theoretical refinements and extensions.[19] No effort towards emancipatory social transformation will succeed, ultimately, without incorporating—without reduction of—the nationalist movement. Nor, on the other hand, will nationalists succeed beyond a simple, and by itself deficient, racial/ethnic nationalism without a class analysis unless it is desired that the class divisions, and all of the problems that come with them, are to be reproduced in a nationalist "heaven." The truth, to be socially realized, is to be found elsewhere.

Notes

1. The University of Chicago Press: Chicago, 1978, pp. 1–2.
2. "Racial Domination in Advanced Capitalism: A Theory of Nationalism and Division in the Labor Market,"*Labor Market Segmentation*, Richard C. Edwards et al., eds., (Lexington, Mass.: D. C. Heath, 1975), pp. 173–216.
3. An early manifesto of what becomes a tradition of critique and praxis bearing his name is Marx's letter to Arnold Ruge, "For a Ruthless Criticism of Everything Existing," in *The Marx-Engels Reader*, 2d ed., Robert C. Tucker, ed., (New York: W. W. Norton, 1978), pp. 12–15.
4. *Ibid.*
5. Trent Schroyer, *The Critique of Domination*, (Boston: Beacon Press, 1975), p. 15.
6. Nicos Poulantzas, *Political Power and Social Classes*, Verso Edition, (London: NLB, 1973), pp. 67–8, emphasis in original. The discussion that follows is drawn from this work by Poulantzas and from his *Classes in Contemporary Capitalism*, Verso Edition, (London: NLB, 1975).
7. *Ibid.*, p. 63, emphasis in original.
8. Poulantzas, op. cit., *Classes in Contemporary Capitalism*, pp. 14, 16.
9. *Ibid.*, p. 21.
10. *Ibid.*, pp. 15, 23.
11. *Ibid.*, p. 23.
12. Marx, "The German Ideology," Tucker, *op. cit.,* p. 172.
13. The concept of "nationality" or "national" is used here to refer to groupings of persons based on shared characteristics (race, culture, aspirations, etc.), which they appropriate *self-consciously* as unifying factors in terms of which they come together and seek to perpetuate their existence, and in terms of which they effect liberating social practices.
14. Lezek Kolakowski, *Main Currents of Marxism*, Vol. 1: *The Founders*, (Oxford: Clarendon Press, 1978), p. 1.
15. The distinction between laws arrived at deductively and those achieved inductively is an important one and impacts on the notions of "necessary" and "universal" that are central to the concept of "law," hence is important for an explication of "law" as employed by Marx. However the matter can not be taken up here.
16. "Left-nationalist" is a term for which I am indebted to Manning Marable with whom I shared many hours of intense discussion about Black Nationalism (June 10–11, 1980, New York City). See Manning Marable, "Through the Prism of Race and Class: Modern Black Nationalism in the U.S.," *Socialist Review* (May/June), 1980.

17. See, for example, the discussion of class stratifications among African-Americans, within the context of a class-race analysis, in Abdul Hakimu Ibn Alkalimat and Nelson Johnson, "Toward the Ideological Unity of the African Liberation Support Committee: A Response to Criticisms of the ALSC Statement of Principles adopted at Frogmore, South Carolina, June-July, 1973," Greensboro, North Carolina, February 1–3, 1974.

18. See the critique of late twentieth century Black Nationalism as "fantasy" by Theodore Draper in his *The Rediscovery of Black Nationalism*, (New York: Viking Press, 1970).

19. See John Bracey, *et al.*, eds., *Black Nationalism in America*, (New York: Bobbs-Merrill, 1970); Sterling Stuckey, *The Ideological Origins of Black Nationalism*, (Boston: Beacon Press, 1970); Alphonso Pinkney, *Red, Black, and Green: Black Nationalism in the United States*, (New York: Cambridge University Press, 1976); and Maulana Ron Karenga, "Afro-American Nationalism: Beyond Mystification and Misconception," *Black Books Bulletin*, Vol. 6, No. 1 (Spring 1978), pp. 7–12.

Unfinished Lecture on Liberation–II

Angela Y. Davis

One of the striking paradoxes of the bourgeois ideological tradition resides in an enduring philosophical emphasis on the idea of freedom alongside an equally pervasive failure to acknowledge the denial of freedom to entire categories of real, social human beings. In ancient Greece, whose legacy of democracy inspired some of the great bourgeois thinkers, citizenship in the *polis*, the real exercise of freedom, was not accessible to the majority of people. Women were not allowed to be citizens and slavery was an uncontested institution. While the lofty notions affirming human liberty were being formulated by those who penned the United States Constitution, Afro-Americans lived and labored in chains. Not even the term 'slavery' was allowed to mar the sublime concepts articulated in the Constitution, which euphemistically refers to "persons held to service or labor" as those exceptional human beings who did not merit the rights and guarantees otherwise extended to all.

Are human beings free or are they not? Ought they be free or ought they not be free? The history of Afro-American literature furnishes an illuminating account of the nature of freedom, its extent and limits. Moreover, we should discover in Black literature an important perspective that is missing in so many of the discourses on the theme of freedom in the history of bourgeois philosophy. Afro-American literature incorporates the consciousness of a people who have been continually denied entrance into the real world of freedom, a people whose struggles and aspirations have exposed the inadequacies not only of the practice of freedom, but also of its very theoretical formulation.

The central issue in this article (based on the course entitled "Recurring Philosophical Themes in Black Literature") will be the idea of freedom. Commencing with the *Life and Times of Frederick Douglass*, we will explore the slave's experience of bondage as the basis for a transformation of the principle of freedom into a dynamic, active struggle for liberation. We will then examine the ideas of the great twentieth century Afro-American thinker, W. E. B. DuBois, and will proceed to trace Black ideological development in literature up to the contemporary era. In conclusion, we will compare the writings of a few representative African and Caribbean writers to the works of Afro-Americans. In each instance, the notion of freedom will be the axis around which we will attempt to develop other philosphical concepts such as the meaning of knowledge, the function of morality, and the perception of history peculiar to an oppressed people striving toward the goal of collective liberation.

Before actually approaching the material, we should familiarize ourselves with some of the questons we will pose as we explore the nature of human freedom. First of all, is freedom an essentially subjective experience?; is it essentially objective?; or is it rather a synthesis of both these poles? In other words, should freedom be conceived as an inherent characteristic of the human mind, whose expression is primarily inward? Or is it a goal to be realized through human action in the real, objective world? Freedom of thought? Freedom of action? Freedom as practical realization? Freedom of the individual? Freedom of the collective? Consider, for instance, this aspect of the philosophy of freedom proposed by the French Existentialist, Jean-Paul Sartre. Because it is in the nature of the human being to be 'condemned to freedom,' even those who are held in chains remain essentially free, for they are always at liberty to eliminate their condition of slavery, if only because death is an alternative to captivity. Considering the African's real experience of slavery on this continent, would you attempt to argue that the Black slave was essentially free since even in bondage, a person retains the freedom to choose between captivity and death? Or rather would you detect a basic incompatibility between this notion and the real prerequisites of liberation? Would you agree, in other words, that when the slave opts for death, the resulting elimination of the predicament of slavery also abolishes the fundamental condition of freedom, i.e., the slave's experience of living, human reality. Nat Turner and Denmark Vesey met with death at the conclusion of the slave revolts they so courageously led, but was it death they chose or was it liberation for their people even at the risk of death for themselves as individuals?

The slave who grasps the real significance of freedom understands that it does not ultimately entail the ability to choose death over life as a slave, but rather the ability to strive toward the abolition of the master-slave relationship itself.

The first part of the *Life and Times of Frederick Douglass*, which is entitled "Life of a Slave," traces both a material and philosophical journey from slavery to freedom. The point of departure is occasioned by the following question posed by Frederick Douglass the child: "Why am I a slave? Why are some people slaves and others masters?" Douglass, of course, has rejected the usual religious explanations based on the belief that God's will was responsible for Black people being condemned to lives of bondage and for the slave-masters being bearers of white skin. As the question itself implies, Douglass has also challenged the credibility of all other apologetic theories regarding slavery in the history of Western ideas.

The slave is a human being whom another has absolutely denied the right to express his or her freedom. But is not freedom a property that belongs to the very essence of the human being? Either the slave is not a human being or else the very existence of the slave is itself a contradiction. Of course, the prevailing racist ideology, which defined people of African descent as subhuman, was simply a distortion within the realm of ideas based on real and systematic efforts to deny Black people their rightful status as human beings. In order to perpetuate the institution of slavery, Africans were forcibly compelled to live and labor under conditions hardly fit for animals. The slaveholder class was determined to fashion Black people in the image of those

131

subhumans described in the ideology justifyng the oppression meted out to slaves. In this sense, it was the slave-holder whose consciousness was a slave to the socio-economic system that relegated to him the role of oppressor. The master's notion of freedom, in fact, involved this capacity to control the lives of others—the master felt himself free at the expense of the freedom of another. As the conscious slave certainly realized, this merely abstract freedom to suppress the lives of others rendered the master a slave of his own misconceptions, his own misdeeds, his own brutality and infliction of oppression.

If the slave-holder was entrapped within a vicious circle, there was a potential exit gate for the slave: the slave could opt for active resistance. These are the reflections Frederick Douglass offers on his childhood experience of observing a slave resist a flogging: "That slave who had the courage to stand up for himself against the overseer, although he might have many hard stripes at first, became while legally a slave virtually a free man. 'You can shoot me,' said a slave to Rigby Hopkins, 'but you can't whip me,' and the result was he was neither whipped nor shot." In this posture of resistance, the rudiments of freedom were already present. The stance of self-defense signified far more than a simple refusal to submit to a flogging, for it was also an implicit rejection of the entire institution of slavery, its standards, its morality. It was a microcosmic effort toward liberation.

The slave could thus become conscious of the fact that freedom is not a static quality, a given, but rather is the goal of an active process, something to be fought for, something to be gained in and through the process of struggle. The slave-master, on the other hand, experienced what he defined as his freedom as an inalienable fact: he could hardly become aware that he, too, had been enslaved by the system over which he appeared to rule.

To return to a question we posed earlier—is it possible for a human being to be free within the limits of slavery—we can argue that the path toward freedom can only be envisioned by the slave when the chains, the lash, and the whipping post of slavery are actively challenged. The first phase of liberation must thus involve a rejection of the material conditions and ideological images contrived in the interests of the slave-holder class. The slave must reject his/her existence as a slave. In the words of Frederick Douglass, "(n)ature never intended that men and women should be either slaves or slaveholders, and nothing but rigid training long persisted in, can perfect the character of the one or the other." Slavery is an alienation from the human condition, a violation of humanity that distorts both parties, but that fundamentally alienates the slave from the freedom to which every human being ought to have a right. This alienation can remain unacknowledged and unchallenged, or it can be recognized in such a way as to provide a theoretical impetus for a practical thrust in the direction of freedom.

The most extreme form of human alienation is the reduction of a productive and thinking human being to the status of property: "Personality swallowed up in the sordid idea of property! Manhood lost in chattelhood! . . . Our destiny was to be *fixed for life*, and we had no more voice in the decision of the question than the oxen and cows that stood chewing at the haymow." "The slave was a fixture," Frederick Douglass compellingly argued. "He had no choice, no goal, but was pegged down to one single spot, and must take root there or nowhere." The slave exercised no control whatsoever over the external circumstances of his/her life. On one day, a woman might be living and working among her children, their father, her relatives, and friends. The very next day she might be headed for a destination miles and miles away, journey far beyond the possibility of ever again encountering those with whom she had enjoyed intimate contacts for years. For the slave, "(h)is going out into the world was like a living man going into the tomb, who, with open eyes, sees himself buried out of sight and hearing of wife, children, and friends of kindred tie." Describing a related experience, Frederick Douglass presents a moving account of his grandmother's last days. Having faithfully served her master from his birth to his death, having borne children and grandchildren for him, she is disdainfully dismissed by her original master's grandson. This old woman is banished from the plantation and sent into the woods to die a horrible solitary death.

Although unwittingly, Frederick Douglass' owner reveals a way for the young boy to become cognizant of his alienation as a slave. "If you give a nigger an inch he will take an ell. Learning will spoil the best nigger in the world. If he learns to read the Bible it will forever unfit him to be a slave. He should know nothing but the will of his master and learn to obey it." In other words, as long as the slave accepts the master's will as the absolute authority over his/her life, the alienation is absolute. With no effective will of one's own, with no realizable desires of one's own, the slave must seek the essence of his/her being in the will of the master. What does this mean? In an important sense, it is the slave's consent that permits the master to perpetuate the condition of slavery—not, of course, free consent, but rather consent based on brutality and force.

Having overheard his master's observations on the revolutionary potential of knowledge, Frederick Douglass reflects: " 'Very well,' thought I, 'Knowledge unfits a child to be a slave.' I instinctively assented to the proposition, and from that moment I understood the direct pathway from slavery to freedom." Looking closely at these words, we detect once again the theme of resistance. Douglass' first enlightening experience regarding the possibility of a slave asserting his yearning for freedom involved resistance to a flogging. He later discovers resistance in the form of education, resistance of the mind, a refusal to accept the will of the slave-master, a determination to seek an independent means of judging the world around him.

As the slave who challenged his master to whip him and threatened to physically resist his aggressor's violent lashes, Frederick Douglass appropriates his master's insight—i.e., learning unfits a person to be a slave—and vows to use it against his oppressor. Resistance, rejection, physical and mental, are fundamental moments of the journey toward freedom. In the beginning, however, it is inevitable that knowledge, as a process leading to a more profound comprehension of the meaning of slavery, results in despair. "When I was about thirteen years old, and had succeeded in learning to read, every increase of knowledge, especially anything respecting the free states, was an additional weight to the most intolerable burden of my thought—'I am a slave for life.' To my bondage I could see no end. It was a terrible reality, and I shall never be able to tell how sadly that thought chafed my young spirit."

The child's despair must give way to an emerging consciousness of his alienated existence. He begins to seek freedom as the negation of his concrete condition—in fact, it seems to be present as the negation of the very air he breathes. "Liberty, as the inestimable birthright of every man, converted every object into an asserter of this right. I heard it in every sound, and saw it in every object. It was ever present to torment me with a sense of my wretchedness, the more horrible and desolate was my condition. I saw nothing without seeing it and I heard nothing without hearing it. I do not exaggerate when I say that it looked at me in every star, smiled in every calm, breathed in every wind and moved in every storm."

Frederick Douglass has arrived at a consciousness of his predicament as a slave. That consciousness at the same time is a rejection of his predicament. But enlightenment does not result in *real* freedom, or even a mental state of pleasure. Referring to his mistress, Douglass says: "She aimed to keep me ignorant, and I resolved to *know,* although knowledge only increased my misery." Moreover, the slave has not simply rejected his individual condition and his misery does not simply result from his consciousness of his alienation as an individual. "It was *slavery* and not its mere *incidents* that I hated." True consciousness involves a rejection of the institution itself and all of the institution's accompaniments.

As he moves down the pathway from slavery to freedom, Frederick Douglass experiences religion as a reinforcement and justification of his yearning for liberation. Out of the doctrines of Christianity, he deduces the equality of all human beings before God. If this is true, he infers, then slavemasters are defying God's will and should consequently suffer God's wrath. Freedom, liberation, the abolition of slavery, the elimination of human alienation—all these visions are given a metaphysical foundation. A supernatural being wills the abolition of slavery and Frederick Douglass, slave and believer, must execute God's will by striving toward the aim of liberation. Of course, Douglass was not alone in his efforts to forge a theology of liberation on the basis of the Christian doctrine. Nat Turner's rebellion and John Brown's attack were among the innumerable anti-slavery actions directly inspired by Christianity.

Christianity, when it was offered to the masses of slaves, was originally destined to serve precisely the opposite purpose. Religion was to furnish a metaphysical justification not for freedom, but rather for the institution of slavery itself.

One of the most widely quoted, but least understood passages in the writings of Karl Marx concerns religion as the 'opium of the people.' This is generally assumed to simply mean that the function of religion is to counsel acquiescence toward worldly oppression and to redirect hopes and yearnings of oppressed people into the supernatural realm. A little suffering during a person's lifetime in the real world is entirely insignificant in comparison to an eternity of bliss. But what is the larger context of Marx's assertion, which is contained in the opening paragraphs of his *Introduction to a Critique of Hegel's Philosophy of Right? "Religious* suffering is at the same time an *expression* of real suffering and a *protest* against real suffering. Religion is the sigh of the oppressed creature, the sentiment of a heartless world, and the soul of soulless conditions. It is the *opium* of the people. The abolition of religion as the *illusory* happiness of men, is a demand for their *real* happiness. The call to abandon their illusions about their condition is a *call to abandon a condition which requires illusions."* In other words, it is true indeed that real wants, real needs, and real desires can be transformed into impotent wish-dreams via the process of religion, especially if things appear to be utterly hopeless in this world. But it is also true that these dreams can revert to their original state—as real wishes, real needs to change the existing social reality. It is possible to redirect these wish-dreams to the here and now. Frederick Douglass attempted to redirect aspirations that were expressed within a religious context and, like Nat Turner and countless others, placed them within the framework of the real world. Religion can play a potentially revolutionary role since—for oppressed people, at least—its very nature is to satisfy urgent needs grounded in the real, social world.

In his work, *The Peculiar Institution,* Kenneth Stampp extensively discusses the role of religion as a vehicle of appeasement for Black people, as a means of suppressing potential revolt. In the beginning, he observes, Africans were not converted to Christianity, because this might have established for the slaves a solid argument for freedom. However, the slave-holding colonies eventually began to pass legislation to the effect that Black Christians were not to become free simply by virtue of their baptism. Stampp formulates the reasons why slaves could be allowed to enter the sacred doors of Christianity: "Through religious instruction, the bondman learned that slavery had divine sanction, that insolence was as much an offense against God as against the temporal master. They received the Biblical command that servants should obey their masters and they heard of the punishments awaiting the disobedient slave in the hereafter. They heard, too, that eternal salvation would be their reward for faithful service and that on the day of judgment God would deal impartially with the poor and the rich, the black man and the white."

Thus those passages in the Bible emphasizing obedience, humility, pacifism, patience, were presented to the slave as the essence of Christianity. On the other hand, those passages that emphasized equality, freedom, and happiness as attributes of this world as well as the next—those that Frederick

Douglass discovered after teaching himself the illegal activity of reading—were eliminated from the official sermons destined to be heard by slaves. Thus a censored version of Christianity was developed especially for the slaves and one who emulated the slave-master's piety would never strike a white man and would believe that his master was always right even though the oppressor might violate all human standards of morality. Yet there is no lack of evidence that new criteria for religious piety were developed within the slave community: the militant posture of a Frederick Douglass, a Harriet Tubman, a Gabriel Prosser, and a Nat Turner, and the fact that the Christian spirituals created and sung by the masses of slaves were also powerful songs of freedom demonstrate the extent to which Christianity could be rescued from the ideological context forged by the slaveholders and imbued with a revolutionary content of liberation.

Frederick Douglass' response to Nat Turner's revolt is revealing: "The insurrection of Nat Turner had been quelled, but the alarm and terror which it occasioned had not subsided. The cholera was then on its way to this country, and I remember thinking that God was angry with the white people because of their slaveholding wickedness, and therefore his judgments were abroad in the land. Of course it was impossible for me not to hope much for the abolition movement when I saw it supported by the Almighty, and armed with death."

Note on the Author

This article is based on the initial lecture given by Angela Y. Davis in her first course, "Recurring Philosophical Themes in Black Literature", Fall 1969, at the University of Los Angeles, Department of Philosophy. The lecture was printed and distributed by the Angela Y. Davis Defense Committee under the title "Unfinished Lectures on Liberation", and subsequently distributed by the Department of Philosophy, Morgan State University. This article is a revision of that initial plunge into the doing of philosophy and forms the second installment in an on-going analysis. A. Y. Davis teaches philosophy at San Francisco State University, Ethnic Studies Department and recently authored *Women, Race & Class*, 1981.

VI

Cornelius Lacy Golightly
1917–1976
c. 1972

138

B. Ideal Theory

Ethics and Moral Activism
[1972]

Cornelius L. Golightly

In a 1959 essay written in honor of the Dewey Centennial Charles L. Stevenson stated:

> Since the second World War we have had much work on meta-ethics; but we have had, quite regrettably in my opinion, very little work by philosophers that resembles work within ethics proper. Perhaps that is because on these relatively specific topics, one so *obviously* [Stevenson's italics] has to know so much about cause and effect relationships. Most philosophers still like to feel that they have a special subject matter, well insulated from anything that the social scientists, and scientists in general, have to tell them. That is not healthy for philosophy; and it is all to likely to lead to an ethics that continues, as of old, to plead for its ultimates—the fact that one is totally ineffectual being decently concealed by an impressive terminology. Let us hope that Dewey's influence will help to counteract this. . . . And if we may hope that Dewey's work will eventually take its established place in the ethical tradition, we may also hope, and with confidence, that ethics will eventually cease to be confined to the classroom and the library and will take on an active role in guiding our practical life.[1]

These remarks were made on a ceremonial occasion and it is understood that the language is partly ceremonial. Any polite philosopher, whatever his persuasion, might be expected to make similar statements at a commemorative celebration in honor of a philosopher who was deeply involved in public affairs. Charles L. Stevenson's statement was chosen, however, both because of his status as an eminent metaethical philosopher and because he has always insisted that the ultimate purpose of metaethics is that its results be applied to practical moral situations. Indeed, it seems clear that the most abstract and detached professional moral philosophers have always insisted that, while philosophical ethics may be done for its own sake, the ultimate test of the soundness of any ethical theory is its applicability to practical moral situations.

In the decade of the sixties moral philosophers increasingly became concerned with taking an active role in practical affairs. Some of this was the result of prodding from the countercultures—the youth rebellions, Black nationalism, and the Third World politics. Also, the exacerbation of our perennial domestic problems plus the strain of the unpopular Vietnam war produced university crises that reached even the most detached philosophy departments. Philosophers joined other academics in the movement of universities and their knowledge into the market place.

Philosophical moral activism and the offering of moral advice for the guidance of practical life raises a family of vexing problems. Some of these are alluded to in the quotation from Stevenson. Another sort involves the problem of authority and value. In what way or ways is ethics an authority on or for the values of practical life? The problem is crucial for an understanding of the difference between philosophical moral activism which Stevenson is endorsing and citizen moral activism which may be engaged in by both philosophers and nonphilosophers alike. The difference between the role of the scholar as scholar-participant in practical affairs versus the role of the scholar as citizen-participant in practical affairs is one facet of the current angry debates about the politicizing of knowledge and the university.

A simple heuristic device to keep the problem in clear perspective is to follow Stevenson's lead and speak of ethics rather than individuals taking an active role in guiding practical life. This is cumbersome, for we know that ethics as a discipline exists only in activities, utterances, and writings of individuals. Still the device will enable us to remember that when the term moral philosopher is used in the present discussion we mean that we are concerned with his status as an authority in the field of ethics, not that of citizen. Ethics and ethical philosopher, moral philosophy and moral philosopher are equally synonymous as we shall use them. We are concerned primarily with the problem of the moral philosopher *qua* moral philosopher who seeks to guide practical life. Philosophical moral activism is clearly distinct from citizen activism by philosophers. Both are desirable but they should not be confused. Ethics, although willing, cannot easily "take an active role in guiding our practical life." Meaningful and effective participation, however, is not impossible if moral philosophy recognizes the nature and limits of its authority.

Authority, Knowledge, and Value

If ethics as an intellectual discipline takes an effective role in guiding our practical life it seems that it can do so only on the basis of the authority derived from its superior knowledge about value. Thus, of the many meanings of authority, three related meanings are applicable to ethics in the role of moral activism. First, ethics must be established as an expert on or having superior knowledge about value. In the sense of this meaning ethics is an authority on value. A second applicable meaning, related also to expert information, is that of authority as an accepted source of advice on value. The third pertinent meaning of authority is the power to influence or persuade because of expert knowledge about value. The first meaning of authority, that is, knowledge about value, is consistent with neutrality about practical affairs. The second casts ethics in the role of reactor rather than actor. The third seems to suggest a kind of deliberate moral activism. We shall be concerned with the role of ethics in each of these three modes.

In neither of these three meanings of authority is ethics politicized. The authority of ethics as knowledge about value does not imply authoritarian ethics. "In authoritarian ethics," as Erich Fromm is quoted in the American Heritage Dictionary of the English Language, "an authority states what is good for man." Authority for ethics, which we shall discuss later, is clearly distinct from the authority on ethics which we are discussing. If knowledge is politicized, that is, if inquiry is not free but subject to the command of the state, then "knowledge" on value could become authority for value. Blatant examples based on historical experience would be state declarations that Aryan knowledge is superior to Jewish knowledge or that Soviet knowledge is better than non-Soviet knowledge. Also, it must be recognized that if knowledge is subverted to ideology then advice is corrupt and coercive; and if rational argument is permitted to degenerate into propaganda, then persuasion is politicized. These possible dangers are sufficient to cause some moral philosophers to abjure philosophical moral activism entirely. Our only answer to this difficulty is to remember that bias and subjectivity, both conscious and unconscious, can infect all intellectual inquiry whether pure or applied. Further, experience proves that the motivation for free and untrammeled inquiry is sufficiently strong to make an objective body of knowledge possible. The motivation for objectivity is in a sense forced upon inquiry because knowledge consists of claims about what is real. What is false simply cannot be made true either by state decree or wishful thinking. If it is correct that authority is never *sui generis* but derivative always from some source, then the authority of simple truth as knowledge about reality is conferred by reality. The external world of value is the final source of the authority of ethics as knowledge about value.

Ethics As Knowledge About Value

Ethics as a discipline, that is, a field of intellectual inquiry, is concerned with knowledge about value. There has been much discussion about the distinction between knowledge and valuation or fact and value. By contrast there has been insufficient attention to the question of the nature of knowledge about value. By habit, we divide knowledge about ethics into three traditional branches: descriptive, normative, and analytical or metaethical. Descriptive ethics is acknowledged to be a field of social science. Normative ethics and analytical ethics, however, are felt to be the special subject matter of philosophers, "well insulated from anything that the social scientists, and scientists in general, have to tell them." As Stevenson has said, "That is not healthy for philosophy."

Since we are considering ethics as a field of intellectual inquiry about values I propose that in considering ethics as an authority on value the distinction between descriptive ethics on the one hand, and normative and analytical ethics on the other, should be blurred deliberately. It should be clear at the outset that we are not at the moment seeking to blur the distinction between fact and value but rather to minimize traditional distinctions between facts about value. Knowledge about value can be conceived as unified. In this sense knowledge claims about value, whether made by scientists or philosophers, have the same generic status of synthetic assertions. Because they are about practical experience, the knowledge claims of normative ethics and analytical ethics have equal right with descriptive ethics to be called either true or false.

There is, unfortunately, an ambiguity in the meaning of normative ethics for the term is applied to two distinct types of activity. One activity is the making and justification of particular (and general) moral judgments; the other is the activity of dealing with general questions about what is right or good and the development of the general outlines of a normative theory which would serve as an aid to making particular (and general) moral judgments. The first activity is essentially a type of verbal moral behavior. As such it is part of the data of descriptive ethics, analytical ethics and normative ethics when normative ethics means the second activity. It is normative ethics in the second sense that I suggest should be merged with analytical ethics. Having already blurred the distinction between descriptive ethics and both analytical ethics and normative ethics we thus would have a unified discipline concerned with knowledge about ethics. Moral philosophy thus loses its present external insularity from social science and its internal insularity from fellow philosophers who are equally concerned with developing a body of knowledge about ethics.

We are not denying that the distinctions between the three branches of ethics are logically distinct but rather asserting that all consist of synthetic knowledge claims about ethics. What is needed presently if there is to be any generally accepted authoritative knowledge about ethics is the unification of the knowledge of moral philosophy into a coherent whole. In one sense this is neither a novel nor a radical point of view. It is a return to the earlier pre-specialization way of doing ethics that has not been abandoned by some philosophers. William K. Frankena adopts a similar point of view but possibly not for our explicit reason of trying to unify the consensus of beliefs about value. Frankena, after describing descriptive ethics, metaethics and normative ethics writes:

> Many recent moral philosophers limit ethics or moral philosophy to ['analytical,' 'critical,' or 'meta-ethical' thinking], excluding from it all questions of psychology and empirical science and also all normative questions about what is good or right. In this book, however, we shall take the more traditional view of our subject. We shall take ethics to include meta-ethics as just described, but as also including normative ethics of the second kind, though only when this deals with general quetions about what is good or right and not when it tries to solve particular prolems as Socrates was mainly doing in the *Crito*. In fact, we shall take ethics to be primarily concerned with providing the general outlines of a normative theory to help us in answering problems about what is right or ought to be done, and as being interested in meta-ethical questions mainly because it seems necessary to answer such questions before one can be entirely satisfied with one's normative

theory (although ethics is also interested in meta-ethical questions for their own sakes). However, since certain psychological and anthropological theories are considered to have a bearing on the answers to normative and meta-ethical questions, as we shall see in discussing egoism, hedonism, and relativism, we shall also include descriptive or empirical thinking of the first kind.[2]

Despite the similarity of Frankena's approach (which is the same as that of many technical moral philosophers) to our proposal, there is a fundamental difference in what we have been suggesting. Moral philosophers still work as individuals in what is traditionally conceived as the insular philosophical field of inquiry about ethics. Our proposal is not that philosophical ethics simply use the data of descriptive ethics but that there be unification of all intellectual inquiry about ethics into a single field of synthetic inquiry. I refrain from using the terms "scientific ethics" or "empirical ethics" partly because they have at times been used by naturalistic and pragmatic moral philosophers to describe their findings in ethics and to blur the distinction between what is fact and what is value. That question is not at issue here. I also do not use the term "scientific ethics" because the term "scientific" always has the connotation of the precision that is derived from the use of the scientific method. What I am advocating is in the spirit of Aristotle's advice in the *Nicomachean Ethics*:

> We must be content, then, in speaking of such subjects and with such premises to indicate the truth roughly and in outline, and . . . to look for precision in each class of things just so far as the nature of the subject permits.[3]

The Unificaton of Ethical Inquiry

Although, following Aristotle, we have just entered a disclaimer for a scientific ethics, Thomas S. Kuhn's discussion of the role of the paradigm in the natural sciences is instructive. Trained in theoretical physics and gravitating toward the history of science, Kuhn spent a year at the Center for Advanced Studies in the Behavioral Sciences. Of this experience he writes:

> . . . spending the year in a community composed predominantly of social scientists confronted me with unanticipated problems about the differences between such communities and those of the natural scientists among whom I had been trained. Particularly, I was struck by the number and extent of the overt disagreements between social scientists about the nature of legitimate scientific problems and methods. Both history and acquaintance made me doubt that practitioners of the natural sciences possess firmer or more permanent answers to such questions than their colleagues in social science. Yet, somehow, the practice of astronomy, physics, chemistry, or biology normally fails to evoke the controversies over fundamentals that today often seem endemic among, say, psychologists or sociologists. Attempting to discover the source of that difference led me to recognize the role of what I have since called "paradigms." These I take to be universally recognized scientific achievements that for a time provide model problems and solutions to a community of practitioners.[4]

There are, of course, paradigms in the social sciences and in philosophy if the term is applied to communities that are considerably less than global in size. For the moment, let us assume that any valid theory about articulating concepts and evaluating evidence in synthetic knowledge as we have used the term is necessarily continuous with theories of the natural sciences. Kuhn's description of the transition from the preparadigm to the postparadigm period in the development of a scientific field thus seems applicable to some obvious transitions in the field of moral philosophy. Before a transition occurs, "a number of schools compete for the domination of a given field. Afterward, in the wake of some notable scientific achievement, the number of schools is greatly reduced, ordinarily to one, and a more efficient mode of scientific practice begins. The latter is generally esoteric and oriented to puzzle-solving, as the work of a group can be only when its members take the foundations of their field for granted."[5] In the social sciences and moral philosophy, of course, the competing schools are rarely, if ever, reduced to one. However, twentieth-century moral philosophy clearly has been dominated successively by three paradigms although the preparadigm modes of thought continue in the lingering adherents to the earlier schools. I speak, of course, of intuitionism or nonnaturalism, naturalism, and emotivism or noncognitivism.

Emotivism as a metaethical theory has dominated moral philosophy for at least three decades. The paradigm or "disciplinary matrix" of emotivism as stated (but not necessarily originated) by A. J. Ayer in 1936 was dramatically revolutionary and readily understood. Ethical statements are not about either natural nor nonnatural properties, are neither true nor false, and their function is not to define nor describe but to express attitudes of the speaker and to arouse feelings and stimulate action in auditors.[6]

The emotivist paradigm provided a foundation for the "generally esoteric" and "normal puzzle-solving research" (Kuhn's terms are not pejorative) that has characterized the notable revisionist achievements of Charles L. Stevenson in America and the so-called Oxford philosophers of England and their followers. The development and maturation of this paradigm by its community of practitioners has had a salutary effect upon moral philosophy as a whole. At the very least it seems to have developed a consensus that feeling and emotion as well as knowledge and belief are important elements in our moral behavior. Thus moral philosophy turned again toward the descriptive ethics of social science but in a way that was complementary rather than contradictory to the prevailing naturalism of, say, John Dewey and his followers.

It is obvious that the emotivist theory makes both factual and logical claims. The purely logical claim is that exclamations and commands are neither truth nor false. The factual claim is that moral utterances even when stated as prima facie propositions are forms of emotional rather than cognitive behavior. Elsewhere we have suggested how a comprehensive, vigorous, and sound theoretical system covering verbal and nonverbal behavior in cognitive, cathectic, and evaluative modes can help resolve this complex question.[7] What seems necessary if progress in moral philosophy is to continue is a new paradigm, disciplinary matrix, or set of examplars that would unify the three branches of descriptive, normative, and analytical ethics into a single conceptual system.

Authority for Value

The authority for value, that is, authority as a source of value, is always derived from the group or community as a whole. Authority as a source for value is the indispensable framework of human association for it organizes the values of the community into the archetypal hierarchy of prescriptions, permissions, and prohibitions.

The most important values of a group are interpreted for action as prescriptions and prohibitions. Roughly these obligations are what ethical philosophers call "right" or moral values. Again, roughly, the permissions of a society or group are its nonmoral values or "good." The authority for both right and good comes from the community. What the society seriously considers obligatory or right eventually becomes a matter of law. Law is simply a declaration that the power of the community will be committed to enforce certain values.

The nature of authority for value is essentially a problem in descriptive ethics. Because we have been insisting on the unification of knowledge about ethics it will be helpful to use here the descriptive ethics of Dewitt H. Parker, a moral philosopher who perceived that "morality is indissolubly connected with every branch of human activity" and that "the study of ethics rests on the study of values." In the following passage it seems clear that what Parker calls "duty, law, convention, command or an equivalent" is what we have described as authority for value.

> In every ethical situation four or five factors may be distinguished:
> (1) duty, law, convention, command or an equivalent; (2) a person or
> persons who will enforce duty, if necessary; (3) a person subject to duty;
> and (4) finally, an organized group to which all persons concerned in
> the situation belong, and from which, in the last analysis, all duties and
> commands issue. Certain variations in this structure are possible
> without affecting its essential character. For example, it may happen in
> a given case that the entire community will be law enforcer as well as
> law giver, as in loosely organized frontier communities; or it may
> happen, as in fact is usually the case with civilized and highly organized
> barbarous communities, that the laws are given by a few, or even by
> one, distinguished individual—priest, king, or legislator—who speak in
> the name of the group. So long as it is recognized that such persons do
> represent the group, it may be found convenient to admit them as a
> fifth distinct item in the ethical situation. Again, it may happen that
> this fifth class is identical with the person or persons in the second
> category, as in the family; yet the two functions, of law giver and law
> enforcer, are obviously separate.[8]

Authority on Value and Moral Activism

Ethics as a discipline concerned with knowledge about value obviously is neither law giver nor law enforcer. How, then, can ethics "take on an active role in guiding our practical life" without becoming politicized? There appear to be several operationally definable roles in which ethics *qua* ethics can legitimately be involved in moral activism. First, the data of ethics as fruits of inquiry can be made available to the community for the community's use in developing its prescriptions, permissions and prohibitions. Applied ethics in this sense consists of the cognitive content of the comprehensive body of ethical theory being focussed upon the practical problems of social and political reform. However, action must be limited to consultation and recommendations that are open-ended because knowlege itself is open-ended. In this limited fashion it seems permissible for a professional body of moral philosophers to take the initiative in focussing public attention to the applicability of moral theory to moral action. However, ethics *qua* ethics, even when applied does not make specific value judgments. Only citizens *qua* citizens legitimately can do that.

Another mode of moral activism is indirect but probably more effective. Moral philosophy, for the sake of clarity and convenience, habitually uses simple and perhaps trivial moral acts for detailed metaethical analysis. We suggest that moral philosophy deliberately choose some of the complex social issues for expert clarification. Increasingly this is being done but it is still the exception rather than the rule.

In the same vein, moral philosophy has been involved too much with the moral judgments of the individual and the moral disagreements between individuals. This procedure is applicable to homogeneous communities but is fairly arid for the social problems of a society with a variety of countercultures. Today the most pressing "disagreements in attitude" are not between individuals but between the dominant culture and its subcultures, or between subculture and subculture. The cry for "relevance" that comes from the youth rebellion, Black nationalism, and the Third World is basically a plea that moral philosophy examine their objections to, or disagreements in attidude with, the authority of the dominant group. The problems of group conflict are difficult because they involve specific moral topics. As Stevenson observed about such topics, "one so *obviously* has to know so much about cause-and-effect relationships." Nevertheless, if ethics hopes to be accepted as an authority on value its cognitive content must be applicable to the first-order value problems of the community. It should be clear from our discussion that although moral philosophy may use these concrete problems for discussion it does not pronounce particular moral judgments on them.

Our third mode of moral activism focuses upon the moral philosopher as an active participant in practical affairs. The moral philosopher as an authority on value uses his expert knowledge about value to influence the community's choice of values. This is nothing more than citizen activism by a citizen who is well informed. Knowledgeable moralists, like knowledgeable ecologists and experts in other fields, can be good citizens. Yet there remains a difference between a man and his knowledge that the public recognizes. The authority of knowledge is both logically and empirically separable from the persuasive power of men as citizens.

Moral activism forces the testing of the cognitive content of moral philosophy in the demanding laboratory of practical human experience. The danger that a particular moral theory may prove to be unsound is counterbalanced by the possibility it may prove to be sound and thus possibly contribute to the public good. Meaningful inquiry about human affairs moves in a circular process from knowledge claims to practical testing and back again to a refinement of the knowledge claims. Moral activism thus contributes to the development of a better ethics as knowledge about value.

Cornelius L. Golightly
Wayne State University

Notes

1. Charles L. Stevenson, *Facts and Values: Studies in Ethical Analysis* (New Haven and London: Yale University Press, 1963), pp. 114–116.
2. William K. Frankena, *Ethics* (Englewood Cliffs, N.J.: Prentice Hall, Inc., 1963), pp. 4–5.
3. Aristotle, *Nicomachean Ethics*, Bk. I, Chap. 3, 1094^b, 19–26.
4. Thomas S. Kuhn, *The Structure of Scientific Revolutions*, 2d ed. (Chicago: The University of Chicago Press, 1970), p. vii–viii.
5. *Structure of Scientific Revolutions*, p. 178.
6. A. J. Ayer, *Language, Truth, and Logic* (London: Victor Gollancz, 1936).
7. Cornelius L. Golightly, "Value as a Scientific Concept," *The Journal of Philosophy*, 53 (1956), 233–245.
8. Dewitt H. Parker, *Human Values: An Interpretation of Ethics Based on a Study of Human Values* (New York: Harper and Brothers, 1931; republished, Ann Arbor, Michigan: George Wahr, 1944), p. 200.

Note on the Author

Cornelius L. Golightly (1917–1976) was an ethicist of liberal persuasion and was associated with relating ethical theory and educational practice. At his death, he was Associate Dean and Professor of Philosophy at Wayne State University. He also taught at the University of Wisconsin-Milwaukee, Olivet College, and Howard University. His publishing career spanned thirty-two years and was augmented by his reputation as a philosophical activist.

Alain L. Locke's "Values and Imperatives": An Interpretation

Johnny Washington

I

Alain Locke was a trail blazer in interpreting and analyzing Black culture. He was perhaps most recognized for the leadership he provided to the Harlem Renaissance movement and for his *The New Negro* (1925), a collection of the works of the Renaissance authors and artists. His intellectual activities, however, go far beyond the Renaissance. As will be shown, he made original contributions to value theory.

He became associated with Howard University as an instructor in 1912 and taught philosophy there until his retirement in 1953. In addition to *The New Negro* and other books, Locke wrote over two hundred articles on various subjects including art, music, drama, poetry, culture, education, literature, religion, and philosophy. His philosophic interests were in value theory and he was interested in applying value theory in understanding racial and cultural problems. Besides his Ph.D. dissertation, *The Problem of Classification in the Theory of Value* (1918) and "Values and Imperatives" (1935), and a few others, his technical works in philosophy are limited, though important.

His "Values and Imperatives" is especially important because it is a distillation of his dissertation and it moves in the direction of outlining an entirely new theory of values. But this is merely an outline. Locke never worked out a full-blown theory of values; yet, from "Values and Imperatives" we can get a sense of what direction such a theory would have taken had he developed it.

Locke was no shallow thinker. He had the capacity to penetrate to the core of a problem, interweave diverse ideas, and produce original insights. This is evident in his "Values and Imperatives," which I will try to elucidate. In so doing, I will focus on three of the main problems with which the above essay is concerned. Among other things, he wanted to demonstrate: (1) how objective values and their standards are grounded in subjective experience; (2) how value conflicts arise; and (3) how value conflicts can be reduced.

To begin, let us consider briefly the relationship Locke had with the American philosophic tradition of Pragmatism. His philosophy had its origin partly in that tradition, though he did not want to be associated with that tradition and often criticized it. A consideration of such criticisms will throw light on Locke's own position.

James, Royce, Santayana, and Perry were among Locke's Harvard teachers. Locke would use, but not be limited to, various features of James', Royce's, and Santayana's theories. Locke integrated into his theory of values

James' principles of pluralism and value relativism. He insisted, as James had done, that a society organized on the principle of pluralism will allow for the freedom and uniqueness of individuals and groups. Further, as in the view of James, Locke argued that values have their basis in feeling and that their standards are relative to individuals and ethnic groups. Both James and Locke's pluralism-relativism views were formulated in opposition to philosophic absolutism, as expressed in the works of Royce and German idealists. James and Locke held that absolutism was incompatible with the plurality of facts and values. Locke went further to say that traditional absolutism tended to promote the attitude of value bigotry, that is, absolutism, which is usually formulated in a monistic reference-frame, insists on a single value creed.

II

"Values and Imperatives" was written in the conviction that American philosophy and other contemporary philosophical movements have not offered an adequate theory of values. One of Locke's objections to American philosophy was that in its flight from traditional metaphysics it associated itself too closely with experimental science. American philosophy went wrong by accepting science's criterion of value, which stresses experimental results. The founder of Pragmatism, Charles Peirce, had as his goal to transform philosophy into science, or, as the case may be, transform science into philosophy. He was preoccupied with the theory of meaning. The meaning of scientific beliefs, Peirce maintained, could be determined only by subjecting such beliefs to experimental analysis, so as to ascertain what *practical bearing* the objects of the beliefs would have on their environment. The investigation, he maintained, must be conducted in conformity with the methodology of science. In Peirce, we get a philosophy that subscribed to the methodology of science as its epistemological model. Truth and meaning no longer attained by rational speculation, but by observing what practical bearing an idea had on its environment.

Subsequently, James and Dewey gave a different twist to American philosophy by placing a greater emphasis on the pragmatic consequences of the actions of the individual. In their view, ideas, beliefs, and theories were merely tools for actions and were to be tested in and through their consequences. This stress on practice, Locke felt, gave rise to a certain type of absolutism which he calls ". . . a universal fundamentalism of values in action."[1] Thus, the common man, influenced by the virtues of Pragmatism, created absolutist attitudes towards the objects of his practical interests and projects this as ". . . valid for all situations, all men and all times."[2] Locke did not think that American philosophy in its reaction against traditional metaphysics had dispelled absolutes. American philosophy had merely transposed absolutes from the realm of Being, as it were, to the realm of practice, manifested in the actions and attitudes of the intellectual and the common man. The trouble with this

149

type of absolutism, Locke argued, was that it bred value conflicts among individuals and groups and encouraged value bigotry.

Both James and Dewey, and to some degree Royce, in formulating their value theories, gave attention to the emotional side of human experience. And both James and Dewey allowed for what may be called the principle of plurality together with the principle of relativism. In this regard, Locke had no problem with their value theories. What Locke found problematic is that their versions of Pragmatism placed too much emphasis on consequences and not enough emphasis on preferences and attitudes. These, in Locke's view, were just as important as pragmatic consequences. He wrote:

> Human behavior, it is true, is experimental, but it is also selectively preferential, and not always in terms of outer adjustments and concrete results. Value reactions guided by emotional preferences and affinities are as potent in the determination of attitudes [values] as pragmatic consequences are in the determination of actions. In the generic and best sense of the term 'pragmatic,' it is as important to take stock of the one as the other.[3]

Locke held that an effective value theory that pays attention to the emotional side of human experience should be developed along the line of the works of Brentano, ". . . father of modern value-theory."[4] Brentano's value theory, Locke suggests, demonstrated as Locke himself wished to demonstrate, that objective values and their standards were in the subjective realm of the valuing process, not in the realm of rational absolutes.

It would be misleading to say that Locke opposed all forms of absolutism. Clearly he opposed traditional absolutism and the type of absolutism that Pragmatism offered in the name of "the philosophy of common sense" and the practical life. Locke was interested in a theory that allows for what he called functional absolutes—flexible, and yet firm enough to provide objectivity. Such absolutes, as will be seen, rest in feelings and have their origin in the valuing process. In coming to grips with this problem of functional absolutes, Locke suggests that he was offering a solution to the most difficult problem of contemporary philosophy, a problem that most contemporary philosophers side-stepped.[5]

III

Central to Locke's resolution of the subjectivism versus objectivism problem is what he called feeling-reference or form-quality.[6] By this he meant the basic feelings that underlie and create the various types of values and their absolute norms. Often he used the terms "feeling-reference" and "form-quality" interchangeably with "attitudes" and "preferences" and they correspond to his other technical term, "value-mode." By "value-mode" he had in mind what we normally mean in the usage of such terms as the "moral," "religious," or "aesthetical" in making distinctions between different types of value situations. We are accustomed to regard these as objective features of the

150

world. The relationship between attitudes and value-modes consists in this: we evoke or enjoy a certain attitude as we are valuing a given situation. The attitude in question creates, moulds, and shapes the value-mode and its standard, determines the nature, as it were, of the value, and induces us to regard the situation as good, ugly, or holy. Locke identified four such attitudes that constitute the unity and diversity of values: exaltation, tension, acceptance or agreement, and repose or equilibrium. These correspond respectively to different value-modes. Thus, the attitude or feeling of exaltation creates the religious value and its norms; the attitude or feeling of tension creates the moral value and its norms and so on. Stereotypes also play a fundamental role in this connection; they act as filters, as it were, through which a scene is judged, and they play a key role in acting as mind-sets that sustain values. But Locke was careful to point out that values are not fixed. Values shift as our attitudes shift, that is, a given scene may in one instance be regarded as ethical; in which case the feeling of tension would be the determining factor. In another instance, that same scene, perceived by the same individual or another individual, may be regarded as religious, in which case the feeling of exaltation would be the determining factor.[7]

Locke suggested that stereotypes were means by which values are fixed and stabilized.[8] He seems to be using "stereotypes" in ways similar to their use by traditional philosophers such as Peirce, James, and Dewey of the term "habits"—James regarded habits as the "fly-wheel of society." As for the general or universal element of values, Locke held that the categorical imperative, which was universal, was given in the immediate context of the valuing process.

> It [the categorical imperative] supplies the clue to the functional value
> norma,—being felt as good, beautiful, etc.—and we have this event in
> mind when we say that in the feeling-reference to some value-mode,
> some value ultimate becomes the birthmark of the value.[9]

Thus, each basic attitude of exaltation, tension, etc., creates its own categorical imperative.

Kant's categorical imperative which is universal and absolute lay outside human nature; it existed in rationality alone and confronts the human will as a rational necessity. Locke's categorical imperatives lay in human nature, that is, in basic attitudes, and involved a psychological urgency or necessity ". . . to construe the situation as of a particular qualitative form-character."[10] Such then is how we arrive at our absolutes, which are functional and flexible, not eternal principles derived from God, or some other transcendent law-giver.

Locke's conception of values and absolutes closely resembles Santayana's. Santayana explains the ways in which absolutes are created thus:

> Our conscience and taste establish these ideals; to make a judgment is
> virtually to establish an ideal, and all ideals are absolute and eternal for
> the judgment that involves them, because in finding and declaring a

thing good or beautiful, our sentence is categorical, and the standard
evoked by our judgment is for that case intrinsic and ultimate. But at
the next moment, when the mind is on another footing, a new ideal is
evoked, no less absolute for the present judgment than the old ideal was
for the previous one.[11]

Santayana's basic position was that all values spring from the irrational side
of our nature. "If any preference or precept," Santayana maintained, "were
declared to be ultimate and primitive, it would thereby be declared to be irrational, since mediation, inference, and synthesis are the essence of rationality."[12] Similarly, insofar as Locke emphasized the feeling side of values, which
he regarded as primitive, he shared Santayana's view that values are largely
irrational. Locke, however, did not go to the extreme position, which holds
that the rational faculty plays no role in the valuing process.[13]

Locke's other technical notions have to do with two types of polarities:
"the value-polarity" and "the Jungian polarity." To grasp the meanings of
these notions, it will be instructive to see what their functions are and how
they fit into the over-all value scheme. These polarities are subdivisions for
each value-mode—the religious, ethical, logical, and aesthetical. The value
polarity discriminates for each value-mode negative and positive values. Similarly, the Jungian polarity discriminates for each value-mode ". . . an introverted and an extroverted variety of value. . . ."[14] The latter pertains to the
end towards which the value is directed. Introverted value is directed to the
individual where it is individualized. Extroverted value is directed to the community where it is socialized. Consider, for example, the religious value-mode
whose underlying feeling-form is that of exaltation. Where the value is of the
introverted type, the value is centered on the individual, individualized, in which
case the religious value is enjoyed as inner ecstacy. Its positive value is regarded as holiness; its negative value regarded as sin. In this case, the predicates "holy" and "unholy" apply respectively. The religious mystic who
withdraws from the world is representative of the introverted type of value.
On the other hand, where the value is of the extroverted type, it is manifest
in the community, socialized, and shared among members of the community;
in which case the value is enjoyed by the community as religious zeal. Its
positive value is regarded as salvation; its negative value is regarded as dam-
nation. In this case, the predicates "good" and "evil" apply respectively. Locke
claimed that the religious reformer who confronts the world, seeking to transform it, is representative of the extroverted type of value.

Let us take as our next illustration the ethical value-mode. Its underlying feeling is that of tension, which in Locke's view, is felt in situations of
conflicts and choosing. Where the value is the introverted type, individualized,
the tension is felt in the realm of conscience, and the situation is ethical. Its
positive value is that of conscience; its negative value, temptation. By contrast,
in the case of the extroverted value, the tension is felt as a duty, motivating
the individual's or group's outer behavior, and the situation is of the moral
type. Its positive value is that of right; its negative value, crime. To the intro-

vert, the positive and negative predicates "good" and "bad" apply respectively; to the extrovert, the positive and negative predicates "right" and "wrong" apply respectively. And so on for the other two categories, the logical and the aesthetical.

One must keep in mind that the concept feeling or attitude offers the key to understanding Locke's view of values. He held that by focusing on a single factor, namely feeling or attitude, he offered a novel explanation of how value mergings, transfers, and conflicts occur, both in the individual and within the community. Dewey and certain other traditional value theorists attempt to explain value conflicts and convergences by focusing almost exclusively on ends, ideals, and consequences. But such theorists, in Locke's view, have difficulties in explaining why we often shift value predicates from one category to another; why, for example, we might apply the predicate "beautiful" to a logical proof; apply the predicate "noble" to an ethical deed.[15]

Locke writes:

> We are aware of instances, for example, where a sequence of logical reasoning will take on an aesthetic character as a 'beautiful proof' or a 'pretty demonstration,' or where a moral quality or disposition is appraised not as 'good' but as 'noble', or again, where a religious ritual is a mythical 'reality' to the convinced believer but is only an aesthetic, symbolic show to the non-credal spectator.[16]

Locke held that the traditional way of accounting for the use of such predicates assumes that they are being used only metaphorically.[16] But Locke does not accept such an explanation. He thinks that something else is at issue. In fact, he holds that the use of such predicates in these inappropriate ways (that is, inappropriate from the standpoint of traditional theories) is evidence in support of his alternative theory: that attitudes that create values are not fixed, that the value and its predicate vary with attitude. And what may be regarded as an inappropriate predicate is in functional relation and agreement with the attitude or value in question.[17]

IV

I have been concerned mainly with explaining, among other things, the dynamic relations and interconnectedness among values. The analysis has centered primarily on the individual seen in isolation from others. However, as was previously noted, one of Locke's main philosophic interests in "Values and Imperatives" lay in explaining the nature of internal value conflicts that occur within the various value fields—the religious, the ethical, the aesthetical, etc. He devoted attention to these in the latter part of his essay. Here, he also, as one might expect, alludes to the nature of what may be considered "external conflicts," which arise when one group seeks to impose its value creed on others. He considers racial problems as instances of such value conflicts. As Locke puts forth his solution to value conflict, he seems to collapse the distinction between internal and external conflicts.

At the outset, Locke rejects traditional explanations of such conflicts and their resolutions—explanations that usually hinge on the means-ends and the value series analysis. Additionally, in the old way of considering the problem, value conflicts were thought to have sprung from questions of the priority of Beauty, Truth, and Good. But he holds that modern scientific relativism ". . . has at least cooled these erstwhile burning issues and tempered the traditional debate."[18] But in the field of values, in Locke's view, the scientific methodology and outlook has its limitations. What science can do is to teach us that absolutes in the traditional sense of the value Trinity do not exist; that all values are relative; that ". . . values are based not upon priority and precedence, but upon parity and reciprocity."[19] Beyond that, science can do very little in resolving conflicts within the value arena, because the conflicts are rooted in our psychological make-up. Such conflicts are due to the value-polarities mentioned above: ". . . repose and action, integration and conflict, acceptance and projection, as attitudes, create natural antinomies, irresolvable orders of value. . . ."[20] As one might suspect, people such as Peirce and Dewey were more optimistic about the role of science in solving such value conflicts. Locke was not so optimistic. He reminds us that all values, including the absolutes of the value trinity, are largely rationalized projections of our preferences and attitudes. And because these are natural adversaries from which conflicts arise, there is little else science can do.[21]

If we relate this view to the Black experience, a well-known example comes to mind; namely, the historical conflicts that existed between W. E. B. DuBois and Booker T. Washington. Their conflicts came to the fore in questions concerning the education of Black people, which, for the purpose of this discussion, may be subsumed under the rubric of the moral situation. It will be remembered, however, that Washington was one of the most politically visible and active men of both the white and Black races. His philosophy stressed the importance of providing the Black rural masses training in the vocational areas, so that they might obtain the skills needed to make a living. Blacks were asked to postpone their political rights, acquire laboring skills, and accept segregation. DuBois' educational philosophy emphasized educating what he called, the "Black Elite." The Black Elite were to be educated, not so much in vocational skills, but in the humanities, arts and sciences; educated in the areas that develop character and culture. Once educated, the Black Elite, he argued, would in turn provide leadership to the Black masses. Such an educational program, as envisaged by DuBois, would provide Blacks with the tools to enjoy their social and political rights as citizens. DuBois' political philosophy wavered between racial integration and separation. As a scholar, DuBois was somewhat withdrawn from the Black masses. As a social leader and educator, Washington was directly in contact with the Black masses. The former is representative of the introverted type,[22] the latter of the extroverted type. The value orientation of each, if Locke's theory is correct, pulled the Black community into opposite directions. Hence, the conflicts between DuBois and Washington were, by their very nature, irresolvable. At times, both DuBois and Washington acted as though their respective values were absolute mandates issued from God. But in Locke's view, such values are to be understood as being merely preferences and attitudes projected as "absolutes" to which their respective followers expressed loyalty.

Of course, Hegel, Marx, Fanon, and other dialecticians placed a positive value on such conflicts, especially on external conflicts, without which, in their view, there would be no social progress and ultimately no social harmony. Locke was interested in social harmony, but he did not place a great deal of positive value on conflicts. In fact, he held that society should organize itself around certain principles which will allow for the reduction of conflicts. Attention has already been brought to the importance he placed on the principles of pluralism, relativism, and loyalty, which he thought lead to the reduction of conflicts. The first and foremost step that American society must take in the reduction of conflicts is to pay more serious attention to axiology. But he had in mind an axiology that was his own, which recognizes that feelings are the basis of values and recognizes that value ultimates are functional, not eternal, principles. In this regard, and in view of the fact that value conflicts are rooted in psychological make-ups, that is, rooted in the Jungian polarity, there is no way to altogether eliminate such conflicts. What we can do, Locke held, was to find ways to control these ". . . by understanding how and why, to find principles of control from the mechanisms of valuation themselves."[23]

V

Though the various value-modes are inherently incompatible, Locke held that they were also complementary in human experience. Another way to put this is that the various value-groups, including the values of ethnic groups and others, could be made complementary. How? He insisted that individuals and groups must develop an attitude of tolerance for the values of people outside their own value-field; for example, the people in the value-field of, say, religion should be tolerant of people in the value-field of morals, and the other way around. Whites must be tolerant of the cultural values of Blacks, and conversely. This in effect meant being loyal to one's own group values while being open to the values of others outside of one's group. In this context, Locke also evoked the principle of social reciprocity, which he regarded as a key principle required to reduce all types of conflicts, the internal as well as the external. In order to effectively combat value conflicts and to allow for the complementary character of values, he suggested that it is not sufficient to develop a detached attitude towards the values of others. Something more is required; that something more is what he called the principle of social reciprocity. By this he meant that groups must share values; value-groups, cultural-groups, ethnic-groups, and the like must give and receive from each other so that each may enrich the other. In this way, he hoped, the myths of value superiority and the attitudes that promote value-bigotry, value-monopoly, and racism could be dispelled and society could move in the direction of promoting social harmony.

Although Locke indeed believed that the principles of tolerance and social reciprocity, along with certain other principles mentioned above, would lead to the open society where universal harmony prevails, I am not in total agreement with his view. I object to his notion of tolerance. In the first place, it has a negative connotation, suggesting passivity and indifference. As a practical matter, the principle of tolerance might be effective in reducing internal conflicts within the various value-fields. In the field of religion, for example, despite the historical ideological differences, Protestants and Catholics alike in Ireland and elsewhere might come to enjoy a greater degree of unity, if there were an increased recognition among them that each group needs to be tolerant of the values of the other. However, the principle of tolerance, I am led to believe, is less effective at the practical level when extended to the racial situation.

The racial situation in America is a complex one. It involves many factors: economic, social, historical, pride, prejudice, myths, and past and present injustices, among others. What is wrong with Locke's notion of tolerance is that, as it stands, it suggests that the larger society and ethnic minorities relate to one another on a "live-and-let-live" basis—the literal meaning of "tolerance." This "live-and-let-live" philosophy may signal to the larger society and to minorities messages that may forestall social changes, which might ultimately result in a better society. The larger society, which treats Blacks and other minorities unjustly, may come to interprete Locke's "tolerance"—though Locke certainly did not intend this interpretation—to mean that matters will automatically and gradually work themselves out in the best interest of all, only if society adopts a "hands-off" policy in dealing with minorities. Such "hands-off" policy, many people have come to believe, will exonerate the larger society from its past wrong-doings. Similarly, Blacks and other minorities may come to interpret "tolerance" to mean that it is permissible to let the larger society "off the hook" as it were; that Blacks and other minorities need not remind the larger society that they were—and still are—victims, and seek redress.

I think that tolerance and mutual respect among the various ethnic groups in this society can be achieved only when the larger society takes actions to off-set the historical and present injustices Blacks and others have suffered. In this way, the larger society can gain a sense of self-respect and thus be in a position to extend this feeling of respect to others. Such actions required to off-set injustices have to be translated in terms of providing minorities with adequate housing, schooling, employment, and other essentials of life. Blacks and other minorities also have key roles to play before this mutual tolerance and respect can be enjoyed. They have to continue to struggle, so as not to lose the ground that was gained in the Civil Rights movements of the 1960s and early 1970s; and by continuing the struggle Blacks and others may gain new ground, which they deserve, and may achieve a new sense of identity and purpose. These qualities are preconditions for self-respect; and self-respect is a precondition for tolerance, and tolerance like any other worthwhile aim cannot be achieved without rigorous effort—without a struggle, in the words of Hegel.

Moreover, in a capitalistic, pragmatic society such as ours, a society shot through and through with the racial problem of the larger society denying freedom and justice to its minorities, it is not altogether clear that the larger society will readily express the attitude of tolerance towards Blacks and other minorities, if no creative conflicts or struggles are involved. The history of the United States clearly attests to this. Nor is it altogether clear, as Locke seems to suppose, that if the larger society develops an appreciation for the cultural values of minorities and if minorities do the same for the larger society, the attitude of mutual respect among the various groups would automatically follow. Further, I am of the conviction that many of the tensions and conflicts that occur among social groups in this society stem from the economic contradictions that pervade our capitalistic society. That what would move in the direction of reducing conflicts among certain social groups is a reorganization of economic institutions so that people on all levels of society can enjoy its wealth. Economic reciprocity comes before cultural reciprocity, because the former is the basis for the latter.

Locke himself recognized the role that economic conditions play in creating social conflicts. He sees his position as being not far removed from Marxism. He writes:

> This sounds Marxian, and is to an extent. But the curtailing of the struggle over the means and instrumentalities of values will not eliminate our quarrels and conflicts about ends, and long after the possible elimination of the profit motive, our varied imperatives will still persist. Economic classes may be absorbed, but our psychological tribes will not thereby be dissolved.[24]

Though Locke's position seems to border on Marxism, he did not think that the reorganization of economic institutions would make much difference in reducing conflicts among the "psychological tribes." This may in part be true. As he holds, the value-polarities will remain in human nature. Granted that, my position is that if the economic institutions are reorganized in conformity with the ideal of Marxism, this may result in the distribution of economic goods equally among the introverts and the extroverts and other groups, thus creating the conditions where people might come close to realizing the ideal of social harmony.

Notes

1. Alain Locke, "Values and Imperatives," in *American Philosophy Today and Tomorrow,* Sidney Hook and Horace M. Kallen (eds.): (New York: Lee Furman, 1935), p. 314.
2. Ibid., p. 318.
3. Ibid.

4. Ibid.
5. Ibid., p. 319.
6. Ibid., p. 324; here, also, he presents a description of his entire value scheme.
7. Ibid., . 321
8. Ibid.
9. Ibid., p. 320
10. Ibid., p. 322.
11. George Santayana, *The Sense of Beauty: Being the Outline of Aesthetic Theory:* (New York: Dover Publications, Inc., 1955), p. 9.
12. Ibid., p. 14.
13. Locke, "Values and Imperatives," p. 322.
14. Ibid., pp. 322–323.
15. Ibid., p. 325.
16. Ibid.
17. Ibid., pp. 325–326.
18. Ibid., p. 326.
19. Ibid.
20. Ibid.
21. Ibid., p. 327.
22. DuBois' personality is difficult to classify; he was a complex man. Like most scholars, he was withdrawn from the world. Seen in that light, he certainly is of the introverted type; yet, in his political activities at times he exemplifies the qualities of the extrovert. Perhaps it would be safe to say that he occasionally bordered on extroversion.
23. Locke, "Values and Imperatives," p. 328.
24. Ibid., p. 331.

Note on the Author

Johnny Washington is Assistant Professor of Philosophy, Rensselaer Polytechnic Institute, having previously taught at Tuskegee Institute. He is noted for his work in value theory and is currently preparing a book, *Alain Locke and Philosophy: A Quest for Cultural Pluralism.*

Liberalism and Liberation

Berkley B. Eddins
Essie A. Eddins

Liberalism today finds itself in practical and theoretical disarray. Widespread doubts about the efficacy of the liberal approach to human and social problems have their counterpart in—if not causal relation to—uncertainties about the theoretical soundness of liberal social theory. The situation in the United States provides dramatic evidence for this assessment of liberalism's status. The civil rights movement is without direction as it moves into the areas of employment, housing, education, and health care. The "move to the right" in the national temper has called into question the customary "liberal" solution of increasing governmental involvement in social matters, only grudgingly allowing such activity as to maintain system equilibrium. Moreover, the burden of proof is now on the side of those favoring ERA, school integration, affirmative action in employment, reform in school financing, abortion funding, national health care planning, and rational direction of the economy under the leadership of the (Federal) government.

On the theoretical side, Roberto Unger's "total critique" of liberal social theory and jurisprudence in *Knowledge and Politics*[1] presents the most serious challenge to liberalism, as it goes to the very heart of any social theory, its philosophical foundations. According to Unger, liberalism, having abandoned the doctrine of "intelligible essences" of the Greeks and Medievalists, is left without an objective basis for reality, knowledge, and value. Moreover, liberalism's Neo-Hobbesian theory of human nature (where man is a creature of subjective desire for comfort and glory) leads it to concentrate on the exchange-transactional mode of human activity, and consequently, to regard law and other aspects of decision making as coercive. Upon such a theory, justice becomes merely formal and procedural, consisting of finding workable rules and scrupulous procedures, rather than the promotion of some social "good," or value. Now, it is beyond the scope of this present paper to attempt to provide an answer to Unger, but we shall be concerned to examine liberalism (mainly as a social philosophy) with respect to its implications for liberation.

It is important to keep in mind that there is a difference in emphasis and approach between "social philosophy" and "political philosophy." Now, traditionally, it has been said that political philosophy is concerned with the issues of "power," whereas social philosophy is much wider, being concerned with the nature of man and his development. Of course, these characterizations are oversimplifications, as the question of the devolution of power may

Reprinted, with revisions by Berkley and Essie Eddins, from *Social Theory and Practice*, vol. 2, no. 1, Spring, 1972 (The Kaufman Memorial Issue, Berkley Eddins, Guest Editor).

well be one that hinges upon commitments concerning man and his destiny—
properly social philosophy issues. But these characterizations do suggest that
the relationship between social and political philosophy is one of subsumption
of the latter to the former. In order to illustrate this, let us include a discussion
of two other endeavors, so that we have the following four-fold classification
in order of generality, reading from bottom to top:

1. Social philosophy
2. Political theory or philosophy
3. Political science—descriptive and prescriptive
4. Practical politics

Now, we can see that practical politics is guided by descriptive and prescriptive political science; descriptive and prescriptive political science are rationalized or justified by an appeal to political theory, which in turn rests upon
some social philosophy: a theory of human nature of the good, of the good
society, and of human destiny.

The campaign for the passing of the Civil Rights Act of 1964 is a dramatic example of the interrelationships holding between these levels and concerns. There was, of course, the area of practical politics: getting enough votes
and seeing to it that the bill was kept alive for a vote on the floor. This involved
a knowledge of various procedures peculiar to the Congress, as well as a
knowledge of the structure of power and privilege extending into the home
districts of the Senators and Representatives. No doubt, certain "rules" of
politics were brought into play, such as, "Insure bipartisan support early in
the campaign," or "Keep the White House ostensibly in the background, but
exerting pressure, nevertheless." The campaign had, of course, a real concern
with equalizing the exercise of power, and this involved our political philosophy concerning rights, liberty, and freedom. Lastly, the social philosophy
aspects: the moral and religious appeals; the appeals to a theory of human and
natural right; the argument from history, certainly all set the tone and provided the impetus for the successful conclusion of the campaign. Since social
philosophy logically subsumes the other three endeavors under it, we may take
issues falling initially under these endeavors as social philosophy issues. We
shall, thus, feel free to show the implications of liberalism for liberation on
the first three levels, but principally from the level of social philosophy.

Prominent among the many complex events of today are the "liberation" movements, especially of women and Third World peoples, including
groups in the United States. There can be little doubt that the character, configuration, and complexion of these movements pose great and searching questions for the future of liberalism, both as an organon of analysis and as a
directive for programmatic change. Those of us who are sympathetic to these
movements (and also adherents to liberalism) may very well wonder if liberalism is still fruitful as an analytic tool and policy guide. But we find ourselves in an anomalous situation, in which we could be throwing out the "baby"

of reform for oppressed groups along with the "bath" of searching and intensive criticism of our own stance. This is especially likely—to anticipate later discussion—if we are at all honest about the morality, analytic cogency, and practical effectiveness of traditional liberalism, particularly as it has been concerned with the interests of groups, rather than with the well-being of individuals.

It was such a concern with the vitality of liberalism that led Arnold Kaufman to write *The Radical Liberal*. In that book Kaufman characterizes what he calls the "heart of liberalism" as follows:

> Liberalism is a political theory, and therefore provides a guide to the making of public policy. All liberals share the belief that the ultimate aim of public policy is the protection and promotion of each person's equal opportunity to develop his potentialities as fully as possible. The limits of possibility for the individual are partly set by unalterable biological, physical, and social circumstances. But additional moral limits are set by the constraints of civility—those traits of character that make possible stability, mutual trust, collective regard for human welfare, and justice in the organization of society.[2]

Whatever else liberalism has meant, it has had as its focus the concern for the individual: for his freedom, his prerogatives, and his self-development. As William Orton puts it (in *The Liberal Tradition*) liberalism of whatever type or period has its hallmark "in the fact that it takes the actual living person, the concrete human being, both as starting point and final criterion."[3]

We may thus identify four main tenets of liberalism: (1) an emphasis on the individual as the locus of value; (2) a doctrine of inalienable, if not "natural" rights; (3) consideration of the individual under the guise of "status," rather than that of "contract"; and (4) the belief that there should be limitations on the exercise of power and "public" justifications offered for its use. The first two tenets are self-explanatory, but the latter two call for brief clarifications. As Sir Henry Maine points out (in *Ancient Law*[4]), liberalism's emphasis on the freedom of contractual behavior was necessary to overcome the historic seats of "status," such as tribal and familial connections. But it is plausible to conclude that liberalism was (and is) able to substitute *true status* for that which was accidental and artificial, and hence, spurious. This tenet, then, clarifies and deepens the first tenet about the individual, *in that the individual is of worth, intrinsically, apart from any contractual relationship into which he might enter.* So that, we now understand that although contractual behavior was, at that time, a necessary expression of individualism, the core meaning of individualism, nevertheless, is status, not contract. With respect to the last tenet about limits on power, the identification of the sector that is to be limited may vary, giving a particular flavor to the character of one's "liberalism." Thus, the "New Deal-Fair Deal-Great Society" liberal is wary of private sector abuses of power, whereas the conservative (yesterday's "liberal") is wary of public sector abuses of power, rather than private sector abuses as formerly.

Classical liberalism, then, asks the questions, "What are the perceived needs of the individual? What are his wants? How can society be arranged to enhance want-satisfaction, and what form of polity may be most useful in bringing this about?" It was the belief of classical liberals (such as Locke and Jefferson) that the socio-political order exists to respond to the perceived needs, wants, and satisfactions of men, whatever their state of enlightenment of insight into themselves, sophistication, moral sensitivity, or moral autonomy.

Now, revisionist democrats, or interest-group liberals (such as Schumpeter, Bell, and Lipset[5]) see the virtue in democracy, not as to what it might do for the individual, but because it is a good way of parcelling out power. More generally, they revise the terms of the democratic dialogue from those of individual satisfactions, wants and perceived needs, to those of the conditions that make for political and other kinds of stability in society. Thus, the "stuff" of their investigation are gross institutions and processes. These processes are primarily involved with the competition for power, especially as embodied in group activity. By concentrating on competition for leadership, they meet the requirements of democracy; and the emphasis on gross competition between and among groups is a more palpable datum or reality, something that is much more easily conceptualized and manipulated than "needs, wants, and satisfactions," which may be arcane, individualistic, and linked to spiritualism or idealism. The countervailing power theorist, the revisionist democrat, is a *realist* who deals in the reality of power. The stuff of his society is gross institutions as they countervail against one another. The activities of groups in their competition for leadership give character and flavor to social life. Interest group liberals believe that we have reached the consensus as to what society is to be about—all that remains now is the proper way of parcelling out power. We are democratic because we wish this competition to be fair, however; there are "rules" of political behavior; there are rules of the game, so to speak. These rules have to do with tradeoff bargaining; the bringing in of novelty and the absorption of change in the system; the social control of individuals; a regularized and routinized way of conducting business. (We are reminded of Max Weber's "case-hardened rationality.")

One of the most serious consequences of the countervailing power, or revisionist democratic thesis is that it allows—nay, compels—one to say that nothing is any good unless it has been tried in the fires of competition. What this does, then is to underscore antagonisms; it sets group against group; it sets person against person; it exacerbates conflict; it substitutes "contract" for status; it establishes as the measure of a person, indeed the status of a person, how this person might be used as a chip in the poker game that is bargaining, or a high card in this poker game. It suggests, moreover, that rights must be won and gained through the process of bargaining; through the process of advocacy, making a case in the so-called marketplace by the use of political instruments that are already established. So that, what it does is to subject man to the pain, suffering, and anguish of the competitive life. Moreover, countervailing power democracy appeals to the worst in human nature; it gives one no sense of the whole. It makes for an illiberal ignoring of the reality and the interest of the individual. It functions as a disguised ideology, which really underscores and underwrites the *status-quo*. It does not make a provision for the formation of new groups, for how shall groups get power, except by the taking of power or the relinquishing of power by the older groups? It does not rule out, moreover, the possibility of coalition and, in fact, coalitions are themselves a fact of life.

We are compelled, therefore, to examine more closely the criticisms of interest-group democracy, especially the claim that it is by its very character conservative rather than liberal or liberating. It has been characterized as giving its blessing to the status quo; as propounding an ideology and consecrating a system of dominant values so that the only questions remaining have to do with reshuffling the customary institutional arrangements rather than with examining the basic ideology or value-system itself. Indeed these very institutional rearrangements by which power is parceled out are said themselves to favor those who already possess the power. In short, interest group liberalism, with its stress on activities of groups, turns out to be "illiberal" in that it does not enhance the capacities of the individual. Since the means by which decisions are made in a group may or may not be democratic, it does not safeguard his participation in decision-making. But, on the other hand, if the individual is not part of a group, he may be without an effective voice in the decision-making of the larger society.

With respect to Black liberation, branches of the Federal Government have, partly by circumstance, and partly by design, been cast in the role of advocate. Time and again, the Supreme Court has given the definitive ruling in a matter of civil rights. The Congress, under the prodding of the Executive Branch, has enacted legislation such as the statutes implementing the "war on poverty." Theodore Lowi's analysis of the government's "activist" approach provides us with additional and incisive criticisms of interest-group liberalism.[6]

Similar to its actions in creating regulatory agencies from among the constituencies involved (and leaving the administering of laws to the prerogatives of the agencies), the government's actions are seen by Lowi as lacking a respect for the proper formalism inherent in the "rule of law"; and we have had many abuses of privilege in the poverty program. What is even more disquieting from *our* standpoint, is that interest-group advocacy throws Blacks and the cause of Black liberation into the power struggle. Existing antagonisms are exacerbated, and Blacks become exposed to the perils of what for some people is nothing less than mortal combat.

Lowi suggests also that interest-group liberalism has caused the government to resort to the most harsh measures before it has exhausted less harsh ones. For example, it places the burden for the eradication of unequal education via bussing squarely on the shoulders of the white blue-collar class, precisely the one that is least likely to want to conform; or to have the respect for, or the moral starch to conform to, the law. The "program approach" makes it appear that problems have been solved when in fact they have not, and indeed may have created others equally unsettling to the body politic. Liberal politicians substitute the rhetoric of liberalism for the reality of social reform.

Governmental action has tended to reinforce the ghetto through its policy of encouraging its rehabilitation, while at the same time making it possible for non-blacks to flee to the suburbs; and via its housing policies has deliberately promoted the separation of city from suburbs. It has also put its blessing upon educational districts as taxing agents. Indeed, Lowi suggests that the notion of a corporate city is unconstitutional in that it is an out-and-out delegation of power to the city by the legislatures.

Interest-group liberalism, by giving its blessing to "community control" (which is an extension of the privileges of those in the suburbs with respect to housing and education), itself fosters the evil of separatism and saps the classical civil rights movement of what was once its greatest strength, its moral impulse. In the context of group-interest, it has become all but impossible to appeal to basic morality.

Lowi's last criticism, which goes to the heart of the matter, is echoed by Robert Paul Wolff in *The Poverty of Liberalism*.[7] Wolff points out that we have lost contact with any overarching, unifying system of values that would tie men together; owing to the mechanism of interest groups, they are rather being kept apart, separated from the very conditions conducive to their best self-development. In fact, according to Wolff, we are faced with an anomalous situation in which deviance on the part of groups is tolerated (in fact fostered and encouraged), while deviance on the part of individuals is not only frowned upon but militantly extirpated.

The criticisms of democratic pluralism found in the writings of Lowi and Wolff are well-founded and equally well-taken. But considered by themselves, they could, if acted upon, result in a paralysis of action, owing to our inability to conceive of a notion of countervailing power that is not self-defeating. Arnold Kaufman gave similar criticisms of interest-group liberalism (or countervailing power democracy). In a brief passage he states:

> All the criticisms of pseudo-realism already developed apply to
> exclusive reliance on a democracy of countervailing power.
> Preoccupation with power is ideologically influenced. The democratic
> process prescribed is immoral because it squanders human rights and
> potentialities. It is self-defeating because it undermines the very
> conditions of deliberative citizenship. It is unrealistic because it is the
> worst possible way to insure that political leadership will have the
> managerial skills necessary to function most effectively in pursuit of
> liberal aims. But basically its pessimistic cast is self-fulfilling. By
> diminishing liberalism's political reach, it forfeits many liberal aims
> that are within liberalism's grasp. In the end, Freud's principle fully
> applies to those who place exclusive reliance on the countervailing
> power conception. Each such individual is governed by deep-rooted
> internal prejudices into whose hands his practicality unwittingly plays.[8]

This reference to Freud's principle is both dramatic and theoretically sound: it is as if nature itself were taking its revenge on the psyche of the person who conceives of human action in terms of countervailing power. Searching for power rather than moral alternatives, we experience a paucity of imaginative ideas. If "power" does not work, if the arrangements made do not pan out, then we are left to invoke a conspiracy or a demonic theory of behavior. Since we are confounded because things do not work, we assume there must be something either inherently wrong with the black person—or with the youth, or with the Indians, or with the Chicanos, or with any other group to whom we have in a sense "given" power—who does not use that power either wisely or successfully. Even before that, we tend to look upon the powerless as some-how cursed because of that powerlessness; we come to believe there must be some cosmic reason why these people are unable to avail themselves of power and to win the rights and privileges other groups have won for themselves. In this way, exclusive reliance on countervailing power debilitates the liberal struggle in that it causes one to become obsessed with powerlessness. As a result, some may simply opt out of the struggle, or become "co-opted," if they stay in. Clearly, exclusive reliance on power politics—on countervailing power politics—either when practiced by government, or allowed to go on by gov-ernment, leads to the weakening of the liberal cause.

As forceful as they are, Kaufman's criticisms do not lead him to pron-ounce final judgment upon interest-group liberalism. True to his belief that political analysis must be informed not only by flexibility but by reasonable-ness (and here he is echoing what John Dewey[9] says about the role of intel-ligence), Kaufman not only finds a place for countervailing power democracy, but also looks forward to a kind of dialectical interplay between countervailing power and participatory democracy, or as he puts it, between Madisonian and the Rousseauean democracy. Kaufman sees here some midpoint yet to be gained from understanding the necessity for liberation and social reform in terms of both countervailing power and participatory democracy. As politi-cian, activist, and theoretician, Kaufman believed that liberalism must get behind the vague yearnings and the explicit programs of the diverse move-ments for liberation; that being authentically liberal means being the liberal-activist; that liberalism must not disdain, or stand aloof from these move-ments; that it must apply, or better still, sanction what he calls the politics of radical pressure. By this he means that any tactic whatsoever that will bring about a given end must be applied. This does not mean that any tactic *must* be applied simply for the sake of application, nor that *all* tactics must be used. Only those tactics that will work in a given situation—when one keeps up steady pressure on power centers by direct action, propaganda, boycotts, lit-igation, *etc.*,—must be applied.

We can now look at Kaufman's dialectical synthesis between Rous-seauean and Madisonian democracy. Kaufman promoted a kind of creative tension between the processes of countervailing power and participatory or developmental democracy. Where he differs from Wolff and from Lowi is in the worth that he ascribes to the politics of countervailing power. For instance, the system of countervailing powers "does provide that degree of protection from interference by corporate powers, public and private, that is essential to the functioning of participatory institutions. And it does create that floor of material benefits that the maligned welfare state affords; and without which a democracy of participation will not last very long."[10] What is being claimed here is that even though one may deplore the inadequacies of the poverty program, unless the government did in a fundamental respect step in and direct the distribution of power (even creating power centers that are antagonistic to the existing ones, and becoming the advocate of those centers), then the notion of participatory democracy will go down the drain. The one set of conditions will allow the other to grow.

In the nature of the case, facing the realities of social and political life we shall have to work through groups and group interest, at least for a long while yet. But, and this is a point made by Wolff, we must not confuse conflict of interest politics and conflict of power politics. We may, without too much of a quarrel, agree with Wolff that

> . . . the government quite successfully referees the conflict among
> competing powers—any group which has already managed to
> accumulate a significant quantum of power will find its claims attended
> to by the federal agencies. But legitimate interests which have been
> ignored, suppressed, defeated, or which have not yet succeeded in
> organizing themselves for effective action will find their
> disadvantageous position perpetuated through the decisions of the
> government.[11]

Granted, therefore, that we shall still have to work through interest groups—this does not obviate or obscure the greater goal of society's attention to the development of the individual. It is still possible to agree with Christian Bay, who is against the "pluralist liberal concerned with the rights of the majority, the greatest happiness of the greatest number, and particularly those political and economic rights that are so dear to the majority or the most favored individuals.[12] He is interested rather in the "self-development or the needs, wants, and satisfactions of even the least favored individual in this society."[13]

We now turn to the formulation of alternatives to interest-group liberalism. We agree with Wolff that we must find a conceptual alternative to liberalism's "private satisfactions and public justice." Until now we have taken the atomic individual as basic. We look upon his wanting, valuing, and striving as the primary reality and then take his relationships to other men as problematic, making the configuration of society dependent upon the satisfaction of private wants; and somehow out of this we expect something called public justice. We seem to be involved here not merely in the why's and wherefore's of political, of social, of institutional arrangements (that is, we are no longer thinking as political scientists or political philosophers concerned mostly with the devolution of power), but must go beyond this to the level of social philosophy, and develop a theory of man and of human destiny, a philosophy of

166

history that leaves room for the moral aspirations of men. This is the value in Wolff's suggestion that we move toward the recognition and the establishment of several kinds of communities: the affective, the productive, and the rational.[14] We need some overarching conception of man and of human destiny that is not reached by the concern with power.

Lowi's suggestions for reform have to do with the reinstitution of what he calls "progressivism": civil rights, voter rights, the kinds of legislation passed in the late fifties and early to mid-sixties. He is for the recovery of the rule of law in government, and would do away with the separation between the making and the administering of the law. In this scheme there would be a clear understanding as to how laws would be carried out, what exact procedures would be applied. There would be less left to the prerogative of this or that administrative body or council. In this way a certain dimension of morality could be restored to government and to the political process.[15] Clearly, what Lowi has in mind is to avoid all those undesirable events involved in the role of government as an "advocate" of group interests. What we would like to see would be some way of safeguarding both the right and capacity of group, *as well* as individual, action. There are legitimate purposes to be served by group activity, group pressure, and even group identification. And there may even be a way that government can play the role of "advocate" effectively, without harming the cause of the very groups and persons it seeks to help.

From the above analyses of interest-group liberalism, which is the dominant variety today, and considering also other contemporary expressions (of liberalism), we may now summarize what has happened to the classical tenets of liberalism.

1. *The emphasis on the individual as locus of value.* From the standpoint of interest-group liberalism, groups and their interaction, rather than individual interest, are taken as central. But when attention *is* centered on individuals, these turn out to be those who have attained a certain position of power in society. (Note the consequences for "status over contract.") Moreover, the interest-group liberals share with the descendants of classical liberalism the characterization of men as egoistic, atomic, but rational individuals, to the extent that interest-group liberals think about the individual at all.

2. *Inalienable, if not "natural" rights.* There are these rights, to be sure, but they are mainly economic and political, and largely formal, rather than substantive. They now have more of a utilitarian than a "natural law" basis. They are established in a system of public rules, rather than as part of the values that the society seeks to enhance, especially as ends or goals.

3. *Status over contract.* Both interest-group and traditional liberals seem to reverse the order, making our contractual relations, as evidenced in the exchange-transactional mode of behavior paramount. In fact, life becomes defined in terms of these relationships. But, as Corinne Gilb points out in a perceptive study of the professions and government, we have moved "from status, to contract, to status as the basis of many private rights."[16] An example of this would be the position enjoyed by one of the health professions, or by the members of a large industrial labor union.

4. *Limitations on the exercise of power; "public" justifications.* To the extent that justifications of power merely ratify and rationalize the *status-quo*, interest-group liberalism falls away from this historic tenet of liberalism. But it is still "liberal," in that it still wants certain features of decision-making that limit (regulate) the use of power. It can even be enlightened about these rules and can wish for (provide for) their use to result in fairness in the system. Interest-group liberalism, however, might not necessarily be alive to abuses of power in the private sector and their effects on the society as a whole.

How then, may the classical tenets of liberalism be fully recovered? This question is highly important, since it appears that only a liberalism that is strong as a social philosophy can rationalize and give direction to inquiry and strategy concerning (black) liberation at the levels of political theory, political science, and practical politics. Can liberalism be "critical" about its foundations? With this question in mind, let us consider these tenets for a final time.

Individualism may very well be established, but *primarily* on the basis of "needs"—objectively established, rather than being a function of perception—rather than "wants." We cannot here provide the complete analysis, but powerful theoretical grounding for a theory of needs may be found by investigations such as those carried on by John Wild,[17] Abraham Maslow [18] and Arnold Kaufman.[19] Wild has a "modern" theory of "natural law," which fits in very well with Maslow's "scientific" notion of organismic health and Kaufman's notion of a need as fitting in with the "conative structure of our nature." Moreover, Kaufman maintains that a "shift from wants to needs" would constitute a "genuine liberation of liberalism."[20] A theory of needs would provide a naturalistic and scientific basis for a theory of rights, and for the affirmation of equality.

Inalienable, if not "natural" rights would have a justification in some realistic description of human nature, rather than in adventitious wants, which may be largely subjective and hard to universalize and generalize upon. Furthermore, they would not merely exist as a result of a "decision to have them in the system," but as based upon a theory of human nature which could be offered for critical analysis. Moreover, we could update the list of rights to go beyond the narrowly economic, mainly political, and largely formal, to the substantive freedoms (human rights)—the amenities of society (jobs, housing, education, and health care). Equality would become more than a "postulate of the system," having a basis in a defensible theory of human nature.

Power would be seen as a positive good and as a social resource. It would be seen as an organic property of society, rather than something for which to compete. Having the concept of power as a social resource, one may very well use government as the proper agent of society, using power to bring about equity in society. Today's "critical" liberal would be alive to the possibility of abuses of power from the private sector. As such, he would not automatically ratify the so-called "power ground rules," but would recognize them as artificially and contingently established by those whose chief interest is in maintaining themselves in power and arrogating unto themselves social prerogative.

Replacing interest-group liberalism with a more critical view will enable us to reestablish the *status* of the individual as a bearer of worth, rights and dignity over whatever *contractual* relationships into which he may enter. The de-emphasis on elite or interest-group competition will enable us to prevent the dialectical movement (pointed out above) from "status, or contract, to status," where the latter is but the hardening of a contractual relationship, and again, an arrogation of the prerogative of society. If we are to be serious about rights, which is what liberation is all about, then individuals must be deemed as having *status* as the proper subjects of rights.

The standpoint of being "critical" about liberalism is also able to appreciate the contributions (as well as limitations) of interest-group liberalism. *The ideal situation would be to promote both participatory democracy and interest-group democracy under a "higher pluralism," free both from the crass concern with power and from the vacuity of rhetoric without reality—of formal democracy without substance.* But it is imperative that the liberal recognize that, with respect to the liberation movements, he must work with the materials at hand; that to be authentically liberal, he must get behind these group movements, even *running the risk* of exacerbating conflict; for if nothing is done in the way of group activity, then very little will be done, given the so-called "ordinary processes" of decision-making. In other words, the individual may be hallowed, but he is at the same time powerless.

What is proposed, then, is that we look upon the securing of political, social, and economic rights (through interest-group activity) as a halfway house and a prerequisite both to full individual participation in the determination of the goods and values of the society and to the highest development of the capacities of the individual. Here again, as Dewey suggested, part of the office of liberalism is to understand the legitimate yearnings and aspirations of the powerless and to mediate between social movements; to help bring about the transition from old to new; to be, as it were, an interpreter of the one to the other social group. At the same time, the liberal stance will afford the standpoint from which inquiry into the quality of life will be made, and suggestions for the amelioration of the quality of life will be given. Pluralism as liberalism means that there must be a plural search for meaning and values and that the systematic exclusion of any quarter be repudiated. And full participation means participation not only of groups but of individuals.

Liberalism has as its counterpart in the theory of knowledge a kind of objectivism; that is to say, liberalism believes that truth or cogency will be determined by the interplay of ideas and suggestions, each of which must be measured against the reality of our social situation. There must be no positions that are preemptive of that field: "Every tub must stand on its own bottom." If the traditions of civility and fair play are adhered to, justifications of positions will be formulated in terms that will satisfy the need of individuals for justifications. There will be tolerance of individuals as well as of groups. Should such a society come into existence, we would find no grounds for the denial of participation in the determination of the goods of the society—its rules, values, and institutions—by anyone or any group on the basis of artificial characteristics such as race, sex, or ethnic or national origin. But if we are to be realistic, we must realize that the extension of participation to the various groups previously excluded can properly come about *only if* the society is changed in interesting (if not in fundamental) respects. For instance, the enjoyment of economic self-sufficiency on the part of Blacks would appear to be enhanced by the general improvement of the economic conditions in America—full employment, full production, wise government regulation, etc. The same would apply to the case of women.

Consider the enjoyment of political rights. These would appear to be enhanced by the improvement in the political machinery allowing a change in the rules, for instance, by which delegates to the Democratic national convention are to be elected, necessitating a greater percentage of Blacks and women. This is, of course, a practical matter, but it reintroduces the dilemma of Madisonian and Rousseauean democracy: the system itself will not be improved unless and until you have the participation or at least the representation of the interests of these groups, even if improvement is to be measured by individual standards. The interests and impetuses toward liberation will have to be represented by groups and persons *having a measure of power—* indeed persons *within the power structure itself!*

It would appear then that the liberal is being called upon once more to spearhead the movement so that he must be concerned, in spite of what might be said about the virtues or the non-virtues of pluralist democracy, with the "welfare of the majority and the greatest happiness of the greatest number" as well as, or as a prelude or a means to the welfare of the "least favored individuals." Christian Bay acknowledged this in a later article, but cautioned that liberal democracy must be judged "*strictly* as a means to the ends of freedom."[21]

To be sure, one has to say that if democracy does not work for the least of individuals, then it does not work for any; that countervailing power or the competition for power is simply not enough. It may be, however, that the liberal has accepted the "power and ground rules" with insufficient caution: the great struggles, the great social, political, economic struggles are themselves about power. We are suggesting that they will have to continue to be about power to a great extent. Insofar as they seek for equity, the groups that are pressing for liberation are talking about power and the lack of power. But a real and cruel dilemma is that not only will the power-game prove self-defeating, but the powerless are, in effect, being called upon to effect transformations in the hearts of men as a precondition of their own (group) liberation. For all its emphasis on the dignity of the individual, the American political process has largely been controlled by the activity of groups competing for power. In order for there to be meaningful improvement in the condition of oppressed groups, there must be significant modification in our dominant ideology and in our social, economic, and political arrangements. To bring this modification about, concerted action must be taken by and in the name of the oppressed groups.

It is safe to conclude that liberation necessarily and essentially must entail "persuasive and effective political activity" (practical politics); access to, and knowledge of the system (political science); theories about power, its rationale and devolution (political theory); and a theory of human nature and of the good society (social philosophy). Central to this latter emphasis is what a person determines to be a worthwhile "quality of life." Paradoxically, the question of quality of life sits squarely astride the question of liberation; it must be related to the fight for equity or equality. But a more fundamental issue is the quality of one's aspirations and whether or not the instruments of society shall have a *truly liberating influence.* One way of rescuing liberalism from its concern with power or from its concern with political instruments and equity is to remind the liberal that at the base of his doctrine is something called the freedom of aspiration: the unfettering of man's spirit. The current movements for liberation in the United States are to a large extent cast in the old mold of liberalism; while liberalism is not exclusively concerned with countervailing power, it has shown an exaggerated concern for equity and equality to a concomitant detriment to the quality of life itself.

What seems to be at stake here is the rescue not only of the liberal dialogue from a concern with power, but the rescue of social philosophy from political science and even from political philosophy. At the heart of our concerns is the establishment of a philosophical anthropology. Social philosophy is *sui generis* and concerns itself with the nature of man, of human destiny, and the nature of the good life, as well as of the good society; as such, it is more than a concern with power, with the competition for power, or the correctness of political decisions. What we are seeking in liberation is the reopening of the search for insight into the nature of man and for the kind of cooperative organization of those activities which could be recommended as being good and proper for all mankind.

Liberation movements, while they may have quite correctly and admirably as their goals the seeking of equity and equitable access to the exercise of power and decision making, nevertheless may, in fastening on those goals, be *illiberal* in their larger implications and dimension. What we seek is the capacity to participate equally in the determination of what we eventually agree upon as proper human activity for a specifically *human* being. We seek a search for the proper kind of human *praxis* whereby society is seen simply as a means for enhancing this search and not systematically abrogating, clamping down, or cutting off the search in an arbitrary and unwarranted manner. True liberation has to do with breaking off not only the institutional fetters which affect the group in a systematic way, but breaking off the ideological fetters which seem to work against the search for insight into the character of man.

If liberalism is to be a means to liberation, we conclude, it must be that form of classical liberalism that has critically recovered the historic tenets of liberalism (on the level of social philosophy), rather than that revisionist form of liberalism known as interest-group liberalism, which is mainly concerned with exercises of power (on the levels of political science and political theory). But paradoxically, this latter form of liberalism must be employed to its fullest extent, as effectively as possible, as an auxiliary instrumentality and strategy within the larger thrust of the now more critical mainstream classical liberalism. Interest-group liberalism, for example, *a la* coalition politics, can be used to reinforce and buttress widespread efforts to secure the rights and amenities of society for hitherto neglected groups. But critical classical liberalism can also show us why we must go beyond the stage of liberation thus achieved to true liberation, which has implications for institution-building as well as for personal development. This is why the tenets of liberalism must be recovered in the form prescribed above—by way of a philosophical anthropology that is defensible in the best theoretical terms we can employ.

Notes

1. Roberto M. Unger, *Knowledge and Politics* (New York: The Free Press, 1975), p. 32.
2. Arnold S. Kaufman, The *Radical Liberal* (New York: The Atherton Press, 1968), p. 4.
3. William Orton, *The Liberal Tradition* (New Haven: The Yale University Press, 1946), p. 33.
4. Sir Henry Maine, *Ancient Law* (New York: Scribner's, 1864).
5. See such thinkers as Joseph A. Schumpeter, *Capitalism, Socialism, and Democracy* (New York, Harper and Row, 1942); Daniel Bell, *The End of Ideology* (New York: Collier, 1961); Seymour M. Lipset, *Political Man* (Garden City: Doubleday, 1960).
6. Theodore Lowi, *The End of Liberalism* (New York: Norton, 1969), chs. 8, 9, 10.
7. Robert Paul Wolff, *The Poverty of Liberalism* (Boston: The Beacon Press, 1968), especially ch. 4, "Tolerance."
8. Op. cit., p. 45.
9. John Dewey, *Liberalism and Social Action* (New York: Capricorn Books, 1963), ch. II, p. 41ff.
10. Kaufman, op. cit., p. 66.
11. Wolff, op. cit., p. 167.
12. Christian Bay, "Needs, Wants, and Political Legitimacy," *Canadian Journal of Political Science*, 1 (Sept., 1968), p. 24.
13. Ibid.
14. Wolff, op. cit., ch. 5.
15. Lowi, op. cit., pp. 96–97.
16. Corinne L. Gilb, *Hidden Hierarchies* (New York: Harper and Row, 1966), p. 5.
17. John Wild, *Plato's Modern Enemies and the Theory of Natural Law* (Chicago: The University of Chicago Press, 1953).
18. Abraham Maslow, *The Farther Reaches of Human Nature* (New York: Viking Press, 1971).
19. Arnold S. Kaufman, "Needs, Wants, and Liberalism," *Inquiry*, 14 (June, 1971), p. 192.
20. Ibid., p. 195.
21. Christian Bay, "Behavioral Research and the Theory of Democracy," in Henry S. Kariel, ed., *Frontiers of Democratic Theory* (New York: Random House, 1970), p. 347 (emphasis supplied).

Note on the Authors

Essie A. Eddins is Assistant Professor of Nursing at New York University. She has taught and lectured at State University of New York, Buffalo, Erie Community College, Georgetown University and D'Youville College. She co-authored with Berkley B. Eddins several book reviews, among them is Richard Wasserstom, ed., *Today's Moral Problems* MacMillian Publishing Company, 1975, *Teaching Philosophy*, Spring, 1976.

Berkley B. Eddins is Professor of philosopohy, State University of New York at Buffalo, New York. He has also taught at Howard University and the University of Colorado. He is noted for his work in the philosophy of history and liberal social theory. His works include *Appraising Theories of History*, Cincinnati: Ehling Press, 1980, and "The Structure of Social Philosophy: Its Problems, Issues, and Concepts," *International Journal of History and Political Science*, August 1968.

173

Self-Respect: Theory and Practice

Laurence Thomas

We begin life as rather frail creatures who are quite unable to do much of anything for ourselves. If all goes well we end up as healthy adults with a secure sense of worth. At the outset of our lives, there are two things that are generally thought to enhance significantly the likelihood of our turning out to be adults of this sort: (i) our being a continuous object of parental love (or, of course, a permanent parental surrogate) and (ii) the acquisition of a strong sense of competence with respect to our ability to interact effectively with our social and physical environment.[1] It is obvious that whereas the latter continues to be important throughout our lives, the former does not. Of course, we may continue to value the love of our parents; the point, rather, is that as adults our sense of worth is not, if we develop normally, tied to our being loved by our parents. Does this mean, then, that the only important sense of worth to be countenanced among adults is that which turns upon their having a sense of competence? One reason to be skeptical that this is so is just that love, and therefore parental love, has so very little to do with a person's performances. I believe that self-respect can be seen as the social analogue, for adults, to the sense of worth that is generated by parental love. My aim in this essay is to show the importance which this line of reasoning has for both moral theory and social philosophy.

I

It will be instructive to begin this section with a brief look at the role that parental love, as opposed to parental praise, plays in the life of the child. Indeed, what I shall have to say will be all too brief; however, I believe it will be enough to at least give one a feel for why I take self-respect to be the social analogue for adults to the sense of worth that is generated by parental love.

Praise, being a form of approval, is conceptually tied to a person's performances. There can be no such thing as serious praise for behavior of which we disapprove. Insincere praise is empty and sometimes cruel. Love, on the other hand, has precious little to do with a person's performance. It constitutes both an acceptance of a person and a concern for his well-being, which is not tied to what he does. It is unconditional, not because one may never cease to

This essay develops and refines a view which I have developed in a number of essays: "Morality and Our Self-Concept," *The Journal of Value Inquiry* (12) 1978; "Rawlsian Self-Respect and the Black Consciousness Movement," *The Philosophical Forum* 9 (1978); and "Capitalism versus Marx's Communism," *Studies in Soviet Thought* 20 (1979). Permission from the editors of these journals to draw upon these essays is gratefully acknowledged.

love an individual, but because there is nothing which a person can do that constitutes a conceptual bar to loving him. Thus, one can have the most genuine love for a person whose behavior one disapproves of in every way. The person can even be one's enemy. (The Christian commandment to this effect is thought to be difficult, not conceptually impossible.)

Now, whereas both parental love and praise both play a most important role in the child's life, the very fact that the child is very dependent upon his parents for food, shelter, and protection should make it obvious why parental love plays yet a more significant role in the child's life than parental praise. A child would be in an awful way if his being provided with these things were conditional upon his doing what his parents deemed praiseworthy. Because learning how to do as one's parents have instructed one is precisely what one does as a child, the fear of parental rejection would loom large in the life of a child for whom receiving these benefits was contingent upon his doing what his parents deemed praiseworthy; for he would be constantly fearful of failing to behave in this way. Moreover, if a child's receiving parental protection were made contingent upon this sort of thing, then out of fear he would be more reluctant to engage in exploratory behavior. This is because he would lack the assurance that his parents would protect him when things got out of hand for him. This would be unfortunate for the child, since engaging in exploratory behavior is one of the chief means by which the child acquires a strong sense of competence.[2]

As no doubt one has already surmised, the significance of parental love lies in the fact that, first of all, it allays, if not precludes entirely, the child's fear of parental rejection; second, it minimizes the child's fear of engaging in exploratory behavior. For, as a result of being the continuous object of parental love, the child comes to have the conviction that the reason why he matters to his parents is just that they love him, and not that he has this or that set of talents or that he behaves in this or that way. Parental praise, as important as it is,[3] could never instill in the child a conviction such as this. As a result of parental love, the child then comes to have a sense of worth that does not turn upon either his abilities or his behavior. This sense of worth is, I want to say, the precursor to self-respect.

To the fact that there are many ways in which persons can be treated is added morality, a conception of how persons ought to be treated. The primary way in which a rights-based moral theory does this is by postulating a set of basic rights, which each person has simply in virtue of being a person. Creatures other than persons may have a subset of these rights; and some creatures, as well as other things, may have none of these rights. (For the purposes of this essay, I shall be concerned with only a rights-based moral theory.[4]) Persons, then, have full moral status; some creatures other than persons have partial moral status; and still others, along with other things, have no moral status at all.[5] While I shall offer an illustration of these points below (§3), we can, on the basis of these remarks alone, say what self-respect comes to. A person has self-respect, I shall say, if and only if he has the conviction

175

that he is deserving of full moral status, and so the basic rights of that status, simply in virtue of the fact that he is a person. Having self-respect, then, is not so much a matter of being able to give a run-down of what one's basic rights happen to be as it is a way of viewing oneself vis à vis others from the moral point of view. Everyone, including oneself, is equally deserving of full moral status and so of being treated in accordance with the basic rights that come with that status. And the reason for this is just that one is a person.

It is clear that, understood in this way, self-respect makes no reference at all to the abilities of persons, since a person is no less that in view of what her abilities are. If it is one of our considered moral judgments that a person's moral status ought not to be a function of what her natural endowments are or how she behaves, then this judgment is captured by the view of self-respect that I am putting forth. What is more, it follows, on my view, that in order to have self-respect, a person need not have a morally acceptable character. For the belief that one is deserving of full moral status is certainly compatible with the belief that one's moral character is not up to par. And this underscores the fact that self-respect, as I conceive of it, does not turn upon a person's abilities. For there can be no question but that having a morally acceptable character calls for abilities and capacities that we do not all possess equally. Consider, for example, such moral virtues as honesty and kindness. The former calls for a considerable measure of resoluteness, a strong will one might say; the latter is intimately connected with the capacity for sympathetic understanding. And it is a brute fact about this world that individuals differ with respect to these capacities.[6] As one might surmise from the fact that I do not take self-respect to be tied to having an acceptable moral character, I am not offering a Kantian account of this notion.[7] This, I believe, is a strength rather than a weakness of the account that I offer, though I shall make no attempt to defend this claim here. (But see the next section, concluding paragraph.)

Thus far, I have merely offered an account of self-respect; I have not argued for its soundness. The argument that I shall offer will draw upon two examples from the black experience in the United States (§3); however, that argument will presuppose an appreciation for the difference between self-respect and self-esteem. So, before I begin it, a brief discussion about this latter concept is in order.

II

William James defined self-esteem as the ratio of a person's successes to his aspirations:[8]

$$\text{SELF-ESTEEM} = \frac{\text{SUCCESSES}}{\text{ASPIRATIONS}}$$

Contemporary psychologists have made no theoretical advance over James' notion of self-esteem.[9] They consider it to be the sense of worth that an individual has, which turns upon his evaluation of his ability to interact effectively with his environment, especially his social environment. It is of utmost importance to note that self-esteem is quite neutral between ends in that the successful pursuit of any end towards which a person aspires can contribute to his self-esteem. If a person has the appropriate aspirations, then being any one of the following can be a significant source of self-esteem for her or him: being a good parent, the first woman to sit on the United States Supreme Court, a gigolo, a call girl, a highly regarded academician, a highly regarded member of one's religious faith, a racist or a sexist.[10] Of course, it may be that we are more likely to value some ends rather than others; indeed, this may be so precisely because the society in which we live encourages the pursuit of some ends rather than others. None of this, though, militates against the point that self-respect is neutral between ends.

Now, as James's formula makes clear, the more (or less) in line our successes are with our aspirations, the higher (or lower) our self-esteem will be. From this it straightforwardly follows that, other things equal, the well-endowed are favored to have high self-esteem, since the well-endowed, in comparison to those whose natural assets are minimal, have fewer ends that are beyond their reach. There are more things that the well-endowed can do successfully. Given the premise that people differ with respect to their natural assets, it seems implausible to suppose that everyone can have (equally) high self-esteem. For, if anything like what Rawls calls the Aristotelian Principle and its companion effect are sound,[11] the displays of complex talents and skills by others will cause some to aspire beyond their reach. After all, any and every person could be a great janitor or typist, say, if only he should try, whereas it is far from obvious that any and every person could be a great physicist or artist, if only he should try. In any society where people are free to attempt to pursue the ends of their choosing, it is virtually inevitable that the talents of some will fail to match their aspirations and, therefore, that some will have low self-esteem. If I am right in this, then, although it may be that social institutions are unjustly arranged, if undermining the self-esteem of persons is the very point of the arrangement, it would be a mistake to suppose that this is so simply because such institutions do not guarantee that each member of society will have (equally) high self-eteem. As we shall see (§5), this is a very important respect in which self-esteem differs from self-respect.

I have said that if a person has the appropriate aspirations, then the successful pursuit of any end can contribute significantly to his self-esteem. I want to conclude this section with the observation that the aim to lead a morally good life is no exception to this claim. A person's high self-esteem can turn just as much upon his moral accomplishments as it can upon his accomplishments in sports or the academy. Naturally enough, we may think of self-esteem that turns upon the former as moral self-esteem. And just as the failure to measure up to our nonmoral aspirations occasions nonmoral shame, the failure to measure up to our moral aspirations occasions moral shame. I have bothered to make this point explicit in order to show that we can capture an important Kantian insight in the absence of a Kantian conception of self-respect. If we assume that everyone morally ought to aspire to lead a minimally decent moral life, then we can rightly say that there is a sense of shame—indeed, moral shame—that a person rightly feels in failing to do so. This we can say without saying that such a person must view herself or himself as not being deserving of full moral status., Thus, in order to experience moral shame a person need not lack self-respect. Self-respect, as I conceive of it, cannot be the source of moral shame; but, as these remarks make clear, the account of self-respect offered leaves room for such shame. I have not taken it out of the picture; rather, I have merely shifted its location.

III

I have offered an account of self-respect, which I have argued is distinct from self-esteem. I turn now to argue for the soundness of the account offered. As I remarked, I shall do this by drawing upon two examples from the black experience.

By definition (or so it seems) an Uncle Tom is a black who lacks self-respect. I do not know whether or not Booker T. Washington was an Uncle Tom; nor shall I be concerned to take a stand on the matter. I do know, however, that he has often been called an Uncle Tom.[12] What has been the force behind this epithet? Well, it is obvious that no one familiar with his life could have ever meant that he was lacking in talent or, in any case, that he set his sights too high. For this was a man who, though he was born a slave, went on to found an academic institution, The Tuskegee Institute. This is not something that a minimally talented person is apt to do; and he did as much as any black could have reasonably hoped to do, life being what it was for blacks then. What is more, Washington was held in high esteem, for both his accomplishments and his views, by a great many blacks and whites, which undoubtedly served to enhance his self-eteem. (*This point is compatible with the view of self-esteem presented, since our conviction that we are performing well the tasks that we have set out to perform is secured or, at the very least, supported by the admiration and esteem that we receive from others. And holding the right views is one of the many aims that a person may have.*[13]) Washington was most surely a man of considerable self-esteem, as defined here; and it is rather implausible to suppose that, in calling him an Uncle Tom, people have meant to deny this.

Nor is it plausible to suppose that, in calling him an Uncle Tom, people have meant to cast aspersions upon his moral character. At any rate, not even W. E. B. DuBois, his staunchest contemporary critic,[14] took Washington's flaw to be that he had a morally corrupt character. On the contrary, what had made him seem so vulnerable to the charge of being an Uncle Tom is that he appeared to be too accepting of the status quo. It was the prevailing view of whites back then that blacks were not socially prepared for full-fledged citizenship and, therefore, that social intercourse between blacks and whites, political participation on the part of blacks, and rights given to them should be kept to a minimum. It has seemed to a great many that, in his "Atlanta Exposition Address,"[15] it is precisely this view that Washington, himself, endorsed. If he did endorse this view, then the charge that he was an Uncle Tom seems fair enough. But, for all we know, and it is certainly not implausible to suppose this, Washington may have been a very shrewd and calculating black whose public stance was designed to appease the status quo in order to assure continued financial support from whites for the educational endeavors of blacks. If so, then I should think that a great deal more has to be said before one has a convincing case that he was an Uncle Tom. For, even if one should find fault with this strategy, the fact that it was a strategy, which did not reflect Washington's actual beliefs about how blacks should be treated, designed to advance the cause of blacks would be reason enough to resist labeling him an Uncle Tom.

But, now, suppose that Washington did subscribe to the prevailing view about blacks then, why would this warrant the charge that he was an Uncle Tom and so lacked self-respect? Before answering this question, I should first like to say a word about the sort of rights that come with having full moral status.

Both animals and persons have a right not to be treated cruelly. Only the latter, however, have a right to be treated fairly; hence, animals have only partial moral status, whereas persons have full moral status. Inanimate things have no moral status at all. They have nothing resembling a right nor are there any duties owed them; though, to be sure, what one does to or with an inanimate thing may constitute a moral wrong in that one is thereby violating some right or duty.[16] In any event, what is clear is that possession of the rights mentioned has absolutely nothing to do with having a morally good character. This is most obvious in the case of animals, since they lack the capacity for such. And to see that this is so in the case of persons, observe that if the right to be treated fairly were grounded in having a morally good character, then we could not, contrary to what we presently hold, treat a criminal unfairly by punishing him more harshly than he deserves nor could we treat one criminal more (or less) fairly than another, since, by hypothesis, criminals lack a morally good character. But, needless to say, we can do both of these things. *Mutatis mutandis*, the argument holds for the right that persons have not to be treated cruelly. Now, I take it to be equally clear that possession of the rights mentioned also has absolutely nothing to do with the talents or abilities of persons. This view has general acceptance, so I shall not bother to argue the case. Whether or not there are other rights that persons have in virtue of having full moral status, the two that I have mentioned, especially the right to be treated fairly, will suffice for our purposes.

The right to be treated fairly is a very powerful right in that it ranges over other rights, institutional ones, in particular, in the following way: First, fairness rules out irrelevant grounds for having institutional rights such as the right to vote. Thus, the grandfather clause,[17] to take an example, is ruled out by considerations of fairness as a requirement for having the right to vote.

Second, fairness requires (a) that with respect to the same rights, the grounds for having them be the same and (b) that equal protection be given to the same rights. So, as I indicated, the right to fair treatment applies to rights that persons do not have simply in virtue of the fact that they have full moral status. To have the conviction that one is deserving of fair treatment in virtue of the fact that one is a person is to have a fundamentally important conviction and a tremendous sense of worth; accordingly, I shall assume that a person who has this conviction has self-respect.

It should be easy enough to see how what has just been said applies to Booker T. Washington. If, in fact, he believed that blacks were not deserving of full-fledged citizenship; if, in particular, he believed that the franchise was something of which blacks should have to prove themselves worthy, then he is quite vulnerable to the charge that he was an Uncle Tom. As is the case now, the right to vote was not, during Washington's time, something that had to be earned: one needed only to be born in this country and to reach the age of majority. This is how whites were treated then; and Washington should have believed, regardless of what he maintained publicly, that considerations of fairness required that blacks be treated in the same way. If he, or anyone else, did not see that it was unfair that blacks should have to earn this fundamentally important right, when whites did not have to do so, then he failed to see that, even in the case of institutional rights, a person's claim to fair treatment is not secured by either his social standing as determined, say, by his wealth and mastery of the social graces or the hue of his skin. If so, then the charge that he was an Uncle Tom, and so lacked self-respect, would appear to be warranted. This claim holds even if Washington himself had earned the right to vote, since he was mistaken in thinking that he had to earn it.

If, indeed, Washington did lack self-respect, and I have not maintained that he did, I suspect it is because he did not allow the law to be subject to any significant moral criticism. He was an extreme legal positivist, one might say.[18] I say this because a person might argue, with some plausibility, that Washington viewed the equality of the races as a moral ideal, but thought that social institutions were at liberty to determine how this moral ideal would be realized. There is no surer sign, however, that a person lacks self-respect than that he should hold this view. For, at the very minimum, morality is about how persons should treat one another; and this is done primarily in the context of and, therefore, is largely influenced by the social institutions of society. Anyone who subscribes to extreme legal positivism has so little appreciation for this fact that it would seem that the very point of morality itself escapes him. As these remarks suggests, I do not take extreme legal positivism to be a very coherent view at all. It is an unfortunate fact, and a testimony to the tremendous power of social institutions, though, that incoherence is no bar to what people can be socialized to believe. Still, if the charge that Washington lacked self-respect can be made to stick, saddling him with this incoherent view would be preferable to saddling him with the view that equality for blacks was not even a moral ideal. To my mind, at any rate, it is not very likely that

Washington believed the latter; nor is it very likely that he lacked self-respect. For he was far too determined and labored far too hard to better the conditions of blacks during his time. I seriously doubt that this could be said of a person who lacked self-respect.

The Civil Rights Movement (CRM) of the 1960s provide us with another illustration from the black experience that supports the account of self-respect presented in this essay. At the outset, I should acknowledge that as a result of the CRM, the self-esteem of many blacks was enhanced as business and social institutions in the United States opened their more privileged positions to blacks in increasingly greater numbers and as various aspects of black culture and history gained greater appreciation in the American mainstream. And it is clear that both the collective pride and self-esteem of blacks was enhanced.[19] I take as evidence of this the change in hairstyles and, most importantly, the fact that the term 'black', which hitherto had been considered a most disparaging term, replaced 'coloured' and 'Negro' as the accepted term for referring to persons of African descent.

Now, as significant as the changes that I have just described were, the CRM wrought yet a more fundamental change in the lives of blacks. It enhanced their self-respect. It secured or, in any event, made more secure the conviction on the part of blacks that they are deserving of full moral status and, therefore, of the right to fair treatment. One must remember, after all, that the CRM did not straightaway result in the vast majority of blacks going on to pursue careers that greatly enhanced their self-esteem. Nor did it result in each black discovering in himself talents that hitherto had gone unnoticed by him. And although it is certainly true that the physical features of whites came to be a less important yardstick by which blacks measured their own physical attractiveness, the end result was not that all blacks got to be beautiful. Thus, if the success of the CRM were to be judged along these lines only, then it would have to be deemed a failure. But, in at least one very important respect a failure it was not.

A person did not need to acquire a new career, to discover new talents in himself, or to consider his physical appearance improved in order to feel the effects of the civil rights movement. For, the raison d'etre of this movement was not to secure these things as such. Rather, it was to stir the conscience of the American people, to arouse their sense of justice, and to move them to end the injustices that blacks have suffered.[20] *The* goal of the civil rights movement was to secure the conviction on the part of both blacks and whites that blacks were deserving of full moral status and, therefore, of just and fair treatment. In order for blacks to see themselves in this light, a new career, or whatever, was far from necessary. Of course, given what the unjust treatment of blacks came to, the just treatment of blacks could not help but have a positive effect upon their self-esteem. (I take justice to be subsumable under fairness.[21] Nothing of substance turns on the talk about justice here.)

However, it would be a mistake to generalize from the civil rights movement to the conclusion that whenever a group of people, who have been treated unjustly, are treated justly their self-esteem, as well as their self-respect, will be enhanced. For the unjust treatment of people does not, as a matter of logic, involve denying the fact that they have the talents and abilities to pursue, with hope of success, and to appreciate the ends of the academy and the other professions. If it did, then we would be logically committed to the absurd view that we could not treat unjustly those who lack the natural endowment to pursue such ends. This last remark points to why self-respect is a more fundamental sense of worth than self-esteem. It could turn out, given our abilities, that so few ends are within our reach that our having low self-esteem is all but inevitable. But not so with self-respect, since it is not, in the first place, a sense of worth that turns upon what our abilities happen to be. Thus, observe that in the 1960s what blacks demanded, in the name of justice and fairness, is that they be allowed the freedoms, opportunities, and privileges to which others had been so long accustomed. What they did not demand, and rightly so, is that they be given the natural assets to do as others do. It is because blacks had a claim to the enhancement of their self-respect that they had a claim to the enhancement of their self-esteem. Sometimes the importance of the latter, as in the case at hand, is derivative upon the importance of the former; the importance of self-respect, however, is never derivative upon the importance of self-esteem.

In this section, I have drawn upon two examples from the black experience in the United States to support the account of self-respect offered in this essay. Using the life of Booker T. Washington and the lives of blacks during the civil rights movement, I have tried to show, respectively, that the sense of worth that the former lacked, purportedly, and the latter gained could not have been simply self-esteem. For, what the former lacked, if anything, was a proper conception of himself from the moral point of view; and what the latter gained or had enhanced was just such a conception of themselves. In the wake of this the self-esteem of the latter was also enhanced. To lose sight of this fact is not only to fail to understand the significance of the civil rights movement, but to fail to grasp the importance of distinguishing between two important, but very different senses of worth, namely, self-respect and self-esteem.

IV

Since self-esteem has to do with the assessment that persons make of their abilities, there are some rather reliable indicators of whether or not a person has (high) self-esteem or lacks it (has low self-esteem). For example, the former tend to be more self-confident and independent than the latter, and they are more inclined to believe that what they do will be well received by others.[22] Since, on the other hand, self-respect has nothing at all to do with the assessment that persons make of their abilities, one naturally wonders whether or not there are any reliable indicators of whether or not a person has this sense of worth. I believe that there are.

It will be remembered that those who have self-respect have the conviction that they are deserving of fair treatment simply by virtue of the fact that they are persons. However, there can be both good and bad reasons for tolerating unfair treatment, for not insisting upon being treated fairly, as I shall illustrate in what follows.

In 1955, Mrs. Rosa Parks became a hero to the people of Montgomery, Alabama, when she refused to follow one of the Jim Crow practices insisted upon by the driver of the bus on which she was riding, namely that of moving to the back of the bus in order to accommodate white passengers.[23] The three other blacks who were on the bus at the time followed the bus driver's command, but Mrs. Parks remained seated. Her arrest was the catalyst of the black civil rights movement.

In retrospect, we might be inclined to say that Mrs. Parks had self-respect, but not the three blacks who followed the bus driver's command. But this is not as obvious as all that. When she first boarded the bus, which was nearly empty, she took the first seat behind the section reserved for whites. The bus driver's command to move to the rear of the bus came after all of the seats had been taken which meant that Mrs. Parks would have had to stand had she moved. That she did not want to stand seems clear, that she was insisting on her rights out of self-respect is not so clear. We do not know the reason why she did not move; we do not know the reason why the other three did move. But suppose that she refused to move out of considerations of self-respect, it does not follow that she alone had self-respect. For each had a self-interested justificatory reason for obeying the bus driver's command, given the way blacks were treated in the South back then for standing up to whites. That a person has self-respect does not mean that he has to put his life on the line.

As I remarked, when Mrs. Parks first boarded the bus, she sat in the black section of the bus (the other three blacks did as well). What was her reason for doing this? (1) Is it that she did not mind this Jim Crow practice so long as she did not have to stand? Or, (2) is it that she did not want to invoke an outbreak of hostility towards her? Or, (3) is it rather that her income was a major part of the family income and she was concerned not to do anything that would result in a major loss in the family's income?

It is conceivable that the answer to all three of these questions is an affirmative one. If, though, the answer to (1) is affirmative, whereas the answer to (2) and (3) is negative, then there would be a strong presumption that she lacked self-respect. If, on the other hand, the answer is affirmative to the second question, but negative to the others, then she acted out of self-interested reasons, and justifiably so. And if the answer is affirmative to (3) only, then her action, although not a self-interested one, was nonetheless justified. Finally, suppose, though it seems rather unlikely, that Mrs. Parks' reason for sitting in the black section when she first boarded the bus was that she is a "good" black who knows her place in a public setting, and that one of her aims was to continue to convey this impression to whites. Well, although we have here a self-interested reason why Mrs. Parks took the black section of the bus, this self-interested reason, far from rebutting the presumption that she lacked self-respect, would seem to confirm just this lack in her part.

The case of Mrs. Parks illustrates quite clearly the important place that reasons have in determining whether or not a person has or lacks self-respect. And by way of our embellishment of the case, we hit upon the extremely significant point that acting out of self-interested reasons does not always suffice to rebut the presumption that a person lacks self-respect. This is as it should be, surely; for we should hardly want to say that lacking self-respect precludes having self-interested reasons for acting.

Self-interested and other-regarding reasons, then, may suffice to rebut the presumption that a person lacks self-respect, though she tolerates unfair treatment. Reasons of this sort are justificatory ones. They are reasons that recommend this or that course of action. However, there can be good nonjustificatory reasons why a person fails to insist upon being treated fairly. These are good excuses. Consider the case of accommodating slaves in the Old South. It may have been futile for them to insist upon being treated fairly; and they may have not done so for just this reason. Or, they may have grown weary from insisting upon such treatment either because previous efforts along this line were so futile or because doing so had brought them so much suffering. Unfortunately, it is so easy for excuses of this sort to mask the fact that a person no longer has the conviction that he is deserving of fair treatment. Thus, in spite of the fact that they will gain nothing and bring nothing but suffering to themselves, sometimes an oppressed people must protest the injustices visited upon them just to convince themselves that this conviction has not slipped away.[24] The ideal may have it that we fight for what we believe. To this, reality demurely adds: But if we fight first, then we will surely come to believe.[25]

V

It is obvious that the social institutions among which we live have a most profound affect upon the way in which we view ourselves. This essay would be incomplete if I said nothing about what ought to be the connection between having self-respect and living amongst social institutions. In view of the fact that having self-respect calls for having the conviction that one is deserving of fair treatment and that the social institutions of society ought to be fairly arranged, it is almost too obvious for words that I want to say that the social institutions of society are fairly arranged if and only if they are conducive to every member of society having self-respect. But this needs to be explained.

To have self-respect is to have certain beliefs. However, it clearly will not do to maintain that the social institutions of society are fairly arranged if and only if every member of society has the appropriate beliefs. There are too many things, which might prevent a person from having the apropriate beliefs, that have nothing to do with any social institutions being unfairly arranged. Let us say, then, the social institutions of society are fairly arranged and, therefore, conducive to everyone having self-respect if and only if from the standpoint of such institutions everyone is justified in having the beliefs for which self-respect calls, since to be justified in believing a proposition does not entail believing that proposition. This much alone enables us to say when there is a strong presumption that the social institutions of society are not conducive to some of its members having self-respect and so are not fairly arranged, as the following argument will show.

Let L represent the class of persons in a given society who lack self-respect. And let K represent any class of persons that is identifiable by the fact that all of its members share the same biological or social characteristics, for example, all are of the same sex, or share the same ethnic or religious background. If the social institutions of society are fairly arranged, and so conducive to everyone having self-respect, then barring some special explanation, no K-like *class* should turn out to be a subclass of the L-class.[26] This, of course, is not to say that no *member* of the K-class will be a member of L, but rather that not all of the members of any such class will be members of L. If there is a K-class that is a subclass of L, then there is the presumption that the social institutions of society are not conducive to members of that class having self-respect and, therefore, that the members of that class are not being fairly treated by such institutions. Hence, there is the presumption that society is to blame for the lack of self-respect on the part of the members of that class. Observe that these remarks do not apply, *mutatis mutandis*, to self-esteem, since social institutions that are fairly arranged are not thereby conducive to persons having (high) self-esteem. In any event, the idea here is a very straightforward one. If all the members of a heterogeneous class are justified in believing a proposition to be true, then, barring some special explanation, the class of persons who fail to believe the proposition to be true should not be identifiable on grounds other than that its members fail to believe that the propostion is true.

The mark of a sexist or racist society is that its social institutions target people on the basis of either their gender or skin color.[27] The remarks in the preceding paragraph bring into sharper relief the reason why that targeting is so morally repugnant.

A final comment. I believe that the arguments of this section bring into sharper focus the difference between self-respect and self-esteem. For observe that it would be most implausible to suppose that the social institutions of a society are fairly arranged if and only if they are conducive to everyone having (high) self-esteem. One of the things that political theorists differ about is the latitude that justice or fairness gives society in the arrangements of its social institutions. I have a hunch that one reason why there is so often an impasse between political theorists is that they fail to distinguish between self-respect and self-esteem. Liberals cannot really mean that the social institutions of a society are fairly arranged only if the members of society have (high) self-esteem, though they can mean this about self-respect. And libertarians cannot really be indifferent to whether or not the social institutions of society are conducive to the members of society having self-respect, though they can be about self-esteem.

Indeed, I believe that the failure to take seriously this distinction is one reason why Marx's critique of capitalism founders somewhat. A capitalist society, to be sure, is compatible with persons having low self-esteem. But, I see no reason to suppose that a communist society is not. Any economic system that is compatible with persons valuing ends that are beyond their reach is compatible with persons having low self-esteem. Both capitalism and Marx's communism are compatible with this. And if we suppose, for the sake of argument, that the social institutions of Marxist society would be conducive to everyone having self-respect, suffice it to say there is no conceptual bar to a capitalist society being conducive to everyone having self-respect.

After all, the United States, which is unquestionably (thought to be) a capitalist society, could have had a different history, surely. American slavery need not ever have existed, nor the Jim Crow practices of the Old South. Educational practices need not ever have required the Supreme Court's *Brown v. Board of Education* decision in 1954, and so on. If racism had never existed in this country, it would not follow that all blacks would have led fulfilling lives, and so all would have had high self-esteem. However, it would follow that their moral status would never have been called into question; indeed, it would have been affirmed. If these remarks, sketchy though they may be, are sound, then, as I have claimed, the social institutions of a capitalistic society can be conducive to persons having self-respect.

VI

In the introduction to this essay, I made the claim that self-respect is the social analogue to the sense of worth engendered by parental love. That must have seemed to be a quite controversial claim those many pages ago. I hope it is less so now. Self-respect, I have tried to show, is a sense of worth that is not in any way tied to a person's abilities. It is a moral sense of worth. It is among social institutions that we live; and these institutions can be conducive to our having self-respect. Not only that, it is of the utmost importance that social institutions are conducive to persons having self-respect, just as it is of the utmost importance that parents love their children. The reason why both of these claims are true has nothing whatsoever to do with the talents and abilities of persons. Now, if drawing upon the black experience has made it easier to see that self-respect is the social analogue to the sense of worth that is engendered by parental love, then our indebtedness to that experience may very well be greater than many have been inclined to suppose.

Notes

1. In connection with (i) see, e.g. John Bowlby, *Child Care and the Growth of Love* (Baltimore: Penguin Books, 1953), with (ii) see, e.g., Robert W. White, *Ego and Reality in Psychoanalytic Theory* (New York: International Universities Press, Inc., 1963). For arguments that support both (i) and (ii) see, among others, H. Rudolph Schaffer and Ch: . ,.s K. Crook, "The Role of the Mother in Early Social Development," in Harry McGurk (ed), *Issues in Childhood Social Development* (London: Metheun and Co., 1978) and M. Rutter, "Early Sources of Security and Competence," in Jerome Bruner and Alison Garton (eds), *Human Growth and Development* (Oxford: Oxford University Press, 1978).
2. See White, ch. 3.
3. For the way in which I have unpacked the difference between parental love and parental praise, I am much indebted to Gregory Vlastos, "Justice and Equality," in Richard Brandt (ed), *Social Justice* (Englewood Cliffs, N.J.: Prentice-Hall, 1962). See section II especially. I have also benefited from the following essays: Ann Swidler, "Love and Adulthood in American Culture" and Leonard I. Pearlin, "Life Strains and Psychological Distress Among Adults." Both are in Neil J. Smelser and Erik H. Erikson (eds), *Themes of Work and Love in Adulthood* (Cambridge, Mass.: Harvard University Press, 1980).
4. For two excellent discussions regarding the difference between a rights-based moral theory and a duty-based moral theory, see Ronald Dworking, *Taking Rights Seriously* (Cambridge, Mass.: Harvard University Press, 1977), ch. 6, and W. L. Sumner, *Abortion and Moral Theory* (Princeton, N.J.: Princeton University Press, 1980), chs. 3, 5. The notion of self-respect, as I understand it, can be accommodated in a utilitarian framework; however, it would seem that it would only have derivative importance in that framework.
5. As far as I can tell, my use of the term "moral status" exactly parallels Sumner's use of the term "moral standing." See chs. 1 and 4 of his abortion book.
6. For an eloquent statement of this point, see Bernard Williams' essay "The Idea of Equality" in his *Problems of the Self* (Cambridge: Cambridge University Press, 1973).
7. I am guided here by what Kant says in the *Lectures on Ethics* in the section "Proper Self-Respect" and his second formulation of the Categorical Imperative: "Always act so that you treat humanity, whether in your own person or in another, as an end, never merely as a means"
8. *Principles of Psychology*, v. I, "The Consciousness of Self."
9. Roger Brown in *Social Psychology* (New York: The Free Press, 1965) writes that James has "written, with unequaled sensitivity and wisdom, of the self as an object of knowledge, as a mental construction of the human organism" (648). Stanley Coopersmith, *The Antecedents of Self-Esteem* (San Francisco, Calif.: W. H. Freeman and Company, 1967) writes "Earlier psychologist and sociologists such as William James . . . provided major insights and guidelines for the study of self-esteem. Their formulations remain among the most cogent on the topic, particularly their discussions of the sources of high and low esteem" (27).
10. On the relevance of self-esteem to being a sexist or racist, see my "Sexism and Racism: Some Conceptual Difference," *Ethics* 90 (1980), and my "Sexism, Racism, and the Business World," *Business Horizons* 24 (1981).
11. *A Theory of Justice* (Cambridge, Mass.: Harvard University Press, 1971), p. 426.
12. For a discussion of the life of Booker T. Washington, see, among others, John Hope Franklin, *From Slavery to Freedom*, 3 ed. (New York: Random House, 1967), ch. 21, and Charles E. Silberman, *Crises in Black and White* (New York: Random House, 1964), ch. 5. And for the story of his life, see, of course, Washington's autobiography *Up From Slavery* (Boston, Mass.: Houghton, Mifflin, 1901).

13. Cf. Coopersmith, ch. 3
14. *The Souls of Black Folk* (Chicago, Ill.: A. C. McClurg, 1903).
15. Consider the following passages from the address, which is to be found in Washington's autobiography, *Up From Slavery*, ch. 14:
    —No race can prosper till it learns that there is as much dignity in tilling a field as in writing a poem. It is at the bottom of life we must begin, and not at the top.
    —In all things that are purely social we can be as separate as the fingers, yet be one as the hand in all things essential to mutual progress
    —It is important and right that all privileges of the law be ours, but it is vastly more important that we be prepared for exercising these privileges.
16. A great many creatures are capable of having expectations about how others will treat them or behave. See, e.g., Daniel C. Dennett, *Brainstorms* (Cambridge, Mass.: The MIT Press, Bradford Books, 1978), pp. 274/5. But, only persons, or so it seems, are capable of having a conception of how others ought to treat them or behave; only persons are capable of having a conception of how they ought to treat others or behave. This capacity it seems to me is the mark of moral agency. And a being has full moral status, I want to say, if and only if it is a moral agent. Along with moral agency comes the capacity for moral character, a capacity that animals unequivocally lack.
17. Cf. William A. Mably, "Louisiana Politics and the Grandfather Clause," *The North Carolina Historical Review* 13 (1936).
18. On legal positivism, see H. L. A. Hart, *The Concept of Law* (Oxford: Oxford University Press, 1961) and Martin P. Golding, *Philosophy of Law* (Englewood Cliffs, N.J.: Prentice-Hall, 1975).
19. I cannot stop here to distinguish fully between pride and self-esteem. I trust that the following remarks will suffice. Suppose that I have just learned that one of my ancestors of long ago was an African king. This is very likely to enhance my pride, but not my self-esteem; since I will not come to think, nor will I expect that anyone else will or should do so, that I am better able to accomplish the tasks that I set for myself. A person's self-esteem may be out of proportion to his actual accomplishments, but this does not mean that he has foolish pride. For this a person has when he puts himself on the line in a reckless way: either there is no need to prove himself or it is obviously not worth doing so. Although an unexpected accomplishment in a fun and casual game of sports is likely to swell my pride, it will do little for my self-esteem, since I do not really aspire to do well in sports. Finally, there is what I would prefer to call derivative self-esteem (collective self-esteem)." If $\emptyset$ is an end that is valued by society at large and, as it happens, persons of kind K tend to be the most successful at pursuing $\emptyset$; and if the association between end $\emptyset$ and people of kind K becomes strong enough, then being of kind K can itself suffice to enhance a person's self-esteem. The self-esteem that comes with being a member of a high socio-economic class is perhaps the most striking example of this. The temptation to suppose that collective pride and self-esteem must come to the same thing should be resisted. To see this, one need only to let the example with which I began this discussion hold for an entire group.

    In any event, I should mention in connection with the self-esteem of blacks the work of Morris Rosenberg, *Conceiving the Self* (New York: Basic Books, 1979). It turns out that the integration of lower-class black children into predominantly white middle-class schools has had the undesirable effect of lowering the self-esteem of black children, whereas lower-class black children who attend predominantly black schools prove to have very high self-esteem. The explanation for this, of course, is that such black children are made more aware of their lower class status. See Rosenberg, ch. 4.

20. See Rawls' discussion on the role of civil disobedience in *A Theory of Justice*, pp. 382–391

21. This is Rawls' insight, which is first stated in his "Justice as Fairness," *The Philosophical Review* 68 (1958). To put it most intuitively, justice is simply fairness backed up by rules of enforcement, especially legal ones. We speak of the sword of justice, not the sword of fairness. Talk about the virtue of justice, as exhibited in the just man, is not all that much at odds with this point, if one supposes that the mark of the just man is that he does what should be required of him whether or not this is so. He does not treat others *unfairly* although he could easily get away with doing so. I owe this point to Paul Ziff.

22. Coopersmith, ch. 3

23. The story of Mrs. Rosa Parks is to be found in Martin Luther King, Jr., *Stride Toward Freedom* (New York: Harper & Row, 1958), pp. 43–46, 48–54.

24. This point is nicely developed by Bernard Boxill, "Self-Respect and Protest," *Philosophy and Public Affairs* 6 (1976).

25. This point is most cogently developed in Daryl J. Bem, Beliefs, *Attitudes, and Human Affairs* (Belmont, Calif.: Brooks/Cole Publishing Company, 1970), ch. 6.

26. Thus, suppose that a society is homogeneous in its make up. Or, suppose that all the members of a K-class are new to society, and that the effects of unfair treatment that they received in their former society have yet to wear off. Explanations of this sort are what I have in mind.

27. It is generally supposed that gravely unjust societies target some identifiable group in this way. But as I have tried to show this surmise is mistaken. See my "Law, Morality, and Our Psychology Nature," forthcoming in *Social Justice* in Michael Brody and Dray Brooke (eds.), (Bowling Green, OH: Bowling Green Studies in Applied Philosophy, 1982).

Note on the Author

Laurence Thomas, noted for his interest in the relevance of psychology to moral theory, is an Associate Professor of Philosophy at the University of North Carolina at Chapel Hill. One of his most well-known essays is "Ethical Egoism and Psychological Dispositions," *American Philosophical Quarterly*, 1980 and "Morality, the Self, and our Natural Sentiments," in I. D. Irani and Gerald Myers (eds.), *Emotions: Philosophical Studies*, 1983.

Self-Respect and Protest

Bernard R. Boxill

Must a person protest his wrongs? Booker T. Washington and W. E. B. Dubois debated this question at the turn of the century. They did not disagree over whether protesting injustice was an effective way to right it, but over whether protesting injustice, when one could do nothing to right it oneself, was self-respecting. Washington felt that it was not. Thus, he did not deny that protest could help ameliorate conditions or that it was sometimes justified; what he did deny was that a person should keep protesting wrongs commited against him when he could not take decisive steps to end them. By insisting on "advertising his wrongs" in such cases, he argued, a person betrayed a weakness for relying, not on his "own efforts" but on the "sympathy" of others. Washington's position was that if a person felt wronged, he should do something about it; if he could do nothing he should hold his tongue and wait his opportunity; protest in such cases is only a servile appeal for sympathy; stoicism, by implication, is better. Dubois strongly contested these views. Not only did he deny that protest is an appeal for sympathy, he maintained that if a person failed to express openly his outrage at injustice, however assiduously he worked against it, he would in the long run lose his self-respect. Thus, he asserted that Washington faced a "paradox" by insisting both on "self-respect" and on "a silent submission to civic inferiority."[1] and he declared that "only in a . . . persistent demand for essential equality . . . can any people show . . . a decent self-respect."[2] Like Frederick Douglass, he concluded that people should protest their wrongs. In this essay I shall expand upon and defend Dubois' side of the debate. I shall argue that persons have reason to protest their wrongs not only to stop injustice but also to show self-respect and to know themselves as self-respecting.

Washington's detractors charge that his depreciation of protest was appeasement; his defenders maintain that it was prudence. Detractors and defenders therefore agree that black protest would have been a provocation to the white South. A provocation arouses an individual's resentment because it challenges his moral claim to a status he enjoys and wants to preserve, thus black protest would have challenged the white South's justification of the superior status it claimed. Washington did not disapprove of every attempt to effect greater justice, he rejected protest in particular. Thus his frequent efforts to urge America to reform were consistent with his position. Since his remonstrations were received considerately, and not at all as provocation or

I am grateful to Tom Hill and Jan Boxill for helpful discussions and to the editors of *Philosophy & Public Affairs* for valuable comments and criticisms.

protest, they must have avoided making the kind of challenge protest presumably presents. Therefore, an analysis of them should suggest what protest is.

Washington always failed to press the claim that black people are victims of America's racial injustice. He frequently implied, and sometimes stated explicitly, that the white perpetrators of injustice were economically and, especially, morally the people most hurt and maimed by racial injustice and that, by comparison, the black victims of injustice suffered only "temporary inconvenience."[3] From this kind of reasoning it is easy to conclude that the morally compelling ground for reform is to save, not so much the victims of injustice, but its perpetrators because their "degradation" places them in greatest need.

The notion that because it implies guilt and ultimately moral degradation, inflicting injustice is a greater evil than suffering it is, of course, part of the Christian tradition and before that, the Socratic. Washington seems, however, to be one of the few to use it as an argument for social reform. Whether he really believed it is completely irrelevant. What is pertinent is that this was the consideration he thought prudent to present to America and that he hoped would be efficacious in motivating reform. This consideration, though urged insistently, did not arouse resentment. America, apparently did not mind being accused of degradation— as long as its affairs, its advancement, and its moral salvation remained the center of moral concern. For, as I have indicated, Washington did explicitly draw the conclusion that the morally compelling ground for reform was the moral salvation of white America.[4]

The idea that being a perpetrator is worse than being a victim is, of course, true in the sense that the person guilty of perpetrating injustice is morally worse than the person who must endure it. But, it does not follow from this that the perpetrator of injustice suffers greater evil than his victim or that the ground for seeking justice is to save the unjust man. As I have argued in another essay, such a position can be maintained only if the victim has no rights. For, if the victim has rights then the perpetrator's duty is not to avoid degrading himself but to respect those rights. To claim that the victim of injustice has rights is thus to challenge the transgressor's arrogant assumption that his own advancement, economic or moral, is the sole legitimate object of social policy. Washington never challenged white America's assumption that its advancement justified the reform he advocated, because he never claimed that black Americans had rights. Black protest would have affirmed that they do.

Because protest emphasizes the wrongs of the victim and declares that redress is a matter of the highest urgency, a person who insistently protests against his own condition may seem to be self-centered and self-pitying. He appears to dwell self-indulgently on his grievances and to be seeking the commiseration of others. Washington, for example, criticized Frederick Douglass for constantly reminding black people of "their sufferings"[5] and suspected that persistent protesters relied on "the special sympathy of the world" rather than on "their own efforts."[6] This is an important charge since the self-respecting person is self-reliant and avoids self-pity. It is not answered by the claim that people have rights, for having rights does not necessarily justify constant reiteration that one has them. The charge is answered, however, by a closer consideration of what is involved in claiming a right. The idea that the protester seeks sympathy is unlikely, since in claiming his rights he affirms that he is claiming what he can demand and exact, and sympathy cannot be demanded and exacted. The idea that the protester is self-pitying is likewise implausible, since a person who feels pity for himself typically believes that his condition is deplorable and unavoidable, and this is not all what the protestor affirms. On the contrary, he affirms that his condition is avoidable, he insists that what he protests is precisely the illegitimate, and hence avoidable, interference by others in the exercise of his rights, and he expresses the sentiment, not of self-pity, but of resentment. Protest could be self-indulgent if it were a demand for help, and it could show a lack of self-reliance if it claimed powerlessness. But, in insisting on his rights, the protestor neither demands help nor claims powerlessness. He demands only noninterference. What Frederick Douglass protested against, for example, was interference. He scorned supererogatory help. "Do nothing with us," he exclaimed, "And, if the Negro cannot stand on his own legs, let him fall."[7]

It follows from the above that when a person protests his wrongs, he expresses a righteous and self-respecting concern for himself. If, as we assume, the self-respecting person has such a concern for himself, it follows that he will naturally be inclined to protest his injuries. Would he always have good reason actually to give vent to his indignation? Protest, it seems, is the response of the weak. It is not a warning of retaliation. The strong man does not waste too much time protesting his injuries; he prevents them. Why then should the weak, but self-respecting, person protest his wrongs? Surely if either protest or whining will prevent injury, the self-respecting person will protest rather than whine. For protest is self-respecting. Though it cannot compel the transgressor to reform, it tells him that he should be compelled to reform and that he is being asked no favors. But, if as Washington's defenders aver, protest often provokes persecution, why should a weak and vulnerable people protest? What good could it do? If it will help, why can't a self-respecting people pretend servility? But it seems that people do protest their wrongs, even when it is clear that this will bring no respite and, instead, cause them further injury. W. E. B. Dubois exhorted black people, "even when bending to the inevitable," to "bend with unabated protest."[8] Is this mere bravado? Or does a person with self-respect have a reason to protest over and above the hope that it will bring relief?

It may be argued that he does; that he should protest to make others recognize that he has rights. But, though a person who believes he has a right not to be unjustly injured also believes that others wrong him if they injure him unjustly and that they should be restrained from doing so, it is not clear that he must want them to share his conviction that he has this right. Why should he care what they believe? Why, just because he believes that he has

192

a right, should he desire that others share his belief? There is no reason to suppose that the self-respecting person must want others to believe what he believes. Though he believes that the morally respectable ground for not injuring him is that he has a right not to be injured, it does not follow that he must want others to act on morally respectable grounds. Self-respect is a morally desirable quality but the self-respecting person need not be a saint. He need not want to make others moral. To this it may be objected that he nevertheless has a good reason to convince others of his rights, because the surest and most stable protection from unjust injury is for others to be restrained by solid moral convictions. This may be true. But it does not show that a person will want others to respect him just because he respects himself. Even the person who fails to respect himself may want the surest and most stable protection from unjust injury, and thus may want others to respect him. And, in general, for the protection of his rights, the self-respecting person cannot depend too heavily on the moral restraint of others. His self-reliance impels him to seek the means of self-defense. Secure in the conviction that it is legitimate to defend himself, he is satisfied if others respect him because they fear him.

Alternately, it may be proposed that the self-respecting person will want others to respect him because he wants to remain self-respecting. For unopposed injustice invites its victims to believe that they have no value and are without rights. This confident invitation may make even the self-respecting fear that their sense of their own value is only prejudiced self-love. It may therefore be argued that since protest is an affirmation of the rights of the victim, the self-respecting victim of injustice will protest to make others recognize, and in that way reassure him, that he has rights. Frederick Douglass, for example, once referred to this acknowledgment as the "all important confession."[9] But, though the self-respecting need to reassure themselves that they have rights, they would disdain this kind of reassurance. It is inappropriate because unanimous acknowledgement of a proposition does not imply its truth but only that everyone avows it. It is not self-respecting because it shows a lack of self-reliance. The self-respecting person cannot be satisfied to depend on the opinions of others. This is not to question the proposition that is difficult to believe what everyone denies and easy to believe what everyone affirms. It is to say that, even while he concedes this, the self-respecting person will want to have his conviction of his worth rationally based.

But it is not clear that the self-respecting person has good reason to protest, even if he does want others to respect him. Washington, for example, understood that social acknowledgement was important but condemned protest. He argued that to be acknowledged as worthy citizens black people would do better to develop the qualities and virtues that would make them economically valuable members of society. Washington was right. For though protest is an uncompromising claim that the victim of some injury has a right not to be injured, it does not follow that protest is therefore a likely way of getting others to agree. To affirm something, no matter how sincerely and passionately, may be an indifferent way of persuading others of it. And protest is, essentially, an affirmation that a victim of injury has rights. It is not an argument for that position. Typically, people protest when the time for argument and persuasion is past. They insist, as Dubois put it, that the claim they protest is "an outrageous falsehood,"[10] and that it would be demeaning to argue and cajole for what is so plain. Responding to a newspaper article that claimed "The Negro" was "Not a Man," Frederick Douglass disdainfully declared, "I cannot, however, argue, I must assert."[11]

It may be objected that though protest is not plausibly designed to persuade others that the victim of some injury has value or rights, it is designed to compel them to acknowledge that he is a moral being. This issue is raised by Orlando Patterson in his essay "Toward a Future that has no Past"[12] Speaking of a slave's stealing as "an assertion of moral worth"—that is, as protest—Patterson points out that by screaming, "You are a thief," the master admits that the slave is a moral being, since it is in the act of punishing him as a thief that the master most emphatically avows the slave to be a moral being. If the slave's stealing is indeed an act of protest then, as I have indicated, protest need not be designed to promote conciliation. Further, since what the slave wants to hear is that he is a thief, his aim is surely not to be acknowledged as an economically valuable asset but as a being who is responsible for his acts. Finally, though this concession is made loudly and publicly and, by all accounts, sincerely, it is nevertheless absurd and paradoxical. For though the master calls the slave a thief, and thus a moral being, he continues to treat him as a piece of property. Still, it may seem that the slave wins a victory. At least, even if it is painful, he enjoys the satisfaction of forcing a most unwilling agent to treat him as a moral being. This argument has considerable force. For a self-respecting person no doubt desires to be treated as a moral being. But it is not clear that a master must, in consistency, deny that a slave is a moral being. If he wants to justify himself, what he must deny is that the slave has rights. And, even if to be consistent he must deny that the slave is a moral being, it is not clear that the slave can always get the master to call him "thief." Or, even if he does, it is not clear that the master must admit that he uses the word in any but an analogical sense. And, it is not true that property cannot be punished without absurdity. Animals, for example, are routinely punished without absurdity and with no implication that they are anything but property.

It may finally be argued that affirming one's rights may be necessary to keeping the sense of one's value simply because doing so is an essential part of having self-respect. This must first be qualified. It may be false that one believes that one has rights. Thus, since lying cannot be an essential part of anything valuable, merely affirming that one has rights cannot, without qualification, be essential to keeping the sense of one's value. The argument must therefore be that protest is necessary to keeping the sense of one's value if one believes that one has rights. But why should one affirm what one believes, however deeply and firmly one believes it? To this it may be proposed that the self-respecting person wishes to seem to be what he is; he is, we may say, authentic. But, though authenticity may be a virtue, it is not clear why the self-respecting person must be authentic. To say that someone has self-respect is certainly not to say that he has all the virtues. Further, it is not evident that authenticity is necessarily one of the qualities that the self-respecting person believes to be valuable about himself. Neither is it clear, without further argument, that the self-respecting person's authenticity can be derived from the fact that he is convinced he has rights. Secret convictions seem possible. In the second place, even if the self-respecting person is authentic and wishes to seem to be what he is, it does not follow that he has to say what he is, unless saying what he is, is part of what he is. But this latter proposition is just what is at issue. The self-respecting person may protest because he believes he has rights. He does not believe he has value only if he protests.

Besides meting out injury incommensurate with the victim's worth and rights, uncontested and unopposed injustice invites witnesses to believe that he is injured just because he is wicked or inferior. Oppressors, no doubt, desire to be justified. They want to believe more than that their treatment of others is fitting; they want those they mistreat to condone their mistreatment as proper, and therefore offer inducements and rewards toward that end. Thus, even the self-respecting person may be tempted at least to pretend servility for some relief. But he will find that such pretense has its dangers; it shakes his confidence in his self-respect. I shall argue that the self-respecting person in such straits must, in some way, protest to assure himself that he has self-respect.

Since self-respect is valuable, it contributes to an individual's worth. But a person can have self-respect and few other good qualities. Since all men have inalienable rights, there is always a rational basis for self-respect, but a person may have an inflated and false sense of his worth. He may be utterly convinced, on what he falsely believes to be rational grounds, that he is much better than he really is. He may be mean and cowardly and cut an absurd figure, but insofar as he has faith in himself, he has self-respect. Consequently, when an individual desires to know whether he has self-respect, what he needs is not evidence of his worth in general but evidence of his faith in his worth. I argued earlier that protest is an indifferent way of getting others to acknowledge and thus to confirm that one has worth. But it may be an excellent way of confirming that one has faith in one's worth. For, as the preceding discussion should suggest, evidence of faith in one's worth is different from evidence of one's worth in general.

A person with a secure sense of his value has self-respect. This does not mean that he cannot lose it. It is a contradiction in terms, however, to suppose that anyone with self-respect would want to lose it. A person would want to lose his self-respect only if he feared that his belief in his worth was false or irrational, or, for some other reason, undesirable. But a person cannot be securely convinced of what he fears is false or irrational. And if a person believes that something has worth, he cannot believe that it is desirable to be ignorant of it. Hence, the person with self-respect cannot want to lose it.

Moreover, the self-respecting person cannot be oblivious to, or unconcerned about, the question of his self-respect. He must be aware that he believes he has value and that this is important. A person can have a belief and be unaware of having it, or have a sense of security and be unable to specify what he feels secure about. But the self-respecting person does not merely believe in his worth or have a vague sense of security. He feels secure about his belief in his worth. Thus, since a person cannot feel certain about something and be unaware of what he feels certain about, the self-respecting person must be aware that he believes he has value. And, for reasons already stated, he must believe that this belief is desirable. This does not mean that a person with self-respect must be continuously agitated by the fear of losing it. But it would be a mistake to urge further that only the confident, self-assured person who can take his self-respect for granted really does have self-respect. This would be to confuse self-respect with self-confidence. People sometimes do lose their self-respect. Thus to the extent that he is reflective, the person with self-respect will concede the possibility of losing it. And, though he may be confident of retaining it, he need not be. For, what he is sure of is that he has worth; not that he will always be sure of this. Whether he has this confidence depends on matters other than his self-respect. Though he may not be servile, a person may properly fear that, because of what he is doing or because of what is happening to him, he will become servile.

He may also fear that he is already servile. If he has self-respect he will be aware that he entertains the belief that he has worth and that he should be convinced of it, though he need not be sure that he is convinced of it. For he will probably also know that servile people too can value and persuade themselves that they have the self-respect which they lack. Thus, not only may a person with self-respect fear losing it; he may fear not having it. And this in not untypical. The early Christian may have had faith but doubt that he had it; to abolish his doubt he often sought the test of martyrdom. The courageous man may test his courage in order to know it. Though such tests may incidentally develop qualities they are meant to test, their main function is to discover to the agent a faith he may have, but of which he is not certain.

In sum, a person with self-respect may lose it. He may not be confident of always having it. He may not even be sure that he really has it. But if he does have self-respect, he will never be unconcerned about the question of his self-respect. Necessarily he will want to retain it. But no one will be satisfied that he has something unless he knows that he has it. Hence, the self-respecting person wants to know that he is self-respecting.

To know this he needs evidence. The need for such evidence must be especially poignant to the self-respecting person when, to prevent injury, he pretends servility. Observers often cannot agree on how to interpret such behavior. The "Sambo" personality, for example, is supposed to typify the good humored, ostensibly servile black slave. Sambo was apparently very convincing. In *Slavery: A Problem in American Institutional Life*, Stanley Elkins suggests that Sambo's "docility" and "humility" reflected true servility. On the other hand, other historians suspect that Sambo was a fraud. Patterson, for example, argues that Sambo's fawning laziness and dishonesty was his way of hitting back at the master's system without penalty. Thus, Patterson sees Sambo's "clowning" as a mask, "to salvage his dignity," a "deadly serious game," in which "the perfect stroke of rebellion must ideally appear to the master as the ultimate act of submission. Patterson is persuasive, but true servility is possible. Sambo could have been genuinely servile. Certainly every effort was made to make him so. There is therefore room for uncertainty. Further, it is not clear that Sambo can himself definitively settle the question. The master could have reason to suspect that Sambo's antics were a pretense only if he had evidence that they were. But if he is to know that he is not servile, Sambo too needs such evidence.

It may be pointed out that if Sambo's ostensible servility was his way of "hitting back," he was providing evidence of self-respect all along. But this must be qualified. Unless it is already known to be pretense, apparent servility is evidence of servility. If Sambo gave a perfect imitation of servility, neither he nor his master could have any reason to think he was anything but servile. If his pretense is to provide him with evidence of his self-respect it must, to some discernible extent, betray him. Patterson may be right that the "perfect stroke of rebellion must seem to the master as the ultimate act of submission,"[13] but the deception must succeed, not because it is undetectable, but because the master is so blinded by his own arrogance that he cannot see that what is presented as abasement is really thinly disguised affront.

If the above argument is sound, only consummate artistry can permit a person continuously and elaborately to pretend servility and still know that he is self-respecting. Unless it is executed by a master, the evidence of servility will seem overwhelming and the evidence of self-respect too ambiguous. But, as I have argued, the self-respecting person wants to know he is self-respecting. He hates deception and pretense because he sees them as obstacles to the knowledge of himself as self-respecting. If only occasionally, he must shed his mask.

This may not be so easy. It is not only that shedding the mask of servility may take courage, but that if a person is powerless it will not be easy for him to make others believe that he is taking off a mask. People do not take the powerless seriously. Because he wants to know himself as self-respecting, the powerless but self-respecting person is driven to make others take him seriously. He is driven to make his claim to self-respect unmistakable. Therefore, since nothing as unequivocally expresses what a person thinks he believes as his own emphatic statment, the powerless but self-respecting person will declare his self-respect. He will protest. His protest affirms that he has rights. More important, it tells everyone that he believes he has rights and that he therefore claims self-respect. When he has to endure wrongs he cannot repel and feels his self-respect threatened, he will publicly claim it in order to reassure himself that he has it. His reassurance does not come from persuading others that he has self-respect. It comes from using his claim to self-respect as a challenge.

Thus, even when transgressors will not desist, protest is nevertheless directed at them. For the strongest challenge to a claim to self-respect and one which can consequently most surely establish it as true will most likely come from those most anxious to deny that it has any basis. Protest in such straits is often unaccompanied by argument showing that the protester has rights, for what is relevant to his claim to self-respect is not whether he has rights but whether he believes he has them.[14]

Notes

1. W. E. B. Dubois, "Of Mr. Booker T. Washington and Others," in *Negro Social and Political Thought 1850–1920,* ed. Howard Brotz (New York, 1966). p. 514. Hereafter cited as Brotz.
2. W. E. B. Dubois, ed. William M. Tuttle, Jr. (New Jersey, 1973), p. 48.
3. Booker T. Washington, "Democracy and Education," in Brotz, p. 370.
4. Ibid.
5. Booker T. Washington, "The Intellectuals and The Boston Mob," in Brotz, p. 425.
6. Ibid., p. 429.
7. Frederick Douglass, "What the Black Man Wants," in Brotz, p. 283.
8. *W. E. B. Dubois,* p. 43.
9. Frederick Douglass, "What are the Colored People Doing For Themselves?" in Brotz, p. 208.
10. W. E. B. Dubois, "The Evolution of the Race Problem," in Brotz, p. 549.
11. Frederick Douglass, "The Claims of the Negro Ethnologically Considered," in Brotz, p. 228.
12. Orlando Patterson, "Toward a Future That Has No Past—Reflections on the Fate of Blacks in the Americas," in *The Public Interest,* no. 27 (Spring 1972), p. 43.
13. Ibid.
14. I have argued that the person with self-respect has a special reason to protest wrongs committed against him. It may be asked whether he also has a special reason to protest wrongs committed against others. As I have indicated, though he possesses one important quality—self-respect itself—he need not possess all or most of the other morally desirable qualities. He need not, for example, be altruistic or care much about others. If he does conceive of himself as having duties to aid others, however, he will want to defend his right to be that sort of person and will accordingly protest interferences with that right. Typically, he will have occasion to do this when his efforts to prevent wrongful injury to others are interfered with.

Racial Integration and Racial Separatism: Conceptual Clarifications

Howard McGary, Jr.

Blacks in the United States have endured economic powerlessness, second-class citizenship, problems of personal identity, and a lack of self-determination as a result of racial discrimination. Black theorists in this country have proposed numerous approaches in their attempts to solve these problems. I shall focus on two conflicting approaches frequently tendered as solutions. The first is the racial separatist approach; the second is the racial integrationist approach. Both approaches take a variety of forms, and both have enjoyed support by black Americans.

In what follows I will compare and contrast the integrationist thesis with the separatist thesis, but I shall not attempt to decide between them. Instead I shall only attempt to clarify some of the conceptual issues and arguments that underlie the dispute and make some suggestions about how policy makers can benefit if they are clear about the conceptual issues involved in the dispute.

There is intense controversy as to what a race is. In fact, some have even argued that there are no races.[1] For the purpose of this paper, I shall assume that there are races and, in particular, that there is a black race. I shall be exclusively concerned with the separation or the integration of the black race with the white race, but perhaps some of what I say can be naturally extended to the question of the integration or separation of any two races.

I

When we think of blacks who have advocated racial separatism as a way of eliminating or solving race related problems, we think of Edward W. Blyden, Martin R. Delany, Marcus M. Garvey, the early Malcolm X, the Nation Islam under the leadership of Elijah Muhammad, and the Black Cultural Nationalist movements of the 1960s with figures like Maulana Ron Karenga and Imamu Amiri Baraka.[2] The rallying cry of these individuals and movements was that blacks were being contaminated and destroyed by the present economic arrangement and by an alien white culture and value system. For them complete or partial separation of the races was the most effective and morally acceptable means of halting the degradation that blacks faced.

We must be careful at this juncture and point out that although all the individuals and groups listed above shared the belief that the races must be separated in order to achieve well being and self-determination for blacks, they differed in the specifics of how to achieve these ends. Garvey and the Nation of Islam stressed the importance of economic self-determination[3] whereas culture separatists like Baraka and Karenga emphasized cultural identification.[4] When I say that they stressed different things I do not mean that they completely ignored what the other group stressed.

Some separatists have been racial chauvinists, although it is possible for a person to support separation without advocating one race as being superior or unique. For example, one might merely believe that talent and abilities are correlated with racial groups, and that the abilities and talents possessed by all races are equally important, but that it would be prudent to separate the races in order to maximize human happiness. Then one must produce evidence that human happiness will, in fact, be promoted or is more likely to be promoted under such an arrangement.

Other separatists, like Garvey, have not been chauvinistic, but maintained that the races ought to be separate in every way. Garvey's argument was a consequentialist one because he believed that given the circumstances, the only practical means to achieve self-determination for blacks was through separation from whites. This consequentialist argument is popular amongst some separatists. But other separatists choose to justify their stance on deontological claims about the virtues of keeping the races pure. For example, the Nation of Islam, under the leadership of Elijah Muhammad, categorically supported the position that the races ought to separate in all areas of life.[5] This position is more controversial than a consequentialist position like Garvey's because it involves absolutist claims about differences between races and the things that may be correlated with these differences.

Cultural separatists, unlike separatists who stress the economic and political importance of keeping the races separate, place a great deal of emphasis on things like a person's self-concept. They believe that blacks in America suffer because they reject their black identity and by rejecting their identity and accepting integration or biological amalgamation deny their own creative possibilities. The separatist believes that this leads to a life without a sense of meaning or purpose. Some cultural separatists see complete separation of the races as a necessary but not a sufficient condition for blacks to achieve meaningful and purposeful lives, whereas others think that complete separation is unnecessary. For the latter, all that is required is that blacks be aware of their culture, take pride in it, and keep their cultural institutions separate from whites.

II

Now that we have set out some of the various kinds of racial separatisms' let us examine arguments in favor of them. I shall not assess all the arguments that have been propounded, but those I scrutinize are representative.

Many blacks who have supported racial separatism to achieve economic self-determination appeal to statistics that compare the economic circumstances of blacks and whites. Numerous publications have made available the statistics that reveal the vast economic inequalities that exist between blacks and whites. But these discouraging statistics nonetheless tend to underemphasize blacks' lack of control over industry, commerce, land, finance, communication, and the professions. Black separatists have claimed that the disparities in these areas are so great that blacks could never become full participants in such an economic system. This claim seems to be based upon the practical failure of economic integration in America. The claim is questionable.

Merely because blacks have a history of economic inequality in this country, one cannot conclude that in a racially mixed society one could never resolve the economic inequalities that exist between blacks and whites. Since no concerted effort has been advanced, one may not conclude that such an effort could never be successful. Does the separatist claim that in a society consisting of one racial group there will be no disparities in incomes? If he does, then his claim is obviously false. Japan is a capitalistic society consisting of only one racial group, yet large disparities in incomes and economic powerlessness of person exists. Although the existence of economic disparities are relevant, they do not by themselves support the separatists' thesis, but economic inequalities of our society do have a bearing on the subject.

One of the most compelling economic arguments for separatism concentrates on the problems one faces in trying to upgrade a previously excluded group. Proponents of this argument usually articulate their intuitions regarding these problems in an uncritical manner. They and their opponents tend to be overly emotional and fail to examine the vital points in question. Still the discussions are not entirely unreasonable. For example, when the black separatists remarks:

> It is crazy to think that blacks can integrate in the areas of jobs and education. White people can't make the commitments necessary to insure equal opportunity, which are necessary if economic racial integration is to be taken seriously.

The black separatist believes that whites will not make the necessary commitments because; (1) some are malevolent; (2) some will feel that it is against their interest, and (3) others feel integration will harm various American institutions. Professor Sidney Hook articulates the latter view with regard to government affirmative action programs. Hook contends that when the Department of Health, Education and Welfare requires from universities actual evidence of their efforts to equalize employment opportunities for minorities, the result is adverse to quality education at our universities.[6]

Worries like Hook's reflect the enormous moral and legal problems associated with achieving racial equality. So far, issues such as compensatory education for black Americans and other racially oppressed groups and the preferential hiring of blacks are still hotly debated. I am not suggesting that settling these issues will bring about racial equality, but rather that they bear directly on it. However, the worries articulated above will not serve to vindicate the conclusion that racial separatism is required to eliminate the problems that blacks face.

The two claims examined above—that past and present inequalities suggest the impossibility of equality in the future and that whites lack the commitment needed to create inequality are reservations advanced by separatists against integrationist policies. Perhaps the economic difficulties can be avoided if the society is willing to redistribute wealth and take certain compensatory measures. There is an argument, however, for the claim that the integration of the races deprives people of culture and self-worth. If this argument is sound it is a more formidable criticism than the two economic reservations.

III

Leroi Jones (Amiri Baraka) and Maulana Ron Karenga at one time advanced the view that racial integration would deprive blacks of culture and self-worth.[7] They felt that racial integration deprives black people of a culture that they already have or that they ought to regain because it involves the grafting of black people onto the white culture. They felt that when this is done blacks will be forced to accept a culture that developed in western Europe, one that ignores black art forms and black values. Jones and Karenga concluded that blacks must recover and maintain the positive aspects of their culture.

Before we can evaluate the cultural separatist position we must have a clear understanding of what separatists have meant by culture. The term 'culture' has been used interchangeably by separatists with terms like ethnicity and race. According to many sociologists this is a mistake. For example, Orlando Patterson feels that we should distinguish cultural groups from ethnic groups. He defines an ethnic group in terms of how symbolic objects are used to ". . . maintain group cohesiveness, sustain and enhance identity, and establish social networks and communicative patterns that are important for the group's optimization of its social and economic position in the society."[8] For Patterson, "a cultural group is simply any group of people who share an identifiable complex of meanings, symbols, values and norms."[9] Patterson also stipulates that there need not be any conscious awareness of belonging to a culture in order to be a member of a cultural group.

Space prevents us from getting embroiled in a discussion of the differences between cultural and ethnic groups. In my examination of the literature by black cultural separatists, I have found that they have taken 'culture' to mean more than the sometimes conscious and sometimes unconscious sharing of symbols, values, and norms. The cultural separatist operates with a concept of culture that includes Patterson's definition of ethnicity.

There is, of course, an obvious objection that might be raised against the position that integration deprives blacks of their culture. The objection is this: surely one cannot argue that some blacks don't willingly participate in, study, and cherish various aspects of white culture. Furthermore, these blacks might derive satisfaction and, in some cases, economic gain from this activity.

Is such an objection persuasive? I think not. Because some blacks receive financial and social benefits at a high cost, it is not good reasoning to assume that other blacks should be willing to pay these costs. The black cultural separatists believe that the game is rigged because the major cultural and economic institutions are set up to guarantee that blacks cannot fully participate unless they are willing to forego their own culture in order to benefit from American institutions. The recent National Broadcasting Company white paper on race relations in America pointed out that many blacks who are economically secure are still extremely dissatisfied. This dissatisfaction, according to the separatist, can be traced to the fact that in American institutional settings blacks are forced to adopt a culture other than their own.

If such a reply is to be compelling then we must have a clear idea of the things blacks must forego in order to benefit from American cultural and economic institutions. What are they? One thing that has often been mentioned is self-respect. As I interpret the position of the cultural separatists, they are maintaining that in the past all forms of racial integration have amounted to the elimination of the cultural identity of blacks and that this has and continues to damage the self-concept of blacks. When we talk about our self-concept, two concepts come to mind: self respect and self-esteem. Writers have sometimes proceeded as if these two concepts are synonymous. This is a mistake. Although there are important similarities between the two concepts, there are important differences. In order to adequately assess their position we should now take note of an important difference between the two concepts.

We esteem a person in reference to his abilities and talents as compared with the abilities and talents of others. A crucial aspect of self-esteem is the fact that the opinions of others are crucial to a person's assessment of whether or not he feels that he is worthy of esteem. Self-respect on the other hand, does not necesssarily depend upon the assessment of others. In fact, the person who stands steadfast in spite of the negative assessment of others might be thought, under appropriate conditions, to epitomize the self-respecting person.

An important feature of self-respect is that one tragic or disgusting episode late in a person's life can justify our describing the person as lacking in self-respect, irrespective of his abilities and talents. There are certain acts that the self-respecting person will not do and when possible, allow to be done to him. The racial separatist believes that to acquiesce in the denial of one's culture is one such act. One might question whether this is true. I doubt that it is always the case that failing to protest a serious wrong serves to undermine a person's self-respect. For there certainly are cases where it is in ones's interest or the interest of one's loved ones to acquiesce in a wrong or injustice. If this is so, blacks may not go along with the denial of the their culture simply for the sake of doing it, but rather to obtain goods that are necessary for their survival. In such cases, it is not clear that in doing so they undermine their self-respect.

The cultural separatist could grant that such cases do exist and that it is sometimes morally preferable to place great value on other things like saving the lives of one's loved ones, but that the price for such deeds may be our self-respect. Consider the case of a black worker, in a white environment, who is required to minimize or give up her identification with her culture in order to care for and protect her children. She does so willingly, but she still detests what she has to do. Even though her actions do not flow from a defective character, they nonetheless are her actions, therefore, she must accept some responsibility for them. In such cases, the separatist might argue that a person's self-respect is still undermined.

If this particular line of argument in the final analysis is not compelling, then there is a similar argument that may be more supportive of the separatist position. In the argument stated above the cultural separatist concentrates on self-respect of black Americans. There is another aspect of the black experience that illustrates the separatist point. This aspect is revealed graphically by Marcus Garvey. Garvey wrote:

> The only wise thing for us . . . Negros to do, is to organize the world over, and build up for the race a mighty nation of our own in Africa. And this race of ours that cannot get *recognition and respect* in the country where we were slaves, by using our ability, power and genius, would develop for ourselves a nation that would get as much respect as . . . any other. . . .[10]

Garvey is focusing on self-esteem because he feels that blacks receive very little recognition from most U.S. whites for their deeds and accomplishments. Recognition by others plays an important role in developing good self-esteem. William James put the point this way:

> A man's social "me" is the recognition which he gets from his mates . . . no more fiendish punishment could be devised than that one should be turned loose in society and remain absolutely unnoticed by all the members thereof.[11]

The separatist claims that blacks are not generally recognized by many of the cultural and economic institutions of our society because blacks are thought to be expendable or of little consequence in the realization of the basic goals and values of these institutions. Garvey proposes that blacks expend their energy developing their own institutions rather than attempting to modify institutions controlled by whites. His solution is the total separation of both races, but all separatists need not take such an extreme position. The moderate separatist could argue that blacks should strive to control some institutions, but not to exclude whites from participating in these institutions. In doing so blacks can gain recognition and legitimation for black achievements. Of course, recognition is a necessary but not a sufficient condition for blacks to develop a healthy self-concept. The communication of respect by one's peers is also necessary, but the separatist believes that this will occur when blacks separate from whites and begin to support each other.

204

Another argument frequently advanced by separatists has as one of its important premises the fact that blacks, unlike any other group, were brought to this country and brutally stripped of their culture, language, and religion. Black separatists, of all varieties, have argued that this caused blacks to lose important traditions and values and that this has contributed to people other than blacks having too much influence on the shaping of black lives. Given these things separatists feel that blacks must (1) realize that it is absolutely necessary that they decide their own destinies and (2) be aware that this could entail a radical departure from Anglo-American traditions and values.

Integrationists and separatists accept the fact that black slaves were robbed of their African heritage, but they disagree over the truth of (1) and (2) above. Integrationists have granted that blacks and whites are different but not so different that they cannot be integrated into American society. For this reason integrationists believe that there is no need for blacks to adopt things like traditional African values or to stress the differences that exist between blacks and whites. Because they don't except these things they don't put stress on black self-determination, but on things like class viability. Separatists, on the other hand, have felt that the racial, the ethnic or the cultural question is more fundamental because of its importance to self-determination, therefore it must be addressed before questions of class inequities.

The above arguments by the extreme or the moderate separatist are persuasive if we accept the following claims:

(1) that white racism is endemic in white American society, that it is central to the culture and economic interest of the white majority,
(2) that racial identification is functional from the standpoint of economic, psychological, and social development.
(3) that racial separatism can be a democratic solution to the race problem, and
(4) that a supportive bond can/does exist between blacks.

The empirical evidence needed to support these claims is sparse. Although I do not feel that racial separatists of any variety have shown that racial separatism is the best or only solution to the race problem in the United States, perhaps they have cast doubt on integration as a solution. But before drawing any conclusions, one should look carefully at the integrationist position.

IV

The major figures and movements within the integrationist camp include: Frederick Douglass, Booker T. Washington, Martin Luther King, Jr.; The National Association for the Advancement of Colored People, The Southern Christian Leadership Conference, and the National Urban League.[12] The basic underlying assumption of the black integrationist position is that American institutions can be designed so that blacks can enjoy, along with whites, economic, political, and social security as well as self-respect. Integrationists reject the black separatist contention that white racism is so deeply woven into the fiber of American institutions that it cannot be unwoven. The major advocates of the integrationist position thus reject the separatist proposal as unwarranted. They also feel that separatism is immoral because it stresses the differences between human beings rather than similarities. However, it should be noted that even though Douglass, Washington, and King all supported the idea of blacks becoming completely integrated into all areas of American life, they did not advocate or feel that this would entail biological or cultural amalgamation. Whether or not they are right or wrong depends upon whether or not any numerical minority can integrate into a culture different from its own and still maintain their own cultural or ethnic identity.

The term "integration" has been used by different people to mean different things. Some people have taken this fact as proof that the term cannot be defined. For example, Malcolm X in his *Autobiography* wrote: "The word has no real meaning. I ask you: in the racial sense in which it's used so much today, whatever 'integration' is supposed to mean, can it precisely be defined?"[13] Such a conclusion is incorrect. The word can be defined.

Unfortunately most attempts to define 'racial integration' have been unsuccessful. This, in large part, is due to a failure to derive a definition from the experiences and ideas of black and white Americans. Instead people have tried to define the term 'integration' in general (or in the abstract) and then placed 'racial' in front of it. Understood in this way, it is impossible to have a useful working definition of 'racial integration'. On the other hand, when we examine some of the writings of black and white Americans we discover several definitions of the term.

One proposed definition of racial integration does not preclude separatism. According to this definition racial integration refers to the condition where an individual of any race can safely make the maximum number of voluntary contacts with others. If racial integration in this sense were to be achieved all racial barriers to association would be eliminated except those based on ability, taste, and personal preference. This position is advanced by those who give weight to the freedom of the individual.

Despite the apparent compatability of integration and separatism, when integration is interpreted in this manner, most of the planning for integration is based on racial integration interpreted as racial balance. According to the racial balance account, individuals of each racial group should be distributed in a manner such that the desirable areas of life contain a representative cross-section of the population. This appears to be the position adopted by the National Association for the Advancement of Colored People and other civil rights groups. Needless to say, efforts to achieve racial balance have been fraught with practical difficulties. Some of these difficulties were mentioned in section II, so there is no need to rehash them here. However, it is worth noting that most efforts to strike racial balance have concentrated on how to desegregate blacks rather than on how to desegregate whites. The consequence of such efforts has been to adopt methods and goals that may not correspond to the interest of the black masses. This objection must be addressed by those who equate racial integration with racial balance.

In theory, integration allows for the coexistence of racial identities within a single socio-economic framework. Amalgamation, on the other hand, requires that the different racial identities become absorbed into one body. In theory, this distinction is clear, but in reality, racial integration often becomes interpreted as racial amalgamation. Both racial amalgamation and racial balance have the following consequence: they both assume that members of the races in question should not have the complete freedom to separate on the basis of racial preference. Thus the critics of integration have argued that both approaches violate something that we give great weight; namely individual liberty. Their objection is that if we respect people's choices or preferences then it is doubtful that there is a morally acceptable way to move to a racially amalgamated or a racially balanced society.

The integrationist position depends upon the following basic assumptions for its validity: (1) that there are not unresolvable differences between blacks and whites, and (2) that problems confronting blacks have as their root cause biased or unjust institutional design or they are the consequence of a systematic failing.

Whether or not these assumptions are true is still a matter of much discussion. We cannot settle these issues here. What I want to do now is to extract what I take to be some of the valuable points that emerge from the debate between the integrationist and the separatist.

V

In order to appreciate and assess the points raised by the integrationist and separatist, we must discuss ends. One might assume that the ends of the integrationist and the black separatist are identical. Historically both sought to eliminate the problems confronting blacks, but they differed radically on how to achieve this end and in their respective interpretations of the problems that blacks face. Although some integrationists and separatists believe that they share the same ends, not all do.

Most integrationists sought to integrate blacks into the white culture rather than vice versa. This, on the surface, appeared to be acceptable because whites enjoyed advantages and opportunities that blacks did not enjoy. So, by making blacks more like whites, they felt that they could eliminate the disadvantages and inequalities that blacks faced. Cultural and economic separatists vigorously opposed such a solution, even though they too wanted to eliminate these disadvantages and inequalities. But they did not feel that blacks could achieve these things by integrating into white society. Carmichael and Hamilton declare this position:

> Clearly "integration"—even if it would solve the educational problem—
> has not proved feasible. The atlernative presented is usually the large
> scale transfer of black children to schools in white neighborhoods. . . .
> Implicit is the idea that the closer you get to whiteness, the better you
> are.[14]

Carmichael and Hamilton are echoing the separatist rejection of the assumption that the white Anglo-Saxon ideal is the best for defining social arrangements and providing solutions to the problems that black experience.

Another important difference, in terms of ideals, between the integrationists and separatists of all varieties is the belief by the integrationists that
he is entitled to judge what is best for all people (black and white). Malcolm
X asserts this point quite clearly in response to a question asked by a white
person in the audience at a meeting before his death: "What contributions
can youth, especially students who are disgusted with racism, make to the
black struggle for freedom?" Malcolm X's response was: "Whites who are
sincere should organize among themselves and figure out some strategy to break
down prejudice that exists in white communities . . . this has never been
done."[15]

The separatist does not feel entitled or obligated to define what strategies are appropriate for races other than his own. It does not follow that he
wishes ill on other groups. His point is simply that he does not have the information or shared experience to know what other groups need and how their
needs ought to be met. If the separatist advocates a strong notion of group
self-interest, then to be concerned only for the interest of one's own group may
entail the violation of the interest of other groups. This would be something
that the separatist would have to live with if he is to be consistent.

When we look closer we discover other differences in ideals. The separatist rejects the ideal of individualism, and endorses collectivism. He feels
that one of a person's primary, if not ultimate, obligations is to the race of
which he is a part. The cultural separatist Ron Karenga wrote:

> There is no such thing as individualism, we're all black. The only thing
> that saved us from being lynched like Emmett Till or shot down like
> Medger Evens was not our economic or social status, but our absence.[16]

All racial or cultural separatists put the interest of blacks as a cultural and
racial group before their own personal welfare and, of course, before the welfare of other groups.

One might interpret the separatist as denying individual freedom. In
other words, individual blacks, under the separatist ideal, are not free to adopt
other racial identities. The separatist would reply that the sense of individual
liberty being employed in this type of objection is an illusion. For all separatists the social realities are such that it is impossible for a black person to
adopt a racial identity other than his own, unless his physical appearance allows him to pass for white. But even then he must be on guard to prevent his

heredity from being discovered. If his identity is revealed, he will be identified as black irrespective of his physical appearance or temperament and thereby subjected to the indignities that all blacks face regardless of their socio-economic standing. One drop of black makes the person black, but many drops of white blood does not suffice to make the person white.

The ideals of the biological and cultural amalgamationists and the proponents of racial integration as racial balance come under attack from those who value personal freedom. Given the present social realities, in order to achieve either of these ideals a society would be forced to disrespect the preferences of its members who choose to retain distinct racial identities and establish social institutions that excluded people with racial identities different from their own. This is an attack on personal autonomy. Unlike the racial separatists' rejection of individual preferences this rejection is done in spite of the social realities rather than because of them.

VI

Where does all of this leave us? What I think that our discussion suggests is that activists and policy makers are going to have to further clarify their goals. This will involve paying close attention to the aspiration and values of those who will be affected by their policies. To date much of their efforts have been expended on the means to achieve vague ideals. If they are to clarify their ideals, they must learn from the integrationist and the separatist.

Black and white communities are a reality everywhere in the United States. The policy maker should not ignore this reality. It has not been demonstrated that equality, fairness, or justice requires that we eliminate these communites. In the past, policy makers have sought to meet the immediate needs of the disadvantaged, rather than expanding the resources of the disadvantaged, so that they can be in a position to interpret and meet their own needs. The black separatist stresses the importance of blacks having a healthy self-concept, which involves having certain resources which will give them control over their own lives.

The key term here is 'resources'. What I mean by resources is the control that individuals and groups have over issues and objects that are in their interest. The assumption is that the more control a person has over things that matter to him the better off he will be, other things being equal. Rational self-interested people thus try to maximize their control over things that matter most to them. It might also involve striking alliances with people with different interests in order to gain control where individually one is weak.

Blacks having control over their own lives is a theme that runs through all of the black separatist literature. Yet you do not find that theme stressed in the integrationist literature. The integrationist places emphasis on the welfare of blacks rather than on control or group autonomy. Integrationists appear to believe that there is no point in having control if this does not promote one's welfare in regard to the basic necessities of life. The integrationists feel that this is the case with black Americans, and they concentrate on promoting welfare rather than control. For them, as long as welfare is achieved, whose efforts produce it is secondary. Although the separatist is not indifferent to the welfare of blacks, he does not believe that the welfare or good self-esteem of blacks can be fully secured unless blacks have control over their lives.

This point can be illustrated by focusing on the issue of forced busing. What are the goals of forced busing? Hopefully not to simply have black and white children sitting together in the same classroom, but to produce quality education for all and to contribute to better race relations. Some policy makers have clearly failed to see this. The lesson to be learned from the dispute between integrationists and separatists is that rather than expending energy and money to force people to integrate or separate, we should start with the social realities as they are and provide members of all groups with the opportunity and resources to shape their own lives. Given the present social realities would not a voucher system for the financing of public education create better education for all and give black parents and children more control over their education? Have black policy makers fully explored this possibility?

The separatist, as we have seen, focuses on controlling one's resources and the need to avoid being deprived of one's culture. Although not all of the separatists arguments are cogent, these two points deserve further consideration. Policy makers must not ignore these two points. They should seek to determine the proper relationship between controlling one's resources and satisfying ones's wants and needs. They should also examine in a very comprehensive way the relationship between race and culture.

The integrationist arguments are not totally persuasive either, but they do reveal some compelling points. For example, their stress on improving the welfare of the blacks rather than group self-determination is a point that warrants careful scrutiny. Policy makers must determine whether the emphasis on welfare rather than self-determination will eliminate the subjugation of blacks and promote better race relations. In doing this they will need to decide whether or not black group self-determination is a necessary condition for individual black Americans to enjoy certain basic rights that are taken for granted by most white Americans. They will also need to decide whether or not trying to eliminate racial distinctions all together or keeping them and playing down their importance is the best way to promote good race relations.

There are no simple answers or solutions to the complex questions and problems raised above. However, becoming clear about the nature of the question or problem is an indispensable first step towards an anwer or a resolution. If we are to adequately address the problems above, we must also work closely with people from all branches of human inquiry and attempt to bridge the gap between the framers of policy, the practitioners, and the political and social theorists.[17]

Notes

1. See Ashley Montagu, *Man's Most Dangerous Myth: The Fallacy of Race* (New York: Oxford University Press, 1974) and Ashley Montagu, *Race, Science and Humanity* (New York: Van Nostrand Reinhold, 1963).
2. See Edward W. Blyden, "The African Problem and the Method of its Solution" and Martin R. Delany "The Condition, Elevation, Emigration, and Destiny of the Colored People of the United States" (abridged) in *Negro Social and Political Thought 1850-1920* (ed.) Howard Brotz (New York: Basic Books, Inc., 1966); Marcus Garvey, *Philosophy and Opinions of Marcus Garvey on Africa for the Africans* (London: Frank Cass and Co., Ltd., 1923); Tony Martin, *Race First* (Westport, Conn.: Greenwood Press, 1976); Malcolm X (with assistance of Alex Haley) *The Autobiography of Malcolm X* (New York: Grove Press, 1965); Elijah Muhammad, *Message to the Black Man in America* (Chicago: Muhammad Mosque of Islam No. 2, 1965); Leroi Jones, "The Need for a Cultural Base to Civil Rites and B power Moments" in *The Black Power Revolt* (ed.) Floyd B. Barbour (New York: Collier Books, 1968), pp. 136–144; and Maulana Karenga, *The Quotable Karenga* (copyright by U.S. Organization, 1967), pp. 1–7 and 9–14.
3. Garvey, *op. cit.*, pp. 49–50 and Elijah Muhammad, *op. cit.*
4. Jones, *op. cit.* pp. 136–144 and Karenga, *op. cit.*, pp. 1–7.
5. Muhammad, *op. cit.*
6. Sidney Hook, "Discrimination Against the Qualified," *New York Times*, Op-Ed page, November 5, 1971.
7. Jones, *op. cit.*, pp. 140–144 and Karenga *op. cit.*, pp. 1–7 and 9–14.
8. Orlando Patterson, *Ethnic Chauvinism: The Reactionary Impulse* (New York: Stein and Day, 1977) p. 102.
9. Ibid., pp. 104–105.
10. Garvey, *op. cit.*, pp. 42–43, emphasis added.
11. William James, *Psychology: The Brief Course*, (ed.) Gordon Allport (New York: Harper and Row, 1961).
12. See, Brotz, *op. cit.*, pp. 203–331 and pp. 356–371, and Martin L. King, Jr., "I Have a Dream", *Negro History Bulletin*, 1968, pp. 16–17.
13. Malcolm X, *The Autobiography*, p. 275.
14. Stokely Carmichael and Charles V. Hamilton, *Black Power* (New York: Random House, 1967), p. 157.
15. Malcolm X. *Malcolm X Speaks* (ed.) G. Breitman (New York: Grove Press, 1966), p. 221.
16. Maulana Ron Karenga, "From the Quotable Karenga" in *The Black Power Revolt* (ed.) Floyd B. Barbour (New York: Collier Books, 1968), p. 190.
17. I wish to thank the New York Society for the Study of Black Philosophy, Brian McLaughlin, and Irving Thalberg for their comments on an earlier draft of this paper. I also thank Rutgers University for a Minority Faculty Development Grant that provided partial support for this project.

Note on the Author

Howard McGary, Jr., is Assistant Professor of Philosophy, Rutgers University. His areas of specialization are social and political philosophy, ethics, and philosophy and the Black Experience. He is noted for his views on reparation and discrimination. He authored "Justice and Reparations," *The Philosophical Forum*, 1977–78.

Society, Culture, and the Problem of Self-Consciousness: A Kawaida Analysis

Maulana Karenga

I. Introduction

If the problem of self-consciousness appears as only a problem of philosophy, it is first because it has been abstracted from the social context in which it rises and is posed. This abstraction no doubt is due to a conscious or unconscious deference to traditional philosophy that "presupposes a permanent, though varying, distance between reality and its philosophical interpretation."[1] At such a deferential distance, it is no wonder that one cannot see that all human thought and practice are socially rooted and can only be understood and explicated in a given social context. Second, such an abstraction from social context suggests a failure to recognize and accept the fact that the ultimate task of philosophy is not only to comprehend reality but also to change it. Thus, as Fanon argued, "reality, for once, requires a total understanding. On the objective level as on the subjective level, a solution has to be supplied."[2] It is within the context of these initial assumptions about society and social consciousness that this paper is organized and developed. The social context in which the problem is posed is the USA; the problem of self-consciousness to be treated is that of the African American and the philosophical or ideological framework within which the analysis takes place is Kawaida.[3]

Kawaida, as an ongoing self-conscious thrust toward synthesis of the best of nationalist, Pan-Africanist, and socialist thought, approaches the problem of Black self-consciousness within the framework of several fundamental assumptions. First, Kawaida argues that the problem of self-consciousness is, in fact, a problem of ethos, which is defined "as the sum of characteristics and achievements of a people which define and distinguish it from others and give it collective self-consciousness and collective personality."[4] Secondly, Kawaida posits that the problem of ethos or collective self-consciousness is in essence both a problem of culture and a task of cultural and social struggle.

Culture is defined as the totality of a peoples's thought and practice, which occurs in seven basic areas: mythology (sacred and secular), history, social organization, economic organization, political organization, creative production (arts and science), and ethos (collective self-definition and consciousness). Kawaida asserts that ethos is ultimately developed and defined by achievements in the other six areas of culture. "Ethos, then, as a social and historical product, a product of social and historical practice by a people to shape the world in its own image and interests."[5] Put another way, ethos rises from social and historical action that translates as a people's struggle to overcome all opposition—natural and social—and realize themselves. And self-realization as both a cognitive and practical enterprise is a cultural project and process.

Self-realization here has a double meaning, i.e., *to know* and *to produce* oneself. "Thus, to realize themselves, a people must know themselves and produce themselves, and both *self-knowledge* and *self-production* are rooted in social and historical practice."[6] Now, if the totality of a people's thought and practice is its culture, then both self-knowledge and self-production can be defined as the cultural construction of self and reality. For as a people creates itself, it does so in a given social context. Thus, it engages in self and social construction at the same time, creating its own particular culture in the process. Culture, then as a particular socio-historical process and product, becomes the central medium, mode, and mirror of self assertion and, therefore, self-identity. It is, perhaps, clear at this point that I am using culture and cultural context as comprehensive categories in a similar manner as socialist writers use "social context" and "social conditions," etc. The main exception is that culture is used as a *particular* product of a given people in the process of knowing and creating itself, and introducing itself to history and humanity.

Given the above, a third asumption of this paper is that the human being is essentially a cultural being. This contention challenges Marx's philosophical anthropology, which posits the human being as essentially a *gattung-swesen* or species being. For though the image of humans may transcend a given socio-historical or cultural context, the concrete human is rooted in a cultural reality. The Marxist view of the human being as species being is an abstraction from his/her socio-historical particularity, i.e., his/her cultural particularity, an abstraction inspired by a normative aspiration and assumption of other-directedness and a rational perception of human's need for each other in social labor. But such a being without socio-historical specificity is one without socio-historical reality. For real humans live in a particular time and place, shape their world in their own image and interests, filling it with both symbols and substance that identify and distinguish them. They are therefore cultural beings in the general and specific sense, and it is their cultural construction that becomes the empirical content of human existence. Cultural construction in both the general human and *people-specific* sense then becomes the central mode by which humans distinguish themselves from animals and each other. Thus, as we shall see later, if cultural construction or the reality and value of a people's culture is denied, doubted, or deformed, it poses not only a problem of self-consciousness, but also of self-construction that shapes and determines self-consciousness.

A fourth fundamental assumption that informs this analysis, then, is that a people creates and recognizes itself through struggle against four basic oppositions: (1) nature; (2) society; (3) others; (4) self, and thru the achievement this struggle produces. As a people struggle to overcome these oppositions, then, it defines itself and informs the world of its difference and distinctiveness, i.e., its ethos. Thus, *a people comes into being and knows itself by its achievement*, i.e., its cultural construction in a definite socio-historical context. *And through its efforts to become and know itself, it achieves.* Given this, it is a fundamental Kawaida contention that a people whose achievements are minor or whose knowledge of its history and the possibilities it suggests is deficient, develops a self-consciousness of similar characteristics. Moreover, in a social context that denies and deforms a people's capacity to realize itself, the problem of self-consciousness is a problem of practice as well as of thought. The problem, then, as suggested at the outset appears as it is, one with both a theoretical and practical dimension and demanding critical and corrective solutions in both the area of social theory and practice.

II. Critique of Problems

In the context of the above, then, the problem of Afro-American consciousness is defined by four basic factors: (1) internal fragmentation; (2) alienation; (3) ideological deficiencies; and (4) the lack of a body of self-conscious intellectuals who could serve as a vanguard in transformation and transcendence of this defective consciousness and the social conditions that created and sustain it.

The problem of fragmented Black consciousness was posited as early as 1897 by W. E. B. DuBois in an essay entitled, "Strivings of the Negro People." Recognizing the social roots of this fragmentation, DuBois described the American social system as "a world which yields (the Black person) no self-consciousness, but only lets him see himself through the revelation of the other world."[7] He categorizes this defective consciousness as a "double consciousness" having two defining aspects. First, it was "a peculiar sensation; . . . a sense of always looking at oneself through the eyes of others, of measuring one's soul by the tape of a world" that is hostile and contemptuous. Secondly, this defective form of consciousness was defined by its being a feeling of "twoness," i.e., of being African and American and having "two unreconciled strivings, two warring ideals in one dark body whose dogged strength alone keeps it from being torn asunder." DuBois concludes positing that the history of the Afro-American is, in fact, a "history of this strife—this longing to attain self-conscious manhood, merge his double self into a better truer self."

The problem of fragmentation, then, as posed by DuBois rests in having a derivative and split consciousness. By derivative I mean that it emanates from the judgment and assignment of value by the rulers of society. And by split I mean that the consciousness lacks wholeness and unity and therefore is deprived of a solid identity. For identity by definition denotes and necessitates oneness and specificity. This split, then, results in an identity crisis reflected in the various names Blacks call themselves, i.e., Moors, Creoles, Bilalians, Ethiopians, Coloreds, Americans, just human, etc., and the ensuing debates around these. This psycho-historical aspect of the problem of self-consciousness is rooted in three basic socio-historical processes African Americans encountered: (1) land and labor dispossession; (2) deculturalization; and (3) dehumanization.

Land and labor dispossession occurred as a result of Europe's conquest of Africa, which involved Africans being enslaved and brought to the U.S. where their labor was used to enrich the slaveholder. "The removal from our ancestral land was at the same time a removal from a clear point of identity-reference, an eternal reminder of who we are and what we've done in our historical becoming."[8] This caused *historical amnesia*, a loss of historical memory, which is a clear aspect of the identity crisis.

Likewise, the European dispossession of African labor—mental and manual— was in fact appropriation of their productive capacity, i.e., appropriation of their capacity to produce and know themselves through that production. Thus, they became strangers to themselves, for they had no way to recognize and confirm themselves. As enslaved Africans, their labor and the products of it belonged to their slaveholder. Though they created them, their products were not recognizable as theirs, and thus were not a means of self-recognition for them.

It is in recognition of this that Cabral establishes the link between history, culture, and the productive process, arguing that not only does imperialism deny the historical process of Africans by interrupting and usurping "the process of development of productive forces" but also "by denying the historical development of a dominated people," (it) also denies their cultural development.[9] Thus, deculturalization was a corollary to dispossession. At the core of this process was the thrust to de-Africanize the African, transfor him or her into a nonhistorical and noncultural being with no historical memory to draw from and no future to look for outside a servile association with white history and future. This de-Africanization involved the destruction of African families and family forms, customs, views, and value systems and the denial and deformation of African history. It is only through the amazing internal strength and struggle of African Americans that they were able to offer significant resistance to these processes and make them less successful than the slaveholder intended.[10]

Logically linked with the dispossession and deculturalization process is the process of dehumanization. Dehumanization, as a psychocultural process, flows from the European's deformation, denial, and destruction of Black people's history. As Touré states, what Europe sought to do was pretend it was dealing with beasts, to allege "the barbarity of Africans" and thus "give birth to [their] estrangement from the human race."[11] This, of course, was done not because it was rational, but to create and maintain a justification for their conquest, exploitation, and oppression of African peoples. And here the history of a people is not simply the *record*, but also the *struggle* of that people in the process of shaping the world in their own image and interest. Deprived of records of what they had done in Africa and of the ability to define themselves thru self-determined productive activity, they had no socio-historical evidence of who they were. *This problem of African identity is directly related to the problem of human identity. For there is no way to be human except by being a certain kind of human.* Torn between DuBois' two worlds on one hand and attempting to escape the "Tarzanic" deformation and denial of African history on the other, the African American found him/herself in the midst of an identity crisis that was rooted in and reflective of a truncated and troubled self-consciousness.

The second factor that defines the problem of Afro-American self-consciousness is alienation. The problem of alienation was posed by Hegel as estrangement of consciousness from external objects in the world.[12] But Hegel reduced alienation to a problem of thought that is solved by thought, and he reduces the objective world to a fantasy, or a phenomenal expression of consciousness that is ultimately solved by the "negation of the negation" i.e., negation in consciousness of the existence of objects that negate consciousness. This exclusive congitive overcoming of alienation is an essential expression of philosophical idealism and was, of course, challenged by Marx.

Marx criticized Hegel's concept on several levels as Avineri notes.[13] First, he rejected Hegel's identifying the existence of objects with alienation. Second, he defined alienation as a state of consciousness resulting from defective relationships between humans and objects. Third, Marx criticized Hegel's reduction of humans to their inner self, isolated from fellow humans. Fourth, he opposed Hegel's denial of humans' practical self-creation and becoming through socio-historical practice rather than through mere contemplation. And for Marx, the essential social practice was social labor which shaped human conditions and consciousness. Finally, Marx opposed the political implications of Hegel's epistemology, which ultimately leads to conservatism and quietism, an impotent and detached contemplation of the world rather than an active self-conscious practice to change it.

Respecting the merits of the contentions above, alienation as an analytical concept will be used in this paper to mean a state of consciousness characterized by estrangement and separation of humans from themselves, each other, their species, nature, their labor, and the products of their labor.[14] In a word, it is estrangement and separation of humans from all or anything through which they can realize themselves, i.e., know and produce themselves. Given the social basis of consciousness, alienation is both—psychological and social, or rather psycho-social. For alienation as a state of defective consciousness is rooted in and reflective of denied, deformed, and destroyed possibilities inherent in humans and the social world they bring into being. It is a fundamental Kawaida contention that the social conditions of Blacks are in conflict with the demands of their development. The developmental demand of freedom is challenged and checked by the social chains imposed on them. Their necessary and historically based identity as Africans is challenged by their oppressor's racist redefinition of them as "niggers" and "negroes," i.e., non-historical beings whose relevance and reality are derivative of and dependent on the oppressor.

Under such social conditions they cannot see themselves as self-defining creators of culture, society, or the world. For the capitalist and racist social conditions under which they live deforms the purpose and identity of their labor, reduces it to a commodity, and forces them to work in their oppressor's interest rather than their own. Thus, the historical vision of the possibility of a total person—self-conscious, creative, other-oriented, multidimensional—is denied, deformed, and concealed. Moreover, social conditions conceal the African Americans' identity as African, challenges their identity as human and forces them into class and race roles which deny their need to free, fulfill and realize themselves. These conditions, then, produce three fundamental kinds of alienation: (1) class, (2) race; and (3) human.

Class alienation and the problem it poses for consciousness and the social practice necessary to end it are well developed by Lukacs.[15] By class alienation is meant the estrangement and separation imposed by class divisions in capitalist society. The majority of Afro-Americans, as predominantly working class, are not only alienated from their labor and its products, but split from other classes both within the Afro-American national community and in American society. Forced to sell their labor under exploitative and oppressive conditions, Afro-Americans suffer an alienation similar to other American workers. In a word, their labor, which should be a self-creating, self-defining, and self-confirming activity appears to be no more than a means to survive. Thus, the Afro-American worker does not fulfill or realize him/herself in work, but denies and deforms him/herself in it. For it debases rather than develops and is an animal burden rather than a means to human self-realization. If humanity is defined as the negation of animality, and labor, the essential human activity, is reduced to the pursuit of biological (animal) needs, then the implications are clear and unsettling.

The problem of worker alienation and the defective consciousness this produces is further complicated for Afro-Americans by the socio-economic reduction of them to a permanent underclass set off from the rest of the American working class by systematic racist discrimination. Such separation represents division within a division, a process and phenomenon that cannot but further increase alienation in Black consciousness. Blacks, then, are not simply alienated from their labor as workers, but also as Blacks. Thus, class alienation is augmented by the factor of race and the Afro-Amercian is blocked on another level of self-recognition and self-realization. Consciousness in turn is split again along race lines and racial alienation joins class alienation as a fundamental problem of Black self-consciousness.

Racial alienation is rooted in social conditions created by the theory and practice of racism. Racism is essentially a system of denial and deformation of the history and humanity of Third World people (people of color) and their right to freedeom based exclusively or primarily on the specious concept of race.[16] By designating race as a specious concept I mean to expose its social basis and motivation. For race is not so much a biological or scientific term as it is a category constructed to facilitate the oppression and exploitation of

Third World peoples. In that role, race becomes and remains a bio-social category designed to assign human worth and social status using Europeans as the paradigm of humanity and social achievement. Racism as social thought and practice expresses itself in three basic ways, i.e., as: (1) imposition; (2) ideology; and (3) institutional arrangement.

As an act of imposition, racism means the interruption, destruction, and appropriation of a people's history in racial terms. This can be translated also as an appropriation of their labor or productive capacity, for labor as the essential process through which a people creates, defines, develops, and confirms itself is an essential act of history. Therefore, the appropriation of African labor interrrupted African history and began the dialectical process of African underdevelopment and European overdevelopment.[17] It also meant as Blauner notes, "the establishment of salvery as an institution along color lines" and " the consolidation of the racial principles of economic exploitation."[18] Second, racism expresses itself as ideology, an elaborate system of pseudo-intellectual categories, assumptions, and contentions negative to Third World peoples and serving as justification of the imposition and reinforcement of the institutional arrangement. Racism, not satisfied with the appropriation of Black history and labor, seeks to deny and deform Black humanity. The need, as Europe defined it, was to create a nonhistorical dehumanized being who could not merit freedom and equality even by his own justification and dared not attempt rebellion. To do this, Europe developed three basic ideological forms of racism, which may be termed absurdities: (1) religious; (2) biological; and (3) cultural.

Religious absurdities involved using God to underwrite claims of Black heathenism and the manifest duty and destiny of ersatz white "saviors." Biological absurdities pushed Blacks further to the edge of humanity and left them little basis to claim humanity or demand freedom and equality. As religious absurdities "heathenized" Africans, biological absurdities objectified them, denied their intellectual capacities, and gave them sexual powers and motives that reflected Europe's fears and self-evaluation rather than the reality of African sexuality. Finally, cultural absurdities revolved around the claim of white genetic superiority based on cultural superiority as "evidenced" by the assumed white creation of all that is good and real in the world. However, the link between alleged white genetic superiority and cultural superiority was not and cannot be established, could not expain the "Oakies" or the average white man, and conveniently forgets the dreadful state of Europe when the first African civilization was created and to which Europe through Greece owes an immeasureable debt.[19] Also, it is obviously an embarrassingly inflated claim on the genetic and cultural level that seeks to pose world culture as a white construction instead as the human product it clearly is.

Finally, racism expresses itself as institutional arrangement, a construction to consolidate and perpetuate both the imposition and ideology that justifies it. This translates as a system of political, economic, and social structures that insure white power and privilege over Third World peoples. These structures, procedures, and practices in courts, schools, the job market, politics, etc., limit and deny access and equal treatment to Afro-Americans and other Third World peoples. At the same time, these institutional arrangements appear to prove Third World social and historical incompetence by structuring and insuring it. Thus, racism as institutional arrangement "denies members of a subjugated group the full range of human possibility that exists in society" and inevitably poses a problem of self-consciousness.[20]

Although there is a tendency among many Marxists to reduce racial alienation and oppression to class alienation and oppression, it is incorrect and analytically unproductive to do so. For regardless of the classical Marxist focus on and contentions about economic or class realities, race or ethnicity is a fundamental and necessary category of social analysis also. It is clearly reductionist to pose race or ethnicity as mere ephiphenomena given the fact that such particularities are constitutive of human and social identity and in a racist social context, determine life-chances and social treatment. It is for this reason that Fanon, realizing the deficiency of Marx's analysis in regard to race and racism, suggests a rethinking of Marx's philosophy to deal with these fundamental categories of social and human existence.[21] In the process of such rethinking, Fanon discovers that in the context of racist social oppression, the African is not only denied the capacity to realize him/herself through labor, but also his/her very reality as human being is challenged. Thus, the European speaks of the African in zoological terms, divides the world into racial compartments in the strictest Manichaean terms, and the African suffers alienation not only as a worker, but also cultural-racial alienation as a Black person, denied both history and humanity. This too limits and deforms possibility and therefore is a fundamental problem of self-consciousness.

In addition to class and racial alienation, human alienation also poses a serious problem of self-consciousness for Afro-Americans. The social limitations imposed on Blacks as a race and as nonrulers and nonowners are at the same time limitations on their humanity in terms of the power to effectively define and develop themselves as both persons and a people. It is a fundamental Kawaida contention that "to deny and deform human possibility is to deny and deform human essence. For *human essence is human possibility.*"[22] Whereas animals are limited by genetic programming, humans are defined by their unlimited potential of self-construction and self-realization. However, unfree, oppressive and exploitative social conditions can and often do deny, deform, and destroy this potential as well as knowledge of it.

The conditions of the ghetto and/or the subordinate social position of Blacks as a racially hated and limited group are such limiting conditions and thus contribute to the problem of Black self-consciousness. Trapped in a deforming, alienating, and alienated context, Afro-Americans begin *to confuse actuality with potentiality and the established order with the eternal order.* Shaped by the imperatives of capitalism and racism, their true identity as both African and human is concealed under layers of externally imposed false and insubstantial identities and roles. Alienated from their own humanity, many become the obscene caricatures of Europe against which Fanon warned.[23] And in this they clearly exhibit and underline another key aspect of the problem of self-consciousness.

A third problem of self-consciousness that Afro-Americans face is rooted and reflected in what can be called ideological deficiency. This ideological deficiency is defined by the lack of a people-specific coherent system of views and values that would give them a moral, material, and meaningful interpretation to life and that would at the same time demand their allegiance and a corresponding practice. The general need for a people-specific ideology for Afro-Americans is found in the function of ideology as an action-related system of ideas and in their objective interest in overcoming the cultural and political-economic hegemony of the dominant society and self-consciously creating a higher level of human life.

One does not have to be a Marxist to concede that "the ideas of the ruling class are in every epoch the ruling ideas, i.e., the class that is the ruling material force of society, is at the same time its ruling intellectual force."[24] If this is so in every epoch, it is also so in every society. To break this cultural hegemony and lay the basis for a practical challenge to its political-economic corollary, an effective alternative ideology is necessary. In the U.S., the ruling class and the ruling race overlap to form a ruling *race-class* that imposes both racist and capitalist views on society creating what can be called a false consciousness among its members.

The falsity of this form of social consciousness can be argued using Geuss' evaluative criteria, i.e., its epistemic, functional, and genetic properties.[25] Epistemically, its falseness is established by its advancement of views unsupportable by valid evidence and its tendency to evaluate the epistemic status of its beliefs to the level of universal facts. Thus, claims are made that human nature is the nature of members of a capitalist/racist society, that money, greed, and class are universal and forever. Functionally, its falseness is expressed by its masking of social contradictions and its thrust to legitimize and stabilize the hegemony of the ruling race-class and support reprehensible social practices. Finally, the ideology of the ruling race-class is revealed as a false form of social consciousness by the fact that is emanates from and is only the partial and distorted view of reality of the ruling race-class that advances its interest at the expense of a critical and/or correct consciousness for members of society. The need then is to intervene in the process, break the monopoly the ruling ideology has on Afro-American minds, and begin to lay the basis for a critical Afro-centric alternative that will not only help eliminate the problem of Black self-consciousness but also the social conditions that created and sustain it.

A final problem of Black self-consciousness is the lack of a body of Afro-American intellectuals who self-consciously become the vanguard in the thrust to transform and transcend both the problem of consciousness and the social conditions in which it has its roots and reality. Upon first perception, this problem might seem one of strategy rather than one of philosophy and consciousness. However, the Kawaida approach to philosophy and consciousness stresses the indissoluble bond between thought and doing, theory and practice. Thus, the passive receipt of knowledge and/or the pure mental process of knowledge is rejected as the paradigmatic mode of consciousness. Consciousness is posed here as the discovering, receiving, and shaping of knowledge, suggesting the need of an active intervention in social reality to establish and validate itself. Self-consciousness then, is and must be at it best, *active self-knowledge*, grasping and confirming self through shaping the social reality in which it is rooted and of which it is reflective.

It is within the context of this philosophic stance that the problem of self-consciousness becomes a problem of self-conscious practice designed to correct and expand consciousness. And this requires a body of intellectuals who become the vanguard in the thrust to achieve this task. The problem, however, is further complicated if those assigned such an historical vocation suffer deficiencies or problems themselves and fail to assume this designated role. This failure and the problems surrounding it are posed by Cruse as a definite crisis. Cruse remains an unavoidable reference in understanding the problems, or to use his term, the crisis of the Afro-American intellectual. He posited that this crisis is defined essentially by the problems of social marginality, alienation, cultural identity, and ethnic commitment. Focusing in on the "old guard" intellectuals, Cruse argues that "The failures and ideological shortcomings of this group have meant no new directions, or insights have been imparted to the (Black) masses."[26] In fact, he continues, "This absence of positive orientation has created a cultural void that has spawned all the present-day tendencies toward nihilism and anarchism evident in the ideology of the young."

Moreover, Cruse maintains correctly that the criticism of America's socio-cultural system by the Black intellectual is hollow and ineffective on two counts.[27] First, the Black intellectual "is beset by his own cultural identity problem" and thus, merely adds another cultural negative to one of the already identified. Second, the Black intellectual has contributed his/her "bit of illusion to the total Americanization fantasy" through integrationist thrusts and thus becomes suspect and a subject for critical analysis him/herself for such cultural and political accommodation and acquiescence. But Cruse does not deny or reduce the role Black intellectuals can and must play. His critique of the dimensions of their crisis is joined by correctives that place on them the responsibility of cultural leadership in the broadest and most essential terms.

There is, however, a class dimension to this problem that revolves around the fact that such a vanguard will for the most part undoubtedly come from the Black middle class, which faces severe problems of integrationist fantasies, political timidity, and the traditional opportunism characteristic of petty bourgeois classes in general. Although Frazier[28] had made the classic criticism of this class, Cruse's criticism of the Black intellectual is a simultaneous criticism of the class from which they came and all the negatives this implies. The crux of the problem of the middle class as a source of cultural and political vanguard seems to be this: "Having no historical mission itself, it cannot provide one for the masses; having built its influence and hopes on service to whites, it cannot urge or imagine power of self-determination for the masses."[29] Differing from other middle classes in its lack of a national consciousness and mission, it has paradoxically become a key part of the problem as well as a vital part of its solution.

III. Towards Correctives

If the problem of self-consciousness is a problem of theory and practice, then its solution must be achieved on those two levels. It is important to state that in the final analysis, all theoretical problems of humans in social life must be solved in practice. Thus, ultimately any demand to solve the theoretical problem of Black self-consciousness must be accompanied by a practical demand to end the social conditions that caused and sustain it. At this point, the introduction of the need for a cultural revolution that precedes and makes possible the political struggle seems unavoidable. Kawaida defines cultural revolution as the ideological and practical struggle to transform persons and a people and to build structures to insure, maintain, and expand that transformation. Given this definition, cultural struggle or revolution is important not only in the preparation of political struggle, but also in the very process of it. This is what Cruse means when he states that, "There can be no real Black revolution in the United States without a cultural revolution as a corollary to the scheme of 'agencies for social change.'"[30] Political revolution then is struggle to reorder the unequal power and wealth relations in society and thus lay the basis for each person and people to fully realize and fulfill themselves. Therefore, though we begin on the cognitive level of knowing and interpreting the world, the need to change it practically will still pose a fundamental human problem.

For the purpose of analysis, the various aspects of the problem of Black self-consciousness can be solved within the framework of: (1) ideological development; (2) creation of a self-conscious intellectual vanguard; and (3) social struggle in the broadest sense of the word. There is no human activity "from which every form of intellectual participation can be excluded," Gramsci argues.[31] "*Homo faber* cannot be separated from *homo sapiens*." In fact, at an advanced level of life, thought not only accompanies practice, but always preceeds it—if conscious and favorable results are anticipated. Thus, there is a need for theory to guide practice and to be tested and refined by practice as well as by more theory. This must not simply be a theory of self-consciousness abstracted from society, but rooted in an understanding of the social roots of consciousness and the dialectical relationship and requirements of change in both consciousness and society.

Afro-Americans, however, cannot simply have a general theory, they must have an Afro-centric theory, i.e., one that rises from, is focused on and on behalf of them. This is necessary not only to free themselves from the racist impositions of society, but also to proactively and self-consciously shape their life in their cultural image and interests. This same need is recognized for other race/ethnic solidarities. Cruse recognized this need, noting that the structure dynamics of American society "demands that each (ethnic) group produce for itself a native radical intellectual trend. . . ."[32] It is important to state here, however, that the task and intention suggested above is not to create an alternative false consciousness for Afro-Americans, but to provide them with a negation of ruling race-class ideology and the basis for a critical Afro-centric conception of reality and the possibilities and methods of changing it. It is the ruling ideology that prevents Afro-Americans from perceiving their objective situation and real interests. Thus, if they are to liberate themselves socially, they must free themselves ideologically or more precisely, culturally.

This intellectual thrust, as Kawaida contends, must not only be Afro-centric, but also critical and corrective in its understanding and provision of solutions in the seven basic areas of culture.[33] Without such a grand and synthetical approach to social theory, the task of breaking through the current defective mode of consciousness and making Blacks self-conscious agents of their own lives and liberation is not only impossible but unthinkable. For in the absence of effective and sufficient categories to conceive of a project, it is unlikely it will be initiated or completed.

It is for this reason that Kawaida stresses—some argue "overstress"—the indispensability of cultural revolution in both the preparation and process of political struggle. This dialectical relationship between culture and politics is argued by Fanon, Cabral, and Toure. Fanon notes that "well before the political or fighting phase of the national movement," culture, struggle, and production teaches impatience, awakens sensibilities, and makes "unreal and unacceptable the contemplative attitude or the acceptance of defeat."[34] Cabral contends that a people "are only able to create and develop a liberation movement because they keep their culture alive . . . because they continue to resist culturally even when their politico-military resistance is destroyed."[35] And Toure argues that "Resistance and then the offensive will be organized first of all in the cultural field."[36]

Given the role of culture and its importance to liberation, Kawaida argues in the Cabralian tradition for a selective analysis of the view and values of *popular culture* with an eye and aim toward building a self-conscious *national culture*. In fact, Kawaida argues that one of the key aspects of the cultural crisis Blacks face is the predominance of popular culture as opposed to national culture.[37] The problem suggested here is found in the definition and contrast between them. Popular culture is defined as the essentially unconscious fluid reaction to everyday life and environment. In contrast, national culture is defined as the "self-conscious, collective thought, and practice through which a people creates itself, celebrates itself, and introduces itself to history and humanity." Examples are the Black National Anthem and other self-conscious classical and current Black Music, Kwanzaa, the nation flag (Black, Red, and Green), intellectual products of the Harlem Renaissance and the Sixties, etc. The argument here is that "To be really creative, culture must be self-conscious in conception, construction and selection."[38] Only then can a people's self-creation, self-celebration, and self-introduction to history and humanity be all it should be.

Finally the emphasis placed on ideology emanates from the assumption of the constructive nature of human consciousness. By this is meant that cognition, the act and fact of knowing, constitutes not only the grasping of reality, but also shaping and changing it. This assumption derives from an epistemology that rejects a simple reflective theory of cognition. Accepting this view, one can see how the epigrammatic Marxian assertion that "social being determines social consciousness" tends to minimize the role self-active knowledge plays in changing circumstances. For if humans can only be products of circumstances, they cannot be also producers and thus can never create themselves and society in their own image and interests. In all fairness to Marx, it is not he who imposed such a mechanistic interpretation of the materialist doctrine. It was and is the vulgar Marxists who have made dogma out of his philosophy and method.

Thus cultural revolution, and the ideological development that stands at the center of it, also solves the question of the identity crisis. For an Afrocentric ideology would, of necessity, contain within it a self-definition based on historical and current facts, i.e., *historical origin* and *social location*. Using such concrete criteria one would define him/herself an Afro-American or any variation that did not contradict these two unavoidable realities. Moreover, the sense of fragmentation of consciousness DuBois posited is eliminated by the assumption of a self-conscious synthesis of the two aspects and by cultural and political struggle that leads to an enlarged sense of self and its socio-historical importance.

But it is clear that the cultural revolution cannot happen by itself. Like the political struggle, it must be formulated and led by a self-conscious vanguard. The critical and corrective consciousness necessary to redefine oneself in thought, achieve liberation, and realize oneself in practice demands a self-conscious agency of social change. As Gramsci correctly argues, "A human mass does not 'distinguish' itself, does not become independent in its own right without, in the widest sense, organizing itself and there is no organization without intellectuals, that is without organizers and leaders."[39] These people, who are "specialized in the conceptual and philosophical elaboration of ideas," produce theories or ideology that give a people or social group its homogeneity, awareness of its status and function in society and the possibilities inherent within it and the society in which it finds itself.

DuBois suggested the fundamental role of the intellectual vanguard in his call for a Talented Tenth, which will "guide the Mass away from the contamination and death of the Worst in their own and other races."[40] Moreover, this vanguard would be leaders and the positors of ideals of the community and would "direct its thought and head its social movements." Cruse and Frazier though criticizing the intellectuals still posed a similar role for them.[41]

The problem, however, is that the intellectuals, often for reasons of class, do not always assume their acknowledged historical vocation. Cabral recognizing the class doubts and timidity the petty bourgeois intellectuals face, gives them a choice of either betraying the masses and their historical role or committing *class suicide* and being reborn "completely identified with the deepest aspiration of the people to which they belong."[42] This may be called the education of the educators and requires transformed thought, not only thru contemplation of social reality, but also self-conscious practice to change it. This movement toward self-consciousness and active commitment reflects a dialectical relationship between the masses and the intellectuals who raise each other to higher levels of thought and practice as they interact and act collectively to transform society.

Finally, the creation of a critical and corrective ideology and a self-conscious vanguard is only a prelude to social struggle that will not only change and raise the consciousness of Afro-Americans but also their conditions. The assumption is that the ideology will pose the broad social struggle as a national vocation, a self-conscious sense, and choice of mission that reflects a positive and expansive identity, purpose, and direction. This national vocation will reflect the clarity, correctness, and effectiveness of the nation or ethnic nation's values and views of self, society, and the world and the possibilities inherent in each. Marcus Garvey, the father of modern Black Nationalism, posed the task of nation-building, stating that, "The race needs workers at this time, not plagiarists, copyists and mere imitators; but men and women who are able to create, to originate and improve, and thus make an independent racial contribution to the world and civilization."[43]

Moreover, the broad social struggle that leads to the ideological and social liberation of African Americans will not only liberate them and the U.S. from its current class and racial negatives, but will in fact bring the whole of humanity closer to full and final liberation. For to free themselves, Afro-Americans must free this country from the class and racial alienations and oppressions that plague it, i.e., its capitalist-racist structure and functioning. Thus, "our historical mission of freeing ourselves, in turn, becomes a contribution to freeing others ruled and controlled by the U.S."[44] in other parts of the world. In a word, the class and racial situation of Afro-Americans is such that the problem of their liberation is in fact a problem of social and human liberation. For they cannot liberate themselves without destroying the social conditions and structures that not only enslave them, but also others in and outside the U.S. Thus, as self-conscious agents of their own liberation, Afro-Americans not only contribute to social and human liberation, through the destruction of inhuman conditions and structures, but also by serving as historically important examples of active self-knowledge and the human possibility it reflects.

225

Moreover, as part of the Third World, African Americans belong to the rising tide of history. If one accepts the analytical assumption of the rising and declining tendencies in history, it seems obvious that Third World peoples are on the rise, stepping back on the stage of human history as self-conscious, free and productive peoples. A critical consciousness of necessity will place Afro-Americans in these ranks. As DuBois noted at the turn of the century, Afro-Americans have a key role in making "a world where men know, where men create, where they realize themselves and where they enjoy life." As part of the historical Black vanguard, he saw in Blacks ". . . stirrings of a new desire to create, of a new will to be, as though in this morning of group life, we had awakened from some sleep that at once dimly mourns the past and dreams a splendid future."[45]

Work and struggle, building and becoming, then, are the keys to de-alienation, self-recognition, and self-realization. Afro-Americans' real self will unfold as they move from self and social concealment to self-conscious construction of self, society and the world, making history with collective will and consciousness. It is in the midst of this cultural and historical construction that they will transform themselves "from a vaguely distinct and unconscious (ethnic nationality) into a clearly defined self-conscious historical personality, proud of its past, challenged by its present and inspired by the possibilities of its future."[46] History as the path to the future, then, is littered with theoretical problems that ultimately were or will be solved through social practice and the comprehension of that practice. Such is the future of the problem of Black self-consciousness that finds its solution in the dialectical relationship between philosophy's comprehension of society and its practical contribution to changing it.

Notes

1. Shlomo Avineri, *The Social and Political Thought of Karl Marx* (New York: Cambridge University Press, 1976), p. 136.
2. Frantz Fanon, *Black Skin, White Masks* (New York: Grove Press, 1967), p. 11.
3. Maulana Karenga, *Kawaida Theory: An Introductory Outline* (Inglewood, Calif.: Kawaida Publications, 1981a); *Essays on Struggle: Position and Analysis* (San Diego: Kawaida Publications, 1978).
4. Karenga (1981a), op. cit., p. 90.
5. Ibid.
6. Ibid.
7. W. E. B. DuBois, *W. E. B. Dubois, A Reader* (ed.) Meyer Weinberg (New York: Harper & Row Publishers, 1970), p. 20.
8. Karenga, (1981a) op. cit., p. 92.
9. Amilcar Cabral, *Return to the Source* (New York: African Information Service and PAIGC, 1973), pp. 42–43.

10. John Blassingame, *The Slave Community* (New York: Oxford University Press, 1979).
11. Sekou Toure, "A Dialectical Approach to Culture," *The Black Scholar*, 1, 1 (November), p. 4.
12. Charles Taylor, *Hegel* (New York: Cambridge University Press, 1972).
13. Avineri, op. cit., p. 97ff.
14. Bertell Ollman, *Alienation: Marx's Conception of Man in Capitalist Society* (New York: Cambridge Universtiy Press, 1976).
15. Georg Lukacs, *History and Class Consciousness* (Cambridge, Mass.: The MIT Press, 1973).
16. Maulana Karenga, "The Problematic Aspects of Pluralism: Ideological and Political Dimensions," in *Pluralism, Racism and Public Policy* (eds.) J. Bermingham and E. Clausen (Boston: G. K. Hall & Company, pp. 223–246, 1981b), pp. 96–97.
17. Walter Rodney, *How Europe Underdeveloped Africa* (Washington, D.C.: Howard University Press, 1974).
18. Robert Blauner, *Racial Oppression in America* (New York: Harper & Row Publishers, 1972), p. 21
19. George James, *Stolen Legacy* (San Francisco: Julian Richardson Associates, 1976).
20. Blauner, op. cit., p. 41.
21. Frantz Fanon, *The Wretched of the Earth* (New York: Grove Press, 1968), pp. 39–40.
22. Karenga, (1981a), op. cit., p. 100.
23. Fanon (1968), op. cit., p. 315.
24. Karl Marx and Frederick Engels, *The German Ideology* (New York: International Publishers, 1976), p. 64.
25. Raymond Geuss, *The Idea of A Critical Theory* (New York: Cambridge University Press, 1981), p. 13ff.
26. Harold Cruse, *The Crisis of the Negro Intellectual* (New York: William Morrow & Company, 1967), p. 99.
27. Ibid., p. 452.
28. E. Franklin Frazier, *Black Bourgeoisie* (New York: Macmillan Company, 1970).
29. Karenga (1981a), op. cit., p. 105.
30. Cruse, op. cit., p. 475.
31. Antonio Gramsci, *Selections From Prison Notebooks* (New York: International Publishers, 1973), p. 9.
32. Cruse, op. cit., p. 468.
33. Karenga (l981a), p. 17.
34. Fanon (l968), op. cit., p. 243.
35. Cabral, op. cit., p. 69.
36. Toure, op. cit., p. 11
37. Karenga (1981a), op. cit., p. 18.
38. Ibid., p. 19.
39. Gramsci, op. cit., p. 334.
40. W. E. B. DuBois, "The Talented Tenth" in *The Negro Problem* (ed.) Ulysses Lee (New York: Arno Press and the New York Times, pp. 31–76, 1969), p. 75.
41. Cruse, op. cit.; Frazier, op. cit.

42. Amilcar Cabral, *Revolution in Guinea* (New York: Monthly Review Press, 1969), p. 110.
43. Marcus Garvey, *Philosophy and Opinions of Marcus Garvey* (ed.) Amy Jacques-Garvey (New York: Atheneum, Volume II, 1977), pp. 23–24.
44. Karenga (1981a), op. cit. p. 110.
45. DuBois (1972), op. cit., pp. 362–363.
46. Karenga (1981a), op. cit., p. 114.

Note on the Author

Maulana Karenga is a well-known cultural nationalist theorist. He has published extensively and lectured both nationally and internationally. At present, he is Associate Professor, Black Studies Department, California State University , Long Beach. His latest book is entitled *Introduction to Black Studies.*

Liberation Strategies in Black Theology: Mao, Martin, or Malcolm?

William R. Jones

Invariably, participants in liberation struggles find themselves embroiled in an unavoidable debate. The heart of this debate is the appropriate model and supporting theory of social change required to eradicate economic, social, and political oppression. This dispute has assumed preeminent importance in the black church and its avant-garde movement, black theology.

An examination of this issue in the context of black theology reveals that the theological and socio-political ethics of Martin Luther King, Jr., is the inescapable, but not always acknowledged, backdrop for the discussion. Indeed, it does not do violence to our understanding to affirm that the debate reduces to the question of the adequacy and serviceability of his strategy of nonviolent resistance. Having said this, however, one should not conclude that black theology speaks with a single voice on this matter. The issue of the legitimacy of violence as a strategy of economic, social, and political liberation, for instance, splits black theology into the opposing camps of James Cone,[1] Albert Cleage,[2] and Joseph Washington[3] against Major Jones[4] and J. Deotis Roberts.[5] In the midst of this diversity, however, I discern a consensual trend: an evolution away from or beyond King's position. Black theology has flirted with, but skirted, the game plan of Mao, tasted the offerings of King, but moved on to sample another dish in the theological and ethical smorgasbord—a repast that bears the unmistakable spice of Malcolm X's socio-political ethics.

My purpose in this essay is to advance a critical and comparative analysis of King's political and theological ethics and, thus, explain this accelerated evolution that has carried black theology closer to Malcolm X than is commonly understood and acknowledged. A comparative treatment of Mao's, Martin's, and Malcolm's respective strategy for social change will provide the critical apparatus by which we will illuminate substantial difficulties in King's blueprint for eradicating oppression.

I

To accomplish the goal of black liberation, black theologians and clergy have pondered the question: What is the most appropriate way to correct the gross maldistribution of power that underlies oppression? In this regard, they have encountered three main choices of "weapons" for radical social change, and these weapons can be correlated as strategies with the transformationist models of Mao Tse-tung, Martin Luther King, Jr., and Malcolm X, which we will analyze in turn.

Chairman Mao argues: "Political power grows out of the barrel of a gun. . . . It is only by the power of the gun that the working class and the labouring masses can defeat the armed bourgeoise and landlords; in this sense we must say that only with guns can the whole world be transformed."[6] Mao also argues for the necessity of and inevitability of revolutionary wars.

> Revolutions and revolutionary wars are inevitable in class society, and
> without them it is impossible to accomplish any leap in social
> development and to overthrow the reactionary ruling classes and
> therefore impossible for the people to win political power.[7]

Thus, Mao contends that those in power respond only to an equal or superior force; they are not moved, as Gandhi and King suppose, by the sight of the undeserved suffering of the oppressed. Nor are their consciences' pricked by the miserable plight of the poor. If the plight of the wretched of the earth troubled the oppressor, oppression could never establish a toehold. The fact that the poor are kept poor and powerless, age after age, is categorical evidence, according to Mao, that appeals to conscience and reason alone will be woefully ineffective. Or as the anecdote goes: "Prayer is fine in prayer meeting, but not in a bear meeting."

The fact of the matter, Mao tells us is that the focus of the problem is not the untroubled conscience of the oppressor, rather it is his superior might and weapons. Accordingly, the appropriate antitoxin is not to prick his conscience but to muzzle his firepower. "When we say that imperialism is ferocious," Mao continues, "we mean that its nature will never change, that the imperialists will never lay down their butcher knives, that they will never become Buddhas, till their doom."[8] In sum, the oppressor will lift his foot from the oppressed man's neck only when he sees a gun barrel, bigger than his own, aimed at his defenseless head.

The other feature of Mao's strategy to be accented is the principle of "dirty activism."[9] Dirty activism invokes the dogma that you must fight fire with fire and force with an equal force. The biblical injunction of "an eye for an eye" expresses the same maxim. Thus dirty activism reduces to the conviction that it is legitimate and/or necessary to utilize similar tactics and instruments of power and destruction that my opponent employs against me. As Mao insists: "We are advocates of the abolition of war; we do not want war: but war can only be abolished through war, and in order to get rid of the gun it is necessary to take up the gun."[10]

II

At the other end of the spectrum stands King. Violence and the gun, he warns, are impractical and immoral ways for achieving social justice. Violence "is impractical because it is a descending spiral ending in destruction for all."[11] Or as he so often admonished: "The old law of an eye for an eye leaves everybody blind."[12]

The end of violence and counterviolence is self-destruction. All who take the sword will perish by the sword. Thus, for King, "the choice is no longer between violence and nonviolence. It is either nonviolence or nonexistence."[13]

The "fight fire with fire" approach, King contends, only multiplies the violence until both oppressor and oppressed are ultimately consumed in a cascading conflagration.

> The nonviolent resister not only refuses to shoot his opponent but he also refuses to hate him. . . . In the struggle for human dignity, the oppressed people of the world must not succumb to the temptation of becoming bitter or indulging in hate campaigns. To retaliate in kind would do nothing but intensify the existence of hate in the universe.[14]

Thus, against Mao's "only the gun" is matched King's "never the gun" in the struggle for social justice. Opposing the dirty activism of Mao we find the clean activism of King. The clean activist advances a "fight fire with water" approach. Translated into the discourse of interpersonal conflict, clean activism adopts means and "weapons" that are antithetical to those you seek to exterminate. It would invoke the formula of "soul force" against "gun force." And set against Mao's emphasis upon a gross imbalance of power as the precondition for oppression, King seems to localize the problem in "the conscience of the great decent majority who through blindness, fear, pride or irrationality have allowed their consciences to sleep."[15]

Attention should be focused on the larger panorama of theological beliefs that undergird King's and Gandhi's strategy for social change. Central to both is the deep-rooted belief that the universe supports specific ethical norms and practices, while undermining the opposite. "He who works against community is working against the whole of creation."[16] Expressing a similar conviction, Gandhi argued that there is a law of love at work in the universe, and the law of love will work, just as the law of gravitation will work, whether we accept it or not."[17] This law of love, Gandhi and King affirm, requires the practice of nonviolent resistance. Accordingly, only nonviolence will ultimately be successful, because only it is supported by ultimate reality. Based on this understanding, the violent individual or society is akin to the fool who tries to defy the law of gravity.

231

III

Between Mao and Martin stands Malcolm, arguing, for any means necessary. The principle, "any means necessary," has been grossly misinterpreted to yield a meaning that is tantamount to ethical nihilism; namely "everything is permitted" in an absolute sense. The principle, however, cannot be summarily dismissed in this fashion when enunciated by Malcolm and other black theologians, for an unprejudiced analysis yields an all together different meaning. "Any means necessary" identifies (1) a *pluralistic* framework in contrast to the monolithic, one and only one, approach of King. In contrast to King's "no gun and no bullet," Malcolm sanctified the "ballot or the bullet." The strategy utilized by the oppressed, Malcom maintains, is to be dictated by the context, specifically by the severity of the oppression and the character of the oppressor's response to legitimate demands for social justice. The point is clearly stated in the option: "the ballot or the bullet." There is no violence for violence's sake. Neither is violence advanced as the superior or the oppressed's *first* response to their plight. One must also note—and here Malcom opposes Mao's understanding—that the inevitability of violence is not affirmed. Rather, the ballot is to be the first strategy, and only if the oppressor rejects the ballot is the bullet permitted. In sum, what is permissible is contingent upon how oppressively white America continues to act.

> . . . We're at a time in history now where we want freedom, and only two things bring you freedom—the ballot or the bullet. . . . If you and I don't use the ballot and get it, we going to be forced to use the bullet. And if you don't want to use the ballot, I know you don't want to use the bullet. So let us try the ballot. And if the ballot doesn't work, we'll try something else. But let us try the ballot.[18]

Elsewhere Malcom argues that America can spawn a revolution "without violence and bloodshed" if "the black man is given full use of the ballot in every one of the fifty states. But if the black man doesn't get the ballot, then you are going to be faced with another man who forgets the ballot and starts using the bullet."[19]

(2) 'Any means necessary,' in Malcolm's view, is also a call for a *contextual* analysis of means-ends questions, and a contextual treatment of the principle leads to the following derivative guidelines: (a) any means necessary legitimates any means *employed by one's opponent.* "You should never be non-violent unless you run into some non-violence. I am non-violent with those who are non-violent with me. . . . But don't die alone. Let your dying be reciprocal. This is what is meant by equality. 'What's good for the goose is good for the gander.'"[20] Any means necessary does validate *counterviolence,* an eye for an eye, and accordingly, elements of dirty activism are also endorsed. Two points, however, must be made clear if we are to understand Malcolm's position. He sanctioned dirty activism as self-defense as distinct from aggressive action; and, in the framework of contextualism, counterviolence is tantamount to self-defense.

232

And this leads to the next derivative principle: (b) the right and necessity of *self-defense* must be safeguarded.

> Since self-preservation is the first law of nature, we assert the Afro-American's right to self-defense. . . . The history of unpunished violence against our people clearly indicates that we must be prepared to defend ourselves or we will continue to be a defenseless people at the mercy of a ruthless and violent racist mob. . . . We assert that in those areas where the government is either unable or unwilling to protect the lives and property of our people, that our people are within our rights to protect themselves by whatever means necessary.[21]

It is important to identify the elements of the context in which counterviolence is legitimated. Malcolm argues from a context where there is "a history of unpunished violence" against blacks and a demonstrated failure of the government to protect the lives and property of blacks. Moreover, the society must be grounded in an immoral system, e.g., a racist system. "Tactics based solely on morality can only succeed when you are dealing with people who are moral or a system that is moral. A man or system that oppresses a man because of his color is not moral."[22] Further, we have a society that responds only to force or power. "The only real power that is respected in this society is political power and economic power. Nothing else. There's no such thing as a moral force that this society recognizes."[23] Finally, we have a society where violence is inconsistently sanctioned. Nonviolence is not advanced as a matter of principle, as Gandhi and King did, but seemingly approved when it is advantageous to the oppressor and disapproved when it is not.

> If violence is wrong in America, violence is wrong abroad. If it is wrong to be violent defending black women and black children . . . then it is wrong for America to draft us and make us violent abroad in defense of her. And if it is right for America to draft us, and teach us how to be violent in defense of her, then it is right for you and me to do whatever is necessary to defend our own people right here in this country.[24]

IV

Having heard the gospel according to Mao, Malcolm, and Martin, it is fitting to examine why I feel compelled to criticize King. No doubt many readers will think that it is much too soon, especially for a black man, to impeach the thought of this black saint, for truly we have not yet praised him enough. But I have come to this agonizing conclusion: that to advance the goal for which he joyously lived and gloriously died we must ruthlessly pinpoint the real defects in his thought.

Why this bewildering way of praising King? I must be frank—because of the exalted status white Americans have given him. Like the role assigned to Jesus, King has become the Black Messiah, the singular and exclusive pattern for blacks slavishly to imitate in their ethical models. Black leaders are indexed as militants or as violent, not on the basis of their actual thought and action, but by virtue of how far they stray from his footsteps. Because he focalized nonviolence and vicarious suffering as the heart of Christian faith, any other black interpretation of the gospel is suspect. There are other black voices and other black interpreters of Christian faith, but they will not receive respectful attention until King is toppled from his pedestal. As one of King's colleagues is reported to have said after his death: "We've never buried Dr. King, and we won't be able to do anything until we do." Advancement in black ethics will only come, it appears, when black and white Americans can say—and with conviction—"King is dead, long live the King."

Let us rivet our attention on some of the defects—I regard them as lethal—that convincingly undermine his mystical authority as the Black Messiah and negate the hope, however sincere, that he can be the alpha and omega for black theology, ethics, and the liberation struggle in America. I want to show that these defects follow from his studied attempt to sanction nonviolent resistance as the only valid approach for radical social change for all time and in all lands, and from a faulty understanding of the operation and inner logic of racism. Given the demographic situation of blacks in America, I want to show that nonviolent resistance is foreordained to failure. Further, I want to establish that King's astounding view of the deterrent impact that the *sight* of the undeserved suffering of the poor has on the conscience and violent actions of the oppressor suffers from an inaccurate understanding of racism, especially its philosophical anthropology.

Prior to addressing these inadequacies, however, let me say in advance that I believe nonviolent resistance can work, but its success requires a specific set of conditions. These conditions, however, do not obtain in America, and the reason is clear—because of its pervasive racism.

This brings us to a substantial difficulty in King's approach, namely, applying the model in radically different situations. The problem immediately surfaces once we call attention to a neglected feature of nonviolent resistance. There are actually two stages in the strategy, and a different strategy informs each phase. In phase one, the nonviolent resister seeks to convert the oppressor by pricking his reason and conscience. The goal in this context is to persuade the oppressor that his actions are rationally pernicious and morally corrupt. Thus, the pressure to transform the oppressor's actions is his unwillingness to be immoral or irrational.

But if rational and moral persuasion fails, then the nonviolent resister shifts gears to a radically different level of activity, and this point is usually ignored. In this second phase, masses of people are used to short-circuit the unjust institutions and processes. In phase two the goal is to force the oppressor to admit that his resources are inadequate to maintain his unjust institutions and repressive practices. Here the concern is to create a inexorable pressure that forces the oppressor to acknowledge his *impotence*—not his irrationality or immorality. At this level, nonviolent resistance is ultimately a test of power.

King gives a graphic account of this approach in his final work.

> Nonviolent protest must now mature to a new level to correspond to
> heightened black impatience and stiffened white resistance. This higher
> level is mass civil disobedience.

> There must be more than a statement to the larger society, there must
> be a force that interrupts its functioning at some key point . . . that
> dislocates the functioning of a city without destroying it. . . .[25]

> Without violence, we totally disrupted the system, the life style of
> Birmingham, and then of Selma. . . . Our Birmingham struggle came
> to its dramatic climax when some 3,500 demonstrators virtually filled
> every jail in that city and surrounding communities, and some 4,000
> more continued to march and demonstrate non-violently. The city knew
> then in terms that were crystal-clear that Birmingham could no longer
> function until the demands of the Negro community were met.[26]

With this understanding, one feature of Gandhi's India augurs for nonviolent resistance as an attractive and viable strategy for liberation. The oppressed, the native Indians, were the overwhelming *majority*, and the oppressor, the English, the small *minority*. Thus the numerical superiority of the Indians supplied the massive and self-sustaining power to short circuit and dislocate the society—without appealing to the oppressor to support the drive for freedom.

However, the reverse situation obtains in America; it is precisely this power of numbers that blacks in this land lack. Here blacks are the decided numerical minority. Hence, if nonviolence is to succeed here, blacks must urge whites to support the cause of black liberation. Blacks have the impossible mission of persuading pharoah to change his stripes without the impressive fire power at the disposal of Moses and Aaron. Like Pharoah, it seems that the white power structure will not change until God sends the angel of death. I do not think it is too harsh to charge that white commitment to black liberation has been at best token. Few whites are ready to put their bodies and wallets on the line to further black freedom.

One certainty can be gleaned from Gandhi's success and King's failure. If nonviolence is to succeed in America, one ingredient is necessary: the extravagant and selfless commitment of whites to the cause of black liberation. It is exactly at this point that King's theory collapses—if it is made the primary or sole means of radical social change.

King's dream has become a dreadful nightmare because whites have refused to act altruistically, all the while urging blacks to accept the nonviolent strategy, a strategy that is doomed to failure from the start because of white inactivity. Is there any wonder that blacks are suspicious of white glorification of King as the Black Messiah?

V

King's analysis, in concert with Gandhi's, tragically misunderstands how the conscience of the oppressor operates, especially where racial oppression is involved. On more than one occasion Gandhi advanced an extraordinary conviction as one of the controlling assumptions of nonviolent resistance: "the implicit belief that the *sight* of suffering on the part of the multitudes of people will melt the heart of the aggressor and induce him to desist from his course of action."[27] That the conscience of the oppressor will be repulsed by the sight of the undeserved suffering and death of the innocent is argued elsewhere by Gandhi. Suffering unto death at the hands of one's tormentor is an essential feature of what nonviolent resistance entails in response to Nazi-like oppression. Gandhi prescribes: present yourself as "a living wall of men and women and children and invite the invaders to walk over your corpses. . . . The army would be brutal enough to walk over them, you might say. I would then say you will have done your duty by allowing yourself to be annihilated. An army that dares to pass over the corpses of innocent men and women would not be able to repeat that experiment."[28]

The same spirit informs King's moving account of the Montgomery boycott.

> What is the Negro's best defense against acts of violence inflicted upon him? . . . His only defense is to meet every act of barbarity, illegality, cruelty and injustice toward an individual Negro with the fact that 100 more Negroes will present themselves in his place as potential victims. . . . Faced with this dynamic unity, this amazing self-respect, this willingness to suffer, and this refusal to hit back, the oppressor will find, as oppressors have always found, that he is glutted with his own barbarity. Forced to stand before the world and his God splattered with the blood of his brother, he will call an end to his self-defeating massacre.

> American Negroes must come to the point where they can say to their white brothers, paraphrasing the words of Gandhi: "We will match your capacity to inflict suffering with our capacity to endure suffering. We will meet your physical force with soul force. We will not hate you, but we cannot in all good conscience obey your unjust laws. Do to us what you will and we will still love you. Bomb our homes and threaten our children: send your hooded perpetrators and violence into our communities and drag us out on some wayside road, beating us and leaving us half dead, and we still love you. But we will soon wear you down by our capacity to suffer. And in winning our freedom we will so appeal to your heart and conscience that we will win you in the process.[29]

History has etched with the blood of the innocent the glaring error of King's and Gandhi's conviction that though the oppressor may kill the nonviolent at the outset, he will then refrain from further slaughter. In the context of racism Gandhi's prescription is self-initiated genocide. In a real sense the Jews in

236

Germany followed Gandhi's advice, and we all know the outcome—Auschwitz. Nor does it appear that the horror of the slaves' condition made the master's heart bleed and release the battered bodies of our black foreparents from further cruelty.

It is not difficult to pinpoint the obvious defect of this understanding of the oppressor. There is an aspect of racism that is too often overlooked: its hierarchial division of humankind into human and subhuman groups. In a similar way we ignore the ethical importance of where we draw the boundary between human and subhuman reality. To classify something as subhuman justifies treating it as less than human. Based on this understanding it is not accidental that the most inhuman acts in human history have been preceded or accompanied by the redefinition of part of humankind as subhuman, e.g., Nazi Germany and slavery in Amercia.

Perhaps an illustration will clarify the point at issue. In Hinduism the cow is not defined as subhuman. Killing it, therefore, is not permissible. Killing it is tantamount to murder. Our own moral sensibilities are undeniably different, precisely because we draw the boundary between the human and the subhuman at another point. Not only do we slaughter the cow, we barbecue it. From the Hindu perspective we commit a double crime—murder plus cannibalism.

The critical principle to be extracted from the illustration is that if I am sub—human in the eyes of the oppressor, clearly my death and suffering will not have the effect that King and Gandhi suggest. Unless you are a Schweitzer, killing fleas or flies will not upset your moral stomach. To paraphrase King, 'the oppressor will not call an end to his self-defeating massacre because he is not forced to stand before the world and his God splattered with the blood of his *brother*.' The racist will cease his oppression and regard my suffering as underserved only to the degree that he regards me as equally human, as his brother. The presupposition of King's theory, the acceptance of my co-humanity, is simply not present in a racist society. King puts the cart before the horse, for where racism is present the belief that black suffering is underserved is absent.

VI

King's social ethics reflects a problematic analysis of other aspects of racism, violence, and their interconnection. His singular failure was to overlook the gross imbalance of power as the precondition for racism and oppression—until the very last.[30] For King and also for Gunnar Myrdal, the racial problem is traceable to the fact that "the great decent majority through blindness, fear, pride, or irrationality have allowed their consciences to sleep."[31] But is the real source of racism the unenlightened conscience of white Americans? White ignorance of injustice to blacks is not the primary cause of racism. Rather racism, like all oppression, is an exercise in *power*. Racism is a gross imbalance of power where whites can pursue their priorities, be they moral or immoral, unchecked by a corresponding power. The pressing need, then, is a shift in the balance of power rather than a converted conscience.

King's defective analysis of power spills over into his perspective on violence. Two basic errors stand out here. First, King treats violence in an absolutist rather than a contextual framework. His position would be substantially enhanced if violence were defined as an illegitimate and/or excessive use of force against the other. Violence is a power that has gone too far. Based on this understanding of violence, one can only determine the "too far" with reference to a concrete situation. One is pushed inevitably into an untenable position if s/he rejects a contextual definition of violence. Should self-defense, for instance, be equated with violence? Is it violence, if I respond to your force in a manner that is roughly equivalent to the force you direct against me?

Having opted for nonviolent resistance as the only valid approach for radical social change in all lands and for all times, King is forced to give nonviolence all positive characteristics and violence all negative features, and this is a gross misinterpretation of the actual state of affairs. The pedagogical value of counterviolence, for instance cannot be short-changed in a sinful world. My authentic self-understanding, it appears, involves my recognition that I am a man and not God; it demands my awareness of my finitude, that I am not an absolute power. I must acknowledge that my rights end where your nose begins, and this simple, but fundamental, lesson is not likely to be learned when you always turn the other cheek.

For similar reasons, it is necessary to challenge King's familiar preachment that "an eye for an eye" philosophy is immoral because it would ultimately lead to a blind society. It might produce a one-eyed society, but not necessarily a blind one. In the situation where we each have only one eye, we may have the basis for the beginning of authentic inter-personal relations.

The second error in King's analysis of violence emerges in the very definition of the problem. The problem warrants answering not only the Christian character of nonviolence, but the Christian quality of *counter*violence. Oppression itself is initiated and maintained by violence. Thus, the core problem is: what actions are appropriate for the Christian to attack the structures of oppression that are themselves initiated and maintained by violence? The failure to adequately address this problem invariably corners the advocate of liberation in a moral impasse.

Black theologians have also found it necessary to challenge King's thought and practice because there is a clear process of selection and rejection in white America's use of King's thought and practice that is consistent only with its exploitation of him as a guardian of white interests and not as a Black Moses to lead his people from the clutches of Pharoah. How else can one explain why white America remains oblivious to King's and Gandhi's description of *authentic* nonviolence and what this entails for white obligations as they execute their Christian stewardship?

Both King and Gandhi argued that authentic nonviolence obtains only when I have the option between violence and nonviolence, only when I possess the instruments of violence but refuse to use them. "If one uses the method of nonviolent resistance because he is afraid or merely because he lacks the instruments of violence, he is not truly nonviolent. This is why Gandhi often said that if cowardice is the only alternative to violence, it is better to fight."[32] In other words, to be truly nonviolent I must be in a situation of power, not impotence; I must have the gun but put it aside because I am persuaded that nonviolence is the superior morality.

If this aspect of King's thought is accented, then it appears that we are forced to conclude that whites, the oppressor, those in power, fulfill the necessary condition to be authentic practitioners of nonviolence in the struggle for black freedom. Indeed, given this understanding of nonviolence, as Vincent Harding has perceptively suggested, it is problematical that there was ever an authentic nonviolent movement under King's tutelage.[33]

The other model of nonviolence that King invoked so often—the Christian concept of self-sacrificing love[34] where one gives all for one's neighbor without thought of return or reward—seems to lead to the same conclusion. Just as God is claimed to have given himself to man in Jesus Christ, relinquishing his majesty and lowering himself for the salvation of man, so the Christian is to be a Christ unto his neighbor. But once again it is questionable that the black situation conforms to the precondition for self-sacrificing love. If the precondition is an exalted situation, one of power, of freedom, then the obligation seems to fall on whites primarily as the executors of Christian agape.

But perhaps the most compelling testimony of white America's unconscionable exploitation of King as a white guardian is the scandal of its response to his Viet Nam Policy. Whites incessantly pressed his philosophy of nonviolence upon blacks—when faced with the other alternative of a Malcolm X—as the instrument for social, political, and economic change. Yet when King was consistent and advanced the same policy for Americans in Viet Nam, he was dropped like a hot potato. This good for the goose (blacks) but not for the gander (whites) principle unwittingly displays the true status of King in the hearts and minds of white Americans.

If this description of the defects in King's thought is close to the target, if the description of how white Americans have abused his views is accurate, then it should be clear why it is necessary for black theologians to enlarge the model for a liberation ethics. And this can be done only by challenging King's theory of social change.

This essay in some ways is an exercise in futility. If white Americans have exploited the name and deeds of this black hero, exposing the fact will hardly reform them. But that is not my purpose. Rather, these words are a hint to King's black sisters and brothers to scrutinize carefully the black hereos that white America seeks to force upon us. Behind the facade of praise may be another Trojan horse to further the oppression of those King gave his life to liberate. Likewise for the black theologian and ethicist as they undertake the crucial task of formulating a scaffolding that reflects the demands of the oppressed black community and not its oppressors.

King's thought and life should be acknowledged as a giant step forward in the march to black freedom. But we who come after him should not expect that his steps are the only path that we who aim to be free must follow. We will not overcome if we march only to his beat as the distant drummer and ignore the stout cadence of others in the army of black thought and action.

Notes

1. James Cone, *A Black Theology of Liberation* (New York: Lippincott, 1970), pp. 133–34.
2. Albert Cleage, *Black Christian Nationalism* (New York: William Morrow & Co., 1977), pp. xxxvi–xxxvii.
3. Joseph Washington, *The Politics of God* (Boston: Beacon Press, 1967), pp. 138, 145.
4. Major Jones, *Black Awareness: A Theology of Hope* (New York: Abingdon Press, 1971).
5. J. Deotis Roberts, *Liberation and Reconciliation: A Black Theology* (Philadelphia: Westminister Press, 1971).
6. Mao Tse-tung, *Quotations from Chairman Mao Tsetung* (Peking: Foreign Languages Press, 1972), pp. 61–63.
7. *Quotations*, p. 60.
8. *Quotations*, p. 68.
9. The term is borrowed, in part from Jean-Paul Sartre's play, "Dirty Hands," where it is argued that authenticity often requires actions that are outlawed or disvalued by the culture.
10. *Quotations*, p. 63.
11. Martin L. King, *Stride Toward Freedom* (New York: Harper & Row, 1964), p. 189.
12. *Stride*, p. 189.
13. *Stride*, p. 201
14. *Stride*, p. 85.
15. *Stride*, p. 87
16. *Stride*, p. 92
17. *Social and Political Philosophy*, ed. John Somerville and Ronald Santoni (New York: Doubleday and Anchor, 1963), p. 543.
18. *Malcolm X, By Any Means Necessary: Speeches, Interviews and a Letter* by Malcolm X, ed. George Brietman (New York: Pathfinders Press, Inc., 1970), p. 89.
19. *Malcolm X speaks: Selected Speeches and Statements*, ed. George Brietman (New York: Grove Press, 1966), p. 57.
20. *Speaks*, p. 34.
21. *Interviews*, p. 41.
22. *Interviews*, 23.
23. *Interviews*, p. 88.
24. *Speaks*, p. 8.
25. Martin L. King, *The Trumpet of Conscience* (New York: Harper & Row, 1967), p. 15.
26. *Trumpet*, p. 54. Many interpreters of King argue that near the end of his life he moved away from the centrality of nonviolent resistance and was about to declare for black power. I do not find this analysis persuasive. The error lies in the failure to recognize the two phases of nonviolence. As these citations from King's final work evidence, what he was advancing was a more emphatic application of phase two, not a repudiation of nonviolent resistance. I do not see any substantial difference between the alledged "early" and the "later" King.

27. *Social*, p. 539.
28. *Social*, p. 538.
29. *Stride*, pp. 193–94.
30. Martin L. King, *Where Do We Go From Here?* (New York: Harper & Row, 1967). King correctly argues: "Ther is nothing essentially wrong with power. The problem is that in America power is unequally distributed. This has led Negro Americans in the past to seek their goals through love and moral suasion deviod of power and white American to seek their goals through power devoid of love and conscience." This aspect of King's thought must not be ignored. Yet as Vincent has persuasively argued, it is problematical that King ever incorporated this analysis of power into the central skein of his thought. Vincent Harding, "The Religion of Black Power," *The Religious Situation 1968*, ed. Donald Cutler (Boston: Beacon Press, 1968), p. 33.
31. *Stride*, p. 87.
32. *Stride*, p. 83.
33. *Black Power*, p. 33.
34. Black theologians have also roundly denounced efforts like King's to reduce Christian faith and ethics to agape or self-sacrificing love for the other, for they correctly see these efforts as conceptual and ideological tools for the maintenance of oppression. James Cone's criticism is representative of this line of argument:

> By emphasizing the complete self-giving of God in Christ . . . the oppressors can then request the oppressed to do the same for the oppressors. If God gives himself without obligation, then in order to be Christian, men must give themselves to the neighbor in like manner. Since God has loved us in spite of our revolt against him, to be like God we too must love those who . . . enslave us. . . . This view of love places no obligation on the white oppressors. . . . In fact, they are permitted to do whatever they will against black people assured that God loves them as well as the people they oppress.

James Cone, *A Black Theology of Liberation* (New York: Lippincott, 1970), pp. 133–34.

Note on the Author

William R. Jones, Professor, Department of Religion and Director of Afro-American Studies Program at Florida State University, also taught at Yale Divinity School and Howard University. He is well known for his work in liberation theology. His published works include, *Is God A White Racist?* Prolegomenon to Black Theology, Doubleday, 1973, and "Toward a Unitarian Universalist Concept of Authority," *Kairos, An Independent Quarterly of Liberal Religion, May, 1979*, and "Religious Humanism: Its Problems and Prospects in Black Religion and Culture," in *Perspectives in Black Theology, 1978*.

III
Experience Interpreted

The New Negro
[1925]

Alain L. Locke

In the last decade something beyond the watch and guard of statistics has happened in the life of the American Negro and the three norns who have traditionally presided over the Negro problem have a changeling in their laps. The Sociologist, the Philanthropist, the Race-leader are not unaware of the New Negro, but they are at a loss to account for him. He simply cannot be swathed in their formulae. For the younger generation is vibrant with a new psychology; the new spirit is awake in the masses, and under the very eyes of the professional observers is transforming what has been a perennial problem into the progressive phases of contemporary Negro life.

Could such a metamorphosis have taken place as suddenly as it has appeared to? The answer is no; not because the New Negro is not here, but because the Old Negro had long become more of a myth than a man. The Old Negro, we must remember, was a creature of moral debate and historical controversy. His has been a stock figure perpetuated as an historical fiction partly in innocent sentimentalism, partly in deliberate reactionism. The Negro himself has contributed his share to this through a sort of protective social mimicry forced upon him by the adverse circumstances of dependence. So for generations in the mind of America, the Negro has been more of a formula than a human being—something to be argued about, condemned or defended, to be "kept down," or "in his place," or "helped up," to be worried with or worried over, harassed or patronized, a social bogey or social burden. The thinking Negro even has been induced to share this same general attitude, to focus his attention on controversial issues, to see himself in the distorted perspective of a social problem. His shadow, so to speak, has been more real to him than his personality. Through having had to appeal from the unjust stereotypes of his oppressors and traducers to those of his liberators, friends and benefactors he has had to subscribe to the traditional positions from which his case has been viewed. Little true social or self-understanding has or could come from such a situation.

242

But while the minds of most of us, black and white, have thus burrowed in the trenches of the Civil War and Reconstruction, the actual march of development has simply flanked these positions, necessitating a sudden reorientation of view. We have not been watching in the right direction; set North and South on a sectional axis, we have not noticed the East till the sun has us blinking.

Recall how suddenly the Negro spirituals revealed themselves; suppressed for generations under the stereotypes of Wesleyan hymn harmony, secretive, half-ashamed, until the courage of being natural brought them out—and behold, there was folk-music. Similarly the mind of the Negro seems suddenly to have slipped from under the tyranny of social intimidation and to be shaking off the psychology of imitation and implied inferiority. By shedding the old chrysalis of the Negro problem we are achieving something like a spiritual emancipation. Until recently, lacking self-understanding, we have been almost as much of a problem to ourselves as we still are to others. But the decade that found us with a problem has left us with only a task. The multitude perhaps feels as yet only a strange relief and a new vague urge, but the thinking few know that in the reaction the vital inner grip of prejudice has been broken.

With this renewed self-respect and self-dependence, the life of the Negro community is bound to enter a new dynamic phase, the buoyancy from within compensating for whatever pressure there may be of conditions from without. The migrant masses, shifting from countryside to city, hurdle several generations of experience at a leap, but more important, the same thing happens spiritually in the life-attitudes and self-expression of the Young Negro, in his poetry, his art, his education and his new outlook, with the additional advantage, of course, of the poise and greater certainty of knowing what it is all about. From this comes the promise and warrant of a new leadership. As one of them has discerningly put it:

> We have tomorrow
> Bright before us
> Like a flame.
>
> Yesterday, a night-gone thing
> A sun-down name.
>
> And dawn today
> Broad arch above the road we came.
> We march!

This is what, even more than any "most creditable record of fifty years of freedom," requires that the Negro of to-day be seen through other than the dusty spectacles of past controversy. The day of "aunties," "uncles," and "mammies" is equally gone. Uncle Tom and Sambo have passed on, and even the "Colonel" and "George" play barnstorm rôles from which they escape with relief when the public spotlight is off. The popular melodrama has about played itself out, and it is time to scrap the fictions, garret the bogeys and settle down to a realistic facing of facts.

First we must observe some of the changes which since the traditional lines of opinion were drawn have rendered these quite obsolete. A main change has been, of course, that shifting of the Negro population which has made the Negro problem no longer exclusively or even predominantly Southern. Why should our minds remain sectionalized, when the problem itself no longer is? Then the trend of migration has not only been toward the North and Central Midwest, but city-ward and to the great centers of industry—the problems of adjustment are new, practical, local and not peculiarly racial. Rather they are an integral part of the large industrial and social problems of our present-day democracy. And finally, with the Negro rapidly in process of class differentiation, if it ever was warrantable to regard and treat the Negro *en masse* it is becoming with every day less possible, more unjust and more ridiculous.

In the very process of being transplanted, the Negro is becoming transformed.

The tide of Negro migration, northward and city-ward, is not to be fully explained as a blind flood started by the demands of war industry coupled with the shutting off of foreign migration, or by the pressure of poor crops coupled with increased social terrorism in certain sections of the South and Southwest. Neither labor demand, the boll-weevil nor the Ku Klux Klan is a basic factor, however contributory any or all of them may have been. The wash and rush of this human tide on the beach line of the northern city centers is to be explained primarily in terms of a new vision of opportunity, of social and economic freedom, of a spirit to seize, even in the face of an extortionate and heavy toll, a chance for the improvement of conditions. With each successive wave of it, the movement of the Negro becomes more and more a mass movement toward the larger and the more democratic chance—in the Negro's case a deliberate flight not only from countryside to city, but from medieval America to modern.

Take Harlem as an instance of this. Here in Manhattan is not merely the largest Negro community in the world, but the first concentration in history of so many diverse elements of Negro life. It has attracted the African, the West Indian, the Negro American; has brought together the Negro of the North and the Negro of the South; the man from the city and the man from the town and village; the peasant, the student, the business man, the professional man, artist, poet, musician, adventurer and worker, preacher and criminal, exploiter and social outcast. Each group has come with its own separate motives and for its own special ends, but their greatest experience has been the finding of one another. Proscription and prejudice have thrown these dissimilar elements into a common area of contact and interaction. Within this area, race sympathy and unity have determined a further fusing of sentiment and experience. So what began in terms of segregation ecomes more and more, as its elements mix and react, the laboratory of a great race-welding. Hitherto, it must be admitted that American Negroes have been a race more in name than in fact, or to be exact, more in sentiment than in experience. The chief bond between them has been that of a common condition rather than a common consciousness; a problem in common rather than a life in common. In Harlem, Negro life is seizing upon its first chances for group expression and self-determination. It is—or promises at least to be—a race capital. That is why our comparison is taken with those nascent centers of folk-expression and self-determination which are playing a creative part in the world to-day. Without pretense to their political significance, Harlem has the same rôle to play for the New Negro as Dublin has had for the New Ireland or Prague for the New Czechoslovakia.

Harlem, I grant you, isn't typical—but it is significant, it is prophetic. No sane observer, however sympathetic to the new trend, would contend that the great masses are articulate as yet, but they stir, they move, they are more than physically restless. The challenge of the new intellectuals among them is clear enough—the "race radicals" and realists who have broken with the old epoch of philanthropic guidance, sentimental appeal and protest. But are we after all only reading into the stirrings of a sleeping giant the dreams of an agitator? The answer is in the migrating peasant. It is the "man farthest down" who is most active in getting up. One of the most characteristic symptoms of this is the professional man, himself migrating to recapture his constituency after a vain effort to maintain in some Southern corner what for years back seemed an established living and clientele. The clergyman following his errant flock, the physician or lawyer trailing his clients, supply the true clues. In a real sense it is the rank and file who are leading, and the leaders who are following. A transformed and transforming psychology permeates the masses.

When the racial leaders of twenty years ago spoke of developing race-pride and stimulating race-consciousness, and of the desirability of race solidarity, they could not in any accurate degree have anticipated the abrupt feeling that has surged up and now pervades the awakened centers. Some of the recognized Negro leaders and a powerful section of white opinion identified with "race work" of the older order have indeed attempted to discount this feeling as a "passing phase," an attack of "race nerves" so to speak, an "aftermath of the war," and the like. It has not abated, however, if we are to gauge by the present tone and temper of the Negro press, or by the shift in popular support from the officially recognized and orthodox spokesmen to those of the independent, popular, and often radical type who are unmistakable symptoms of a new order. It is a social disservice to blunt the fact that the Negro of the Northern centers has reached a stage where tutelage, even of the most interested and well-intentioned sort, must give place to new relationships, where positive self-direction must be reckoned with in ever increasing measure. The American mind must reckon with a fundamentally changed Negro.

The Negro too, for his part, has idols of the tribe to smash. If on the one hand the white man has erred in making the Negro appear to be that which would excuse or extenuate his treatment of him, the Negro, in turn, has too often unnecessarily excused himself because of the way he has been treated. The intelligent Negro of to-day is resolved not to make discrimination an extenuation for his shortcomings in performance, individual or collective; he is trying to hold himself at par, neither inflated by sentimental allowances nor depreciated by current social discounts. For this he must know himself and be known for precisely what he is, and for that reason he welcomes the new scientific rather than the old sentimental interest. Sentimental interest in the Negro has ebbed. We used to lament this as the falling off of our friends; now we rejoice and pray to be delivered both from self-pity and condescension. The mind of each racial group has had a bitter weaning, apathy or hatred on one side matching disillusionment or resentment on the other; but they face each other to-day with the possibility at least of entirely new mutual attitudes.

It does not follow that if the Negro were better known, he would be better liked or better treated. But mutual understanding is basic for any subsequent coöperation and adjustment. The effort toward this will at least have the effect of remedying in large part what has been the most unsatisfactory feature of our present stage of race relationships in America, namely the fact that the more intelligent and representative elements of the two race groups have at so many points got quite out of vital touch with one another.

The fiction is that the life of the races is separate, and increasingly so. The fact is that they have touched too closely at the unfavorable and too lightly at the favorable levels.

While inter-racial councils have sprung up in the South, drawing on forward elements of both races, in the Northern cities manual laborers may brush elbows in their everyday work, but the community and business leaders have experienced no such interplay or far too little of it. These segments must achieve contact or the race situation in America becomes desperate. Fortunately this is happening. There is a growing realization that in social effort the co-operative basis must supplant long-distance philanthropy, and that the only safeguard for mass relations in the future must be provided in the carefully maintained contacts of the enlightened minorities of both race groups. In the intellectual realm a renewed and keen curiosity is replacing the recent apathy; the Negro is being carefully studied, not just talked about and discussed. In art and letters, instead of being wholly caricatured, he is being seriously portrayed and painted.

To all of this the New Negro is keenly responsive as an augury of a new democracy in American culture. He is contributing his share to the new social understanding. But the desire to be understood would never in itself have been sufficient to have opened so completely the protectively closed portals of the thinking Negro's mind. There is still too much possibility of being snubbed or patronized for that. It was rather the necessity for fuller, truer self-expression, the realization of the unwisdom of allowing social discrimination to segregate him mentally, and a counter-attitude to cramp and fetter his own living—and so the "spite-wall" that the intellectuals built over the "color-line" has happily been taken down. Much of this reopening of intellectual contacts has centered in New York and has been richly fruitful not merely in the enlarging of personal experience, but in the definite enrichment of American art and letters and in the clarifying of our common vision of the social tasks ahead.

The particular significance in the re-establishment of contact between the more advanced and representative classes is that it promises to offset some of the unfavorable reactions of the past, or at least to re-surface race contacts somewhat for the future. Subtly the conditions that are molding a New Negro are molding a new American attitude.

However, this new phase of things is delicate; it will call for less charity but more justice; less help, but infinitely closer understanding. This is indeed a critical stage of race relationships because of the likelihood, if the new temper is not understood, of engendering sharp group antagonism and a second crop of more calculated prejudice. In some quarters, it has already done so. Having weaned the Negro, public opinion cannot continue to paternalize. The Negro to-day is inevitably moving forward under the control largely of his own objectives. What are these objectives? Those of his outer life are happily already well and finally formulated, for they are none other than the ideals of American institutions and democracy. Those of his inner life are yet in process of formation, for the new psychology at present is more of a consensus of feeling than of opinion, of attitude rather than of program. Still some points seem to have crystallized.

Up to the present one may adequately describe the Negro's "inner objectives" as an attempt to repair a damaged group psychology and reshape a warped social perspective. Their realization has required a new mentality for the American Negro. And as it matures we begin to see its effects; at first, negative, iconoclastic, and then positive and constructive. In this new group psychology we note the lapse of sentimental appeal, then the development of a more positive self-respect and self-reliance; the repudiation of social dependence, and then the gradual recovery from hyper-sensitiveness and "touchy" nerves, the repudiation of the double standard of judgment with its special philanthropic allowances and then the sturdier desire for objective and scientific appraisal; and finally the rise from social disillusionment to race pride, from the sense of social debt to the responsibilities of social contribution, and offsetting the necessary working and commonsense acceptance of restricted conditions, the belief in ultimate esteem and recognition. Therefore the Negro to-day wishes to be known for what he is, even in his faults and shortcomings, and scorns a craven and precarious survival at the price of seeming to be what he is not. He resents being spoken of as a social ward or minor, even by his own, and to being regarded a chronic patient for the sociological clinic, the sick man of American Democracy. For the same reasons, he himself is through with those social nostrums and panaceas, the so-called "solutions" of his "problem," with which he and the country have been so liberally dosed in the past. Religion, freedom, education, money—in turn, he has ardently hoped for and peculiarly trusted these things; he still believes in them, but not in blind trust that they alone will solve his life-problem.

Each generation, however, will have its creed, and that of the present is the belief in the efficacy of collective effort, in race co-operation. This deep feeling of race is at present the mainspring of Negro life. It seems to be the outcome of the reaction to proscription and prejudice; an attempt, fairly successful on the whole, to convert a defensive into an offensive position, a handicap into an incentive. It is radical in tone, but not in purpose and only the most stupid forms of opposition, misunderstanding or persecution could make it otherwise. Of course, the thinking Negro has shifted a little toward the left with the world-trend, and there is an increasing group who affiliate with radical and liberal movements. But fundamentally for the present the Negro is radical on race matters, conservative on others, in other words, a "forced radical," a social protestant rather than a genuine radical. Yet under further pressure and injustice iconoclastic thought and motives will inevitably increase. Harlem's quixotic radicalisms call for their ounce of democracy today lest to-morrow they be beyond cure.

The Negro mind reaches out as yet to nothing but American wants, American ideas. But this forced attempt to build his Americanism on race values is a unique social experiment, and its ultimate success is impossible except through the fullest sharing of American culture and institutions. There should be no delusion about this. American nerves in sections unstrung with race hysteria are often fed the opiate that the trend of Negro advance is wholly separatist, and that the effect of its operation will be to encyst the Negro as a benign foreign body in the body politic. This cannot be—even if it were desirable. The racialism of the Negro is no limitation or reservation with respect to American life; it is only a constructive effort to build the obstructions in the stream of his progress into an efficient dam of social energy and power. Democracy itself is obstructed and stagnated to the extent that any of its channels are closed. Indeed they cannot be selectively closed. So the choice is not between one way for the Negro and another way for the rest, but between American institutions frustrated on the one hand and American ideals progressively fulfilled and realized on the other.

There is, of course, a warrantably comfortable feeling in being on the right side of the country's professed ideals. We realize that we cannot be undone without America's undoing. It is within the gamut of this attitude that the thinking Negro faces America, but with variations of mood that are if anything more significant than the attitude itself. Sometimes we have it taken with the defiant ironic challenge of McKay:

Mine is the future grinding down to-day
Like a great landslip moving to the sea,
Bearing its freight of debris far away
Where the green hungry waters restlessly
Heave mammoth pyramids, and break and roar
Their eerie challenge to the crumbling shore.

Sometimes, perhaps more frequently as yet, it is taken in the fervent and almost filial appeal and counsel of Weldon Johnson's:

O Southland, dear Southland!
Then why do you still cling
To an idle age and a musty page,
To a dead and useless thing?

But between defiance and appeal, midway almost between cynicism and hope, the prevailing mind stands in the mood of the same author's *To America,* an attitude of sober query and stoical challenge:

How would you have us, as we are?
    Or sinking 'neath the load we bear,
Our eyes fixed forward on a star,
    Or gazing empty at despair?

Rising or falling? Men or things?
    With dragging pace or footsteps fleet?
Strong, willing sinews in your wings,
    Or tightening chains about your feet?

More and more, however, an intelligent realization of the great discrepancy between the American social creed and the American social practice forces upon the Negro the taking of the moral advantage that is his. Only the steadying and sobering effect of a truly characteristic gentleness of spirit prevents the rapid rise of a definite cynicism and counter-hate and a defiant superiority feeling. Human as this reaction would be, the majority still deprecate its advent, and would gladly see it forestalled by the speedy amelioration of its causes. We wish our race pride to be a healthier, more positive achievement than a feeling based upon a realization of the shortcomings of others. But all paths toward the attainment of a sound social attitude have been difficult; only a relatively few enlightened minds have been able as the phrase puts it "to rise above" prejudice. The ordinary man has had until recently only a hard choice between the alternatives of supine and humiliating submission and stimulating but hurtful counter-prejudice. Fortunately from some inner, desperate resourcefulness has recently sprung up the simple expedient of fighting prejudice by mental passive resistance, in other words by trying to ignore it. For the few, this manna may perhaps be effective, but the masses cannot thrive upon it.

Fortunately there are constructive channels opening out into which the balked social feelings of the American Negro can flow freely.

Without them there would be much more pressure and danger than there is. These compensating interests are racial but in a new and enlarged way. One is the consciousness of acting as the advance-guard of the African peoples in their contact with Twentieth Century civilization; the other, the sense of a mission of rehabilitating the race in world esteem from that loss of prestige for which the fate and conditions of slavery have so largely been responsible.

Harlem, as we shall see, is the center of both these movements; she is the home of the Negro's "Zionism." The pulse of the Negro world has begun to beat in Harlem. A Negro newspaper carrying news material in English, French and Spanish, gathered from all quarters of America, the West Indies and Africa has maintained itself in Harlem for over five years. Two important magazines, both edited from New York, maintain their news and circulation consistently on a cosmopolitan scale. Under American auspices and backing, three pan-African congresses have been held abroad for the discussion of common interests, colonial questions and the future co-operative development of Africa. In terms of the race question as a world problem, the Negro mind has leapt, so to speak, upon the parapets of prejudice and extended its cramped horizons. In so doing it has linked up with the growing group consciousness of the dark-peoples and is gradually learning their common interests. As one of our writers has recently put it: "It is imperative that we understand the white world in its relations to the non-white world." As with the Jew, persecution is making the Negro international.

As a world phenomenon this wider race consciousness is a different thing from the much asserted rising tide of color. Its inevitable causes are not of our making. The consequences are not necessarily damaging to the best interests of civilization. Whether it actually brings into being new Armadas of conflict or argosies of cultural exchange and enlightenment can only be decided by the attitude of the dominant races in an era of critical change. With the American Negro, his new internationalism is primarily an effort to recapture contact with the scattered peoples of African derivation. Garveyism may be a transient, if spectacular, phenomenon, but the possible rôle of the American Negro in the future development of Africa is one of the most constructive and universally helpful missions that any modern people can lay claim to.

Constructive participation in such causes cannot help giving the Negro valuable group incentives, as well as increased prestigé at home and abroad. Our greatest rehabilitation may possibly come through such channels, but for the present, more immediate hope rests in the revaluation by white and black alike of the Negro in terms of his artistic endowments and cultural contributions, past and prospective. It must be increasingly recognized that the Negro has already made very substantial contributions, not only in his folk-art, music especially, which has always found appreciation, but in larger, though humbler and less acknowledged ways. For generations the Negro has been the peasant matrix of that section of America which has most undervalued him, and here he has contributed not only materially in labor and in social patience, but spiritually as well. The South has unconsciously absorbed the gift of his folk-temperament. In less than half a generation it will be easier to recognize this, but the fact remains that a leaven of humor, sentiment, imagination and tropic nonchalance has gone into the making of the South from a humble, unacknowledged source. A second crop of the Negro's gifts promises still more largely. He now becomes a conscious contributor and lays aside the status of a beneficiary and ward for that of a collaborator and participant in American civilization. The great social gain in this is the releasing of our talented group from the arid fields of controversy and debate to the productive fields of creative expression. The especially cultural recognition they win should in turn prove the key to that revaluation of the Negro which must precede or accompany any considerable further betterment of race relationships. But whatever the general effect, the present generation will have added the motives of self-expression and spiritual development to the old and still unfinished task of making material headway and progress. No one who understandingly faces the situation with its substantial accomplishment or views the new scene with its still more abundant promise can be entirely without hope. And certainly, if in our lifetime the Negro should not be able to celebrate his full initiation into American democracy, he can at least, on the warrant of these things, celebrate the attainment of a significant and satisfying new phase of group development, and with it a spiritual Coming of Age.

On the Criticism of Black American Literature: One View of the Black Aesthetic

Houston A. Baker, Jr.

> Words' meanings, but also the rhythm and syntax that frame and
> propel their concatenation, seek their culture as the final reference for
> what they are describing of the world. An A flat played twice on the
> same saxophone by two different men does not have to sound the same.
>
> Imamu Baraka

The corpus of Black American literature might be defined as that body of written works crafted by authors consciously (even, at times, self-consciously) aware of the longstanding values and significant experiences of their culture. By embodying these experiences and values in expressive form, the writer provides one means through which those who share the same culture can recognize themselves and move toward fruitful self-definition. The literature contains deep aspects of the culture, and its Black audience actively benefits from its reflection of the most humane values of a singular whole way of life.

It is, perhaps, easier (as with most definitions) to specify what would not be included here than vice versa. But certain things are clear. First, the corpus of Black American literature is predicated upon culturally-specific values and experiences. Second, the literature must be viewed in a historical spectrum since it serves as a cultural mirror. These considerations seem to place the original definition within the framework of the "Black aesthetic." And insofar as that term indicates a theory that generates a particular conception of Black literature, I am willing to accept it. Theories of literature are essential if one is to have individualizing definitions of the object. It is difficult to speak meaningfully of literature independent of a theorectical context without reducing (or hopelessly expanding) our understanding to such vagaries as: a body of writing in prose or verse, imaginative or creative writings, belles-lettres. While recognizing the need for theories, however, one might raise objections to the insistence of Imamu Baraka that literature is composed exclusively of propagandistic works. And one might shy away from the injunctions of Don L. Lee (Haki Madhubuti) and Larry Neal that writings can only be classified as Black American literature if they demonstrate an affinity with the Black Power concept and with the idiom of the Black urban community.[1]

Despite these reservations, one might recognize the timeliness of a theoretical perspective that treats Black American literature as a distinctive body of writings. With all its authoritarianism, stridency, and downright mistakes, the Black aesthetic is still a positive, transitional point of view that attempts to move the treatment of Black literature away from the ideational and critical frames of reference that have beset it in the past. Moreover, any abuses that have been committed in its name should come as no surprise to the individual who has read the prolific commentary on Aristotle's *Poetics,* or perused the vituperative attacks on Victor Hugo for his violation of the classical unities, or perceived the overwhelming stubbornness and subjectivity of Samuel Johnson.

Literature and criticism exist in the *Lebenswelt.* Firmly rooted in the human condition by their medium, they reflect the glories and shortcomings of their origin. Any new critical perspective, such as the Black aesthetic, is destined to attract both zealous adherents and committed opponents. The battles between the two often lead to vagueness, overstatement, and confusion.

To assert that the time for a new critical theory has arrived and to offer an apology for its more obvious failings, though, is to leap ahead in the argument. There are prior conditions that call for exploration, and certain theoretical considerations must be set forth before one can justify such a course. It will be helpful, I think, to discuss some of the ideational frames that have influenced the criticism of Black literature in America before moving to a treatment of linguistic and historical factors that play an important role in any discussion of the Black aesthetic.

II

The complexity of the American mind in regard to literature is an established fact. Vernon Parrington, D. H. Lawrence, and Van Wyck Brooks demolished the image of the innocent Yankee bumpkin turning out doggerel stanzas. And in recent years, Tony Tanner, Harry Levin, Leslie Fiedler, and Richard Chase have deepened our sense of a serious and brooding intellect behind the body of American literature. It is not, however, the overall picture of the American mind as reflected in literature that is of concern here. Rather, the output—the ideation—of that mind in regard to Black American artistry provides that focus. The responses of eminent or influential white Americans—both literary critics and others—to the creativity of Black Americans reflect certain patterns of ideas that make a number of the judgments rendered on Black American literature understandable. Realizing the diversity and intricacy of American intellectual history, it would be absurd to attempt an exhaustive classification, but three broad categories can be set forth.

It is fitting that a view of these ideational frames begin with Thomas Jefferson. Not only was he eminent among the founding fathers, but also representative. Both his biographers and a recent literary critic, Jean Fagin Yellin, have illustrated the seminal place of his thought in colonial America. Professor Yellin has shown how his view of the Black American in *Notes on the State of Virginia* acts as a paradigm for such later writers as John Pendleton Kennedy, William Gilmore Simms, and Herman Melville.[2] It is the critical component of Jefferson's *Notes* that deserves treatment here.

After lauding Native Americans (Indians) for their simple art work, Jefferson says: "But never yet could I find that a Black had uttered a thought above the level of plain narration; never see even an elementary trait of painting or sculpture."[3] A brief and condescending nod to Black music is followed by his well-known remarks on the first Black American woman (and the second woman in America) to produce a volume of poetry:

> Religion indeed has produced a Phyllis Whately [sic.]; but it could not
> produce a poet. The compositions published under her name are below
> the dignity of criticism. The heroes of the *Dunciad* are to her, as
> Hercules to the author of that poem.

He continues his censure of Black writers with his less-quoted, but more interesting, triade against Ignatius Sancho whose letters were published in England in 1782:

> . . . his imagination is wild and extravagant, escapes incessantly from
> every restraint of reason and taste, and, in the course of its vagaries,
> leaves a tract of thought as incoherent and eccentric, as is the course of
> a meteor through the sky. His subjects should have led him to a process
> of sober reasoning: yet we find him always substituting sentiment for
> demonstration.

While he feels Sancho can be admitted "to the first place among those of his own colour who have presented themselves to the public judgement," he sets him at the bottom of the column when compared to white epistolers.

Jefferson's remarks are in accord with the Humean consensus. David Hume, and a host of others in Britain and America during the eighteenth century, felt that the taste of an intelligent man was sufficient to judge a literary work. The light of common reason guided the man of wit and propriety to those works that best clothed "nature" and felicitously captured what was often thought. Given this milieu, it is not surprising that Jefferson, who felt a sense of moral culpability regarding his Black slaves, was unable to appreciate the folksongs of Black America. They certainly did not satisfy Popean criteria of "What oft was thought, but ne're so well expressed." Moreover, it is hardly striking that he reduces the singers to creatures of mere passion. First, he was concerned to show French naturalists such as Buffon that white Americans stood above many species in the human order. That process of "negative identification," considered so important for American racial attitudes by Winthrop Jordan, was at work. Second, if Black slaves were indeed sentient beings infused with common reason, how could they justifiably be enslaved? How could those clauses in the constitution Jefferson helped to formulate, those pithy statements assuring slavery in America, be sanctioned? Thus, Phillis Wheatley's verses, the products of a remarkable slave, are ranked far below those of Alexander Pope.

Sancho's letters, however, occasion more difficulty. They are the work of a man who was born on a slave ship from Africa but who, as a child, entered the household of the Duke of Montagu. He was one of the most assimilated products of a dark system: tutored by royalty, a friend of Garrick, and a subject for Gainsborough. If any Black man deserved a place in the consensus, it was Sancho, and Jefferson knew it. He, therefore, damns his work with faint praise: he is the first of his race but last in the general lists. Further, he casts doubt on the genuineness of the letters and asserts that it would be difficult to prove ". . . they have received amendment from no other hand." The *coup de grace* is the argument from blood: "The improvement of the blacks in body and mind, in the first instance of their mixture with the whites, has been observed by every one, and proves that their inferiority is not the effect merely of their condition of life." Though Sancho's "condition of life," according to Humean standards, has fitted him for a writer, without Anglo-Saxon blood in his veins he scarcely stands a chance. Both Jefferson's slaveholding and his critical responses to Black authors are proved upon the pulses.

To label Jefferson a simple "no" man vis-a-vis Black American literature would be meaningless. The reason his views deserve notice is that they capture a prevailing American attitude. One is not only dealing with a Humean consensus, but also with a consensus about the human. Jefferson insists that Blacks do not possess that initial seed of hope which elevates Native Americans above them; they lack "a germ in their mind which only wants cultivation." Hedged round by scientific, religious, and political theories that placed the Anglo-Saxon (particularly the European Anglo-Saxon) on the highest rung of the human ladder, Jefferson was capable of articulating only the harshest judgments on works by individuals who could barely approach the ladder, much less scale it. There were, of course, theories of chronological primitivism. They categorized certain British washerwomen and South Sea islanders as noble savages, uncorrupted by the institutions of society. But Jefferson's concession to this point of view was recognition of the Indians. As an empirical observer who believed that human talent would show through regardless of the "condition of life," he found the evidence of the Black man's humanity insufficient. When Benjamin Banneker—the Black mathematician, surveyor, and compiler of almanacs—sent him examples of his work, Jefferson responded with the hope that more evidence of a similar nature would be forthcoming. The irony, of course, is that Banneker thought it necessary to convince a man whose responses were so deeply grounded in his age. The proposition runs as follows: Blacks are not as human (if human at all) as whites, hence one does not expect from them expressions of the human order, e.g., noteworthy creative works.

To move from the colonial to the middle period of American history brings a shift from one proposition to another which is less rigorous in its exclusions. The abolitionists and the pro-slavery advocates of the nineteenth century both endorsed this ideational frame—the former conditionally, the latter determinately. It would be folly for a Black American to lay critical siege to the abolitionists. Yet to turn to two representative white Americans from that group is to come away less than jubilant. William Lloyd Garrison speaks as follows about one of the most significant narratives written by a Black American:

> Mr. Douglass has very properly chosen to write his own narrative, in his own style, and according to the best of his ability, rather than to employ some one else. . . . I am confident that it is essentially true in all its statements; that nothing has been set down in malice, nothing exaggerated, nothing drawn from the imagination.[4]

These words from Garrison's preface to *Narrative of the Life of Frederick Douglass* do serve as an affadavit to the work's authenticity, and the act of prefacing an unknown author's creation is still a common practice. But Garrison's tone implies dominance or control. Since Douglass had indeed written the work himself and had assured Garrison long since of his integrity and imagination, why did the publisher of *The Liberator* feel it necessary to assume the tone of the kindly, leading father? Perhaps, for the same reason he tried (first confidently, then bitterly) to keep Douglass from founding *The North Star.* (One notices, incidentally, the differing intentions of the two publishers in the titles of their newspapers.) When he cried out against the Black publisher's changed and anti-Garrisonian stance in 1851, "There is roguery somewhere," he clarified his earlier paternalism. As long as Douglas was willing to support the Garrisonian point of view and to be guided by the man who would not "retreat a single inch," all was well. But when he manifested that power of reason properly belonging to a human being, Garrison's wrath was unequivocal. Operating on the assumption that slaves needed the direction of whites if they were to move up the scale of civilization, the abolitionist recoiled sharply before the Black man's opinions.

One suspects that Harriet Beecher Stowe would have reacted similarly. Her novel sold over 300,000 copies during its first year, and J. R. Thompson, editor of the *Southern Literary Messenger,* was all the while beseeching Frederick Holmes to blast and sear the reputation of the "vile wench in petticoats who could write such a volume." But reading *Uncle Tom's Cabin* today is often like scanning a tract by a mild racial theorizer. Blacks are impressionable, susceptible to religion, affectionate, fond of the domestic virtues, lyrical, and educable. They are (without a healthy admixture of Saxon blood) like wily children—human, to be sure, but wanting in the white advantages that ensure survival. Their "tropical fervor" and moral sensibility can contribute to the world, but only after they have been converted to Christianity and received a sound Western education, including a course in New England conscientiousness.

Both Garrison and Stowe left firmly in its place that question mark behind the query on Wedgewood's cameo: "Am I not a man and your brother?" They were willing to concede brotherhood, reserving the role of the young and inexperienced sibling for Black Americans. The shift from the colonial to the middle period, therefore, involves reclassification of the Black man as a child, one capable of full, adult, human development. During the years of fervent abolitionism and Civil War, all evidence of Black creative ability was welcomed and praised as a boon to the anti-slavery cause. Slave songs, narratives, verses, and orations offered affecting proof to an evangelical and sentimental age that Blacks were, after all, human.

On one hand, what is described above amounts to revisionism. On the other hand, it simply specifies the form American racial theorizing took during a particular era and in relationship to a select area of the Black experience. Slave narratives sold by the thousands, and the spirituals and work songs were suddenly of interest. But the dominating, condescending tone of the abolitionists is prevalent in even the most sympathetic critiques. After all, one is not expected to devote a great deal of scholarly concern to children, particularly in an age when youngsters are expected to observe the strictest rules when (and if) they are heard.

C. L. R. James has said of the American abolitionist movement:

> History really moves when the traditionally most civilized section of the population—in this case New Englanders representing the longest American line of continuity with the English tradition of lawful sovereignty—joins as coequals with those without whose labor society could not exist for a day—in this case the plantation chattel. Otherwise, history stays pretty much the same, or worse yet, repeats itself.

This may be true of American history in general, but the characteristic relationship between white New Englanders and Black "chattel" in this evolving pattern remained one of the adult prince of civilization to the childlike pauper of the tropics. Arna Bontemps, for example, identifies the appeal of nineteenth-century Black American slave narratives as "not unlike the vogue of the Western story in the twentieth [century]."[5] And William McFeely has spoken of the voyeuristic impulse that led whites to attend abolitionist meetings and to read slave narratives.[6] Considered good and racy adventure stories produced by lowly fugitives, even the best of these narratives (Douglass's, for example) were allowed to go out of print within a few decades after the Civil War. When Lerone Bennett speaks of the "Negro exhibit" at abolitionist meetings, therefore it comes as no surprise that he means the escaped slave himself.[7]

The reason it is absurd to berate the abolitionists, however, is that they applied a dominant point of view in a manner favorable to Black Americans. If the effects were not salutary for literature, they were for body and soul. The pro-slavery faction, by contrast, not only wanted to sear Mrs. Stowe, but also any Black "children" who entertained the idea that they could match strides with the white patriarchs. While the abolitionists endorsed a conditional Black puerility, pro-slavery advocates argued a determinate puerility. According to the latter, Blacks were the intermediate link between man and animal; they could move in one direction only—toward the bestial. As eternal and ebullient children, they demanded the protection of kind and longsuffering masters. The countless doubts about the authenticity of the slave narratives expressed by this group indicate how it reacted to the idea of creative Black Americans. And Since its opinions carried the day in American letters during the post-bellum period, perhaps it is fitting to cite a later illustration of its codes. In 1877, William Owens wrote:

> Travellers and missionaries tell us that the same sweet airs which are so often heard in religious meetings in America, set to Christian hymns, are to be recognized in the boats and palm-roofed houses of Africa, set to heathen words and that the same wild stories of Buh Rabbit, Buh Wolf, and other *Buhs* that are so charming to the ears of American children, are to be heard to this day in Africa, differing only in drapery necessary to the change of scene.[8]

The quotation not only condemns American Blacks, but an entire continent to the prelapserian. Joel Chandler Harris, who was motivated by Owens to begin collecting Black animal tales, simply makes Uncle Remus a childlike figure and designates plantation children as his appropriate audience. Bernard Wolfe surely had the pro-slavery faction and its post-bellum followers in mind when he wrote: "Uncle Remus—a kind of blackface Will Rogers complete with standard minstrel dialect and plantation shuffle—has had remarkable staying power in our popular culture. . . ."[9] He might have added "and our literary culture." Regardless of one's angle of vision, the Black American emerges from the nineteenth-century white perspective as a child-like, lesser member of the human family, an individual whose creative efforts must be judged by standards set for juveniles. From non-being to puerility, from total exclusion to a conditional acceptance is not an overwhelming distance.

One recent writer has skillfully demonstrated that the temper of an age conditions its judicial decisions; he speaks of "racial prejudices which judges share with their fellow men."[10] By changing the phrasing, one could talk of the ideational sets literary critics share with their cultures. The first literary history of America, Moses Coit Tyler's *The Literary History of the American Revolution,* offers an illustration. Here one encounters a denunciation of Phillis Wheatley less scathing than Jefferson's:

> The other prominent representative of the town of Boston in the poetry of this period 1763–1776 is Phillis Wheatly [sic.], a gentle-minded and intelligent slave girl, whose name still survives among us in the shape of a traditional vaguely testifying to the existence of poetic talent in this particular member of the African race. Unfortunately, a glance at what she wrote will show that there is no adequate basis for such tradition, and that the significance of her career belongs rather to the domain of anthropology, or of hagiology, than to that of poetry—whether American or African. Her verses, which were first published in a collected form in London in 1773, under the title "Poems on Various Subjects, Religious and Moral," attracted for a time considerable

curiosity, both in England and in America,—not at all, however, because the verses were good, but because they were written by one from whom even bad verses were too good to be expected.[11]

Tyler's comments are interesting in several respects. They include the Black poet among the representatives of a particular region, and since they follow a condemnation of all New England for its "poetic poverty," their indictment of Wheatley is predictable. There is a kind of gamesmanship, however, in which the left hand takes away what the right has given. Tyler is republican enough to view the abolition of slavery as an absolute moral good, but he doesn't know what to make of those "human brethren" who have been released. His ironical tone—an almost whimsical detachment from the camp that debates whether Africans are capable of artistic expression—cuts two ways. He can be charged with deriding a "tradition vaguely testifying" to the Black's ability, or he can be praised for recognizing the folly that necessitates such a tradition. He seems certain that Wheatley's poems are valueless, but he doesn't know why. Assuredly, Africans are human, but can they produce worthy verse? Tyler is not prepared to answer, and his reference to anthropology almost forces one to see him as a product of the postbellum period. Blacks are lower and somewhat curious specimen for Tyler. Only the *Declaration of Independence* stands in the way of those who would easily keep them down. Republicanism can, thus, accommodate Phillis Wheatley, but it can not view her as an important poet.

Of course, the author of *The Literary History* does not stand alone. White American critics from Barrett Wendell to the latest issue of *Saturday Review* have oscillated between the poles of an overall exclusion of Blacks and an acceptance of them as puerile human beings. At the turn of the century, both Barrett Wendell and William Dean Howells turned a critical eye on the Black American. A quotation from Wendell makes his point of view abundantly clear:

> However human, native Africans are still savage; and although, long before the Civil War, the Southern slaves had shown such sensitiveness to comparatively civilized conditions as to have lost their superficial savagery, and indeed as still to warrant, in many hopeful minds, even the franchise which was ultimately granted them, the spectre of darkest Africa loomed behind them all.[12]

This is a violent yoking together of the ideational frames of Jefferson and the pro-slavery faction. And the effect—no matter how emphatically one points to the *Declaration of Independence* or to the Social Darwinists and outright bigots of the critic's day—is devastating. A contrasting contemporary opinion is offered by Howells's conditional puerility. He felt Paul Laurence Dunbar's dialect pieces and Charles Chestnutt's *The Conjure Woman* were superb because they captured the humor and the limitations of Black America. He would not have understood the Black poet's lament to James Weldon Johnson:

"You know, of course, that I didn't start as a dialect poet. I simply came to the conclusion that I could write it as well, if not better, than anybody else I knew of, and that by doing so I should gain a hearing. I gained the hearing, and now they don't want me to write anything but dialect."[13]

For Howells, a sanguine metaphysics and an optimistic critical stance could be wedded. While the results were often beneficial to Black artists, they were frequently disastrous. Dunbar's poems in literary English—many of them extremely pessimistic—receive only passing notice. Chesnutt's telling analysis of Southern racial prejudice earns the following comment:

The book [*The Marrow of Tradition*] is, in fact, bitter, bitter. There is no reason in history why it should not be so, if wrong is to be repaid with hate, and yet it would be better if it were not so bitter.[14]

Believing that truth could only be extracted from the "large cheerful average of health and success and happy life," Howells hardly expected the Black man to lament or to turn bitter. Morality, for him, penetrated all things, and if those whose range of existence spanned "appetite and emotion"[15] could not reflect this point of view, something was amiss. So the man whom Mark Twain described as like himself—an old derelict—floated on in the strange seas of a complex and racist time, his mind thoroughly shaped by the tenets of an earlier age. He was incapable of raising life itself above the "eternal amenities." How could one expect him to elevate Blacks above the level of an aspiring childhood?

The twentieth-century has, for the most part, offered critical responses in harmony with the three ideational patterns treated above. The new critics, for example, have been so mired in lexis (the word as meaning) and so distrustful of the world of common men that they have usually excluded Black artists. When they have turned an occasional gaze on the Black artifact, they have been so far above its praxis (the word as action) that they have committed almost comic offenses. Robert Bone has been the "new critical" whipping boy of contemporary, outraged Black writers, and Theodore Gross and David Littlejohn have run close seconds.

The political progressives (usually Marxists or Marxist-Leninists) have frequently chosen the domineering, condescending stance of certain abolitionists. Realizing the necessity for a Black advance guard if American social change is to be meaningful, they have enlisted Black artists under their banners. Like the abolitionists, however, these activists have been stung to fierce retorts when the Black man has become too energetic in his own behalf. In *Black Writers of the Thirties,* James O. Young discusses the shifting reactions of the Communist Party to the writings of Langston Hughes and Richard Wright. And Harold Cruse, in *The Crisis of the Negro Intellectual,* gives an even more telling account. Irving Howe's treatment of *Native Son* offers a case in point. In "Black Boys and Native Sons," Howe sees Wright as a paradigm for the Black artist. Ralph Ellison and James Baldwin, by comparison, have adopted false ideals. The critic's article "At Ease With Apocalypse," however, reveals an altered perspective. Here, *Native Son* is labelled a crude book. (One almost hears the cry go up: "There is roguery somewhere.") When it became apparent to Howe (through the responses of Ellison and Baldwin) that Blacks would not tolerate his prescriptive, political formulas, he seems to have turned against even his model Black artist.

There have also been a host of twentieth-century advocates for the determinate puerility of Blacks. Critics such as John Nelson, Louis Simpson, and John Leonard seem agreed on Nelson's list of characteristics: "[the Black man's] irrepressible spirits, his complete absorption in the present moment, his whimsicality, his irresponsibility, his intense superstition, his freedom from resentment." Defined in this manner, the Black writer is expected to provide easy, exotic fare for his white readers. If his work transcends such stuff, he is promoted to a conditional stage where he has a chance of reaching full civilization in his life and "universality" in his writing.

The origins of white responses to Black creativity may be obscured by a plethora of theoretical issues and by endless pages of analysis. Behind these tangible boundaries, however, lie basic ideational, or pre-shaping, patterns that condition what has been a felt rejection. W. E. B. DuBois speaks of that "other world which does not know and does not want to know our power." There is another dimension: a world that *can not* know the Black man's expressive power because it is locked into a narrow trinity of ideation. Van Wyck Brooks divides American literature into three categories: high, low, and middle brow. Analogically, one can compare white American ideational patterns to an amplitude with three stops: exclusion, conditional and determinate puerility. Because the white critic shares this limiting range with his culture, he has seldom been able to enunciate the loud and clear praise of Black creativity that he has bestowed upon white artifacts.

But what if the objects of criticism are located, linguistically and historically, outside this compass? What if Black creativity is the result of a context—a web of meanings—different in kind and degree from that of white commentators? A view of the development of Black American language and a consideration of certain historiographical factors suggest such an eventuality.

III

"Nominalists," writes one philosopher, "make the mistake of interpreting all words as *names,* and so of not really describing their use, but only, so to speak, giving a paper draft on such a description."[16] The reason for such paper drafts, according to Ludwig Wittgenstein, is the belief that there is a determinate standard of knowledge because every word has an essential meaning. If such were the case, words would be "names" referring to an objective (but not necessarily present) essence. The counter argument he proposes is that no determinate standard of knowledge exists. Philosophy, like being it-self, originates in a "speaking situation." When one arrives at a speaking sit-uation, the origins of the conjunction between word and object are already obscured. To discuss "meaning," therefore, is to find oneself, at the outset, detailing an event dominated by language usage, by the user and his physical behavior.

The case of the baby crying, as it is presented in the *Philosophical In-vestigations,* makes this clearer. Jeffrey Price explains that:

> Wittgenstein finds the question of the relationship of lanugage and its object to be the same as the question of the origin of speaking. By asserting that in an infant the expression of pain replaces a situation of unbroken conjunction of certain movements and the condition of the body, Wittgenstein reveals his insistence that the original moments of expression issue in the determinations that form their content. He is grieved that this originality is obscured in our normal thinking, for if we lose sight of the origin and possibilities of speech, its deep aspect will elude us.[17]

In other words, at the original moments of expression, undifferentiated move-ment and words as instances of absolute separation or distinctiveness are com-plicated in a way that pervades all we know. Edward Sapir states the same when he says: "it may be that originally the primal cries or other types of symbols developed by man had some connection with certain emotions or at-titudes or notions. But a connection is no longer directly traceable between words, or combinations of words, and what they refer to."[18] The apparent gulf between the pre-verbal moment—as a complex of physical and, perhaps, emo-tional "activity"—and speech raises, of course, an ancient linguistic issue: the origin of speech.

Noam Chomsky and a number of others espouse a position closer to Leibniz than to Locke, believing that only on the assumption that human beings possess specific mental faculties and innate ideas can one "understand the sci-ence of linguistics or the wondrous ability of the child of tender years to learn how to speak."[19] Opposing this view are the early works of Sapir and Benjamin Lee Whorf and the more recent efforts of Dell Hymes and William Labov who feel that language is an essentially social phenomenon reflecting the ac-cumulated experience of a group and determining to a great extent its world view.[20] Sidney Hook states the dichotomy as follows: "The facts [language as species-specific, manifesting a similarity of development, regardless of the particular linguistic system] are not in dispute but their interpretations are."[21] Chomsky believes the "innateness" determining linguistic competence resides in the individual speaker, while sociolinguists seem to feel that communicative competence is somehow invested by language and society. What one has is idealists facing empiricists with cognitive psychology and countless chimpan-zees in the middle attempting to provide sufficient data to decide the issue.

262

For the moment, however, and for the sake of the present discussion, it seems enough to acknowledge that a gap exists in our understanding of the connection between the pre-expressive instant and the spoken word. This synapse is of adequate proportion to have triggered some recent concern with the whole issue of "privacy" or "private language." It is the "private," or "Black Public" (if you prefer), domain that is of greatest importance for a criticism of Black American literature. LeRoi Jones's Walker Vessels captures this with a fine brevity in *The Slave:* "But listen now. . . . Brown is not brown except when used as an intimate description of personal phenomenological fields. As your brown is not my brown, et cetera, that is, we need, ahem, a meta-language. We need some thing not included here." The experiences of Black and white speakers of English are so bifurcated that it is hard to conceive of a criticism that does not deal with the fundamental distinctions raised by a concern with language.

Coming into English in a trading situation, making contact with the language through restless vagabonds and adventurers in search of wealth, native Africans moved toward a pidgin English. Some indications of a specifically West African pidgin date back to the sixteenth-century. This language was comprised of vocabulary items from various European languages, and it was so regular that syntactic rules generating an infinite number of sentences could be written.[22] But grammatical rules are not the most interesting considerations here. The social and psychological situations of the Africans and their vocabulary borrowings offer more interesting speculations. As they watched whites destroy their internal trade (both slave and other), viewed the introduction of firearms, witnessed Europeans struggling bloodily for commercial advantage, and felt themselves driven from a stable system of social organization to enthrallment in a vast pattern of trade that was to claim millions of African lives, what conjunctions existed between the pre-English instant and the employemnt of English lexical items?

One cannot compare the moments of original significance for an infant and the language contact phenomena that result in West African pidgin English. But one might assume that words like "white," "slave," "freedom" and a host of others had a significance for their Black borrowers that was firmly tied to their psycho-physical circumstances. Since language is never value-neutral, and since the situation and the values of the African were substantially different from those of the white European, the pidgin English of African (and later, Afro-American) speakers must have carried meanings (semantic levels of the lexicon) quite different from those held by Europeans. As a second language, adopted or learned for the purpose of trade, the vocabulary of the two groups who came in contact would have been almost identical. The origin of the distinctiveness between word and object, however, would have been quite different. In the public intercourse between Europeans and Africans, the speaking situation determined meaning. Behind this realm, though, stretched the vistas of origins—deep, only vaguely understood. And along this axis value first attaches itself, a phenomenon that can certainly be observed where language is *learned* by the adult members of a society.

Recognizing the irony/absurdity between the words (concepts) they were borrowing and the brutal realities of the slave trade, Africans were scarcely prepared to adopt in toto the "rules" of the language games of their white exploiters. It becomes clearer with each new critique of the "Sapir-Whorf hypothesis" that language is *not* an invisible garment that drapes itself about the spirit of a person, giving a predetermined form to all its (the spirit's) symbolic expression; hence, the Africans were, indeed, free to reverse the rules.

Wittgenstein, of course, accounted for the possibility of such linguistic behavior. Even though he felt that usage—a speaking situation—gave meaning to words and coherence to human society, he also knew that people were not trapped in a hopeless continuum of language games. They could transcend custom/rules through the act of negation. "Freedom," therefore, can become "not freedom." Another approach here is the poetical one. Langston Hughes says:

> There are words like *Freedom*
> Sweet and wonderful to say.
> On my heartstrings freedom sings
> All day everyday.
>
> There are words like *Liberty*
> That almost make me cry.
> If you had known what I know
> You would know why.[23]

If one commences with the answer Wittgenstein gives to his hypothetical questioner, a perspective totally different from the one that emerges from a discussion of American ideational frames is necessary:

> " 'But doesn't what you say come to this: that there is no pain, for example, without pain-behavior?'—It comes to this, only of a living human being and what resembles (behaves like) a living human being can one say: it has sensations; it sees; is blind; hears; is deaf; is conscious or unconscious."

If the Black man entered the speaking situation with values antithetical to those of the white externality surrounding him, then his vocabulary and the standard forms into which it enters are less important than an attempt to hold the moments of Black, original significance in mind. What I am positing, or speculating on, of course, is the distinct possibility that whites—moving exclusively in a white public realm and unable to move beyond the ideational veil obscuring origins—have taken the Black creative work at its face value, or worse, at a value assigned by their own preconceptions.

Since everyone's reading time is limited, however, (everyone, that is, who has pursued the argument thus far) let me give just two brief examples. The first is offered by Charles Chesnutt's *The Conjure Woman*. Published as a volume of framework tales in 1899, the work's success seemed assured by the earlier reactions to one of its stories. "The Goophered Grapevine" had appeared to white critical acclaim in an 1896 issue of the *Atlantic*. Few readers were aware of Chestnutt's race, and in the heyday of the Plantation School, who would expect a Black American writer to go against the weave of what Oscar Handlin calls the "Linnaean Web."[24] Chestnutt's creation simply seemed one in a long line of opuses dedicated to portraying the Black man as a predial and loveable creature who devoted himself to strumming and a-humming all day in the antebellum South. Howells and other white critics praised the story with these assumptions as their base. Why? Is there an absence of guideposts to a different explication? On the contrary, the very title of Chestnutt's group of stories, speaks of the author's intention. It holds a clue to the origins of *The Conjure Woman's* language as a whole.

John Blassingame writes:

> In addition to these activities [religious and recreational], several other customs prevented the slaves from identifying with the ideals of their masters. Because of their superstitions and belief in fortune tellers, witches, magic and conjurers, many of the slaves constructed a psychological defense against total dependence on and submission to their masters. Whatever his power, the master was a puny man compared to the supernatural. Often the most powerful and significant individual on the plantation was the conjurer.[25]

The historian goes on to point out that by shrewdness and an industrious countermanding of the slave system the plantation conjurer gained control over both Blacks and whites. The real Black protagonist—the motivating force behind the action of all the tales in Chestnutt's volume—is the conjurer. By shaping the life of the entire plantation, a single Black man or woman dictates the ultimate norms and actions of secondary figures in the stories. Such conclusions, of course, can not be drawn simply from the title of the book. They indicate, though, that white critics unimbued with the Black "meaning," of the word "conjurer" were ill-prepared to evaluate Chestnutt's stories. Their referents were all grounded outside that almost exclusively Black domain that assured autonomy, obverse value, a sense of the Black self different from that held by members, or champions, of the Plantation School.

If this seems an example of "justification by the little-known work," one can turn to a later example—Richard Wright's *Native Son*. Having already set forth my own sense of the infrastructure of the novel,[26] I wish to introduce here James Emanuel's all but ignored article on the metaphorical aspects of Wright's classic.[27] Insisting that the book is rooted in a unique experience, Emanual points out a host of recurrent images that accompany Bigger Thomas's progress. Images of crucifixion, confinement, claustrophobia, heat, light all speak of a protagonist hemmed in by a world oblivious to his most pressing drives. The rhetorical structures and vocabulary of the novel are often those of the proletarian tradition of the 1930's and 1940's, but the overall effect produced by a close attention to the work's metaphorical clusters outstrips the responses of the rigidly Marxist critic. The images carry one to the folk level, to the "forms of things unknown," on which Wright's story is based. Grasping only, the bare words "furnace," "flight," "snow," "curtain," etc., the white critic has often missed the point rather than lent point to the novelist's creation. The negation of custom that rumbles mightily through most of the work's pages has been repeatedly misinterpreted by the unaware.

To stop at this point, would be to risk the charge that I am setting forth only a linguistic perspective. But while the case presented here stresses the primacy of being/language/meaning, it also pushes toward a concern for the historical aspects of the critical process. If the quotation from Wittgenstein that speaks of "a living human being" is relevant, so too is R. G. Collingwood's evaluation of Toynbee's philosophy of history:

> . . . his general conception of history is ultimately naturalistic; he regards the life of a society as a natural and not a mental life, something at bottom merely biological and best understood on biological analogies. And this is connected with the fact that he never reaches the conception of historical knowledge as the reenactment of the past in the historian's mind.[28]

For the idealistic historian like Collingwood, the stress is on that mental life which makes historical inquiry possible. Events are intelligible because they have an inside, a thought side, that comes from human agents who think about what they are doing before they act. Obviously, American ideation vis-a-vis the Black man virtually excludes him from history. That which has been considered distinctively Black by white Americans has seldom included the rational, or thought side, of Black American culture. Critics have not felt it necessary to rethink the thoughts of Black historical agents. William Dray's analysis of Collingwood helps to clarify the preceding statement:

> In insisting that the historian must re-think the agent's thoughts, what Collingwood is claiming is that the point of his [the agent's] action cannot be grasped without a piece of vicarious practical reasoning on the part of the historian. The latter, on considering the agent's thoughts, must see that, from the agent's own point of view, what he did really was *the thing to do.*[29]

The historian begins with evidence, those tangible manifestations of a historical event that exist in the present:

> The whole perceptible world, then, is potentially and in principle evidence to the historian. It becomes actual evidence in so far as he can use it. And he cannot use it unless he comes to it with the right kind of historical knowledge. The more historical knowledge we have, the more we can learn from any given piece of evidence; if we had none, we could learn nothing. Evidence is evidence only when someone contemplates it historically.[30]

266

The Black literary text stands "historically dumb" before the critic who possesses no historical knowledge, who is incapable of realizing that the creator of the text was firmly based in a *sui generis* culture that invested what seems a common language (English) with *particular* value. Of course, the critic who believes the author of the Black text has been motivated to write by a kind of pure, primitive instinct is lost from the outset. But the man who fails to attempt the depths of the Black author's language—no matter how liberal he might feel himself to be—will prove equally inept. He will not be able to get at the inside of the event constituted by the creation of the text. A sympathetic and insightful act of "vicarious practical reasoning" is scarcely to be expected from the individual who sees the Black artifact not as evidence of a singular past, but as one object in that vast panoply of world creativity which he must circle in order to prove his catholicity.

The Black text is historical evidence because it is a present, palpable component of the past that formed it. Its creation—despite the mysteries of the artistic imagination—was governed by a thinking agent, by the mental life of a culture. The *sine qua non* that draws the linguistic and historiographical considerations together is the Black person as a thinking human being who possesses the supports, values, and stays of a unique culture. Wittgenstein writes: "When I think in language there aren't 'meanings' going through my mind in addition to the verbal expressions: the language is itself the vehicle of thought."

To grasp fully the significance of the Black text, however, the critic must recognize that the situation of the author was substantially different from that of the white American. He must reach beyond the obscuring veil and seek the origins of the Black word. In order to do this, he must view the text as historical evidence. Set in language, the text is also the vehicle of thought—that source from which the tides of history flow. The proposition governing this section, therefore, might read as follows: the private sector (condition of the body, origins) leads in unbroken conjunction to the word, which is not value-neutral when it is formed. Meaning and its expression are one; hence, in the Black word resides the culturally-specific meaning that grows out of the physical circumstances where language begins. As the vehicle of a rational agent's thought, the language of the Black author (as embodied in a literary text) can be taken as historical evidence. The critic must realize that behind the purely public cast of the Black author's language lie its unique origins and meanings. His evaluation remains a superficial glance at large general properties unless he follows the thread of a Black web of meaning to where it had its spinning.

IV

The significance of the Black aesthetic is that it moves beyond those white American ideational frames discussed earlier. By accepting Black American culture as a *sui generis* way of life, it is capable of extricating from the Black text composed in English those meanings that grow out of a particular cultural situation. The critical work of the Black aesthetician is not rooted in some mysterious affinity between the critic and the text. It does not insist upon the possession of a vaguely-defined "soul." Its realization of the origins of the Black author's language and its willingness to view his created text as historical evidence are grounded on a recognition of the Black man as a fully rational agent. Since white American ideational frames have precluded such considerations, it is not surprising that a perspective—endorsed primarily by Blacks and capable of generating an accurate conception of Black American literature—has come to the fore.

What is the function of those who will champion and develop such a perspective? First, they must steep themselves in manifold historical evidence that has been too long ignored. The literary text is most revealing to the critic who possesses a high degree of historical knowledge. Second, those who would contribute to a just view of Black American literature must be able to move from the broad historical plane to the distinctive Black word. If an altruistic relationship exists between the author and his reader, the latter can not simply lead a work into being. He must lend a consciousness that reveals the text's most important meanings and values. In order to achieve this, he must journey, using all available signs, toward those moments of original significance when the Black word became a discreet entity. The discussion of *Native Son* and *The Conjure Woman* raises issues that fit this second prerequisite.

Third, the critic must attempt to free himself from slavish adherence to the ideational pulls of the critical moment (the time in which his evaluation occurs). The challenge for the critic who endorses a Black aesthetic is to go first to the evidence that is the literary text. Its words and metaphors can carry the historically aware individual toward understanding and insight. "Historically aware" does not mean engagedly activist. The events of the last decade offer ample evidence that the most abysmally unaware are often the most stridently active. The politician (or the active revolutionary) and the literary critic may require the same type of historical cognizance, but their roles should not be conflated. The rhetorical strategies of the militant warrior are usually a hindrance to the critic, whose function is predicated upon a clear grasp and explication of the deep aspects of a culture. A full analysis of *Native Son* may, finally, be more revolutionary in its implications (because it makes clear the whole way of life that is Black America) than an ill-advised injunction to revolt, a hastily tossed grenade, or a spuriously utopian social philosophy that is actually a new totalitarianism. Simply stated, one must beware of saying "right on" or "solid on that" to each voice insisting it is the most committed.

Fourth, the critic who moves toward a Black aesthetic should, indeed, number the stripes on the tulip. When told by authoritarians that only one community of Black folk and its idiom must hold his attention, he might simply point out that the boundaries of Black America are wide. The focus of those championing a Black aesthetic has been the inner-city because they inhabit cities and because literature and criticism (since the eighteenth-century, at any rate) have been based in urban areas. Is Barry Beckham's *My Main Mother* to be ignored or labelled an inexact representation of Black America because it is set in a small New England town? Those who claim to have their fingers on the pulse of a culture have often mistaken the thudding of their own voices for the pumping of the Black heart.

Obviously, the four points stressed include a fuller statement of the reservations mentioned at the beginning of this discussion. They do not speak as forcefully as they might about the timeliness of the Black aesthetic. That should be apparent at this point. To step outside the constricting patterns of ideation that have left a culture unknown and to move back, through language and history, to origins and values is the aim of this new theoretical stance. To generate an informed view of a body of creative works rooted in these beginnings is its most essential work. There are cultural imperatives, then, at the center of its endeavors. While the future of the Black aesthetic is beyond historical ken, one might speculate that the nature of its enterprise makes the Black scholar its most likely practitioner. The furor of contemporary white detractors and the continued appearance of white critical works governed by traditional ideational frames indicate that the Black aesthetic is, at present, a unique possession of the Black American. As it develops and moves beyond the pitfalls that endanger the life of a new theoretical framework, it will be endorsed by all scholars who hope to grasp Black American literature.

One must reiterate Wittgenstein's point, though, that words are not names. In the future, there may be no mention of a "Black aesthetic," but surely there will be individuals dedicated to a theory of Black American literature that stresses the primacy of the Black word and views the Black text as evidence of a people's singular nd accomplished history. A prolegomenon for the future would call for the critic's acceptance of the Black man as the thoughtful agent of his own destiny, an individual who has invested his words with value and his creations with a significance that awaits the discerning investigator.

Notes

1. Books, collections and articles that move toward a statement of the Black aesthetic are: the essays on literature and language in Baraka's (LeRoi Jones's) *Home: Social Essays,* New York: William Morrow, 1966; Neal's "The Black Arts Movement," *Tulane Drama Review* (Summer, 1968), pp. 29–39; Lee's (now Haki Madhubuti's) *Dynamite Voices,* Broadside Press: Detroit, 1971; Neal and Baraka's *Black Fire,* New York: William Morrow, 1968; Addison Gayle's *The Black Aesthetic,* New York: Doubleday, 1971; Stephen Henderson's *Understanding the New Black Poetry,* New York: William Morrow, 1973; and a number of articles in *Black World* (formerly, *Negro Digest*).
2. *The Intricate Knot,* New York: New York University Press, 1972.
3. *Notes on the State of Virginia,* ed. William Peden (Chapel Hill: University of North Carolina Press, 1955), P. 140. The other quotations from *Notes* in my text refer to this edition and can be found between p. 137 and p. 141.
4. *Narrative of the Life of Frederick Douglass* (New York: Signet, 1968), pp. ix–x.
5. *Great Slave Narratives* (Boston: Beacon Press, 1969), p. xviii.

6. McFeely is the author of *Yankee Stepfather,* a biography of General O. O. Howard. After his helpful reading of an essay I had written on Frederick Douglass, we discussed the genre of the slave narrative at length.
7. *Before the Mayflower* (Baltimore: Penguin Books, 1964), p. 137.
8. Quoted from Bruce Jackson, ed., *The Negro and His Folklore in Nineteenth-Century Periodicals* (Austin: University of Texas Press, 1967), pp. 147–148. Owen's remark appeared first in *Lippincott Magazine.*
9. "Uncle Remus and the Malevolent Rabbit," *Commentary,* VII (July, 1969), 31.
10. Unpublished manuscript in progress on racial justice in America by The Honorable Leon Higginbotham.
11. *The Literary History of the American Revolution 1763–1783,* I (New York: Frederick Ungar, 19557), pp. 186–187.
12. *A Literary History of America* (New York: Charles Scribner's, 1900), p. 482.
13. Quoted from James Weldon Johnson, *Along This Way* (New York: The Viking Press, 1968), p. 160.
14. Quoted from Helen M. Chesnutt, *Charles Waddell Chesnutt: Pioneer of the Color Line* (Chapel Hill: University of North Carolina Press, 1952), p. 177. Howells's comment originally appeared in "A Psychological Counter-Current in Recent Fiction," *North American Review,* December, 1901.
15. Howells sets this range in his introduction to Dunbar's *Lyrics of Lowly Life.*
16. *Philosophical Investigations,* trans. G. E. M. Anscombe (New York: Macmillan, 1953), p. 118e. My discussion of Wittgenstein's point of view covers sections 243–415.
17. *Language and Being in Wittgenstein's 'Philosophical Investigations,'* (The Hague: Mouton, 1973), pp. 106–107.
18. "The Status of Linguistics as a Science," in *Culture, Language and Personality Selected Essays,* ed. David Mendelbaum (Los Angeles: University of California Press, 1953), p. 73.
19. Sidney Hook, ed., *Language and Philosophy* (New York: New York University Press, 1969), p. x. The first section of this volume, "Language and Culture," contains extremely interesting commentaries on the work of Sapir and Whorf. It is at this point that I should add a comment—a note of thanks—of my own on the very careful reading of an earlier draft of the present essay by Professor Barbara H. Smith. Professor Smith not only called the works of the sociolinguists to my attention, but also discussed their hypotheses at some length. I would also like to express my gratitude to Professor Michael Peinovich who read the earlier draft and provided helpful suggestions.
20. See: Sapir, *Language;* Whorf, *Language, Thought and Reality;* Hymes, *Foundations in Sociolinguistics* and *Language in Culture;* Labov, *Sociolinguistic Patterns.*
21. Hook, p. x.
22. Books, articles, and sections of texts dealing with the language of Black Americans include: Juanita Williamson's "Selected Features of Speech: Black and White," *CLA Journal,* June, 1970; Kirkland Jones's "The Language of the Black 'In-Crowd': Some observations on Intra-Group Communication," *CLA Journal,* September, 1971; J. L. Dillard, *Black English,* New York: Random House, 1972; Orlando Taylor's "Historical Development of Black English and Implications for American Education," *Speech and Language of the Urban and Rural Poor,* eds. Ronald Williams and Richard Ham (Collection of papers presented at the Summer Institute on Speech and Language of the Urban and Rural Poor—July 14–18, 1969—Ohio University, Athens, Ohio); Philip S. Dale, *Language Development*

(Hinsdale, Illinois: Dryden Press, 1972), pp. 244–254; Victoria Fromkin and Robert Rodman, *An Introduction to Language* (New York: Holt, Rinehart, and Winston, 1974), pp. 258–269. Of course, one of the pioneering studies in this area was Lorenzo Turner's *Africanisms in the Gallah Dialect.*

23. "Refugee in America," in *Selected Poems of Langston Hughes* (New York: Alfred A. Knopf, 1969), p. 290.
24. *Race and Nationality in American Life* (Boston: Little, Brown, 1957), pp. 71–92.
25. *The Slave Community* (New York: Oxford University Press, 1972), p. 45.
26. *Long Black Song* (Charlottesville: University Press of Virginia, 1972), pp. 122–141.
27. "Fever and Feeling: Notes on the Imagery of *Native Son*," *Negro Digest,* XVIII (1968), pp. 16–26.
28. *The Idea of History* (New York: Oxford University Press, 1970), p. 163.
29. *Philosophy of History* (Englewood Cliffs, N.J.: Prentice-Hall, 1964), p. 12.
30. Collingwood, p. 247.

Note on the Author

Houston A. Baker, Jr., Professor of English and former Director of Afro-American Studies, University of Pennsylvania, has also taught at he University of Virginia, Yale University, and Howard University. He is well known for his analysis of symbolic meanings and literary criticisms. His latest book *The Journey Back: Issues in Black Literature and Criticism,* University of Chicago Press, 1980, and recent article, "Generational Shifts and the Recent Criticism of Afro-American Literature", *Black American Literature Forum,* 1981, reflect his on-going concerns.

Negritude, Magic, and the Arts: A Pragmatic Perspective

Albert G. Mosley

A. African Culture in the Americas—Magic and the Arts

The traumatic transfer of millions of Africans from their traditional homes and cultures and their relocation in North and South America is one of the most extraordinary sagas of man's history. The slave ships brought human beings to American shores as captive property and cheap labor. Less obviously but no less significantly, the slave ships brought African beliefs and practices, African attitudes and aspirations. Despite the severity of slavery, Africans have survived and multiplied in the New World. And despite the determined attempt to divorce Africans from their traditional cultural patterns and impose European orientations, African cultural patterns have maintained their influence.

In the New World, African resistance to slavery was most successful in the Caribbean and South America. There, many slaves were able to escape into the forests and establish communities that have continued to exist in virtual isolation from the rest of the world. These so-called "maroon" societies have preserved traditional customs, beliefs, and practices that often have been transformed by outside pressure in their countries of origin.[1] The Bush Negroes of Guiana and Surinam (formerly Dutch and French Guiana), for example, maintain animal taboos, funeral practices, body decorations, deities, child-naming practices, and features such as the ordeal by poison, which mirror in detail parallel practices in Africa. In Brazil, among the Bahia, Yoruba religio-magical practices remain intact to the point that deities are still referred to by their African names, and ceremonies copy in all important respects those still performed in Nigeria. In Cuba, the drums used in the lucumi dances are Bata drums, identical with those used for similar purposes in Nigeria. In Haiti, the Catholic hierarchy of saints and angels has been assimilated into the Yoruba pantheon of gods, retaining characteristic patterns of African worship and spirit possession. One observer writes:

> . . . the pattern of ecstatic possession . . . conforms to standard African practice. Everything that happens makes it look as though the motor memory has proved more lasting and more coherent than memory as recollection. Thus, we find Dambellas Queddo wriggling across the ground or wrapping himself round trees, Ogun puts on a martial expression, and Ezili mimes the act of love-making.[2]

The author gratefully acknowledges the support and facilities provided by the Moton Center for Independent Studies during the completion of this paper.

In North America, Africans were not able to establish similar independent enclaves, either physically or culturally. As a result, it was not possible for them to maintain explicit traditional African cultural patterns. The rigors of slavery and the opposition of protestantism to notions of supernatural causation denied African religio-magical practices a chance for explicit survival.[3] Nonetheless, African attitudes and orientations continued to express themselves. Within a century of his presence on North American shores, the African exerted a vigorous and original influence on the folk art of the country.[4]

Within the antebellum South, antics taken as indicative of the African's natural subservience (such as head scratching, eyes bucking, grinning, stooping, shuffling, etc.) actually served the practical purpose of placating all powerful masters. These antics were developed to such a perfection that even awareness of their aim was no protection against their effectiveness.[5]

From the African slaves developed the major forms of American humor, theater (vaudeville), music (blues, R&B, jazz), and dance. Such achievements have earned worldwide admiration and appreciation.

Not only have African and African-American art forms been accepted as equal in profundity to those produced from the European tradition, but there is a growing recognition that African forms pointed in directions the European tradition was incapable of leading. This has been recognized most explicitly in music and the visual arts. Thus, Leopold Stokowsky, then conductor of the London Philharmonic Orchestra wrote:

The Negro musicians of America . . . have an open mind and an
unbiased outlook. They are not hampered by conventions and traditions,
and with their new ideas, their constant experiment, they caused new
blood to flow in the veins of music. The jazz players make their
instruments do entirely new things, things finished musicians are taught
to avoid. They are path-finders into new realm.[6]

One of the members of the group of French artists and collectors who first began to seriously acquire and study African sculpture wrote:

We came to the realization that hardly anywhere else had certain
problems of form and certain technical ways of solving them presented
themselves in greater clarity or success than in the art of the Negro. It
then became apparent that previous judgements about the Negro and
his arts characterized the critic more than the object of criticism. The
new appreciation developed instantly a new passion; we began to collect
Negro art as art, became passionately interested in corrective
reappraisal of it, and made out of the old material a newly evaluated
thing.[7]

Cubism and its offsprings were the result of this influence in the visual arts. Much the same impact can be traced in dance, humor, and sports.

It is undeniable that African aesthetic patterns have survived to play a dominant role in the evolution of the arts. But granted the continued vitality of Africanism in the areas of religion, magic, and the arts, the question remains: what good are such carry-overs? Considering the discredit in which magical beliefs are held and the view of the arts as mere forms of amusement, what good is it that African influences have predominated in such areas?

B. The Role of Magic in Traditional Cultures

What is magic? Typically, both the magician and the scientist are portrayed as having the same aim, namely, control of the processes of nature. Presumably then, both the medicine man and the scientist wanted to counteract malaria. But although scientific methods actually did lead to knowledge of how to control malaria (the power of lightning and many other processes of nature), magical practices did not lead to such practical knowledge. Thus, magic has been made to appear as a pseudo-science, a carry-over of man's first crude attempts to influence the course of natural events. In line with this orientation, Freud viewed magical practices as a form of neurotic wish fulfillment, in which the believer attempted to satisfy his wishes by carrying out an act representing the state of affairs desired. Magic was thus likened to the fantasizing of children and science to the adult reasoning of European civilization. This way of viewing magic helped reinforce the myth of Europe's progress from its own primitive past relative to Africa's cultural stagnation. But with the peaking of imperialism, Europe's domination of the rest of the world is no longer justifiable by reference to the presumed superiority of its social institutions and cultural forms (e.g., science).[8] In what follows, let us review some recent reappraisals of the role of magic in traditional settings and discuss their implications for African carry-overs in the New World.

Magic, in a view espoused by R. G. Collingwood, was not directed at the natural world; rather, it was directed at the human agents involved in some particular situation. The essence of magic, in this view, is the use of culturally evolved techniques to evoke certain emotions in human agents such that those agents are aided (or hindered) in the performance of certain practical activities:

> . . . these emotional effects, partly on the performers themselves, partly on others favourably affected by the performance, are the only effects which magic can produce, and the only ones which, when intelligently performed, it is meant to produce. The primary function of all magical arts . . . is to generate in the agent or agents certain emotions that are considered necessary or useful for the work of living; their secondary function is to generate in others, friends or enemies of the agent, emotions useful or detrimental to the lives of these others.[9]

This interpretation is supported by an examination of magical practices in the context of traditional settings. If, for instance, something was stolen and one wanted to find out who had done it, one consulted a diviner. Contrary to the stealth with which such an endeavor would be pursued in modern times, in traditional settings such consultations were usually well publicized and typically held in a gathering of all concerned.[10] A primary objective of the divination ceremony was to induce fear in the mind of the thief so that he would be revealed to the trained eye of the diviner.

Another purpose for which magical aid was commonly sought in traditional cultures was to obtain relief from illness. In many parts of the world today and less than a hundred years ago in Europe and America, most medicines and remedies were inert. They had no direct physio-chemical relationship to the bio-chemical nature of the illness. In such situations, a patient's recovery was based, not so much on the physio-chemical reactions triggered by the medication, but rather on the expectations generated in the patient through his interaction with the healer.[11] The success of the healer in nonindustrialized societies depended primarily on his ability to mobilize his patient's hopes, restore his morale, and gain the patient's reacceptance by his group, and only secondarily on the effectiveness of his pharmacopoeia. Such considerations have not been rendered obsolete even with the most modern scientific implements:

> In industrialized cultures, the efficacy of medications and even of some surgical procedures may depend on their capacity to arouse the patient's hopes for cure, as do the shaman's charms and incantations. For example, patients with coronary artery disease have experienced spectacular relief of angina pain and showed greatly improved ability to function following the tying of a blood vessel in the chest wall, which supposedly shuts more blood to the heart. Yet, a mock operation mimicking the real one in all respects except the tying of the blood vessel, has proved equally effective. The ability of placebos—pharmacologically inert pills that serve as symbols of the physician's healing power—to relieve pain even in patients with organic disease is further evidence of *the healing power of emotions and attitudes* aroused by the physician. In fact, since until recent years most medical remedies were either inert or harmful, the reputation of the medical profession actually rested largely on the power of the placebo. Since the effectiveness of placebos lies in their ability to counteract psychonoxious emotional states, it is not surprising that some of the beneficial results of psychotherapy can be duplicated simply by giving the patient a placebo.[12]

Of course, many claims were made for magic that in fact could not be met by its practitioners. The idea, for instance, that a magical ceremony might stop a volcanic eruption is erroneous, but no more so than the idea that application of the appropriate physio-chemical agents can produce mental health. In other words, the primary domain of application for magic has been overextended much as has the primary domain of application for modern science. But such an error should not blind us to the central efficacy of either. The primary function of magic was to supply human beings with the emotional focus needed to insure optimum performance in practical life. Magic might not affect an erupting volcano, but it did affect those human beings facing the eruption by giving them the faith and fortitude and courage to deal with a potentially paralyzing threat.

Professor John Mbiti, in his influential book, *African Religions and Philosophy,* summarizes the duties of medicine-men in traditional African societies as follows:

> First and foremost, medicine-men are concerned with sickness, disease and misfortune. In African societies these are generally believed to be caused by the ill-will or ill-action of one person against another, normally through the agency of witchcraft and magic. The medicine-man has therefore to discover the cause of the sickness, find out who the criminal is, diagnose the nature of the disease, apply the right treatment and supply a means of preventing the misfortune from occurring again. This is the process that medicine-men follow in dealing with illness and misfortune: it is partly psychological and partly physical. Thus the medicine-man applies both physical and 'spiritual' (or psychological) treatment, which assures the sufferer that all is and will be well. The medicine-man is in effect both doctor and pastor to the sick person. His medicines are made from plants, herbs, powders, bones, seeds, roots, juices, leaves, liquids, minerals, charcoal, and the like; and in dealing with a patient, he may apply massages, needles or thorns, and he may bleed the patient; he may jump over the patients, he may use incantations and ventriloquism, and he may ask the patient to perform various things like sacrificing a chicken or goat, observing some taboos or avoiding certain foods and persons—all these are in addition to giving the patient physical medicines.[13]

The radical distinction between mind and body that dominates the positivistic tendencies of modern scientific culture is not made in traditional African culture. There, physical illness and misfortune is assumed to be caused by bad feelings between members of the community. Sudden misfortune or accident was assumed to be ill-will manifesting itself through witchcraft. In order to counteract the noxious influence, a priest, medicine man, or sorcerer was consulted. Treatment involved a thorough airing of the sufferer's problems with the people around him in order that an identification of the bad feelings could be made. The entire process involved not only the sufferer, but also the sufferer's family and friends, with explicit attention to the interests of the recently dead. The treatment was meant to placate the spirits of all concerned. As Claude Levi-Strauss points out, in the case of both shaman and psychoanalyst, the goal was to bring to the conscious attention of the group, feelings, emotions, and attitudes that otherwise might preclude optimum beneficial social interaction.[14]

Of medicine-men in traditional African societies, Mbiti writes:

> They advise and assist on how a man may win more love from his wife; they give help to impotent men; they 'treat' people in order to prosper in business or succeed in politics; they supply various aids to students to 'enable' them to pass their examinations; they perform various rites to

increase the fertility and productivity of the fields and livestock; and barren women (or their husbands and relatives) continually consult them in search of being able to bear children.[15]

Such a list of needs for which magical aid was solicited testifies to the thesis that the purpose of magic was to mobilize the feelings, emotions, and attitudes of human subjects for the achievement of socially valued ends. As we become more aware of the intimate relationship between physiological healing and psychological states, it becomes clear that the patient's emotions and attitudes are a critical factor in therapy.

Medicine men and other specialists in traditional societies who used supernatural agencies in order to relieve suffering were much like psychiatrists of modern western cultures.[16] They are both therapists whose primary aim is to focus emotional influences so as to facilitate human efforts. Many of the medical profession would resist such an identification, pointing to the sophistication of physio-chemical and surgical techniques of modern psychiatry. But technical sophistication is not sufficient for successful therapy. (Witness to that is the medical school joke in which the surgeon declares that the operation was a success but the patient died nonetheless.) Moreover, most of the physical therapies available in modern psychiatry are not new, but have long been used in one form or another by traditional healers and medicine-men. It is only since the wide introduction of tranquilizers during the 1950s that drugs have become a mainstay of western psychiatry. Still, other cultures have used drugs which are generically similar for thousands of years; drugs which often were superior to anything available in western medicine.

Rauwolfia root is a good example. This drug, with the trade name of Reserpine, was introduced into western psychiatry in the 1950's as a major tranquilizer. At the time it was recognized as having been used in India for centuries as a tranquilizer. Later it was found also to have been in wide use in West Africa for many years. In 1925, in fact, a famous Nigerian witchdoctor was summoned to England to treat an eminent Nigerian who had become psychotic there. Armed with his rauwolfia root, the witchdoctor had better medicine to offer the psychotic patient than did any English psychiatrist of that period.[17]

Despite their similarities, however, there are many forms of therapy that are central in traditional magical healing that are used hardly at all in western psychiatry. This is especially true of the use of the arts as therapeutic tools. The use of music, dance, and dramatic encounters to provide the patient and his community with vehicles to express otherwise unverbalized feelings and inclinations remains an unexploited avenue in western culture. It is my contention that the extraordinary impact of Africans in the arts derives from a tradition of using the arts as therapeutic agents. Magic, then, was a means of affecting the emotions and attitudes of human beings for good or ill, and the development of the arts provided nonverbal modes of personal and interpersonal communication.

It is only when viewed from such a perspective that testimonies to the impact of African-American music on the European intelligensia can be appreciated:

> Negro music appeared suddenly (in Europe) after the greatest war of all times. . . . It came upon a bankrupt spirituality. To have continued with Slavic mysticism (Russian music was the great vogue when the World War broke out) would in 1918 have inclined us all to commit suicide. We needed the roar of the lion to remind us that life had been going on for a while. . . . The Negro taught us to . . . come back to the elementary principles of self-preservation.[18]

If it is to a therapist that a person must be referred when he or she is not deterred from a path of self-harm by ordinary forms of social interaction, then it appears that the same may hold true for cultures. I suggest that, through the therapeutic effect of the arts, Africa has had as profound an effect on the European psyche as, through the sciences, the European has had on the African psyche.

The Psychology of Negritude: Communication in Alternative Modes

The expression of emotion is, for Senghor, at the center of traditional African culture. It is the essence of 'Negritude':

> In African society, technical activities are always linked with cultural and religious activities, with art and magic, if not with the realm of the mystical. In technical activities and especially in productive labour, all these have an important part to play. We are dealing with a society based essentially on human relationships, or rather on the relationships between men and the 'Gods', with the animistic society. . . . Emotion is the seizure of the whole being, consciousness and body, by the indeterminate world. It is an erruption of the mystical or magical world into the world of determinism.

> Thus, emotion, though at first it appears a failure of consciousness is, on the contrary, the accession to a higher state of consciousness. It is a 'consciousness of the world', 'a certain way of apprehending the world'. It is complete consciousness, because the subject moved and the moving object are united in an indissolvably synthesis, or, as I have put it, in a dance of love. I have also spoken of it as a higher state of consciousness. As evidence, I wish only to quote this remark from one of the greatest scientific geniuses of the twentieth century. 'The greatest emotion we can experience,' wrote Albert Einstein, 'is the mystical feeling. This is the seed of all art and of all true science.' It is this gift of emotion which explains *Negritude*.[19]

Unfortunately, modern man is prone to think of the expression of emotion as the ejaculation of spasmodic cries and uncontrolled convulsions. For it is the elimination rather than cultivation of emotional expression that has been the dominant orientation of western civilization. The development of the sciences was predicated on the necessity of eliminating subjective factors in order to gain objective knowledge of reality. Thus, knowledge of external reality has been gained whereas knowledge of inner realities has been lost. By viewing thought as the civilized successor to feeling and logic as a proper substitute for empathy, western man has become a prisoner of his successes. Africa's influence through the arts has helped keep alive an undervalued and depreciated key to human health and well-being.

Although increasing levels of technical expertise has characterized the growth of western civilization, Black American art forms has embodied the idea that technical expertise (while required) is no substitute for 'soul'. 'Soul' is the ability to infuse a technical performance with emotional significance, thereby creating a context that incorporates the experiences of the performer with the experiences of the audience. We recognize when a rendition expresses something 'soulful' by the way it makes us feel, though often we are unable to verbalize that significance. Thus, when Louis Armstrong was asked by a reporter for the meaning of jazz, he made his now famous reply: "If you don't know, I can't tell you. . . ." Satchmo does not say that he does not *know* what jazz is, only that he cannot *explain* what it is. Recent developments of psychology and neuro-physiology indicate that Satchmo's reply, like the medicine man's rauwolfia root, was perhaps the most adequate response possible.

The developments to which I refer are indeed very recent.[20] In 1961 Dr. Roger Sperry of the California Institute of Technology began observations of a forty-eight-year-old war veteran who had been hit in the head by bomb fragments during WWII. As a result of the injury the veteran began having severe epileptic fits, and an operation had to be performed to keep him from injuring himself. This operation involved cutting the network of nerves that connect the left hemisphere of the brain with the right hemisphere of the brain. As a result of past evidence, it had been recognized for some time that the left side of the brain controls the right side of the body and the right side of the brain controls the left side of the body. But observations on the behavior of the veteran indicated a totally new psychological dimension was involved in the different functions of the left and right sides of the brain. It seems that different aspects of the reasoning process itself are controlled independently by one or the other hemisphere of the brain.

The veteran, for instance, if given a verbal command, could carry it out with his right hand but not with his left hand. If shown something, he could write the name of it with his right hand but not with his left. If shown the form of a thing (e.g., a cross), he could trace the form with his left hand but not with his right hand. If he touched an object with his left hand (without seeing it) and then was shown the object among other objects, he could not say verbally which one he had touched but he could point to it. If shown a pattern, he could arrange blocks in accordance with it, using his left hand but not his right hand. Observations such as these demonstrated that the left side of the brain controls our verbal and analytical skill, and the right side of the brain controls pattern production and recognition. Normally the collection of nerves connecting the two hemispheres made possible the transfer of information between the two. But when this collection of nerves was severed, it became possible to observe one hemisphere functioning independently of the other.

The right side of the brain is capable of accomplishments in pattern production and recognition that the left hemisphere cannot produce, but only reproduce in verbal form. The right side of the brain, however, can not verbally articulate even its own unique accomplishments. Dr. Robert Ornstein, research psychologist at the Langley Porter Neuropsychiatric Institute and professor at the University of California Medical Center in San Francisco, points out that many people are dominated by one side of the brain or the other. Those dominated by the left hemisphere typically have a problem dealing with pattern productions and body movement, whereas those dominated by the right hemisphere typically have difficulty dealing with logical sequencing and verbal reasoning. Ornstein writes:

> Culture apparently has a lot to do with this. Children from poor black neighborhoods generally learn to use their right hemisphere more than the left—they outscore whites on tests of pattern recognition from incomplete figures, for instance, but tend to do badly at verbal tasks. Other children, who have learned to verbalize everything, find this approach a hindrance when it comes to copying a tennis serve or learning a dance step. Analyzing bodily movements verbally just slows them down and interferes with direct learning through the right hemisphere.[21]

Thus, the evidence suggests that most artists and athletes are dominated by the right hemisphere, most technical analysts, scientists, and writers by the left hemisphere, and that the highest achievements involve the integration of both modes of cognition. Albert Einstein, for instance, wrote that his most creative thoughts came to him first in an unverbalized form, and only afterwards did he attempt to put them into words and formula. These unverbalized thoughts, he wrote, were "of visual and . . . muscular type," and he adds:

> Conventional words or other signs have to be sought for laboriously only in a secondary stage, when the aforementioned associative play is sufficiently established and can be reproduced at will.[22]

Only after he was able to reproduce thoughts in a visual or muscular form was Einstein then able to turn to the laborious job of translating those thoughts into a suitable linguistic form. The arts cultivate this ability to articulate unverbalized thoughts into socially evolved nonverbal mediums of communication.

Freud revolutionized psychology by showing that events experienced without the aid of verbal reference (as in infancy and early childhood, before speech is learned) are remembered nontheless in nonverbal forms. Such thoughts continue to affect us as feelings which we are unable to verbally articulate and sometimes blocks us from dealing satisfactorily with situations encountered later in life. Freud is credited with introducing free association and dream analysis as techniques for bringing the unverbalized presuppositions of our actions to conscious focus. But the use of the arts as psycho-therapeutic techniques has been stifled by a denigration of emotional involvement that has been at the heart of western progress. A reappraisal of the role of magic and the arts is necessary if an adequate assessment of the value of African continuities in the Americas is to be made. For the African influence has been most active in a sphere that otherwise has suffered both cultural neglect and personal atrophy. Only by clearly recognizing the role of magic and the arts in traditional settings, can their pragmatic benefit in the African Diaspora be adequately appreciated.

Notes

1. Roger Bastide, *African Civilizations in the New World* (New York: Harper Torchbook, 1971), Ch 3 passim.
2. Ibid., p. 141.
3. See Keith Thomas, *Religion and the Decline of Magic* (New York: Scribner, 1971), passim.
4. Margaret Butcher, *The Negro in American Culture* (New York: Alfred Knopf, 1971), p. 24.
5. Ibid., p. 25.
6. Ibid., pp. 79–80.
7. Ibid., p. 224.
8. See the Spring, 1978 issue of *Daedalus* (Journal of the American Academic of Arts and Sciences), "The Limits of Scientific Inquiry."
9. R. G. Collingwood, *The Principles of Art* (New York: Oxford Galaxy edition, 1958), pp. 67–68.
10. Thomas, *Religion,* p. 221.
11. Thomas, p. 209ff.
12. Jerome D. Frank, M.D., foreword to *Magic, Faith, and Healing,* ed. Ari Kiev, M.D. (New York: Free Press, 1964), pp. x–xi.
13. John S. Mbiti, *Mbiti, African Religion and Philosophy,* (New York: Doubleday/Anchor, 1969), p. 221.
14. Quoted in E. Fuller Torrey, *The Mind Game: Witchdoctors and Psychiatrists,* (New York: Bantam Books, 1973), p. 17.
15. Mbitit, pp. 222–223.
16. Torrey, *The Mind Game,* p. 1.
17. Torrey, p. 66.
18. Butcher, p. 78.

19. "De La Negritude. Psychologie du Negro-African," quoted in *Senghor—Prose and Poetry*, ed. John Reed and Clive Wake (New York: Oxford paperback).
20. For the following see chapter 3 of Robert E. Ornstein, *The Psychology of Consciousness*. There have been many popular accounts of these developments in *Psychology Today, The New York Times Magazine, Human Nature*.
21. Ornstein, op. cit.
22. Ibid.

Note on the Author

Albert G. Mosley, Chairman, Department of Philosophy, University of the District of Columbia. His areas of specialization are Philosophy of Science, Logic, and African Philosophy. Publications include "The Metaphysics of Magic: Practical and Philosophical Implications," *Second Order: An African Journal of Philosophy*, July, 1978.

Epidermalizing the World:
A Basic Mode of Being Black

Thomas F. Slaughter, Jr.

One of the intriguing things about phenomenology is the manner in which its species of philosophical description tends primarily to disclose for us what is already before us in a new and sometimes deeper light. In that spirit, my intention here is to assemble some familiar notions about Black experience in such a way as to disclose a principle posture of being-Black. Assuming success in that endeavor, I might suggest here that the "posture" considered could well be as fundamental a feature of things as that primal peculiarity of New World Blackness, first enunciated by W. E. B. Du Bois: "double-consciousness."

Reflecting upon Du Bois' formulation in behalf of our own considerations, one wonders what Du Bois might have meant by the "dogged strength" of "one dark body," as he announced double-consciousness:

> After the Egyptian and Indian, the Greek and Roman, the Teuton and Mongolian, the Negro is a sort of seventh son, born with a veil, and gifted with second-sight in this American world—a world which yields him no true self-consciousness, but only lets him see himself through the revelation of the other world. It is a peculiar sensation, this double-consciousness, this sense of always looking at one's self through the eyes of others, of measuring one's soul by the tape of a world that looks on in amused contempt and pity. One ever feels his twoness,—an American, a Negro; two warring ideals in one dark body, whose dogged strength alone keeps it from being torn asunder.[1]

Clearly, Du Bois is articulating a profound predicament. Thus in what follows we run the risk of fostering distorting simplifications of the situation. But with that in mind, it can be noted that among the facets of my body's "dogged strength" is the basic fact that I am me: however many "warring ideals" there may be, I have but one life to live, and as long as I live, I live my body.

Yet, if my being Black therefore has this suggested unity of a lived-body, how then does the duality of double-consciousness come about and persist in its existential prominence? The multiplexity occasioned by double-consciousness is not an existential dimension distinct from a unity constituted by my lived-body. In fact the stubborn primacy of my lived-body is the precondition of double-consciousness. It poses the impossibility of my succumbing totally

* The first draft of this paper was presented as a workshop contribution to the Annual Meeting of the Society for Phenomenological and Existential Philosophy, Vanderbilt University, Nashville, Tenn., October 31–November 2, 1974.

to that thorough denigration (!) of Blackness, apparently intended by the society. Consequently, double-consciousness is precisely the expression of the contradiction posed by this immovable immediacy of my lived-body on the one hand, and the society's apparently irresistible compulsion, on the other, to fashion my physiognomic degradation. My duality of consciousness is the psycho-physical dynamic spanning the socio-physical gap between my own sense of me and the culturally contrived ignominy surrounding my body. This spanning of the social gap is achieved by internalizing that contradiction and suffering it as an integral structure of my own character. Obviously, I exist by now both only through my particular body, but also, only in this peculiar society. And the case is both that my-body-in-this-society induces double-consciousness, and that by now, double-consciousness is my relation through this society to my own body, as this latter crucially is the public, first fact of my existence.[2]

Put differently: my double-consciousness is due in part to the fact that through routine subjective conditioning, I am impregnated with the values and mores of my environing society. But this social environment *and* my routine internalization of it are not only hostile to my individualizing ego; they are so constituted as to be explicitly antithetical to the very being I am to the world through my body. Between me and the surrounding world there exists a split of which by lopsided social contract, my body is the symbol. Blackness embodies the ostracised. Under the duress of racial domination, I undergo the now familiar two-pronged process of externally imposed inferiorization and subsequent internalization of that inferiority. It is thus probable that in my routine state, I carry White hatred of me within me as my own property. Double-consciousness expresses the fact that the essence of my subjugation, as concerns the one aspect of colonized consciousness, is precisely the simultaneous entertainment of two mutually antagonistic basins of self-valuation. Regardless, in the end, a condition, the "inferiority" of Blackness, which in fact is the *result* of a process of domination comes to be perceived as a *cause* of my subjugation. And, this latter perception is both the public's hostile assessment and my self-perception.

Now to this we might add the fact, disclosed by Fanon, that as a correlate to my act of internalizing inferiority, I act also to "epidermalize" the world.[3] I live my world in terms of Black skins and White skins. Fanon uses the notion of a "Manichean world"[4] here to describe the essence of contemporary cultural contact between a dominating Western world and colored, colonized and neo-colonialized people the world over. He thereby invokes the ancient philosophy which conceived the cosmos in terms of a struggle between the principles of Good and Evil. In that scheme, Black was designated the color of evil, and White, the color of 'Right.' By historic tragedy, this essentially metaphysical myth became epidermalized, physicalized, by the now-fading epoch of African enslavement and world colonization. Thus today, on the one hand, White is exclusive; on the other hand, I am my appearance (but yet my double-consciousness). Between our two worlds there can be no adequate communication, save my base participation in the universal zest for survival.

Pursuing a suggestion inherent in Fanon's formulation, we can note further that as I epidermalize my situation, I go beyond the mere color coding of men's skins; I also 'pigmentize' if you will, my total environment. And as an aside clarifying a crucial distinction,[5] it must be mentioned here that to epidermalize and to pigmentize my world are "acts" which are neither psychological nor creative in character. Also, neither the question of philosophical idealism nor the dynamics of mental projection is intended here. "The racist world is *already there.*"[6] Our concern here is *"how it comes to be there for a given mode of Black consciousness."*[7] Thus, something akin to a Husserlian "constituting act" is involved here.

Continuing: I live against the yawn of the universe in a thin film of technological gadgetry. I am totally enveloped in consumer goods. And the White world is the omnipresent possessor of all goods, save some exotic African art facts. On this question of participation and legitimization through 'possession,' the axiology of brains or brawn also comes squarely into play because at this point in the cultural game there appears to be little need to deny the role of my muscle in the scheme of production. The point of contention is the precious pretense that I've masterminded no operations. The White world is the omniscient administrator over all manufactured goods.

My act of pigmentizing the world extends even to the natural world. Today all grains are hybrid; all grass has been sodded; all trees have been seeded; all rivers have been dammed. And throughout, the producer's imprint is White. This maze of relations in its totality imposes itself on me as a massive, irrevocable confirmation of the superiority of the Whiteness which envelopes me. The cultural reflection of this technological present offers no quarter. I am civilized to the smallest detail in a system of instrumental relations which officially shows no trace of my own occupation. In a sense, my being 'borrows.' My existence may be characterized as a state of 'indebtedness.' I own nothing. I just pay rent. The wretchedness of being colonized secretes 'guilt.'

As a second technical aside: Out of my guilt comes the fact that phenomenological access to the truth of my being is never merely descriptive. As Fanon would have it, ". . . every ontology is made unattainable in a colonized and civilized society."[8] My being is judgmental. Quoting Fanon, "the Negro is comparison."[9]

Further, my being frozen out of the system of credits for personal worth creates in me, if you will, a 'thrown-ness.' I am thrown-out-of-mesh with the processes which surround me. I don't belong here. I belong to neither this time nor this place. I am an African person. I come from an ancient past; and I lean toward a cosmic future in wihch the principle of life will mangle the bind of race. The racialized will be the righteous.

Being in the open, outside the system, I begin to question. Through my 'throwness,' the sanctity of the system of credits begins to fade. I act in judgment on it. I gaze on the society's axiological periphery and condemn the arbitrary valorizations of its monopoly market place mentality. I myself in this am beyond the pale. I am exonerated of the decadence I observe because I own nothing. Whereas before, my being to the world through my body was my condemnation, now, by body is my vindication. Blackness enshrines my innocence. I rehabilitate myself.

At this point in the scheme of things, language becomes most crucial. That is, in the absence of real changes in the relations of production and property, *my* changes are executed in the arena of my subjective conditioning. I reappraise my concepts and reverse their valuations.

The trick is that in all of this I use the very language which previously antagonized my existence. It is also the case that in this I have no choice. I own nothing. His is the only language I have.

Again: I'm changing *now*. I'm reaching and moving fast. In my rage I scour my environment for resources to meet my needs. Key among my findings is 'the language,' the very tool so instrumental in the previous process of my devaluation. Thus in order to appropriate it for my own needs, I 'brutalize' the language. I jar the syntax and shuffle its semantics. Through my violence to the language, I mediate the being I was to the world through my body. "Black is Beautiful."

I create a person. But I own nothing. I borrow things. And in the end I give language back to the environing society, revitalized; and in the process, create again progressive momentum among its own.

To sum things then and put a comfortable name on it, the Black man is a perennial cultural rebel, a cultural nationalist. Blackness begins in double-consciousness, the vicious internalization of a vicious socio-political contradiction imposed upon a Black man in a racist society. In the opposition of races, conjunctive with racial subordination, which constitutes the basis of my subjugation, I epidermalize and pigmentize the world. The world is never merely given. It is given always already as a racist world. The ponderous wrap of race in the scheme of things precludes the probability of political revolution for the sake of racial liberation. In the absence of the promise of revolution's requisite material reparations, I respond to the enticements of attempted subjective transformations. Subsequently, in the subjective movement constituting my reaction to my predicament, the imposed division of man by skin is the ironic pivot, my vantage point in my condemnation of the found system's overall inhumanity to man. In my thrust toward personal revaluation, in the absence of real revolution, my skin becomes the very seed of my wrought salvation. Whereas Blackness was my condemnation; Blackness, subjectively revised, is my vindication. Having moved, but yet not having destroyed or fundamentally altered the usurping society, my maneuvers are never only my own. My being is borrowed. My "dues" revolve in the surrounding society, inseminating its soul with "life."

Notes

1. W. E. B. Du Bois. *The Souls of Black Folk,* New American Library, New York 1969, p. 45.
2. Cf. also Frantz Fanon's articulation of the distortion of human consciousness of the body in terms of "corporal schema" vs. "historico-racial" or "racial epidermal" schemata. *Black Skin, White Masks* (New York: Grove Press, 1967, pp. 110–111, p. 112.
3. *Ibid.,* p. 11; see also Fanon, *Toward the African Revolution* (New York: Grove Press, 1969), p. 21, p. 35.
4. Fanon, *Black Skin, White Masks* p. 190–192; see also Fanon, *The Wretched of the Earth,* New York: Grove Press, 1968), pp. 39–42, p. 93.
5-6-7. I am indebted to Professor Robert Stone (C. W. Post College), a friend, who since my first presentation of this paper has made several positive contributions to my thoughts, among which are these clarifying formulations especially those directly quoted here.
8. Fanon, *Black Skin, White Masks,* p. 109.
9. *Ibid.,* p. 211.

Note on the Author

Thomas F. Slaughter, Jr., is Assistant Professor, African-American Studies Department, Douglass College, Rutgers University. He previously taught at Southern Illinois University. His works in African-American studies involve a phenomenological analysis of the black experience.

VII

Leonard Harris
Editor

Select Bibliography of Afro-American Works in Philosophy

Leonard Harris

Listed below are works primarily by professional Afro-American philosophers in social philosophy. Authors whose works lie totally in other fields, or who make no reference to Afro-American situations or use any particular feature of that situation in an example, are not listed. Where known, the dates of deceased authors are included. In addition, to the best of my ability, I have provided a comprehensive listing of the published works of deceased authors as well as the works to date of authors represented in the anthology. I also list works of philosophic import by a variety of authors from various fields. The intent of the bibliography is to serve as a basic guide for further research.

The bibliography is not a comprehensive listing of all works in philosophy by Afro-Americans or by Afro-American philosophers. I have not listed works by Frederick Douglass, Alexander Crummell, Marcus Garvey, W. E. B. DuBois, C. L. R. James, or Martin L. King for example, simply because the listing of their works is far beyond the capacity of available pages here and bibliographies of their works are available in other texts.

There is a historically close link between theology and philosophy. However, given limited space I have tried to focus on social philosophers. The theologians listed whose works are represented in the anthology have had major, direct impact on the development of social philosophy within the profession or were early recipients of degrees in philosophy and wrote articles of philosophic note. Consequently, there is a less than adequate representation of authors from the sphere of the philosophy of religion.

The bibliography is tailored to a limited range of authors and works—works from approximately 1917, by primarily but not exclusively Afro-American professional social philosophers who at least utilized Afro-American situations in the forging of at least one published article, and includes comprehensive listings of published works by deceased authors as well as authors with works represented in the anthology. If the limited range of this bibliography is taken as a small sample of Afro-American works in philosophy, it augurs well for the wealth of philosophic material by Afro-Americans and the need for further research.

Baker, Houston A., Jr.

"Engage Literature and Jean Paul Sartre's *The Flies.*" *The UCLA Graduate Journal.* No. 1 (1967).
"A Decadent's Nature: The Poetry of Ernest Dawson." *Victorian Poetry* VI (1968).
"A Tragedy of the Artist: *The Picture of Dorian Gray.*" *Nineteenth Century Fiction* XXIV, (1969).

"New Year's Eve at Yale," *Liberator* IX (1969).
"The Poet's Progress: Rossetti's *The House of Life.*" *Victorian Poetry* VIII (1970).
"One Black College." *Liberator* X (1970).
"The Environment as Enemy in a Black Autobiography: *Manchild in the Promised Land.*" *Phylon* XXXII (1971).
"Completely Well: One View of Black American Culture." *Key Issues in the Afro-American Experience.* New York: Harcourt, Brace and Jovanovich, (1971).
"Paul Laurence Dunbar: An Evaluation." *Black World* XXI (1971).
Ed., *Black Literature in America.* New York: McGraw-Hill, (1971).
Long Black Song: Essays in Black American Literature and Culture. Charlottesville: University Press of Virginia, (1972).
Ed., *Twentieth-Century Interpretations of Native Son.* Englewood Cliffs, N.J.: Prentice-Hall, (1972).
"The Western University: Culturocentricism and the Interdisciplinary Ideal." *Afro-American Studies* III (1972).
"The Achievement of Gwendolyn Brooks." *CLA Journal* XVI (1972).
"Utile, Dulce and the Literature of the Black American." *Black World* XXI (1972).
"Arna Bontemps: A Memoir." *Black World* XXII (1973).
"A Forgotten Prototype: *The Autobiography of an Ex-Colored Man and Invisible Man,*" *Virginia Quarterly Review* IL, (1973).
"Reports on a Celebration: Dunbar's One-Hundredth Year." *Black World* XXII (1973).
Singers of Daybreak: Studies in Black American Literature. Washington: Howard University Press, 1974.
A Many-Colored Coat of Dreams: The Poetry of Countee Cullen. Detroit: Bradside Press, 1974.
"The Problem of Being: Some Reflections on Black Autobiography." *Obsidian* I (1975).
"The West's Illegitimate Child: A Note on James Baldwin as a Literary and Social Critic." *Maji* II (1975).
"James Emanuel," "Carolyn Rodgers," "Nikki Giovanni," *Contemporary Poets.* London: St. Martin, (1975).
"Is There Anybody There?: Some Black, Aesthetic Notes." *Era* (University of Pennsylvania) XXII (1976).
"Terms for Order: Reflections on Early Black American Literature." Deland, Florida: Everett/Edwards, Inc., (1976). (cassette).
" 'An Intrinsic Ardor': The work of Phillis Wheatley." Deland, Florida: Everett/ Edwards, Inc., 1976. (cassette).
"On the Criticism of Black American Literature: One View of the Black Aesthetic." In *Reading Black* (1976).
Ed., *Reading Black: Essays in the Criticism of African, Caribbean, and Black American Literature.* Ithaca, New York: Cornell University (Africana Studies and Research Center Monograph Series, no. 4), 1976.
Co-ed., *Renewal: A Volume of Black Poems.* Philadelphia Afro-American Studies Program, University of Pennsylvania, 1977. (with Charlotte Pierce-Baker)
Ed., *A Dark and Sudden Beauty: Two Essays in Black American Poetry by George Kent and Stephen Henderson.* Philadelphia: Afro-American Studies Program, University of Pennsylvania, 1977.
"By the Rivers of Babylon: The Diasporic Historian and the Function of History." *Ju-Ju: Research Papers in Afro-American Studies* Spring (1977).
"A View of William Melvin Kelley's *dem.*" *Obsidian* II (1977).
"Renewal," "The Humble Black/Helpful White," and " 'Because I do not hope to know again'." *Obsidian* II (1977).
" 'These are songs if you have the/music': An Essay on Imamu Baraka." *Minority Voices* I (1977).

"The Embattled Craftsman: An Essay on James Baldwin." *The Journal of African-Afro-American Affairs* I (1977).

No Matter Where You Travel, You Still Be Black. (Poems) Detroit: Lotus Press, 1979.

"For Sterling Brown," *Sterling Brown: A Umum Tribute,* Ed., Black History Museum Committee Philadelphia, (1979).

"A Note on Style and the Anthropology of Art." *Black American Literature Forum* XIV (1980) (repr. from *Black History Museum Newsletter* VII (1979).

Black American Literature Forum. (Special Issue on Literary Theory) XIV (1980), Guest Editor.

"Color: A Possible Ending." *Obsidian* V (1980).

"Black Woman," "For Billy and Helen's Second," "Return to my Parents' Home, Christmas, 1979." *Dear Dark Faces: Portraits of a People* Ed. Helen Earle Simcox. Detroit: Lotus Press, (1980).

The Journey Back: Issues in Black Literature and Criticism. Chicago: University of Chicago Press, 1980.

"English as a World Language for Literature." *English Institute Essays.* Ed. Leslie Fiedler, (1981).

"The 'Limitless' Freedom of Myth: Paul Laurence Dunbar's *The Sport of the Gods,* and the Criticism of Afro-American Literature," *The American Self: Myth, Ideology and Popular Culture.* Ed. Sam Girgus. Albuquerque: University of New Mexico Press, 1981.

"Generational Shifts and the Recent Criticism of Afro-American Literature." *Black American Literature Forum* XV (1981).

"Lorraine Hansberry." *Dictionary of American Negro Biography* New York: Norton (forthcoming).

Ed., Three American Literatures: *Essays in Chicano, Native American, and Asian American Literature for Teachers of "American Literature.* (In progress for the Modern Language Association.)

Book Reviews

"Some Late Victorian Attitudes" by David Daiches. *Yale Review* LIX (1969), x, xi, xx.

"Black Pow-Wow, Riot, Homecoming, Cities Burning, Maumau American Cantos." Liberator X (1970).

"The Black Situation," by Addison Gayle, Jr. *Liberator* XI (1971).

"The Quality of Hurt, The Autobiography of Chester Himes." Vol. I. *Black World* XXI (1972).

"Mumbo Jumbo," by Ishmael Reed. *Black World* XXII (1973).

"Blueschild Baby." Black World XXII (1973).

"Flashbacks." Black World XXII (1973).

"Interviews With Black Writers." Journal of Popular Culture Fall (1973).

"The Emergence of Richard Wright." *Journal of Popular Culture* Winter (1974).

"There is a Tree More Ancient Than Eden." Black World XXIII (1974).

"The Passion of Claude McKay." American Literature (1974).

"The Intricate Knot." American Literature (January 1975).

"Where I'm Bound." American Literature (May 1975).

"The Last Days of Louisiana Red." Black World XXIV (1975).

"The Last Days of Louisiana Red." Umum: Black History Museum Newsletter IV (1975).

"Roots." Cross Reference I (1978).

"Time's Unfading Garden: Anne Spencer's Life and Poetry" by J. Lee Greene. *Black American Literature Forum* XXII (1978).

"Images of Africa in Black American Literature" by Marion Berghahn. *Research in African Literatures* X (1979).

Baker, Thomas N. (1860–1941)

"Ideals." (Part I). *Alexander's Magazine* 2 (September 1906).

"Ideals." (Part II). *Alexander's Magazine* 2, (October 1906).

The Negro Woman. (A.M.E. Book Concern, 1912.) Reprinted from the women's edition of the *Christian Recorder* (April 4, 1912).

The Ethical Significance of the Connection Between Mind and Body. Yale University, 1903. (Dissertation).

Baraka, Imamu, A.

"A Black Value System." *Black Scholar* (November, 1968).

Ben-Jochannan, Yosef

We the Black Jews (Spanish Pamphlet: Privately printed), 1949.

An African Nationalist View of Black Power. New York: C.O.R.E., 1966.

Co-authors, K. Webb, H. Brooks. *Africa: The Land, the People, the Culture.* New York: W. H. Sandlier Co., 1969.

Co-authors, K. Webb, H. Brooks. *Southern Lands.* New York: W. H. Sandlier Co., 1969.

Co-authors, K. Webb, H. Brooks. *Southern Neighbours.* New York: W. H. Sandlier Co., 1969.

African Origins of the Major "Western Religions." New York: Alkebu-lan Book Associates, 1970.

Black Man of the Nile. New York: Alkebu-lan Book Associates, 1971.

Africa: Mother of Western Civilization. New York: Alkebu-lan Book Associates, 1971.

Co-author G. E. Simmons. *The Black Man's North and East Africa.* New York: Alkebu-lan Book Associates, 1971.

Black Man of the Nile and His Family. New York: Alkebu-lan Book Associates, 1972.

A Chronology of the Bible: Challenge to the Standard Version. New York: Alkebu-lan Book Associates, 1973.

Cultural Genocide in the Black and African Studies Curriculum. New York: Alkebu-lan Book Associates, 1973.

The Black Man's Religion and Extracts and Comments from the Holy Black Bible. New York: Alkebu-lan Book Associates, 1974.

Extracts and Comments from the Holy Black Bible. New York: Alkebu-lan Book Associates, 1974.

The Need for a Holy Black Bible. Vol. III. New York: Alkebu-lan Book Associates, 1974.

"The African Origins of Judaism, Christianity and Islam." *Black Books Bulletin* 4 (Spring 1976).

"Black Books Bulletin Interviews, Dr. Yosef Ben-Jochannan." *Black Books Bulletin* (Winter 1977).

Bennett, Lerone, Jr.

"Of Time, Space, and Revolution, Beyond Either/Or: A Philosophy of Liberation." In L. Bennett, *Challenge of Blackness.* Chicago: Johnson Publishing Company, 1972.

Berrian, Albert H.

Co-author, Long, Richard. *Negritude: Essays and Studies.* Virginia: Hampton Institute Press, 1967.

Birt, Robert E.

"An Examination of James Cones' Concept of God and its Role in Black Liberation."
The Philosophical Forum (Winter-Spring, 1977–1978).

Boxill, Bernard R.

"Morality of Reparations," *Social Theory and Practice* (Spring, 1972). Reprinted in
Today's Moral Problems, R. Wasserstrom, Ed., *Philosophy Now,* 2d Edition,
Struhl and Struhl, Eds., *Reverse Discrimination,* ed., B. Gross.
"Self-Respect and Protest." Philosophy and Public Affairs (Fall, 1976). Reprinted in
The Politics of Self Esteem, Special Issue of *Nursing Digest* (Fall, 1978).
"The Morality of Preferential Hiring." *Philosophy and Public Affairs* (Spring, 1978).
"Fanon and Dubois on Culture." The Philosophical Forum (Winter/Spring 1977–78).
"What is Equal Education Opportunity." *Proceedings of the Public Policy Conference
on Equality of Opportunity,* California Council for the Humanities in Public
Policy, (1980).
"Sexual Blindness and Sexual Equality." *Social Theory and Practice* (Fall, 1980).
"How Injustice Pays." *Philosophy and Public Affairs* (Summer, 1980).
"Discrimination, Compensation and Self-Respect." Abstract of Invited Paper for A.P.A.
Eastern Division. *Journal of Philosophy* (Fall 1980).
"Democracy and Human Rights in the Third World." Forthcoming, *Dayton Review.*
"Consent and Compensation." Forthcoming, *Proceedings of the Presidents's Com-
mission on Biomedical Research.*
Blacks and Social Justice. Forthcoming, 1983 (In preparation for Rowman and Lit-
tlefield Publishing Company).

Butler, Broadus N.

"High School-College Continuum from the Gifted." *The Gifted Child Quarterly* III
(Winter 1959).
"Amazing Omega Man." *The Oracle* XCIX (September 1959).
"High School Students and College Credit." *School and Society* 87 (December 5, 1959).
With Jiri Kolaji. "Dimensions of Identification." *The Personalist* 41 (University of
Kentucky, Summer 1960).
Prefatory "Comments" to monograph *Impressions of African Art Forms* in the poetry
of Margaret Danner (April 1960).
(Edited) "Which Way Africa" by Honorable Richard S. S. Bright. *The Negro History
Bulletin* XXIV (December 1960).
". . . To do a Better Job?" by Victor A. Rapport (collaborated in writing). *Liberal
Education* XLVII (December 1961).
"The Negro Self-Image." A printed reproduction of a speech delivered June 28, 1961.
Distributed by All-Trades Construction Company, Detroit. Partially reprinted
in *Negro Digest* XI (March 1962).
"In Defense of Negro Intellectuals." *Negro Digest* XI (August 1962).
"The Time of Promise." *The Negro History Bulletin* XXVI (October 1962).
Editor, Special Edition: *The Negro History Bulletin* XXVI (October 1962).
"Scholarships, Fellowships, and Loans in Michigan Colleges and Universities." Mich-
igan Colleges and Universities." *Michigan Yearbooks* IV (1962).
Editorial Columnist: The Michigan Chronicle weekly series beginning March 10, 1962.
Of the more than 250 articles, several were reprinted in other publications, in-
cluding:
"Economic Emancipation Greatest Imperative for Negroes Today." Reprinted in *Cri-
sis Magazine* (May 1962): 262.

"Young Man, Young Women Wake Up." Reprinted in *Congressional Record* 109 (January 10, 1963): A272.

"President Kennedy's Moral Fiber." Reprinted in *Congressional Record* 109 (July 1, 1963): A4170.

"Completely Free by 1963." Reprinted in *Congressional Record* 109 (January 25, 1963): A307.

"In Memorian: John Fitzgerald Kennedy." Delivered in behalf of Wayne County Board of Supervisors, Detroit, Michigan, Tuesday, November 26, 1963. Reprinted in *Congressional Record* 110 (January 7, 1964): A25.

"A Message to Northern Educators." Reprinted by National Scholarship Service and Fund for Negro Students, New York, 1964.

"The Time is Now," *Negro Digest* XII (May 1963).

"A New National Climate and a New Negro Image." Published in microfilm by Southern Education Reporting Service, (November 1963).

Public Assistance in Metropolitan Detroit: A Study by United Community Services of Metropolitan Detroit. A bulletin and report of the research committee. Published by U.C.S., 1964.

"Our 1965 Landmarks: A Century of Negro Freedom, A Half Century of Scientific Negro History." *50th Anniversary Publication of the Association for the Study of Negro Life and History,* Washington, D.C., (February 1965).

"Pressures and Priorities: the Disadvantaged." *Current Issues in Higher Education,* the 20th Annual Meeting of the Association for Higher Education, Chicago, Illinois, March 7–10, 1965.

"The Other Side of the Coin." In *Report of the Plans for Progress Manpower Conference,* Southern University, Baton Rouge, Louisiana, May 5, 1965.

"Reflections Upon the History of American Ideals and the Civil Rights Movements." A lecture to Leverette House Seminar on: The Negro in the United States, Harvard University, Cambridge, Massachusetts, March 4, 1964. Published in Wayne State University *Graduate Comment.* IX (1965–66).

Honors Convocation Lecture: "Race Education and National Purpose," Maryland State College, February, 1966. Reprinted in *Journal of the National Medical Association,* (September 1966).

"Race, Education and National Purpose." *Journal of the National Medical Association* 58 (September, 1966).

"The Detroit Reality." *Negro Digest* XVII (November 1967).

Integration of Detroit Public Schools: Past Problems and Present Promises." *Michigan Challenge* VIII (June 1968).

"Opportunities in Business and Industry." *Michigan Challenge* VIII (June 1968).

"Health Care Systems and Health Care Needs." *Graduate Comment* XI (Wayne State University, 1968), and *Proceedings of Tri-Regional Workshop on Planning and Implementing Social Work Programs in Community Health Services.* The University of Pittsburgh, (March 1968).

"Ruminations on Black Power." Speech to Conference on Business and Economic Future, Texas Southern University School of Business Administration, (April 1969).

"Towards Total Commitment to Educational Opportunity." *Pennsylvania Schoolmaster,* (March 1971).

"The Value of Academic Excellence." *Bulletin of the National Association of Secondary School Principals,* Number 355 (May 1971).

"Black Arts in Higher Education: A Situation Report." *Proceedings of the Second Annual Invitational Workshop on Afro-American Studies.* Bennett College, Greensboro, N.C., (May 1971).

"Education is the Pivot?" *Proceedings of Congress on the Quality of Life.* American Medical Association, Chicago, Illinois, March 22–25, 1972. Also reprinted in book titled *Quality of Life: The Early Years.* (See below.)

"Breaking the Cycles of Poverty." *Proceedings of the Western Hemisphere Nutrition Congress III,* The American Medical Association, Miami Beach, Florida, August 30–September 2, 1972.

"Should Business Government and Private Philanthrophy Support African-American Art?" Conference on Business and the Arts, Louisiana Council for the Performing Arts, New Orleans, Louisiana, November 20, 1972.

"Past Goals, Present Mission and Future Prospects for our Colleges and Universities." *Curriculum Change in Black Colleges IV,* Institute for Services to Education, Atlanta, Georgia, December 4–6, 1972.

"Morality or Legality: That is the Question." *Journal of the National Medical Association* 67 (National Medical Association, May 1975).

"Leadership Development in Higher Education." *Educational Record* 56 (American Council on Education, Winter 1975).

"Two Commentaries." *Presidential Studies Quarterly V.* Center for the Study of the Presidency (Winter 1975).

"Support for Higher Education Within the Black Community." *The Boule Journal* (Sigma Pi Phi Fraternity, Xenia, Ohio) 39 (Summer 1976).

"Founders Dream and American Reality." *The Crisis* 84 (New York: Crisis Publishing Co., February 1977).

"Mordecai Wyatt Johnson: A Model of Higher Education Leadership." *New Directions* 4 (Washington, D.C., Howard University Press, January 1977).

"Unforgettable Clarence Mathews." *Reader's Digest* (December 1977).

"Booker T. Washington, W. E. B. DuBois, Black Americans and the NAACP." *The Crisis* (August 1978).

"The Alienation Syndrome: Twenty Five Years After Brown vs. Topeka." *The Crisis* (Special Edition, June–July, 1979).

"Humanity, U.S. Immigration and Refugee Policy and the Select Commission." *Crisis* 88 (December 1980).

"International Dimensions of Our History and Some Imperatives for Present Afro-American Scholars: The Harvard-Atlanta-Howard-NAACP Connection." *The Crisis 70th Anniversary Edition,* Part I, 87 (November, 1980).

"The Great Debate." *The Crisis 70th Anniversary Edition,* Part II, 87 (December 1980).

"Humanity, U.S. Immigration and Refugee Policy and the Select Commission." *The Crisis* 88 (December, 1981).

"The 1979 Constitution of the Federal Republic of Nigeria and the Constitution of the United States of America: An Historical Comparison." (International Institute of Public Management Research Document, 1980. Delivered and discussed in States in Nigeria, 1980–81).

"The United States Department of Labor Black College Initiative in Historical Perspective." A document prepared for the Bureau of Education and Training of the U.S. Department of Labor, (November, 1981).

A series of articles published in the *Washington North Star* between February and April, 1982, under the following topics:

"African Economic Development: A New Civil Rights Frontier" "Black Americans and Black African Economic Development" "Toward Haitian Refugees: What Manner of America Are We?"

"Report on the Lecture—Discussion Tour of Four African Countries—Nigeria, South Africa, Lesotho, and Zimbabwe; Representing the International Institute of Public Management and the National Association for the Advancement of Colored People; Under the Auspices of the United States International Communications Agency, November 3 to November 20, 1981." Submitted to USICA, IIPM, and NAACP. To be published in 1982.

In Books:

A Pragmatic Study of Value and Evaluation. Doctoral Dissertation, University of Michigan Microfilm, 1952.

"The City of Detroit and the Emancipation Proclamation." A chapter in *Assuring Freedom to the Free,* edited by Arnold Rose, Detroit: Wayne State Univ. Press, 1964.

Introduction to *Images to Grow On,* a book of poetry for children by Eloise Culver. Washington, D.C.: Associated Publishers, 1964.

"The Negro Self-Image." A chapter in Arnold Rose and Carolina Rose, *Minority Problems.* New York: Harper and Row Co. 1965.

Forewords to publications of *The Scholars Statesmen Lectures Series* of Dillard University, 1969–1973:

Assuring Freedom: Scholars Statesmen Lecture Series, No. 1, 1969–70.

The Pursuit of a Culture and Dignity: Scholars Statesmen Lecture Series, No. 3, 1971–72.

Progress in Africa and America: Scholars Statesmen Lecture Series, No. 3, 1971–72.

Achieving Social Justice and Equal Opportunity: Scholars Statesmen Lecture Series, No. 4, 1972–73.

"Education is the Pivot?" *Quality of Life: The Early Years.* Action, Mass.: Publishing Science Group, Inc., 1974.

"Pursuit of Happiness, Not Pleasure", in Warren Marr II and Maybell Ward (Eds.) *Minorities and the American Dream: A Bicentennial Perspective,* New York: Arno Press, 1976.

"Foreword" to Mbrumba Kerina, Namibia: *The Making of a Nation.* New York: Books in Focus, Incorporated. 1981.

Booklet:

Memorial statement prepared for presentation to the Burton Historical Collection, City of Detroit Library, titled: "Another 1963 American Tragedy: Dr. W. E. B. DuBois." Published by W. E. B. DuBois Memorial Committee, Detroit, Michigan, February 4, 1964.

Craftmanship: A Tradition in Black America. New York: RCA Corporation, 1976.

Book Reviews:

Poole, Rosey, *Beyond the Blues.* London: Headley Brothers Lts., (1962).

Bontemps, Arna. *American Negro Poetry.* New York: Hill and Wang Co., (1963).

Rose, Arnold (Ed). *Assuring Freedom to the Free.* Detroit: Wayne State University Press, (1964).

Greenleaf, William. *From These Beginnings.* Detroit: Wayne State University Press, (1964).

Bittle, William E. and Geis, Gilbert. *The Longest Way Home.* Detroit: Wayne State University Press, (1964).

Meier, August. *Negro Thought in America 1880–1915.* Ann Arbor: University of Michigan Press, (1963).

Robert Shogan and Tom Craig. *The Detroit Race Riot, A Study in Violence.* Philadelphia Chilton Co., 1965 in *Michigan History,* (September 1965).

Hope, John II. *Minority Access to Federal Grants-in-Aid: The Gap Between Policy and Performance.* New York: Praeger Publishers, (1976).

Carruthers, Jacob C.

"Further Thoughts on the African Mind." *East African Medical Journal* 37 (1960).
"Futurity and The Black Race in the Western Hemisphere." *Black Books Bulletin* 4 (1976).
"Writing for Eternity." *Black Books Bulletin* 5 (Summer 1977).

Cook, Joyce M.

"The Examined Life." *Bryn Mawr College Alumnae Bulletin* (Fall 1973).
"The Nature and Nurture of Intelligence." *The Philosophical Forum* IX (Winter-Spring, 1977–78).

Daise, Benjamin

"Kierkegaard and the Absolute Paradox." *Journal of the History of Philosophy* (January 1976).
Book review. *International Philosophical Quarterly* (January 1976).

Davis, Angela Y.

Lectures on Liberation. New York: Committee to Free Angela Davis, 1969–71.
"Reflections on the Black Woman's Role in the Community of Slaves," *Black Scholar* 3 (December 1971).
(Ed.) *If They Come in the Morning.* New York: The Third Press, 1971.
"I am a Black Revolutionary Woman." In Phillip S. Foner, (ed.) *The Voice of Black America.* New York: Simon and Schuster, 1972.
"The Legacy of George Jackson." In Phillip S. Foner, (ed.) *The Voice of Black America.* New York: Simon and Schuster, 1972.
"A Conversation with Angela." *Black Scholar* 3 (March-April 1972).
Angela Davis—An Autobiography. New York: Random House, 1974.
"The Struggle of Ben Chavis and the Wilmington 10." *Black Scholar* 6 (April 1975).
"Rape, Racism and the Capitalist Setting." *Black Scholar* 9 (April 1978).
Women, Race & Class. New York: Random House, 1981.

Dixon, Vernon J.

"African Oriented and Euro-American Oriented World Views: Research Methodologies and Economics." *Review of Black Political Economy* 77 (Winter 1977).

Dunham, Albert M.

"The Concept of Tension in Philosophy." *Psychiatry* 1 (February 1938).
"The Concept of Tension in Philosophy." Chicago: University of Chicago, 1933. (Dissertation)

Eddins, Berkley B.

"Staliknecht's Criterion of Existence." *Review of Metaphysics* (September 1953).
"Empiricism, Necessity, and Freedom." *Review of Metaphysics* (March 1963).
"Historical Data and Policy-Decisions." *Philosophy and Phenomenological Research* (March 1966).
"Natural Rights as Foundation of Democracy." *Journal of Human Relations* (Spring 1967).
"Does Toynbee Need Two Theories of History?" *Philosophic Journal* (July 1967).
"The Case for Philosophy of History." *Systematics* (March 1968).
"Punishment and Its Mythological Context." Madden, Farber, Handy, Eds. *Philosophical Perspectives on Punishment.* 1968.

"Is the Consensus Model Necessarily 'Elitist'? A Query for Mr. Oppenheimer." *Sociological Inquiry* (Summer 1967).

"On Evaluating Conceptual Models." *Journal of Conflict Resolution* (December 1967).

"Speculative Philosophy of History: A Critical Analysis." *Southern Journal of Philosophy* (Spring 1968).

"The Structure of Social Philosophy: Its Problems, Issues, and Concepts." *International Journal of History and Political Science* (August 1968).

Co-author Greg Iggers. "Philosophy of History." in "History," *Encyclopedia Americana*, 1968.

"The Covering-Law Model as Speculative Philosophy of History: A Reply to Mr. Loftin." *Southern Journal of Philosophy* (Spring 1971).

"Philosophia Perennis and Black Studies." *Southern Journal of Philosophy* (Summer 1971).

"Liberalism and Liberation." *Social Theory and Practice* (June 1972).

"A Philosopher and Senator Look at the Constitution." *Center Report* (April 1971).

"Presidential Candidates as Social Thinkers." *Center Report* (December 1971).

Appraising Theories of History. Cincinnati: Ehling Press, 1980.

"Justification in Social Theory: Truth vs. Adequacy." *The Philosopher in the Community: Essays in Memory of Bertram Morris.* B. Lang and W. Sacksteder, eds. (Volume forthcoming).

Book Reviews

Rebecca Gross, *Voltaire: Nonconformist,* and David W. Smith, *Helvetius: A Study in Persecution. Dialogue* (June 1966).

Ali Mazrui, *World Culture and the Black Experience;* And R. A. Wasserstrom, *Today's Moral Problems, Teaching Philosophy.* (October 1975, with Essie Eddins).

Joseph Fletcher, *The Ethics of Genetic Control, Teaching Philosophy* (Spring 1976, with Essie Eddins).

William A. Banner, *Moral Norms and Moral Order* (University of Florida Press, 1981). *Journal of Negro Education.* 1982.

Eddins, Essie A.

"Proposed Changes in Health-Care Patterns in the Black Community." *The Journal of the American Orthopsychiatric Association* 42 (March 1972).

Interorganizations Relations: A Study of Decision-Making Among Health Organizers. Health Transactions (Spring, 1980).

Book Reviews:

Ali A. Mazrui, *World Cultural and the Black Experience* (Washington Paperbacks, 1974). *Teaching Philosophy* (Fall, 1975, co-author, B. Eddins).

Richard Wasserstrom, ed., *Today's Moral Problems* (MacMillan Publishing Co., 1975). *Teaching Philosophy* (Spring 1975, co-author B. Eddins).

Joseph Fletcher, *The Ethics of Genetic Control: Ending Reproductive Roulette* (Anchor Press, 1974) *Teaching Philosophy* (Spring 1976, co-author B. Eddins).

Fontaine, William T., (1909–1968)

"Philosophical Implications of the Biology of Dr. Ernest E. Just." *The Journal of Negro History* 24 (July 1939).

"An Interpretation of Contemporary Negro Thought from the Standpoint of the Sociology of Knowledge." *The Journal of Negro History* XXV (January 1940).

"Social Determination' in the Writing of Negro Scholars," *American Journal of Sociology* XLIX (January 1944).

"The Paradox of Counterfactual Conditional Statements." *Journal of Philosophy* 46 (April 1949).
"Avoidability and the Contrary-to-Fact Conditional in C. I. Lewis and C. I. Stevenson." *Journal of Philosophy* 48 (1951).
"Segregation and Desegregation in the United States: A Philosophical Analysis." *Presence Africaine,* Special Edition, Le 1er Congress International des Ecrivains et Artistes Noirs, Nos. 8–9–10 (June–November 1956). (French version, Nos. 24–25, February–May 1959).
"The Means-End Relation and Its Significance for Cross-Cultural Ethical Agreement." *Philosophy of Science* 25 (1958).
"Toward a Philosophy of American Negro Literature." *Presence Africaine* (1958).
"Philosophical Aspects of Contemporary African Social Thought." In *Pan-Africanism Reconsidered.* Ed. John A. Davis. Berkeley: University of California Press, 1961.
Reflections on Segregation, Desegregation, Power and Morals. Illinois: Charles C. Thomas, 1967.
"The Negro Continuum from Dominant Wish to Collective Act." *African Forum* 3 (Spring-Summer 1968).
"Josiah Royce and the American Race Problem." *Philosophy and Phenomenological Research* XXIX (December 1968). Reprinted from William T. Fontaine, *Reflections on Segregation, Desegregation, Power and Morals.* Illinois: Charles C. Thomas, 1967.
"Fortune, Matter and Providence: A Study of Ancius Severinus Boethius and Giordano Bruno." University of Pennsylvania, 1939 (Dissertation).

Frye, Charles

"The Sister." *Afro-American Review* (Spring 1969).
"Roses," *Nommo* (Spring 1970).
"A Feeling . . . A Word." *Afro-American Review* (Spring 1970).
"Ass-Simulation: An Autobiography." *Afro-American Review* (Spring 1970).
"The Psychology of the Black Experience: A Jungian Approach." *Black Lines* (Spring 1973).
"Black Studies as Individuation." *JuJu* (Winter 1974).
"Spiritual Hierarchies: Another Look at the Movement." *Black Images* 3 (Autumn 1974).
"On the Trail of Black Studies." (Book Review) *Journal of Afro-American Issues* (May 1974).
Interdisciplinarity: Coping with Real Life and the Future: Summary Report 1974 Interdisciplinary Evaluation Conference. Washington, D.C.: Institute for Services to Education, 1975. (Co-authors: Lawrence Langer, William Moore, Gary Weaver).
Death and Dying in Western Society: An Interdisciplinary Curriculum Guide. Washington, D.C.: Institute for Services to Education, 1976. (Co-authors: Lawrence Langer, William Moore, Gary Weaver).
"Black Studies at Kent State University: A Case Study." *JuJu, Black Studies Journal of Case Western Reserve University* (Winter 1976).
"Sorcerer, Superman, and Victim: The Hero As Don Juan." *The American Theosophist* (July 1977).
"Black Studies: Definition and Administrative Model." *Western Journal of Black Studies* (June 1977).
"Higher Education in the New Age: The Role of Interdisciplinary Studies." *The American Theosophist* (March 1977).
Toward a Philosophy of Black Studies. San Francisco: R & E Research Associates, 1978.

The Impact of Black Studies on the Curricula of Three Universities. Washington, D.C.: University Press of America, 1976, 1979.

"Einstein and African Religion and Philosophy: The Hermetic Parallel." In *Albert Einstein As An Intercultural and Interdisciplinary Phenomenon: His Influence in All Fields of Thought.* The Proceedings of the International Conference Celebrating the 100th Anniversary of the Birth of Albert Einstein, Hofstra University, November 8–10, 1979.

"Human Origins: Black Studies and the Use of Controversial Materials." *Minority Education* (October 1979).

"The Black Studies Administrator." *Illinois Quarterly* (Summer 1980).

"Deadly Con Men: Black Agents Provocateurs of the 1960's." *Enfield House Journal* (Spring 1980).

Value in Conflict: Blacks and the American Ambivalence Toward Violence. Washington, D.C.: University Press of America, 1980.

Ed., *Level Three: A Black Philosophy Reader.* Washington, D.C.: University Press of America, 1980.

"The Feast." *HooDoo Magazine* No. 7 (1980).

Gayle, Addison

The Black Aesthetic. New York: Doubleday & Company, Incorporated, 1971.
Claude McKay, The Black Poet at War. Michigan: Broadside Press, 1972.
The Way of the New World; The Black Novel in America. New York: Anchor Press, 1975.
The Black Situation. New York: Delta Books, 1975.
Wayward Child: A Personal Odyssey. New York: Anchor Press, 1977.
Richard Wright: Ordeal of a Native Son. New York: Anchor Press/Doubleday, 1980.

Golightly, Cornelius L., (1917–1976)

"A Bible of Mankind and the World of Tomorrow." *New History* (December 1939).
Review of Norman Leys, *The Color Bar in East Africa. Phylon* First Quarter (1942).
"Negro Higher Education and Democratic Negro Morale." *Journal of Negro Education* (Summer, 1942).
Abstracts (German, French, Spanish, periodicals) for *Psychological Abstracts.* American Psychological Association (1943–45).
Studies for the Division of Review and Analysis, Fair Employment Practice Committee. U.S. Government, Washington, D.C., 1943–45. Published in mimeograph form.
Portions of Annual Reports of Fair Employment Practice Committee, written as *Compliance Analyst,* 1943–45. Published by U.S. Government Printing Office, Washington, D.C.
Review of J. R. Shalloo and Donald Young, eds. *Minority Peoples in a Nation at War, Journal of Negro Education* (Spring 1943).
Review of Ben Karpman, *Case Studies in the Psychopathology of Crime,* Vol. 11, Cases 6–9. *Journal of Negro Education* (Spring 1945).
Co-author John A. Davis. "Negro Employment in the Federal Government." *Phylon* Fourth Quarter (1945).
"Social Science and Normative Ethics." *Journal of Philosophy* (September 1947).
"Race, Values, and Guilt." *Social Forces* (December 1947).
Co-author Isreal Scheffler. "Playing the Dozens: A Note." *Journal of Abnormal and Social Psychology* (January 1948).
Review of Ben Karpman, *Case Studies in the Psychopathology of Crime,* Vols. III and IV. *Ethics* (October 1949).

Review of Karl Jaspers, *The Perennial Scope of Philosophy. Philosophy of Science* (October 1950).

"Inquiry and Whitehead's Schematic Method." *Philosophy and Phenomenological Research* (June 1951).

"Legerdemain in Ethics." *Philosophical Review* (April 1952).

"Mind-Body, Causation and Correlation." *Philosophy of Science* (July 1952).

Review of E. Findlay Freundlich, *Cosmology. Philosophy of Science* (October 1952).

Review of G. B. Brown, *Science: Its Method and its Philosophy. Philosophy of Science* (January 1952).

Review of C. Jorgensen, *Two Commandments. Philosophy of Science* (April 1953).

"Freedom in the Arts." *Wisconsin Idea Theatre Quarterly* (Fall 1953).

"The James-Lange Theory: A Logical Post-Mortem." *Philosophy of Science* (October 1953).

Review of Barrows Dunham, *Giant in Chains. Humanist* (December 1953).

"Our Obsolete Southern Liberals." *Progressive* (March 1955).

"Southern Liberals Speak Only for Whites." *Time* (March 21, 1955).

Co-author Roy G. Francis "On Scientific Interference." *Midwest Sociologist* (Winter 1955).

"Value as a Scientific Concept." *Journal of Philosophy* (March 1956).

Review of Abraham Edel, *Ethical Judgment: The Use of Science in Ethics. Philosophy of Science* (April 1956).

Review of Avrum Stroll, *The Emotive Theory of Ethics. Philosophy of Science* (April 1956).

Review of Mario Lins, *Operations of Sociological Inquiry. Philosophy of Science* (April 1958).

Review of G. M. McKinley, *Evolution: The Ages and Tomorrow. Philosophy of Science* (April 1950).

Review of B. Schaffner, ed., *Group Processes. Philosophy of Science* (April 1958).

"W. E. B. DuBois: Negro Who Wanted to Segregate Negroes." *The Milwaukee Journal* (September 28, 1958).

Review of A. J. Johnson, *Whitehead's Philosophy of Civilization. Wisconsin Magazine of History* (Spring 1959).

Ideals and Institutions: An Adult's Guide to American Philosophy. Madison: University Extension Division, 1960.

Review of Editorial Committee of the Lifwynn Foundation, *A Search for Man's Sanity: The Selected Letters of Trigant Burrow. Philosophy of Science* (January 1961).

"Self Serving Research." *University of Wisconsin-Milwaukee* (September 1963).

"De Facto Segregation in Milwaukee Schools." *Integrated Education* (December 1963).

"De Facto Segregation in Milwaukee Schools." In Meyer Weinberg, ed., *Learning Together.* Chicago: Integrated Education Associates, 1964, (Second printing, 1965).

"The Historians and American History." A review of John Higham, Leonard Krieger, and Felix Gilbert, *History. The Humanist* (January–February 1966).

"Counseling, Culture, and Value." In Carlton E. Beck, ed., *Guidelines for Guidance.* Dubuque: W. C. Brown Company, 1966. Reprinted in Carlton E. Beck, ed., *Philosophical Guidelines for Counseling.* Dubuque, Wm. C. Brown Company, 1971.

"Where The Action Is." *University of Wisconsin-Milwaukee Magazine* 1 (July 1967).

"The Negro and Respect for Law." *Chicago Daily Law Bulletin* (April 26, 1968).

"The Negro and the Law Revisited." *Chicago Daily Law Bulletin.* 11th Annual Law Day Edition (April 25, 1969).

"Campus Protests Pose Legal Problems." *Milwaukee Journal,* Law Day USA Supplement (May 1, 1969).

"A Philosopher's View of Values and Ethics." *Personnel and Guidance Journal* 50 (December 1971).
"Ethics and Moral Activism." *The Monist* 56 (October 1972).
"Mind, Self, and Soul." *Probing the Secrets of the Universe.* Proceedings of the Eighth Annual Southeastern Michigan Junior Science and Humanities Symposium, Detroit, Michigan, 1972.
"Ethics and Moral Activism." Abstract in *Review of Metaphysics,* (1973).
"Ethics and Moral Activism." Abstract in *The Philosopher's Index.* Bowling Green University, Ohio, (1973).
"Justice and 'Discrimination for' in Higher Education." *Proceedings of the Center for Philosophic Exchange* 5, SUNY at Brockport, (1974).
Thought and Language in Whitehead's Categorical Scheme. Michigan: University of Michigan, 1941. (Dissertation)

Harris, Leonard

Ed., *JEM Literary Magazine.* Ohio: Central State University, 1968.
"The Myths of Bayard Rustin." *Liberator* (October 1970).
"Crisis in Dominica." *SHANGO* 1 (1973).
Co-author, Clement Williams, "New Jersey Afro-Americans." *The New Jersey Ethnic Experience.* New Jersey: Bicentennial Commission, 1977.
"Black Philosophers—New Class of Scholars." *The Philadelphia Tribune Black History Bulletin* 93 (February 1977).
"Philosophy in Black and White." *Proceedings* (February 1978).
"Philosophy in the Black World: A Negro History Bulletin Heritage." *Negro History Bulletin.* (May–June 1978).
"Philosophic Anthropology and Scientism." *Consequences,* 1979–80 Edition. Anthologized and translated, *Sur la Philosophie Africaine,* ed., Giles Vilasco, Abidjan (1981).
"Critique of Richard Bernstein's *The Restructuring of Social and Political Theory.*" *International Philosophical Quarterly* 76 (December 1979).
"Romanticism and Scientism in Africa." *Presence Africaine.* 1st Quarter (1980).
"Philosophy Born of Struggle: Afro-American Philosophy from 1917." *Philosophical Perspective in Black Studies.* Ed., Gerald A. McWorter, Urbana: Afro-American Studies and Research Program, University of Illinois—Urbana, Illinois. 1982.

Harris, Marquis L.

Four Typical Cosmologies—Development of A Cosmology from Data of Mathematics, Natural, Physical and Social Sciences. Columbus, Ohio: Ohio State University Press, 1934.
Life Can Be Meaningful. Boston: Christopher Publishing House, 1951. 195 pages.
Some Conceptions of God in the Gifford Lectures, 1927–1929. Ohio: Ohio State University, 1933. (Dissertation)

Hill, Charles L. (1906–1956)

The Loci Communies of Phillip Melanchthon. Translated by Charles Leander Hill with a critical introduction by the translater. Boston: Meador Publishing Company, 1944.
The Evangel in Ebony. Boston: Meader Publishing Company, 1960 (Published posthumously by George A. Singleton, manuscript written in 1950).
A Short History of Modern Philosophy from the Renaissance to Hegel. Boston: Meader Publishing Company, 1951.

"Melanchthon's Proposition on the Mass." *Lutheran Quarterly* 6 (February 1954).
"Some Theses of Phillip Melanchthon." *Lutheran Quarterly* 6 (August 1954).
Melanchthon: Selected Writings. Translated by Charles Leander Hill with translator's introduction. Minneapolis: Augsburg Publishing House, 1962. (Published posthumously and edited by Elmer E. Flack and Lowell J. Satre.)
"An Exposition and Critical Estimate of the Philosophy of Phillip Melanchthon." Ohio: Ohio State University, 1938. (Dissertation)

Hodge, John L.

Co-author, D. D. Struckmann, L. D. Trost. *Cultural Bases of Racism and Group Oppression.* California: Two Riders Press, 1975.
"Democracy and Free Speech: A Normative Theory of Society and Government." In *The First Amendment Reconsidered,* (1982).

Holmes, Eugene C. (1905–1980)

"Jean Toomer', Apostle of Beauty." *Opportunity* 10 (August 1932).
"The Negro in Recent American Literature." in Henry Hart. *American Writers' Congress.* New York: International Publishers, 1935.
"Pushkin in America." *International Literature* No. 6 (1937).
"The Negro as Capitalist." by A. L. Harris. *Science and Society,* no. 2 (1937).
"Problems Facing the Negro Writer." *New Challenge* (Fall 1937).
"Educators Fight for Federal Aid." *American Teacher* (May–June 1938).
"Famine." by Liam O'Flaherty. *American Teacher* (March–April 1938).
"Negro College Graduate." by C. S. Johnson. *New Masses* (November 1938).
"Philosophy Takes a Holiday." by Irwin Edman. *American Teacher* (January 1939).
"Guide of Philosophy of Morals and Politics." by C. E. M. Joad. *Science and Society* (Spring 1939).
"Mrs. James Crow: D.A.R." *New Masses* 30 (March 1939).
"Race Against Men." by H. J. Seligmann; "The Negro Immigrant" by R. D. A. Reid. *Science and Society* (Spring 1940).
"Anti-Semitism." Series of articles in *The Chicago Defender* (1944).
"Philosophical Problems of Space and Time." *Science and Society* 24, (1950): 207–27.
"The Main Philosophical Considerations of Space and Time." *American Journal of Physics* 18 (December 1950): 560–70.
"The Kantian Views of Time and Space Evaluated." *Philosophy and Phenomenological Research* (September 1955–56).
The New Negro Thirty Years Afterward: Papers Contributed to the Sixteenth Annual Spring Conference of the Division of the Social Sciences. Co-editor with Rayford W. Logan and G. Franklin Edwards. Washington, D.C.: Howard University Press, 1955.
"Alain Locke—Philosopher." In *The New Negro Thirty Years Afterward.* Washington, D.C.: Howard University Press, 1955.
"A General Theory of the Freedom Cause of the Negro People." *American Philosophical Association,* December 1955. This paper was later published in Percy E. Johnston *Afro-American Philosophies: Selected Readings from Jupiter Hammon to Eugene C. Holmes.* Upper Montclair, N.J.: Montclair State College Press, 1970.
"Alain Locke, Philosopher, Critic, Spokesman." *Journal of Philosophy* 54 (February 28, 1957).
"Alain LeRoy Locke: A Sketch." *Phylon,* 1st Quarter (Spring 1959).
"A Program for African Liberation." *The African* 2 (September–October 1960).

"The Legacy of Alain Locke." *Freedomways* 3 (Summer 1963).
"Social Philosophy and the Social Mind: A Study of Genetic Methods of J. M. Baldwin, George Herbert Mead, and J. E. Boodin." New York: Columbia University, 1942. (Dissertation)

James, George G. M.
Stolen Legacy. New York: Philosophical Library, 1954.

Johnson, Percy E.
"Social Responsibility of the Artist." *The Hilltop,* Washington, D.C. (1959).
"A Preface to New Israel." *Dasein* IV & V (1964).
"Benjamin Pierce's Description of Mathematics." *Dasein* VI (1966).
"Confessions of Whitey: Review of William Styron's *Confessions of Nat Turner." Dasein* VII & VIII (1968).
"New Jazz Poets, Compiled by Walter Lowenfels & Art Berger. *Dasein* VII & VIII (1968).
"Legacy for My Two Adopted Nations: Critical Essay on Bernard B. Fall,, & his Viet-Nam books, especially *Last Reflections on A War." Dasein* VII & VIII (1968).
"Kent State Massacre & Boston Massacre," ms., delivered Montclair State College, during Alternate Seminars," 1968. "Black Theories of History & Black Historiographies, Part I." *Dasein* IX (1969).
"Images or Value: Critical Appraisal of Jeremiah C. McGuire's *Cinema & Value Philosophy." Dasein* IX (1969).
"Afro-American Philosophies: From Jupiter Hammon to Eugene C. Holmes." (Editor.) Montclair State College Press, Upper Montclair, N.J. 1970.
"Phenomenology of Space & Time: An Examination of Eugene C. Holme's Studies in the Philosophy of Time & Space." *New York: Dasein Literary Society,* (1976).

Jones, Gilbert H. (1883–1966)
Education in Theory and Practice. Boston: Richard G. Badger, 1919.
"Lotze and Bowne Eine Vergleichung ihren Philosophsehen Arbeit." University of Jena, 1909 (Dissertation).

Jones, James J.
Survival and the Code of Love. Cheyney State College, 1979.
Race Against Darkness. Cheyney State College, 1980.
The Ethics of Right and the Imperative of Brotherhood. Cheyney State College, 1981.
Natural States and the State of Community, Cheyney State College, 1982.

Jones, Mack H.
"Scientific Method, Value Judgments, and the Black Predicament in the U.S." *Review Black Political Economy* 7 (Fall 1976).

Jones, William R.
"Theodicy and Methodology in Black Theology: A Critique of Washington, Cone and Cleage." *Harvard Theological Review* (October 1971). Included in *The Black Experience in Religion,* ed. C. Eric Lincoln. New York: Doubleday, 1974.
"Toward an Interim Assessment of Black Theology." *The Christian Century* 89 (May 3, 1972).
"Reconciliation and Liberation in Black Theology: Some Implications for Religious Education." *Religious Education* 67 (September–October 1972).

"Theodicy: The Controlling Category for Black Theology." *Journal of Religious Thought* (Summer 1973).

Is God a White Racist? Prolegomenon to Black Theology. New York: Doubleday, 1973.

"Toward a Black Theology." *Mid-Stream* (Fall–Winter 1973–74).

"Crisis in Philosophy: The Black Presence." *Radical Philosophers' News Journal* (August, 1974). Included in *Proceedings and Addresses of the American Philosophical Association* XLVII (1973–74).

"Theism and Religious Humanism: The Chasm Narrows." *The Christian Century* 92 (May 21, 1975).

"Black Theology and Black Higher Education." *Journal of Ministries to Blacks in Higher Education* (1976).

"Power and Anti-Power." *Karios, An Independent Quarterly of Liberal Religion* (Spring 1977).

"Critique of *From Salvation to Utopia: Technological Society in Christian Prospect,*" by Gabriel Vahanian. *Proceedings of the Fifth International Conference on the Unity of the Sciences* (1977).

"Religious Humanism: Its Problems and Prospects in Black Religion and Culture." In *Perspectives of Black Theology,* ed. Rosino Gibellini (Brescia, Italia: Queriniana, 1978). Also published in the *Interdenominational Theological Center Journal* (December 1979).

"The Concept of Authority in Religious Humanism." *Religious Humanism* (Spring 1978).

"The Legitimacy and Necessity of Black Philosophy: Some Preliminary Considerations." *Philosophical Forum* IX (Winter–Spring 1977–78).

"The Church and Urban Policy: Theological Response." *Journal of the Society for Common Insights* II (1978).

"Toward a Unitarian-Universalist Concept of Authority." *Kairos, An Independent Quarterly of Liberal Religion* (May 1979).

Black Theology II, Ed. with Calvin E. Bruce. Bucknell Press, 1978.

"Toward a Humanist Framework for Black Theology." Included in *Black Theology* II. Eds. William R. Jones and Calvin E. Bruce. Bucknell Press, 1978.

Karenga, Maulana

"From the Quotable Karenga," *The Black Power Revolt.* Floyd Barbour, ed., Boston: Porter Sargent Publishers, 1968.

"The Black Community and the University: A Community Organizers Perspective." *Black Studies in the University: A Symposium.* Armstead Robinson, Craig Foster and Donald Ogilvie, eds. New Haven: Yale University Press, 1969. Reprinted in *Black Viewpoints,* Arthur C. Littleton and Mary Burger, eds., New York: New American Library, 1971.

(Participant) "The Measure and Meaning of the Sixties, What Lies Ahead for Black Americans?—A Symposium." *Negro Digest* XIX (November 1969).

"Overturning Ourselves: From Mystification to Meaningful Struggle." *The Black Scholar* 4 (October 1972).

"Black Cultural Nationalism." *The Black Aesthetic.* Addison Gayle, Jr., ed. Garden City, N.Y.: Doubleday and Co., Inc., 1972.

"A Strategy for Struggle: Turning Weakness Into Strength." *The Black Scholar* 5 (November 1973).

"Which Road to Revolution: Nationalism, Pan-Africanism or Socialism?" *The Black Scholar* 6 (October 1974).

"Black Art: Mute Matter Given Force and Function." *Black Poets and Prophets.* W. King and E. Anthony, eds. New York: Mentor Press, 1974.

"In Defense of Sis. Joanne: For Ourselves and History." *The Black Scholar* 6 (July/August 1975).

"In Love and Struggle: Toward A Greater Togetherness." *The Black Scholar* 6 (January/February 1975).

"Black People and the Future—An Interview." *Black Books Bulletin* 4 (Summer, 1976).

"Prisons and Law: Punitive Politics." *The Black Collegian* 6 (January/February 1976).

"Reaffirmation and Change." *Nkombo* 5 (January 1976).

"FESTAC and Pan-Africanism: Continental and Diasporan Considerations." Proceedings—African Studies Conference (California State University, Chico). *African Studies Newsletter* 3 (1977).

"Kawaida and Its Critics: A Socio-Historical Analysis." *Journal of Black Studies* 8 (December 1977).

"Carter and His Black Critics: The Dialogue and Its Lessons." *The Black Scholar* 9 (November 1977).

"Beyond Connections: Liberation in Love and Struggle." *Nkombo* 6 (June 1977).

"The Value and Validity of Ethnic Studies: Towards a Holistic Conception." *The Political Economy of Institutional Change: Proceedings of Ethnic Studies Symposium*. Dan Moreno and Rudy Torres, eds. Irvine, Calif.: UCI Comparative Culture Program, 1977.

"The Crisis in Black Studies: The Ideological Dimension." *Black Studies in White Institutions*. Discussion Papers Series, Hassan Sisay, ed. Chico, Calif.: School of Behavioral & Social Sciences, CSU, Chico, 1978.

Essays on Struggle: Position and Analysis. San Diego: Kawaida Publications, 1978.

"Afro-American Nationalism: Beyond Mystification and Misconception." *Black Books Bulletin* 6 (Spring 1978).

"Chinese Psycho-Social Therapy: A Strategic Model for Mental Health." *Psychotherapy: Theory, Research, Practice* 15 (Spring 1978).

"A Response to Muhammad Ahmad on the US/Panther Conflict." *The Black Scholar* 9 (July/August 1978).

"Inter-Ethnic Conflict in Prisons: Causes and Consequences." *Nkombo* 6 (January 1978).

"Kwanzaa: Concepts and Functions." *Black Collegian* 10 (December/January 1979/1980).

"The Socio-Political Philosophy of Malcolm X." *Western Journal of Black Studies* 3 (Winter 1979).

"From Civil Rights to Human Rights: Social Struggles in the Sixties." *Black Collegian* 10 (February/March 1980).

Kawaida Theory: An Introductory Outline. Inglewood, Calif.: Kawaida Publications, 1980.

Afro-American Nationalism: An Alternative Analysis. Chicago: Third World Press, 1981.

"The Problematic of Cultural Pluralism: Ideological and Political Dimensions." *Pluralism, Racism and Public Policy*. Jack Bermingham and Ed Clausen, eds. Boston: G. K. Hall & Company, 1981.

"Kwanzaa." entry in *The World Book Encyclopedia*. Vol. II, J–K, Chicago: World Book & Childcraft International, Inc., 1981.

"The Black Male/Female Connection." *Black Male/Female Relationships* 2 (1981).

"The African Intellectual and the Concept of Class Suicide: Political and Cultural Dimensions." *The African Culture: Essays and Studies*. Molefi Asante and Doyinsola Aboaba, eds., Buffalo: State University of New York Press (forthcoming).

"Fannon, Cabral and Toure: Toward An African Theory of Cultural Revolution." *The Legacy of Frantz Fanon*. Ed., Hussein Bulhan, (forthcoming).

Book Reviews and Commentaries:

Review essay, "On Wallace's Myths: Wading Thru Troubled Waters." Michele Wallace, *Black Macho and the Myth of the Superwoman.* New York: Dial Press, 1979 in the *The Black Scholar* 8 (May/June 1979). Reprinted in *In These Times* 3 (June 20–26, 1979).

Review essay, "William Marshall's Othello." *The Black Scholar* 8 (September 1976).

Review of Kalamu ya Salaam's *Ibura.* New Orleans: Ahidiana, 1976 in *The Black Scholar* 7 (July/August 1976).

"Reagan and the Right: Beyond Illusion to Concrete Analysis." *Black News* 4 (January 4, 1979).

"Black Politics in 1980: The Problem of Strategy and Structure." *Black News* 4 (October 1978).

"Blacks and the GOP: The Newest Deal." *In These Times* 2 (October 11–17, 1978).

"The De-Afro-Americanization of Malcolm X." *The Voice News & Viewpoint* 17 (May 31, 1978).

"Chinese Theory and Practice on the Nationalities Question." *In These Times* 1 (September 14–20, 1977).

"Malcolm X: His Message and Magnitude." *Voice News & Viewpoint* 15 (May 18, 1977).

"FESTAC: Report From Nigeria." *In These Times* 1 (April 20, 1977).

"Reassessing King's Rich Political Legacy." *In These Times* 3 (May 9–15, 1979).

"Confrontation at Camp Pendleton: Issues and Impact." *Voice News & Viewpoint* (December 22, 1976).

"A Brief Outline of a Philosophy of Black Studies." *Black News* 3 (November 1976).

"African Liberation and Shuttle Diplomacy." *Voice News & Viewpoint* 15 (October 6, 1976).

"William Marshall's Othello: Critique and Commentary." *Voice News & Viewpoint* 15 (August 25, 1976).

"For Amilcar Cabral: A Tribute to His Triumph." *The African World* III (July 14, 1973).

Monographs and Special Publications:

Beyond Connections: Liberation in Love and Struggle. New Orleans: Ahidiana, 1978.

In Love and Struggle: Poems for Bold Hearts. San Diego: Kawaida Publications, 1978.

Kwanzaa: Origin, Concepts, Practice. Inglewood, Calif.: Kawaida Publications, 1977.

The Roots of the US/Panther Conflict: The Perverse and Deadly Games Police Play. San Diego: Kawaida Publications, 1976.

Kwanzaa: May Your Holiday Be With Much Happiness. San Diego: Kawaida Publications, 1975.

Names For a New People: An Authentic African Namebook. Inglewood, Calif.: Kawaida Publications, 1975.

The US/Panther Conflict and the Tackwood Distortions. Los Angeles: Saidi Publications, 1974.

Lee, Carleton, L. (1913–1972)

"God Hath Made of One Heart." *Missionary Herald* (1939).

"Minors of a Minority." *Service Magazine* (1941).

"Toward a Christian Critique of British Socialism." *Journal of Religious Thought* 1 (1949).

"White Hyancinths." *Service Magazine* 15 (February 19, 1951).

"Not Only Bread: Of Bread and Wine." *Service Magazine.* 15 (March 17, 1951).

"Not Only Bread: Life, Death and Re-birth." *Service Magazine* 15 (April 19, 1951).

"On Standing Before Kings." Editorial, *Service Magazine* 16 (August 6, 1951).

"Second Change." Editorial, *Service Magazine* 17 (January 6, 1953).
"The Sound of Race and Clan." *Christian Evangelist* 93 (February 1955).
"Philosophy of Tragedy in Brothers Karamazov." *Tougaloo Southern News* 66 (January 1956).
"Toward a Sociology of the Black Religious Experience Bibliography." *Journal of Religious Thought* 29 (Fall–Winter, 1972).
"The Black Church in America." Book review, *Phylon* 33 (Winter 1972).
Patterns of Leadership in Race Relations: A Study of Leadership Among Negro Americans. Chicago: University of Chicago, 1951. (Dissertation)

Locke, Alain L. (1886–1954)

"The American Temperament." *North American Review* CXCIV (August 1911).
"Steps Toward the Negro Theatre." *Crisis* XXV (December 1922).
"The Ethics of Culture." *Howard University Record* XVII (January 1923).
"Review of Goat Alley." *Opportunity* I (February 1923).
"The Concept of Race as Applied to Social Culture." *Howard Review* 1, 2–3 (1924).
Ed. *The New Negro.* New York: Albert & Charles Boni, Incorporated, 1925. (Reprinted by Atheneum, 1969).
"The New Negro." *The New Negro.* Alain L. Locke Ed., 1925.
"Negro Youth Speaks." *The New Negro.* Alain L. Locke Ed., 1925.
"The Legacy of the Ancestral Arts." *The New Negro.* Alain L. Locke Ed., 1925.
"The Negro Spirituals." *The New Negro.* Alain L. Locke Ed., 1925.
"The Negro Speaks for Himself." *Survey* LII (April 15, 1924).
"Apropos of Africa." *Opportunity* II (February 1924).
"Negro Education Bids for Par." *Survey* LIV (September 1925).
"American Literary Tradition and the Negro." *Modern Quarterly* III (May–July 1926).
"The Negro Poets of the United States." *Anthology of Magazine Verse for 1926.* William S. Braithwaite, Ed. Boston: B. J. Brimmer Company, 1926.
"Review of Weary Blues." *Palms* (October 1926).
Ed. *Four Negro Poets.* New York: Simon and Schuster, 1927.
"The Poetry of Negro Life." *Four Negro Poets.* Alain L. Locke (Editor), 1927.
"Our Little Renaissance." *Ebony and Topaz.* Charles S. Johnson, Editor. New York: National Urban League, 1927.
"The Negro Poet and His Tradition." *Survey* LVIII (August 1, 1927).
"The Gift of the Jungle." *Survey* LVII (January 1, 1927).
Co-editor, Montgomery Gregory. *Plays of Negro Life.* New York: Harper and Brothers, 1927.
"The Drama of Negro Life." *Plays of Negro Life* (Co-editor, Montgomery Gregory), 1927.
"Art Lessons from the Congo. *Survey* LVII (February 1, 1927).
"Review of Fire." *Survey* LVIII (August–September, 1927).
"Art or Propaganda?" *Harlem* I (November, 1928).
"The Negro's Contribution to American Art and Literature." *Annals of the American Academy of Political and Social Science* CXL (November, 1928).
"The 'Negro's Contribution." *World Tomorrow* (June 1929).
"1928: A Retrospective Review." *Opportunity* VII (January 1929).
"The Negro in American Culture." *Anthology of American Negro Literature.* V. F. Calverton, Editor. New York: Random House, 1929.
"Both Sides of the Color Line." *Survey* LXII (June 1929).
"The Contribution of Race to Culture." *The Student World* (October 1930).
"This Year of Grace." *Opportunity* IX (February 1931).
"We Turn to Prose." *Opportunity* X (February 1932).
"Black Truth and Black Beauty." *Opportunity* XI (January 1933).

The Negro in America. Chicago: American Library Association, 1933.

"Toward a Critique of Negro Music." *Opportunity* XII (November 1934).

"The Saving Grace of Realism." *Opportunity* XII (January 1934).

"The Eleventh Hour of Nordicism." *Opportunity* XIII (January 1935).

"Values and Imperatives." *American Philosophy Today and Tomorrow.* Sidney Hook, Horace Kallen, Editors. New York: Lee Furman, 1935.

"Minorities and the Social Mind." *Progressive Education XIII* (March 1935).

The Negro and His Music. Washington D.C.: Associates in Negro Folk Education. 1936.

"Deep River: Deeper Sea." *Opportunity* XIV (January 1936).

Negro Art, Past and Present. Washington D.C.: Associates in Negro Folk Education, 1936.

"Propaganda or Poetry." *Race* I (Summer 1936).

"God Save Reality" *Opportunity* V (January 1937).

"Jingo, Counter-Jingo, and Us." *Opportunity* XVI (January 1938).

"Advance on the Art Front." *Opportunity* XVII (May 1939).

"Negro Music Goes to Paris." *Opportunity* XVII (July 1939).

"The Negro: 'New' or Newer." *Opportunity* XVII (January 1939).

"The Negro's Contribution to American Culture." *Journal of Negro Education VIII* (July 1939).

"Dry Fields and Green Pastures." *Opportunity* XVIII (January 1940).

The Negro in Art. Washington D.C.: Associates in Negro Folk Education, 1940.

Co-editors. Bernhard J. Stern. *When Peoples Meet; A Study of Race and Culture Contacts.* New York: Committee on Workshops, Progressive Education Association, 1942.

"Of Native Sons: Real and Otherwise." *Opportunity* XIX (January 1941).

"Three Corollaries of Cultural Relativism." In *Proceedings of the Second Conference on the Scientific Spirit and the Democratic Faith.* New York, New York, 1941.

"Who and What is 'Negro'?" *Opportunity* XX (February 1942).

"Autobiographical Sketch." *Twentieth Century Authors.* Stanley Kunitz, Howard Haycraft, Editors. New York: Wilson Company, 1942.

"Democracy Faces a World Order." *Harvard Educational Review* XII (March 1942).

"Pluralism and Intellectual Democracy." In *Second Symposium.* New York: Conference on Science, Philosophy and Religion, (1942).

Le' role du Negre dans la culture des Ameriques. Port-au-Prince, Haiti: Imprimerie de l'etat, 1943.

"Whitner Race Relations? A Critical Commentary." *Journal of Negro Education* (Summer 1944).

"Cultural Relativism and Ideological Peace." In *Approaches to World Peace.* New York: Conference on Science, Philosophy and Religion, 1944.

"A Contribution to American Culture." *Opportunity* XXIII (Fall 1945).

"Pluralism and Ideological Peace." *Freedom and Experience.* Sidney Hook and M. R. Konvitz, Editors. New York: Cornell University Press, 1947.

"Reason and Race." *Phylon* VIII (1947).

"A Critical Retrospect of the Literature of the Negro for 1947." *Phylon* IX (1948).

"Foreword," *Witnesses for Freedom.* Rebecca Barton. New York: Harper and Brothers, 1948.

"Dawn Patrol: A Review of the Literature of the Negro for 1948." *Phylon* X (1949).

"Wisdom De Profundis: The Literature of the Negro, 1949." *Phylon* XI (1950).

"Self-Criticism: The Third Dimension in Culture." *Phylon* XI-4 (1950).

"Inventory at Mid-Century: A Review of the Literature of the Negro for 1950." *Phylon* XII (1951).

"The High Price of Integration: A Review of the Literature of the Negro for 1951." *Phylon* XIII (1952).

"The Negro in American Literature." *New World Writing*. New York: New American Library, (April 1952).
"From Native Son to Invisible Man: A Review of the Literature of the Negro for 1952." *Phylon* XIV (1953).
"Values that Matter." *Key Reporter XIX* (May 1954).
(Posthumously, Margarett J. Butcher) *The Negro in American Culture*. New York: Alfred Knopf, 1976.
"The Problems of Classification in Theory of Value." Boston: Harvard University, 1918. (Dissertation)
(For additional bibliographic information see "Memorial Tribute to Alain Locke." *Phylon* XV (1954). Richard Long, "Alain Locke, Cultural Mentor," *Homage to Alain Locke*. Atlanta: University of Atlanta Press, 1970. *The New Negro Thirty Years Afterward*. Rayford W. Logan, Eugene C. Holmes, G. Franklin Edwards, Eds. Washington, D.C.: The Howard University Press, 1955. Alain L. Locke Papers, Howard University; James Weldon Johnson Collection, Yale University; Countee Cullen Papers, Amistad Research Center, Dillard University.)

Lott, Tommy L.

"Motivation and Egoism in Hobbes." *Kinesis* 6 (Spring 1974).

McAllister, Winston K. (1920–1976)

"Toward a Reexamination of Hedonism." *Philosophy and Phenomenological Research* 13 (June 1953).
"Review of Realms of Meaning." *Journal of Negro Education* (1966).
The Compatibility of Psychological Hedonism and Utilitariansim. University of Michigan, 1947. (Dissertation)

McClendon, John H.

"Black Sociology: Another Name for Black Subjectivity." *Freedomways* 20/1 (1980).
"Afro-American Philosophers and Philosophy: A Neglected Theme in Black Intellectual History." *Afro-Scholar Working Papers*—No. 7. Urbana: University of Illinois-Urbana, Afro-American Studies and Research Program. 1981.
"Dr. Holmes, the Philosopher Rebel." *Freedomways* 22/1, 1982.
"The Afro-American Philosopher and the Philosophy of the Black Experience: A Bibliographical Essay on a Neglected Topic in both Philosophy and Black Studies." *Sage Race Relation Abstracts*. (November 1982).

McDade, Jesse N.

"The Ethnicity of Revolution." *Social Praxis* 1 (1973).
"Drugs and the Black Community." *Textbook of Black-Related Diseases*. Ed., Richard Williams. New York: McGraw Hill, 1975.
"The Significance of Hegel's 'das ungluckliche Bewusstein and Dubois' 'Double Consciousness." *A Lute Continua* (September 1976).
"Happy Birthday America: A Priori Truths and A Posteriori Refutation." *Morgan Magazine* (Spring 1976).
"Towards an Ontology of Negritude." *The Philosophical Forum* IX (Winter–Spring, 1977–78).
"Spinoza's Concept of God." *Journal of the Interdenominational Theological Center*. Atlanta, Georgia, (1978).

McGary, Howard, Jr.

"Jogging the Mind." *Creative Living* 3 (Spring 1974).

"Reparations and Inverse Discrimination." *Dialogue* 17 (Journal of Phi Sigma Tau) (1974).

"Justice and Reparations." *The Philosophical Forum* 9 (1977–78).

Co-author, Robert Meir, "Social Justice and Public Policy." *Educational Studies* 8 (Winter 1978).

McKinney, Richard I.

"Our Own Minority." *The Intercollegian* LVI (May 1939).

"Religion in Negro Colleges." *Journal of Negro Education* (Fall 1944).

"Christianity and the Problems of Race Relations." *Missions* XXXVII (February 1947).

Contributor to W. S. Nelson Ed., *The Christian Way in Race Relations.* New York: Harper and Bros., 1948.

"Negro Baptist Theological Schools,"—An Analysis of the Facilities and Programs of the Major Institutions and Agencies Providing Ministerial Preparation for Negro Baptists. Included as Chapter III (pp. 19–60) in Ira De A. Reid, *The Negro Baptist Ministry,* An Analysis of its Profession, Preparation and Practice (Report of a Study Conducted Under the Auspices of the Inter-Convention Committee of the American, National and Southern Baptist Convention) Philadelphia: H and L Publishing Company, 1952.

"A Philosophy of Discipline for a Small College." *Liberal Education* XLII (December 1956).

"Some Aspects of the Teaching of Philosophy." *Liberal Education* XLVI (October 1960).

"Science and Humanities in a Space." *Proceedings of the XIIth International Congress of Philosophy.* Florence, Italy: G. C. Sansone, Editore, 1961.

"Existentialist Ethics and the Protest Movement." *Journal of Religious Thought* XXII (1965–1966).

"Reflection on the Concept of 'Black Theology.' " *Journal of Religious Thought* XXVI (Summer Supplement 1969).

"The Black Church—Its Development and Present Impact." *Harvard Theological Review* 64 (October 1971).

"The Ethics of Dissent." *The Journal of Religious Thought* XXXIX (Autumn–Winter 1972).

Religion in Higher Education Among Negroes. New Haven: Yale University Press, 1945. Reprinted by the Arno and New York Times Press in 1972 as one of a series entitled *Religion in America.*

"A Philosophical Paragraph: 'We Hold These Truths . . .' " in *Common Ground,* Essays in Honor of Howard Thurman. Samuel Gandy Ed., Washington: Hoffman Press, 1976.

A History of the First Baptist Church, 1863–1980, In Light of its Times. Charlottesville: Michie Bobs Merrill Press, 1981.

McWorter, Gerald A.

"The Ideology of Black Social Science." *The Black Scholar* 1 (December 1969).

"The Uses of Philosophy and the Black Experience." *Black Studies Program,* University of Illinois at Chicago Circle, (February 1976).

Ed., *Philosophical Perspectives in Black Studies.* Urbana: Afro-American Studies and Research Program, University of Illinois-Urbana, Illinois, 1982.

Menkiti, Ifeani A.
"The Negro and the Emergence of Africa." *UCLAN Review* VIII (Summer 1962).
"Between Ideology and Philosophy." *Wellesley Alumnae Magazine* (Summer 1976).
"The Resentment of Injustice: Some Consequences of Institutional Racism." *The Philosophical Forum* 9 (1977–78).
Review of P. M. John, *Marx on Alienation* in the *Journal of the American Academy of Religion* XLVI (September 1978).
"Person and Community in African Thought." Richard A. Wright Ed., *African Philosophy* 2d. edition. Washington, D.C.: University Press of America, 1978.
"Criminal Responsibility and the Mentally Ill." *Journal of Value Inquiry* 14 (1980).
Review of Kwasi Wiredu, *Philosophy and an African Culture* (Oxford University Press, 1980), in the *Harvard Educational Review* 51 (February 1981).

Moore, Lewis B. (1866–1929)
Syllabus of a Course of Lectures on the History of Educational Reform. Alabama: Tuskegee Institute Press, 1903.
What the Negro Has Done for Himself. Washington, D.C.: R. L. Pendleton, 1911.
How the Colored Race Can Help In the Problem Issueing From the War. New York: National Security League, 1919.
Biographical Notes; *Crisis* 8 (June 1914); 12 (July 1916); 15 (December 1917); 20 (September 1920); 36 (February 1929).

Moreland, Marc M.
"Samuel Howard Archer: Portrait of a Teacher." *Phylon* X (1949).
"The Welfare State: Embattled Concept." *Phylon* XI (1950).
The Tolono Station and Beyond. Massachusetts: The Christopher Publishing House, 1970.
"Conversation Piece." *New Jersey Herald News,* Syndicated Column, 1952–1970.
The Theory and Problem of Liberty in New England, 1636–1700. Canada: University of Toronto, 1937. (Dissertation)

Mosley, Albert G.
"The Metaphysics of Magic: Practical and Philosophical Implications." *Second Order: An African Journal of Philosophy.* Ile-Ife, Nigeria: University of Ife Press, (July 1978).
Co-author, Eulalio R. Baltazer, *An Introduction to Logic: From Everyday Life to Formal Systems.* Monograph, University of the District of Columbia, 1982.

Murungi, John.
"Being a Black Son in USA." *Journal of Afro-American Issues* (Fall–Winter 1975).
"Towards an African Understanding of Time." *International Philosophical Quarterly* XX (December 1980).
"Mealeau-Ponty's Perspective on Politics." *Man and World* IV (1981).

Nobles, Wade W.
"African Philosophy: Foundations for Black Psychology." *Black Psychology.* Jones, Reginald L., Harper & Row Publishers, New York, 1972.

Outlaw, Lucius T.
"Language and Consciousness: Foundations for a Hermeneutic of Black Culture. *Cultural Hermeneutics* 1 (February 1974).

"Beyond the Everyday Life-World: A Phenomenological Encounter with Sorcery." *Man and World* 8 (November 1975): 436–45.
Panelist, "Hermeneutics and Critical Social Theory." *Cultural Hermeneutics* 2 (February 1975): 371–72.
"Black Folk and the Struggle in 'Philosophy'," *Endarch* 1 (Winter 1976): 24–36; and, in a revised version. In *Radical Philosophers Newsjournal* VI (April 1976).
"American Philosophy and the Unfinished American Revolution: A Program for African-American Philosophy." *Bicentennial Symposium of Philosophy: Contributed Papers,* City University of New York Graduate Center, New York, 1976.
"The Case for Affirmative Action for Blacks in Higher Education: A Critical Review." *Cross Reference* 1 (May/June 1978).
"Honors and Ethical Training: A New Social Ethic?" *Forum for Honors* IX (September 1978).
"The Future of Black People in the United States." *Sojourners* 10 (May1981).

Perry, Rufus, L. M. (1833–1895)

Sketch of Philosophical Systems. Springfield, Mass.: Wiley and Company, 1889.
The Cushite or the Descendent of Ham as Found in the Sacred Scriptures and in the Writings of the Ancient Historians and Poets from Noah to the Christian Era. Springfield, Massachusetts: Wiley and Company, 1893.

Reed, Adolph L.

"Black Particularity Reconsidered." *Telos* (Spring 1979).

Rigsby, Gregory

"Space-Time Concepts in Black Literature." *The Philosophical Forum* 9 (Winter–Spring 1977–78).

Riley, Jerome R. (?)

The Philosophy of Negro Suffrage. Hartford, Conn.: American Publication Company, 1895. (Second Edition, Washington, D.C. 1897).
Evolution or Racial Development. Oglive, New York: Privately Printed, 1901.
Reach the Reached Negro. Atlanta: Byrd Printing Company, 1932.

Rogers, Joel A.

From Superman to Man. New York: Helga M. Rogers, 1957.

Simpson, Lorenzo C.

"On Scientific Knowing." *Yale Scientific Magazine* (February 7, 1968).
"A Critical Note Concerning Marcuse's Theory of Science. *Philosophy of the Social Sciences* (1983).

Slaughter, F. Thomas, Jr.

"The Dialectics of Our Oppression: Rehearsing the Basic Concert." *Black Voice.* Rutgers University, (March 1973).
"Parts of Me in Concert." *Caellian* (College Newspaper), under the title, "Sitting Back and Becoming One of Pharoah (Sanders') Slaves," Douglass College, April 6, 1973.
"The Status of Black Studies Programs at American Colleges and Universities". Co-authors, R. Goldstein and J. Albert, in *The Black Studies Debate.* Eds., J. V. Gordon, J. M. Rosser. Kansas: The University of Kansas, 1974.

"Epidermalizing the World: A Basic Mode of Being Black." *Man and World: An International Philosophical Review* 10 (1977).
"Phenomenological Reflections on Black Studies." *The Annals of Phenomenological Sociology* II (1977).

Smith, John M. (?)
"A Critical Estimate of Plato's and Dewey's Educational Philosophies." *Education Theory* 9 (April 1959).
A Comparison and Criticism of the Educational Philosophies of Plato and John Dewey. Iowa: University of Iowa, 1941. (Dissertation)

Snowden, Conrad
Co-editor, Henry Olela. *Philosophical Inquiry: Student's Manual, Socio-Political Philosophy.* Washington D.C.: Institute for Services to Education. 1971/72/73.

Spady, James G.
"Negritude, Pan Banegritude and the Diopian Philosophy of African History." *A Current Bibliography of African Affairs* 5 Series III, (January 1972).
"Surrealism and the Marvelous Black Plunge in Search of Yemanga and the Human Condition." *Cultural Correspondence,* No. 12–13–14 (Summer 1981).

Thomas, Laurence
"To A Theory of Justice: An Epilogue." *The Philosophical Forum* 6 (1976).
Book Review: Rolf E. Sartorius, *Individual Conduct and Social Norms. New Scholasticism* 51 (1977).
"Human Potentiality: Its Moral Relevance." *The Personalist* 53 (1978).
"Morality and Our Self-Concept." *The Journal of Value Inquiry* 12 (1978).
"Rawlsian Self-Respect and the Black Consciousness Movement." *The Philosophical Forum* 9 (1978).
"Capitalism versus Marx's Communism." *Studies in Soviet Thought* 20 (1979).
"Ethical Egoism and Psychological Dispositions." *American Philosophical Quarterly* 17 (1980).
"Sexism and Racism: Some Conceptual Differences." *Ethics* 90 (1980). Reprinted in *Sexist Language: A Modern Philosophical Analysis.* Ed., M. V. Braggin. Totowa, N.J.: Littlefield, Adams, and Company, 1981.
"Sexism, Racism, and the Business World." *Business Horizons* (July/August 1981).
"Case Study: Should States Require Passenger Protection?" *Hastings Center Report* (July 1981).

Turner, James
Co-author W. Eric Perkins. "Toward a Critique of Social Science." *Black Scholar* 7 (April 1976).

Walton, Hanes, Jr.
The Philosophy of Martin Luther King, Jr. Westport, Conn.: Greenwood Publishing Company, 1971.

Washington, Johnny
Alaine Locke and Philosophy: A Quest for Cultural Pluralism. (forthcoming, Greenwood Press)

West, Cornel

"A Philosophical Perspective on the Participation of Prisoners in Experimental Research," prepared for the National Commission for the Protection of Human Subjects of Biomedical and Behavioral Research and published in public report, 2/1/76.

"Socialism and The Black Church." *New York Circus* (October–November 1979).

Review of Eulalio R. Baltazar's *God Within Process, Religious Studies Review* (January 1979).

"A Philosophical View of Easter." *Dialog: A Journal of Theology* 19 (Winter 1980).

"Reviews of Robert McAfee Brown's *Theology in a New Key* and Albert Munk's *A Synoptic Approach to the Riddle of Existence, Religious Studies Review* (April 1980).

"Black Theology and Socialist Thought." *The Witness* 63 (April 1980).

Review of Paul Homer's *The Grammar of Faith, Union Seminary Quarterly Review* (Spring & Summer 1980).

"Set the Record Straight." *Commonweal* (November 21, 1980). "Liberation Theology in America." (with Sheila Collins) *Commonground* (April 1981).

"Class, Race and Cultural: Comments." *International Ecumenical Congress Proceedings,* Sao Paulo, Brazil: Orbis Press, 1981.

"Nietzsche's Pregiguratoin of Postmodern American Philosophy." *Boundary 2: A Journal of Postmodern Literature,* Special Nietzsche issue (Summer 1981).

Review of John Gunneman's *The Moral Meaning of Revolution, The Journal of Religion* (April 1981).

"Philosophy and The Afro-American Experience." *The Philosophical Forum* IX (Winter-Spring 1977–78).

"Introduction" and "Schleiermacher's Hermeneutics and the Myth of the Given." *Union Seminary Quarterly Review.* (Winter 1979).

"Black Theology and Marxist Thought." *Black Theology: Documentary History, 1966–1979.* (ed. Gayraud Wilmore and James Cone. 1979).

Prophesy Deliverance: An Afro-American Revolutionary Christianity. (Forthcoming).

Wiggins, Forest O.

"Discussion of Mr. Wilkerson's American Caste and the Social Studies Curriculum." *Quarterly Review of Higher Education Among Negroes.* 5 (April 1937).

Review: "Leighton: *Social Philosophies in Conflict.*" *Journal of Social Philosophy* 6 (July 1941).

"William James and John Dewey." *Personalist* (Spring 1942).

"Ethics and Economics." *Phylon* 6 (1945).

"Treason Against Reason." *The Negro* 3 (July 1945).

"Individualism and Individuality." *Personalist* 27 (Winter 1946).

"Reflections on Education." *Quarterly Review of Higer Education Among Negroes* 13 (January 1945).

"The Data and Evaluation of Business." *American Journal of Economics and Sociology* 6 (July 1941).

"What is Property?" *The American Socialist* 2 (September 1955).

"Why Integrate White Students into Negro Colleges?" *Allen University Bulletin* 10 (February 1956).

"Reflections on Education and Politics." *Allen University Bulletin* 21 (February 1957).

"Responsibility of the Scholar." *Faculty Research Edition of the Savannah State College Bulletin.*

"Ideas and Ideals in the Philosophy of William James." *Faculty Research Edition of the Savannah State College Bulletin* 16 (December 1962).

Book Reviews
Norman St. John-Stevas, *The Right of Life. Choice* 1 (June 1964).
Anatol Rapoport, *Strategy and Conscience. Choice* 1 (November 1964).
Hugo Adam, Bedau, editor, *The Death Penalty in America. Choice* 1 (December 1964).
Whitaker Deininger, *Problems in Social and Political Thought. Choice* 2 (September 1965).
"The Moral Consequences of Individualism." Summaries of Doctoral Dissertations 3, 1937–38. Wisconsin: University of Wisconsin Press, 1939. (Dissertation)

Williams, Robert C.

"Moral Suasion and Militant Aggression in the Theological Perspective of Black Religion." *The Journal of Religious Thought* XXX (Fall/Winter 1973–74).
"Afro-American Folklore as a Philosophical Source." *Philosophy of Social Science* (Fall 1976).
"Response to Marx." In *Introduction to Philosophy: A Case Method Approach.* New York: Harper and Row, 1981.
"The Church" in *Christian Theology: An Introduction to Its Traditions and Tasks.* Philadelphia: Fortress Press, 1982.

Wortham, Anne

The Other Side of Racism: Philosophical Study of Black Race Consciousness. Ohio: Ohio State University Press, 1981.

About the Editor

LEONARD HARRIS is a former Portia Washington Pittman Fellow and Moton Center for Independent Studies Fellow. He has lectured at the Inter-University Centre of Postgraduate Studies, Dubrovnik, Yugoslavia; Inter-African Council for Philosophy Conference, Republic of Benin, West Africa; and the University of the West Indies. He is a member of the New York Society for Black Philosophy, Inter-African Council for Philosophy, and the American Society for Social Philosophy. His works have appeared in the *Liberator, Negro History Bulletin, Presence Africaine,* and *International Philosophical Quarterly.* His philosophical focus includes the history of American philosophy, philosophic anthropology, and problems of explanation and justification in critical theory. He is currently an Assistant Professor at Morgan State University.